ß45

CW00925716

D

BLUEWATER
FLY FISHING

Books by
TREY COMBS

THE STEELHEAD TROUT
STEELHEAD FLY FISHING AND FLIES
STEELHEAD FLY FISHING
BLUEWATER FLY FISHING

BLUEWATER

TREY COMBS

FLY FISHING

 LYONS & BURFORD, PUBLISHERS

© 1995 by Trey Combs

ALL RIGHTS RESERVED. No part of this book may be reproduced in any manner without the express written consent of the publisher, except in the case of brief excerpts in critical reviews and articles. All inquiries should be addressed to Lyons & Burford, Publishers, 31 West 21 Street, New York, New York 10010.

Printed in Hong Kong

10 9 8 7 6 5 4 3 2 1

Design by Howard P. Johnson
          Communigrafix, Inc.

Library of Congress Cataloging-in-Publication Data

Combs, Trey.
      Bluewater fly fishing / Trey Combs.
              p.   cm.
      Includes bibliographical references and index.
      ISBN 1-55821-331-7
      1. Big game fishing.   2. Saltwater fly fishing.
  I. Title.
SH457.5.C65   1995
    799.1′6—dc20   95-23916
                                                              CIP

Sold by TSI

Drawings by Mike Stidham

Facing title page: A mixed school of yellowfin and Pacific sailfish off Costa Rica. Photograph by William Boyce.

This book is dedicated to the sport of bluewater fly fishing as defined by the fly-fishing rules of the International Game Fish Association.

Denny Rickards and Roy Rose photographed a moment before releasing the striped marlin. Photograph by Jim LePage.

A skipjack tuna taken on a Mylar popper. Photograph by Trey Combs.

The striped marlin's rise to the popper is a blur. Photograph by Trey Combs.

A fly-caught high seas pink salmon. Photograph by Trey Combs.

A striped marlin ready to be released.

Next page: An Atlantic sailfish is billed off Dakar, Senegal. Photograph by BJ Meiggs.

CONTENTS

ACKNOWLEDGMENTS

My basic theme in *Bluewater Fly Fishing* was simple in concept and not so simple in its implementation: Where should anglers travel in the world to fly fish for a certain species of offshore gamefish? Once at their destination, what methods should they employ to successfully catch the gamefish? My answers to these questions became the subject of this book in large measure because of the generosity of friends and acquaintances who shared my conviction that "offshore" was a legitimate and exciting fly-fishing environment, and one that deserved an introductory guide.

These persons kept my dream alive.

Mark Sosin, Billy Pate, Stu Apte, Chico Fernandez, Winston Moore, Les Eichhorn, Bob Marriott, Cam Sigler, Bob Veverka, Bill Catherwood, Mike Meyers, and Jim Brown, Assistant to the President of the International Game Fish Association, provided information, flies, and memorabilia contributing to my brief history of offshore fly fishing.

An Atlantic sailfish caught on a fly off West Africa's Cape Verde Peninsula. Photograph by Trey Combs.

Mike and Susie Fitzgerald of Frontiers, Bruce Theunissen of African Rod & Rifle Safaris, John Barrett, producer and host of "Fly Fishing the World," Patrick Guillanton and Gerard Aulong of Mako Video Productions, Fred Edworthy, owner of North Island Lodge, Randall Kaufmann of Kaufmann's Streamborn, Frank LoPreste of LoPreste-Dunn Inc., Lani Waller of Lani Waller's Worldwide Angler, Roland Tyak of Beachcomber Fishing in Le Morne, Mauritius, Ray Shirakawa of Shirakawa's Motel in Naalehu, Hawaii, Sonja

Lillvik of Cuzon Guest House, Rick Alvarez, and Steve Jensen gave me opportunities to fly fish for gamefish in areas that contributed directly to the completion of this book.

Steve Jensen, Dick Thrasher, Cliff and Sharon Beatty, Captain Calin Canales, Curpin Merdez, Kevin Shelly, Rob Rohrke, Philippe Sleurs, Christine Herbert, Paul Dutton of the Southern Africa Nature Foundation, Antonio Uribe, Enrique Garcia-Reyes, Captain Richard Chellemi, Captain Robert Trosset, Captain Brett Middleton, Rick Rosenthal, Jim Teeny, Steve Huff, Roland Tyak, Captain Del Dykes, Mike Combs, Dean Butler, Alan "Fish" Philliskirk, Captain Craig "Sparrow" Denham, Captain Bobby Jones, Captain Tim Eckstrom, Rex Nelson of Western Filaments, Steve Shelly, Nanci Morris, Seattle Aquarium, and Barbara Ilchuck, Director of Public Relations, Holiday Inn, Key West, Florida provided invaluable information and assistance.

Special thanks to Mark Tupper, former owner of Costa Rica's Bahía Pez Vela Lodge, who made available to me offshore boats and vast amounts of rod time for Pacific sailfish and blue marlin.

For information on the development and performance of offshore rods and reels, special thanks to Randy Swisher and Jerry Siem of Sage, Gary Loomis and Bruce Holt of Loomis, Bryan Peterson of Thomas and Thomas, Jim Lepage of Orvis, Kate and Bill Howe of Graphite USA, personnel at Seamaster and Tycoon/Fin-Nor, Ted Juracsiy of Billy Pate Reels, Steve Abel (Abel Reels), Jake Jordan of STH Reels, John Harder of Lamson, Jack Charleton (Charleton Reels), Dave McNeese (McNeese Reels), and Joe Saracione.

Bruce Richards at Scientific Anglers sent me production and experimental fly lines, and the latest in fly-line technology. Jim Vincent of Rio, and Rex Nelson of Western Filaments, provided me with leader and backing, and the technology that I needed to know about both.

Many of the anglers who provided me with flies and instructions as to their correct tying were also my companions on a lifetime of offshore trips: Steve Abel, Ron Ayotte, Terry Baird, Ray Beadle, Dan Blanton, George "Chappie" Chapman, Nick Curcione, Rod Harrison, Kate and Bill Howe, Dave Inks, Ralph Kanz, Pete Parker, Bob Popovics, Steve Probasco, Billy Pate, Richard Stoll, Bob Veverka, Steven Vletas, and Lani Waller.

Kim Markus and Ann Black of the Australian Tourist Commission provided important assistance for my fishing in Australia for black marlin.

The following airlines found reasons to provide complimentary flights and promotional fares that made much of my international travel affordable: South African Airways, Avianca, Air France, and Quantas.

Special thanks to Script's Institute of Oceanography, the Billfish Foundation, the National Oceanic and Atmospheric Administration, and the International Game Fish Association for life history information on gamefish and past angling records.

I was able to select photographs from many of the very best angler photographers working today's offshore fly-fishing scene. I am indebted to the following for so wonderfully illustrating my stories: B. J. Meiggs, Neal and Linda Rogers, Marty and Janet Downey, Ray Beadle, R. Valentine Atkinson, Tony Oswald, William Boyce, Terry Gunn, Wendy Hanvold, Dean Butler, Jim Lepage,

Walt Jennings, Tim Leary, Rod Harrison, Bryan Peterson, Rhonda Klevansky, David Linkiewicz, and Bob Stearns.

Paul Boyer painstakingly photographed the fishing flies that appear in *Bluewater Fly Fishing*. I believe that the result are the finest fly plates yet to appear in a saltwater fly-fishing book.

Mike Stidham, an artist who is internationally known for his portraits of fresh and saltwater gamefish, illustrated *Bluewater Fly Fishing*. His dramatic graphite drawings of offshore gamefish appear at the head of each chapter and capture the esssence of the sport.

B. J. Meiggs, pioneer offshore photographer, editor of the book's gamefish chapters, and my companion on many adventures, was key to the completion of *Bluewater Fly Fishing*.

Ed Rice, President of the International Sportsman's Expositions, maintained unflagging faith in this enterprise and never doubted that this steelhead fly fisher possessed the experience to also write knowledgeably about offshore fly fishing.

Lefty Kreh, whose knowledge, reputation, and fame make him fly fishing's lone icon, wrote the Foreword and thus gave *Bluewater Fly Fishing* a significance—and acceptance—that my words and pictures alone would never have gained. I'm tremendously grateful for his efforts in behalf of my book and the sport of offshore fly fishing.

Nick Lyons, my editor and publisher, knew during the years I spent writing *Steelhead Fly Fishing* that I was simultaneously gathering material for this book. Nick, a fly fisher who writes with such brilliant wonderment of trout and spring creeks, and who so willingly identified with my steelhead book, found my offshore environment somewhat alien to his passion for fly fishing. Nevertheless, with all his might he supported this project, the first "how to" saltwater fly-fishing book ever done entirely in color. I will always appreciate Nick's leap of faith.

*Lefty Kreh, the world's best-
known fly fisherman, holds
up a little tunny, or false
albacore, as anglers often
call this superb fly-rod fish.*

FOREWORD

If you enjoy trying to catch fish so big that you have no business going for them, or if you want to offer your fly to a fish that has probably never seen one—then the offshore waters are where you should be. The vastness of the oceans holds many species that will take a fly—up to and including blue marlin. Tackle for the various species varies greatly. What will work for catching a small tuna is totally inadequate on a large, swift wahoo. The selection of lines is vital to success. And, while many inshore anglers may get away with a poor or even a fair knot, only the best knots and connections will stand up to the strain of some of the rough customers you will encounter in blue water.

Few people have the broad experience needed to write a book that gives this important information and much more. Trey Combs is one of those fishermen who has fought the offshore wars and has often won them. This is a solid how-to book for all no-nonsense fly fishermen who want to know everything they need to rig tackle, select the best flies for the job, present the fly, and finally hook, fight, and land those tough bluewater species.

This is not a book you can read, put down, and go to blue water. Instead, this is a well-written book that gives so much information about this area of fly fishing, that you will learn a great deal on the first read. As your offshore skills increase, you will realize that by reading this book again and again you continue to learn something new. It is not simply a book. *It is a manual on how to fish offshore.* Read it carefully, thoroughly, and often, and you can become a competent offshore angler. Bluewater fly fishermen owe Trey Combs a debt of gratitude for writing this excellent book.

—Lefty Kreh

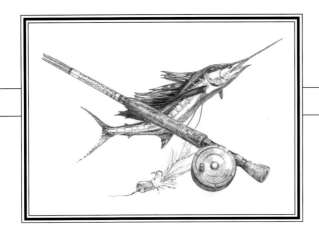

INTRODUCTION

One hundred and fifty years ago, fishing as a sport in North America was almost entirely the province of fly fishermen who pursued trout and Atlantic salmon on the rivers of the northeastern United States and the Canadian Maritimes. Salt water remained, as it had for centuries, the realm of commercial enterprises, the catches generally marketed fresh each day without the benefit of refrigeration. Weekend anglers might charter boats or use their own skiffs to take porgy, sea bass, sheepshead, and weakfish using handlines of tarred cotton. Bluefish were easily secured in season by trolling tin squids from gaff-rigged sloops. From docks and breakwaters, anglers with cane poles and equal lengths of line fished for striped bass and other inshore fish. Big gamefish of commercial importance, the swordfish and bluefin tuna, were harpooned. Other large creatures of the sea, including tarpon, manta rays, and dolphin, were harpooned for sport.

Trout and salmon fishermen turned uneasily to the sea with their rods of greenheart, single action reels, and wealth of flies. Purely as a practical matter, their equipment did not lend itself easily to ocean fishing. As a point of social reference, saltwater fly fishing was déclassé, the debasement of fine craftsmanship for a food fish, a fertilizer fish, or a baitfish. Fly fishing meant gamefish, a trout or a salmon; only a fool would argue otherwise.

Henry William Herbert, described as "America's first great outdoor writer" in George Reiger's *Profiles in Saltwater Angling* (Prentice-Hall, 1973), was

An exhausted yellowfin tuna ready to be netted. Photograph by Tony Oswald.

certainly a maverick, something of a visionary, but no fool. He came to the United States in 1831 from London, the exile forced upon him by his wealthy father for reasons unknown. Herbert taught school in New York City, and by the 1840s turned to writing—first historical novels, but later stories about horse racing, hunting, and fishing, because they were more lucrative. Sporting stories lacked the prestige of novels, though, and Herbert took refuge from the commentary of his times by writing under the pseudonym "Frank Forester." When Forester's fame eclipsed that of Herbert's, particularly in the British press, Herbert chose to move his outdoor writing along under both names.

His collective wisdom on all matters pertaining to saltwater fishing became *Frank Forester's Fish and Fishing of the United States and British Provinces of North America*, by Henry William Herbert, first published in London in 1849. In this encyclopedic tome, the author claimed that, save for the Atlantic salmon, the finest gamefish was the striped bass, and that "the fly will take them brilliantly." He is remarkably specific as to pattern: "The fly to be used is any of the large Salmon flies, the larger and gaudier the better. None is more taking than an orange body with peacock and bluejay wings and black hackle legs; but any of the well known Salmon flies will secure him, as will the scarlet bodied fly with scarlet ibis and silver pheasant wings, which is so killing to the black bass of the lakes."

Herbert may well have been the first person to take shad on the fly when they migrated upriver. He fly fished for herring with a "gaudy peacock tail fly," and sang their praises as gamefish. He did not restrict his attentions to these fish, but advanced the concept that all saltwater fish embodied the best the sport of fishing could offer, and that some deserved recognition as fly-rod gamefish as well.

Herbert was a leader with no followers, for no one rushed to continue his pioneering explorations into the world of saltwater fly fishing. But his writings stand as a remarkably definitive body of fishing literature, and some parts of them must be considered the starting point for American saltwater fly fishing.

Two trends in American saltwater fishing following the Civil War can be identified. Inspired in part by Herbert, Thaddeus Norris wrote *The American Angler's Book*, 1864, and urged anglers to give up handlines for "sporting tackle" when fishing the salt. Norris was hardly the sole instrument of this change, for the idea was gaining common hold, and fishing with rod and reel in salt water soon became a legitimate sport. The second trend that bears most cogently on the history of bluewater fly fishing is the industrial North's "discovery" of Florida.

Forest and Stream, a weekly outdoor newspaper, sponsored expeditions to south Florida in 1873 and 1875. Charles Hallock, the newspaper's owner, and S. C. Clarke, an expert on the identification of gamefish species, took part in these adventures. When Hallock published *Camp Life in Florida*, the story of the two trips, Americans received their first description of the "tarpum," a fish possessing almost mythical strength; it could only be killed with a harpoon that had been connected to a heavy hemp line that was in turn secured to a floating cask.

Only three years later, Dr. James A. Henshall, the self-appointed dean of American bass fishing, wrote *Camping and Cruising in Florida*, an account of his experiences boating around both coasts of south Florida. He described his introduction to the area's flats and natural canals, and the gamefish they held: tarpon, redfish, sea trout, snook, jack crevalle, and ladyfish. Henshall would claim in later years that during this trip he boated the first tarpon ever caught on a fly, doing so with a cane rod, an Atlantic salmon fly, and a Vom Hoff bait-casting reel. Other claims by gear fishermen made their way into print, and by the turn of the century, the tarpon had become a fish of considerable legend, and the focus of many anglers visiting Florida.

Dr. Henshall's experience is most interesting, not so much for the claim he makes for the first fly-caught tarpon, but for the tackle he used. He and other fishermen who came to Florida with 9½- to 10-foot cane rods and sheep-skin books full of Atlantic salmon flies found their direct drive reels hardly equal to the task of saltwater gamefish. Like Henshall, these pioneering fly fishermen used Edwin Vom Hoff's bait-casting reels, "state of the art" at the time. The choice reflected considerable sober thinking on the task before them, a clear recognition that Florida's gamefish in general, and the tarpon in particular, assaulted fly-fishing tackle at a more physical level than their generation had ever experienced on trout and salmon waters.

Holmes Allen may have taken the first fly-caught bonefish in 1924 while fishing a white feather streamer, a meeting apparently surprising each party equally. Within a few years, there emerged a small group of flats anglers who specifically targeted tarpon, bonefish, and permit. This included W. D. "Bo" Crandall, Frank Baxter, Lee Cuddy, and Captain Bill Smith, whose wife, "Bonefish Bonnie," became the first woman to take a permit on a fly.

Homer Rhode, an Everglades National Park ranger, took both bonefish and permit on the fly in 1930. His Homer Rhode Tarpon Fly became the forerunner of the Seaducer Series, while the Homer Rhode Loop Knot is still commonly used.

As Keys fly fishers searched the flats for tarpon, bonefish, and permit, "off-shore" was merely a short ride to the edge of the reef, and the blue water beyond. Lee Cuddy, a Miami tackle manufacturer and legendary flats fisherman who would eventually claim over 2,000 bonefish on the fly, routinely fished blue water for dorado (dolphin) on flies more than 50 years ago.

Joe Brooks, who more than any other angler past or present popularized American saltwater fly fishing, came by his fly-fishing skills naturally. He was a remarkably gifted athlete. As a teenager he signed a professional baseball contract—and was then whisked off to Princeton by his wealthy parents. His collegiate career was short-lived; soon he was playing semipro football in Canada. In later years he both bowled and golfed at the professional level, and he claimed to have once been a sparring partner for Jack Dempsey. Brooks had such a mania for the outdoors that as a young man he would leave his home in Baltimore in the spring and fish south to Florida, then months later hunt his way north back to Maryland, displaying a work ethic that further dismayed his parents. These wanderings in the late 1920s included the company of Tom Loving. The two men became regulars on the shallow flats of the Chesapeake Bay, where striped bass were abundant. Loving, no newcomer to saltwater fly fishing, had developed the first shad fly in 1922, and pioneered fly fishing for largemouth bass in brackish water. Brooks credited Loving with developing a white bucktail that was, he said, the first fly tied expressly for a saltwater species. Surely this fly by Loving became the inspiration for Brooks's own Platinum Blonde Bucktail.

In the late 1930s, Harold Gibbs, a commercial lobster fisherman, was appointed Rhode Island's Administrator of Fish and Game. He pushed the sport of striped bass fishing, and personally pioneered fly fishing for this gamefish. One of the common baitfish that stripers fed on was the Atlantic silversides. Gibbs sought specifically to imitate this fish with a fly of his own design. The fly, which became known as the Gibbs Striper Fly, was about three or four inches long, with a body of silver tinsel, and wings of white goat topped with a strip of blue swan. Gibbs shouldered the fly with barred teal, gave it a red hackle throat, and painted in an eye, usually with a white or yellow iris and a red pupil. This pattern, along with variations of it that imitate other baitfish, survives in common use today for bluewater gamefish. I think this was the first saltwater fly designed to *imitate* rather than simply attract.

During the years immediately after World War II, Joe Brooks became saltwater fly fishing's best known proponent. He lived in Richmond, Virginia, wrote a weekly "how-to" fly-fishing column for the Washington *Post*, and otherwise worked full time as a freelance outdoor writer. In 1947, while attending the Outdoor Writer's Association of America convention in St. Petersburg, Florida, Allen Corson, fishing editor of the Miami *Herald*, told him about bonefish and asked if he thought they could be caught on flies. To find out, Brooks drove south to Islamorada where he booked Jimmie Albright, a famous tarpon guide. The two men fished the flats where Albright caught two tailing bonefish on small streamer flies. "As far as is known," wrote Brooks in *The Complete Book of Fly Fishing* (Outdoor Life, 1958), "that was the first deliberate effort to take bonefish on flies, and it was successful."

The operative word is *deliberate*, for numerous bonefish had already been caught by anglers casting flies for small tarpon, and surely some of these anglers cast more or less *deliberately* for bonefish. No matter, really. Almost overnight Brooks became a huge fan of this gamefish and wrote so enthusiastically of its virtues that a generation of anglers became saltwater fly fishers solely because of bonefish.

Joe Brooks fished Orvis cane rods in salt water (at one time he owned sixty), his favorite a slow action 9½-foot model that weighed 6⅝ ounces. His reel was the Sagueney model manufactured by Otto Zwarg. In the early 1950s it was, at $75, the most expensive fly reel in the world. Using this tackle, Brooks fished inshore and offshore, taking tarpon of over 100 pounds, numerous bonefish, his first permit in 1951 (the first "recorded" permit on a fly), and offshore fish such as dorado and little tunny.

The Rod and Reel Club of Miami Beach, Florida was organized in 1927. It developed various fishing categories based on the type of tackle used: plug, spinning, trolling, and fly. Points were awarded for catches. The accumulation of points took fishers from "Novice" to "Angler" to, eventually, "Master Angler." The club awarded release certificates. Additional details are not important to this history—except the fact that the rules governing the club's fly-fishing category set the stage for the International Game Fish Association's regulations that today determine what is, and what is not, fly fishing.

The Rod and Reel Club of Miami Beach divided fly fishing into "fly light" (no-shock tippet) and "fly heavy" (shock tippet), the latter category established in recognition of the specialized leaders needed for tarpon. Shock tippet length, including all knots, was restricted to 12 inches; no one at the time imagined taking a billfish on a fly. The maximum class tippet was one that, when submitted, tested no more than 12 pounds.

Fred Schrier, who represented *Salt Water Sportsman* magazine for the Middle Atlantic states in the 1950s, advanced to friends the idea of a national saltwater fly-fishing organization. He had for years fly fished for striped bass in Barnegat Bay, New Jersey. Nearby, at Island Beach, New Jersey, Elwood "Cap" Colvin owned a tackle shop on a narrow strip of land that divided the Atlantic Ocean from Barnegat Bay. Immense concentrations of striped bass and bluefish appeared in season on the bay side. Colvin pursued them with a fly rod so single-mindedly that his shop soon became a gathering place for saltwater fly fishermen.

These two men, Schrier and Colvin, formed the Salt Water Fly Rodders of America at a meeting held for interested parties in Toms River, New Jersey in 1960. They began keeping a list of fly-rod records based on catches by the Rod and Reel Club of Miami Beach, as well as other clubs organized with similar goals and ethics—the Virginia Anglers Club, for example. The founders of the Salt Water Fly Rodders of America included Lefty Kreh, Mark Sosin, Louis "Bub" Church, and Charlie Waterman on the East Coast, as well as Larry Green and Myron Gregory on the West Coast.

Even at the time, this group was an astonishing collection of fly-fishing talent. Sosin, a full-time, nationally known outdoor writer, had learned about saltwater fly fishing while chasing down bluefish and striped bass on Barnegat Bay. Kreh, too, wrote and photographed the outdoor fly-fishing scene, and for eight months a year managed the Metropolitan Miami Fishing Tournament sponsored annually by the Miami *Herald.* He had also developed Lefty's Deceiver, the single most effective and widely used saltwater fly in the world today. Thirty years ago, however, many saltwater fly rodders thought that Bub Church was the most innovative saltwater fly tier on the American scene. It had been Church who helped develop what was then Sosin's signature fly, the Blockbuster.

Sosin was the World Records Editor, and in that capacity headed a committee that included Kreh and Church. They processed all record applications and determined whether the fish in question was or was not a legal fly-rod catch. This proved troublesome, for the class tippet needed only to *test* a specified breaking strength. Anglers could—and some did—fish a heavier tippet, submitting it after it had been abraded by a fish—or possibly abraded by the angler on a concrete sidewalk. To call the catch into question became politically difficult, especially if the angler was a fellow club member.

An influential member of the Rod and Reel Club of Miami Beach, and an angler who dramatically expanded the dimensions of offshore fly fishing, was Dr. Webster Robinson of Key West, Florida. In the early 1960s Lefty Regan, a Key West fishing guide since 1946, often skippered for Robinson and his wife, Helen. Regan worked out teasing techniques that brought cobia and amberjack to the surface, and discussed with Robinson the possibility of using similar techniques for billfish. In doing so, Robinson would fish "fly heavy" by club rules: a 12-pound class tippet and a 12-inch shock tippet. Efforts to take an Atlantic sailfish were not initially successful. The Robinsons then chartered a boat in Piñas Bay, Panama. On January 18, 1962, with Helen teasing, Robinson cast, hooked, and boated a 74½-pound Pacific sailfish, the first billfish ever caught on a fly. During the next three seasons, he landed 14 additional Pacific sails on flies. When Robinson expanded his fly fishing to include striped marlin, he fished off the coast of Baja California, and brought along Lefty Regan to skipper the boat. After numerous hookups and broken class tippets, Robinson landed a 145-pound striped marlin, the first marlin of any species taken fly fishing.

Lee Cuddy landed the first Atlantic sailfish on a fly in 1964, and then became the second person to land a Pacific sailfish on a fly. Other anglers soon followed: Stu Apte, Gill Drake, and Guy de Ladene.

Stu Apte, a pioneer of saltwater fly fishing, was born in Miami and raised in the Keys. He became a navy fighter pilot, and for years flew commercial jets for Pan American. He and his wife lived in Little Torch Key, about thirty miles north of Key West. Here in the Keys, Apte became a legend in tarpon fishing circles. By the early 1960s, his fame was such that when Ray Smith, a Texas oilman, built the Club de Pesca (now Tropic Star Lodge) in Panama, he asked Apte to manage it. Managers had come and gone; Apte agreed only to come down and train the captains.

Apte had never taken a billfish on a fly. But Dr. Webster Robinson was a Key West neighbor and Apte soon learned the techniques for teasing in a billfish. Late in 1964 he fished Panama's Piñas Bay and took a 58-pound dorado on 12-pound tippet. The following June, Apte got a 136-pound Pacific sailfish, again on 12-pound tippet, the maximum then allowed. Both records, now 30 years old and among the oldest in saltwater fly fishing, may well stand for another 30 years—enduring testimonials to Apte's remarkable angling skills.

Saltwater fly fishing did not take place only on the East Coast. In the Pacific Northwest, during the 1950s, William Lohrer, George McLeod, Letcher Lambuth, Zell Parkhurst, and Roy Patrick cast long shank candlefish and herring dressings of polar bear for the silver salmon that filled the Strait of Juan de Fuca and Puget Sound late each summer.

Joe Brooks fished Coos Bay, Oregon in the late 1940s with balsa poppers, and landed a striped bass of 29 pounds, 6 ounces. The catch brought national fly-fishing attention to this gamefish, which had been transplanted to the West Coast in 1879. This world record stood for nearly 20 years, until Russell Chatham, the brilliant painter and fly-fishing writer now living in Livingston, Montana, topped it in 1966 with a 36-pound, 6-ounce striper from San Francisco Bay.

Other notable fly fishermen from the Bay area were addicted to striped bass: Hal Jansen, whose Hamada Silversides were among the first flies to involve Mylar piping epoxied over a core of balsa wood; and Myron Gregory, whose lead core shooting heads opened up new vistas in inshore fishing. Include Larry Green, whose original Mylar-covered Beer Belly Streamer found its way offshore under many other names; and Dan Blanton and Bob Edgley, whose Whistler series of flies is one of the most used in saltwater fly fishing, and whose Sea-Arrow Squid has been used by a generation of offshore anglers to cast for offshore gamefish such as albacore.

During the 1960s, inspired by Ray Cannon's articles about his adventures in Baja California, fly fishers began making their way to Mexico for this virgin fishing. Harry Kime, a world-traveled freshwater angler, was among the first of these pioneers. He would fly down with pilot Ed Tabor to Loreto, a tiny village 170 miles north of La Paz, to take yellowtail in the spring, and dorado in the summer. (The largest Pacific yellowtail caught on flies date back to the early 1970s and came from Loreto. Sadly, this fishery has in all ways been badly degraded.) After ten years of spectacular fishing in Loreto, Kime moved to the mainland of Mexico between Mazatlán and Manzanillo. He boated many sailfish and several striped marlin on flies during these years on the mainland.

During the early 1970s, the yellowfin tuna was known as the Allison's tuna in south Florida, and was believed to be a separate species. Fly fishers discovered that these fish could be intercepted along the edge of Bermuda's Challenger Bank. A captain would anchor the boat in 350 feet of water with line so light it could be easily broken. Mates would then chunk up anchovies, the tuna soon picking up the scent and following the chum slick to its source. Anglers that included Bob Stearns, Chico Fernandez, Mark Sosin, and Jim Lopez fished shooting heads connected to 100 feet of Amnesia running line backed with as much as 700 yards of 20- or 30-pound Dacron. Sosin's 56-pound, 6-ounce yellowfin became the first tuna over 50 pounds ever landed on fly tackle. Jim Lopez followed on June 28, 1973 with an 81-pound yellowfin in the newly added 15-pound tippet class, and came back nine days later to boat a 67-pound, 8-ounce yellowfin in the 12-pound tippet class. The records still stand. Arguably, they are the most remarkable in fly fishing. I personally think that Lopez's 12-pound record may prove to be the most durable record in bluewater fly fishing.

Billy Pate, already famous for his catches of huge tarpon, began a most remarkable run at billfish records in the 1970s. Like offshore fly fishers before him, Pate got the essentials from Dr. Webster Robinson—both teasing and bait stitching techniques, along with a handful of cork-bodied poppers with red-painted heads. His first record came on Atlantic sailfish while fishing out of Cozumel, Mexico with Bill Barnes in 1970. That same year he went after the huge striped marlin found off Salinas, Ecuador.

Lee Wulff, whose international celebrity was tied enduringly to his writings about Atlantic salmon, had traveled to Ecuador several years before to fly fish for striped marlin in conjunction with a promotional film for the Garcia Company. At the time, the fly-fishing rules that governed world record consideration were still under the aegis of the Salt Water Fly Rodders of America; Wulff would fish "fly heavy," a 12-pound class tippet, the maximum allowed, and a shock tippet no more than 12 inches long, including all knots. In May, 1967, he landed a 148-pound striped marlin, a world record.

When Pate came to Ecuador, the Salt Water Fly Rodders of America had added a 15-pound class tippet category. Fishing the new class tippet, Pate

XXX B l u e w a t e r   F l y   F i s h i n g

Previous page: Bill Pate fights a large Costa Rican sailfish. Photograph by R. Valentine Atkinson.

boated a 146-pound striped marlin after a fight that lasted nearly two hours. Like Wulff's record, Pate's striped marlin record still stands after thirty years.

When Pate returned to Florida, Helen Robinson told him about a fishing tournament she and Al Pflueger had entered off Cairns, Australia. They were hunting for "granders," the 1,000-pound black marlin that were bringing sport-fishing fame to the area, but they had also encountered many juvenile blacks, fish of 20 to 50 pounds. Pate, of course, understood the fly-fishing implications of these marlin. When he flew to Cairns in 1972, he fished class tippets in the 15-, 12-, 10-, and 6-pound categories, *and took world record blacks in each.* (Pate had given up fishing the big cork poppers popularized by Dr. Web Robinson. He felt that fishing a straight fly resulted in an increased percentage of solid hookups.) To fish a 6-pound class tippet, Pate dressed his white hackled fly on a thin 2/0 hook, and broke off numerous blacks before getting one of 46 pounds, 4 ounces to the boat on September 14, 1972.

Three years later Pate became the first person to take a white marlin on a fly off Venezuela's La Guaira Bank. He had difficulty arranging for a fly-fishing charter, and then experienced a dismal week of fishing. Pate checked out of the Sheraton Macuto Hotel and was driving to the airport when he spotted his captain walking along the coastal road. On a sudden impulse, he stopped and negotiated two more days of fishing from the captain. The next day, Pate boated an 80-pound white marlin, and one day later took a 75-pound Atlantic sailfish, both world records on 15-pound class tippet.

Pate now needed only the blue marlin to claim all six species of billfish on the fly. At the time, no fly fisher had caught even one such blue. Juvenile blues became his obsession. Pate searched for them off Venezuela, Jamaica, and the Keys. During 10 days of fishing off St. Thomas in the Virgin Islands, he raised 20 small blues and hooked 6. "All six cleaned me out," he says of the experience.

Pate had heard rumors of small blues from big game fishermen returning to Islamorada from the Hemingway Tournament held each fall in Havana, Cuba. He and George Hommel, his business partner at World Wide Sportsman in Islamorada, Florida, secured special permission from U.S. officials in 1978 to enter that country and fly fish for six days. On the final day, Pate hooked a blue that immediately sounded, taking out over 900 feet of line. Pate told me, "Every blue I ever hooked sounded. This blue was the only blue I was ever able to bring back."

The marlin started coming up while still green. The angle was such that it became evident the fish would surface beside the boat. Pate, in his soft Carolina drawl, told his captain, "Skip, we're going to get a shot at him." Before the blue could orient itself, the captain hot-gaffed it, and hung on as the fish dragged him along the gunwale and slammed him into the pilothouse. The mate then got a second gaff into the fish, and the first fly-caught blue became history. The marlin weighed 96 pounds.

In June, 1978, the Salt Walter Fly Rodders of America turned the task of world record keeping over to the International Game Fish Association (IGFA). (*Field & Stream* magazine had turned over freshwater fly-fishing records to the IGFA in March, 1978.) The IGFA's class tippet categories—1, 2, 4, 6, and 8 kg—

did not exactly match those of the Fly Rodders. Pate's black marlin record was bumped into the 4 kg category, 8.8-pound test, a 30% increase over 6-pound. Nevertheless, Pate's black marlin record was still in the IGFA's *1994 World Record Game Fishes* book. Starting on June 15, 1994, the IGFA began accepting applications for fly-rod records in the 6-pound (3 kg) tippet class. Whenever they applied, the old 6-pound records from the Salt Water Fly Rodders of America were reinstated. This included Pate's 4 kg black marlin record. (Other 6-pound [3 kg] records reinstated included catches by such famous anglers as Joe Brooks [permit], Stu Apte [tarpon], and Lefty Kreh [jack crevalle].)

Saltwater fly tying through the 1950s and 1960s usually involved attractor-style dressings that didn't imitate any particular baitfish. Joe Brooks's Blondes were a classic case in point. The Platinum Blonde, made entirely of white bucktail, became his signature fly. Mark Sosin's all-white Blockbuster, early all-white examples of Lefty's Deceiver, and expanded versions of tarpon patterns such as Tom McNally's Magnum streamers were other such examples. These flies were effective on many marine species when the fish were feeding naturally on baitfish, or turned on with live or dead chum, or hunting—and thus less cautious—during periods of low light. But when the fish were not in such modes, these

Joe Brooks's December 1963 subscription copy of Outdoor Life *carried a lead article by Brooks on his Blonde series of flies. Bill Gillasch, a professional fly tier and a Richmond neighbor, tied for Brooks. Brooks fished Gillasch's popping bugs for a variety of saltwater inshore gamefish. Joe Brooks memorabilia courtesy of Cam Sigler.*

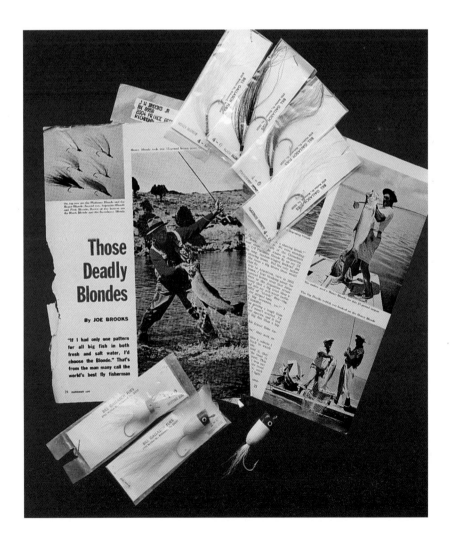

Fly tier: Bill Catherwood. Bill Catherwood's original flies, left row, top to bottom: White Perch, Hair Head Pogy, Giant Tuna Pogy, Raging Squid, Pink Squid. Right row, top to bottom: Hair Head Tinker, Mackerel, Herring, Tinker Mackerel, Hair Head Herring. Catherwood flies courtesy of Bob Veverka.

and any attractor-type flies could get a lot of refusals. At such times, flies that more carefully imitated baitfish could receive more attention.

Popular American saltwater flies representing specific forage fish go at least as far back as Harold Gibbs's Gibbs Striper Fly. But not until Bill Catherwood, a full-time professional fly tier from Tewksbury, Massachusetts, did saltwater fly tying really start to turn from attractor-type flies to flies that imitated the small fish, squid, shrimp, and crabs that made up the diets of marine gamefish. Catherwood's large (often gigantic) flies—called "giant killers" in a 1968 *Outdoor Life* article by Tom MacNally—did more than just imitate. Catherwood's tying methods were revolutionary. To give his flies a true three-dimensional baitfish silhouette, he spun deer hair onto the heads and added glass eyes. He studied the colors reflected by baitfish under various light conditions, and duplicated them by blending shades of marabou to produce both lifelike movement and the desired color. To get exactly the right kind of extra-long saddle hackles for his big flies, he selectively bred his own chickens. The long strands of dyed wool Catherwood used came from the black-faced sheep that lived in his backyard.

Three of his earliest saltwater flies—still among the best of dozens of original Catherwood patterns—are the Mullet, Herring, and Tinker Mackerel. Other dressings imitated sand lance (aka "sand eel," "needlefish"), smelt, chub, and "beakfish"—ballyhoo, and the baby sailfish that he called the "marlinette."

Just about every saltwater fish worth the name *gamefish* has been caught on Catherwood's flies. A few of the many are: Atlantic salmon, black bass, lake trout, tarpon, dorado, most species of tuna, billfish, striped bass, bluefish, jack crevalle, king mackerel, barracuda, and sharks.

Though Catherwood uses only natural materials, I think the single most dramatic addition to saltwater fly tying over the past 20 years has been the synthetic tying materials available now in seemingly endless diversity—the artificial hairs, the Krystal Flashes and Flashabous, and their many variations. These materials, when incorporated into bait-imitating flies by the best of our contemporary saltwater tiers such as Bob Popovics, Joe Branham, Bill and Kate Howe, Pete Parker, Terry Baird, Richard Stoll, Ralph Kanz, and Bob Johns, to name but a few, produce results both dazzlingly lifelike and effective.

A sport develops incrementally, a cause producing an effect, better training producing better athletes, modern technology producing better equipment, and so on. Offshore fly fishing's history, however brief and dramatic, essentially fits this pattern. It's a story of improvements in tackle, fly lines, and flies; a story of new fly-fishing techniques, played out in new and increasingly exotic fishing areas, for gamefish unimagined a generation ago. In this regard, I have watched the bluewater fly-fishing scene hurry along faster than any other in fly fishing, and at times the rod, reel, and line manufacturers frantically play catch-up. But no single curtain lifted to dramatically give dimension to the new world of offshore fly fishing until long-range fly fishing came upon the scene. Then, suddenly, everything in fins became faster, larger, and infinitely more available.

For more than twenty years, long-range fishing boats have been a unique fixture of the San Diego, California angling scene. Called "long-range" because they could motor for weeks on their incredible fuel capacity, the go-anywhere, 90- to 100-foot boats had carried fishers south into Baja California waters for the wealth of gamefish on and around its offshore banks. Yellowfin tuna to nearly 400 pounds, blue, black, and striped marlin, Pacific sailfish, yellowtail, wahoo, and dorado were the targets; finding and hooking them was assured on two counts: The boats filled numerous bait wells with live bait before departure, and each came complete with the world's most sophisticated fish-finding electronics.

Whether long-range boats had application in fly fishing was another matter. Fly fishing is not gear fishing, with its 80-pound test line, heavy rods, and stand-up harnesses. No one beats up on a 100-pound tuna with fly tackle, much less a tuna two or three times that size. Fly fishers need room to cast and keep flies out of each other's way. That means fewer anglers on board, and the cost per angler necessarily increasing. Runaway tuna and billfish can't be followed on a party boat if other anglers are to keep fishing. While high speed rubber skiffs could be used in conjunction with the mothership, the question of whether fly fishers could stand up in one for hours to fight a big gamefish remained.

Steve Abel of reel-making fame put the first trip together in 1991, a mixed group of gear- and fly-tackle enthusiasts who returned to San Diego after a ten-day trip with tales of big tuna and broken gear that traveled like seismic waves

Captain Tim Eckstron fly fishes for skipjack tuna from the transom of the Royal Star.

Nanci Morris poses with a striped marlin she took in January 1995 on a 10-kilogram tippet during a long-range fly-fishing trip she and the author hosted for LoPreste-Dunn Inc. At the time of the catch off Baja California's Pacific coast, the marlin weighed approximately 185 pounds. Officially weighed a week later in San Diego, the marlin weighed 173 pounds and was the largest billfish ever caught by a woman. This marlin and one caught by the author at the same time are pending records with the International Game Fish Association.

through the fly-fishing industry. The next year, and each year thereafter, Ed Rice, president of International Sportsman's Expositions, put LoPreste-Dunn's *Royal Star* under charter for his Blue Water Fly Rod Invitationals. I've been part of these invitationals, and other long-range, fly-fishing charters as well.

During the first invitational, I saw more wahoo caught IGFA legal than ever before in the history of fly fishing, as well as more really large yellowfin tuna, and more record black skipjack. The following year our party raised over 300 striped marlin to teasers in four days, hooked more than 100 on flies, and boated 7, the largest was a world record for Wendy Hanvold, the first woman to take a striped marlin on a fly. Then we broke "old" wahoo and black skipjack records set the previous year.

A year later, in 1994, Wendy Hanvold was joined by two other women, Janet Downey and Nanci Morris. Not only did all three women bill and release at least one striped marlin apiece, they all boated wahoo as well. Harm Seville, seventy-seven years young, became the hero of the trip when he caught—and released—his first striped marlin on a fly. Altogether, more than sixty striped marlin were fought from the skiffs, with about half that number successfully boated and released.

Fighting and ultimately billing a striped marlin at water level in a small rubber skiff was an incredibly up close and personal experience. To then revive

Chico Fernandez, a pioneer in saltwater fly fishing, holds a yellowfin tuna of nearly 50 pounds caught off Bermuda's Challenger Bank. Photograph by Bob Stearns.

Facing page: The author pumps up a striped marlin of Baja, California. Photograph by Janet Downey.

and release such a creature put those fly fishers who experienced it on a spiritual level both wondrous and little traveled.

The tours now seem as much cosmographic as geographic. What is not possible? Is there an ocean that cannot be crossed, a seamount or bank or canyon that cannot be located, an ocean current or water temperature that cannot be detected, a school of baitfish that cannot be located, a pelagic gamefish that cannot be chummed up to waiting fly fishers?

Many species of saltwater gamefish, including swordfish and short-billed spearfish, have not yet been caught on flies. Neither have 100-pound Mexican yellowfin tuna, 200-pound Tongan sailfish, or 300-pound Australian black marlin. Taking new species of saltwater gamefish, and taking other species in sizes thought unimaginable only a few years ago, may best sum up the evolution currently taking place in bluewater fly fishing. We push at what we perceive to be the boundaries of our sport, and find little to restrain us.

BLUEWATER

Fish

PART

1

DORADO

Loreto, Baja California Sur, Mexico

When I first fly fished the Sea of Cortez off Loreto, Mexico, the airport terminal was a thatched hut with a Coke machine, most panga captains had never heard of fly

fishermen, and those few who had thoroughly despised them, calling them *las plumas*, "the feathers," the feminine gender intentional. This was a time when no limits existed in sportfishing, in either size or numbers, and no one gave a second glance to a 40-pound dorado. Gringos got drunk on Cuervo Gold and cases of Pacifico, visited unbelievable hell on the local populace, and filled casket-sized coolers with frozen fillets. These commitments to fish hoggery and bacchanalian pleasures did not please the residents, but they did not displease them either. If gringos on holiday were pigs, they were rich pigs, and that counted for a lot in a village so poor.

Ticon was my first panga captain. Hook-nosed and hatchet-faced with flashing black eyes and a wildly insolent disposition, he reminded me of an Aztec warrior ready to eat the still-beating heart of a vanquished foe. He considered me his unfortunate lot, the worst kind of luck, an attitude that disappointed me, for I was determined not to be his Ugly American. I would be courteous, pleasant, and sober. I would also fish the fly—all in all, a gentleman angler. After one day with me, Ticon may have thought I possessed all these traits, but he thought me an idiot besides, for while he could find dorado for me, I couldn't catch them. On the second morning, he greeted me with contempt, morbidly despaired, and threw my fly rods, gold reels and all,

The author holds a large bull dorado caught off Loreto, Mexico. The fish took a homemade Balsa popper painted to imitate a flying fish, a favorite prey of dorado. Photograph by Mark Mandell.

1

ten feet through the air into the bow of the boat. Then we went fishing.

The object of these cultural transgressions was the dorado, Spanish for "golden," a name perfectly describing a fish that often seems gilded. Hawaiians call it "mahimahi," while on the east coast of the United States it becomes the dolphin—or "dolphinfish," to distinguish it from the sea mammal of the same name. I'd been assured that by any name, this gamefish, which inhabited tropical and temperate seas worldwide, represented bluewater fly fishing better than any other. Few gamefish were faster or more acrobatic and none, my friends insisted, would demonstrate a greater eagerness to eat my flies and poppers.

Loreto's panga captains all had identical routines. They left before dawn and ran eight miles north of town for the southern end of Coronado Island, where they and their anglers jigged for mackerel, often catching two or three at a time and storing them beneath the athwart seat, a primitive but effective live bait well. Ticon had to get all the baits because I couldn't jig with a fly rod, further evidence that *las plumas* were a brotherhood of wimps. I asked to relieve him of this chore, but Ticon, his martyrdom complete, disdainfully waved me off.

We would motor slowly along looking for patches of "weed," rafts of sargasso that might shelter school dorado in the 6- to 15-pound class, or an occasional bull of 20 pounds or more. Without polarized glasses to filter dawn's oily shadows, Ticon still saw dorado I could not, and he would throw a couple of mackerel over the side to stampede them into striking the huge flies I fished on 60-pound, hard nylon shock tippets. The mackerel immediately sounded for their lives, taking the dorado with them, and leaving me staring into a lot of empty water. At the end of the day, when Ticon's peers were hauling great dorado from their pangas, and saw that his boat was empty, they felt pity for him, and damned *la mosca*, "the fly," and any angler demented enough to fish it. The fishermen often gave a few dorado to the panga captains who were free to eat them or to sell them to boost their meager wages. Fly fishing hurt Ticon's pride, and his pocketbook. As the other captains collected their filleting knives and gathered at the fish-cleaning station, Ticon glared at me. I knew what he was thinking, and I was thankful that his knife was still in the panga.

Ticon began fishing for me by running a huge hook through the nose of a mackerel and casting it at the dorado. Sometimes I would see a huge bull come from a considerable distance for the mackerel, attack it crosswise, and run for 50 yards before Ticon struck, either to be fast to the fish or to spit out a string of Spanish curses when the dorado leaped and the mackerel came sailing out of its mouth. When a hooked dorado attracted others, Ticon sometimes held a dozen by the boat so I could cast frantically to them, but they would not take my fly. Ticon would go back to catching dorado and leave me to glumly search through my pile of huge bucktails and Deceivers. Dorado were supposed to eat anything in sight and my flies, buzzing with tinsels in a dozen electric colors, were a reflection of everything I had found to read on the subject. The low point of my descent into self-pity occurred when I cast a red-and-yellow 4/0 Deceiver into a school of 8- to 10-pound dorado, and watched several turn blotchy with shock before they fled in panic. An hour later, Ticon hooked a bull dorado as big as a door and insisted that I take the rod, a fiberglass broomstick anchored at one end by a 6/0 reel that gave out unlubricated, fingernails-down-the-blackboard screeches as the fish tore off a 100 yards of 80-pound line. I was nearly pulled from the panga before gaining my footing and feeling the weight of the fish. I gasped, first at its strength, and then at where my hubristic passion for the fly had led me: Regardless of whether I could or could not hook such a fish on a fly, I could not land it, a depressing realization to come to after five days of casting and sweating in 100-degree heat with a man who could not imagine the source of my stupidity. When I derricked the 50-pound dorado to the boat, Ticon gaffed it and smiled, satisfied that I had grown wiser from the experience.

I had not, for the next day Ticon found me waiting in the predawn darkness again clutching my fly rod. We made short work of the mackerel. I had proven to him that using them did not help me, and after he collected only enough for himself, we set out in near darkness to hunt for dorado. When he saw a single dorado under the first patch of sargasso, I cast and he hissed, "*Grande!*" The fish did not take the fly, and Ticon motioned for me to cast again. This time, when the bucktail landed at the very edge of the sargasso, the bull took it without hesitation. I struck, and the dorado executed the longest run I had ever witnessed, 700 feet across the Sea of Cortez stitched by a series of golden leaps, a dorado so far away so quickly that I wondered whether the miniature on the horizon was indeed my fish. It was, 30 pounds, and when brought aboard I howled and embraced Ticon, who could only laugh and shake his head at a gringo so possessed.

I returned to Loreto again and again; to Baja's "first city," the capital of Baja California for 132 years, to the site of Junipero Serra's first mission in 1769, to Caesar's restaurant and my dinner of lobster and margaritas, and to where, as its merchants proclaim on T-shirts, "the mountains meet the sea." They do, and despite the centuries of human endeavor, I think that nowhere else on this temperate planet do the riches of the sea so contrast to the poverty of the land. The Sierra Giganta forms the east coast of the Baja Peninsula by plunging directly into the sea. Conversely, the western slopes drop gradually across Baja to the Llano de Magdalena and the Pacific. The clouds of late summer moisture that sweep in from the ocean are wrung dry by the time they reach this spine of great mountains. Loreto remains so in the lee of the weather pattern that years may go by without measurable precipitation, a fact registered on the faces of these moonscape mountains that silicate-bearing winds have left eternally wet with desert varnish.

Looking into those mountains, I could believe that sometime in the long ago germinal life returned to the sea to be nurtured to its current state of biodiversity. Beneath my panga, from the aquamarines of white sand shallows to the blue-black depths hundreds of feet below, thrived every imaginable marine organism, from copepod, to 100-pound squid, to the tuna by the shoals and the sailfish, and the striped, blue, and black marlin that hunted them. Dorado lurked under seaweed paddies, and roosterfish raced across the headland flats. Bottomfish filled the ledges and grottoes in dizzying variety. Hammerhead sharks hounded my fly-hooked fish even as manta rays entertained me with high, somersaulting leaps. Porpoises, sea lions, and great baleen whales became daily companions. Frigate birds, boobies, shearwaters, gulls, and terns pursued flying fish, mackerel, anchovies, mullet, and sardines. Coming to understand how these parts related to one another, and thus learning how the dorado and the many other gamefish could best be caught on flies, would take many years. For the most part, I was unable to think of a more useful way to spend my time.

Dorado normally move north into the Sea of Cortez in early June, when water temperatures first break into the eighties. This temperature is insufficient to bring about the rapid growth of sargasso, the mustard-colored weed that gathers in school-sized dorado like a mother hen, and the fish search hard for other types of cover. Dorado will hold under anything: pieces of plastic, newspaper, cardboard, driftwood, even dead turtles and dead whales. Once on a November long-range fly-fishing trip down the Baja Peninsula, our company of anglers aboard *Royal Star* found an estimated 2,000 dorado under a single dead seal. During one Loreto June, an upcountry sawmill dumped tons of coarse sawdust in the ocean. This blew out to sea, formed a drift a mile long, and for a week held some immense dorado. I watched with fascination as terrified flying fish, a favorite food of dorado, spread their huge pectoral fins and eased themselves out on top of the sawdust while huge bulls shouldered their way through the cover.

A generation of anglers considered July *the* dorado month, a time when numbers, size, and sargasso cover all came together, a peak season that had every hotel and panga booked months in advance. August, extremely hot and humid, and susceptible to *chubasco* storms that in only a few hours can sweep the sea clean of sargasso and dorado, has gained a loyal following in more recent years because the fishing can be so extraordinary. I recall one morning in early August when, at dawn, the dorsals of hundreds of cruising dorado could be seen to the horizon. My partner and I together hooked forty dorado that morning. Nearly dead with exhaustion and dehydration, we ordered the panga back to the beach at 11 o'clock.

I call the time between the first light and the moment the sun sends shafts of light deep into the water—about eight o'clock during Loreto's July— "Golden Time," for dorado move freely, are much less wary, and can thus be approached more easily. Large bulls, especially, are more likely to smash a popper at this time. Overcast or coastal fog can extend this time, and I consider either condition a blessing.

I fish two outfits when hunting dorado from a panga. I choose a 9- or 10-weight rod when casting 1/0 to 2/0 Sea Habits, whether Bucktails, Deceivers, or Tubes, and a 10- or 11-weight rod when casting poppers and 4/0 flies, especially at first light. I cast the flies with a monocore running line looped to 28 feet of shooting taper, sink rate IV. The poppers, either a 2/0 cork-bodied Gaines popper or a 2/0 Edgewater rubber popper, are covered with Mylar piping, and coated with epoxy. Like the flies, the poppers cast like bullets, enabling me to get the extra distance I want. I fish them with either a shooting taper, sink rate III or IV, or a Scientific Anglers Mastery Series sinking monocore tarpon line.

A bull dorado caught off Thetis Bank, Baja California. Note the light leader without a shock. When fly fishing for school-size dorado in the 5- to 15-pound range, a hard nylon leader testing only 15 pounds can be safely used. Photograph by Trey Combs.

The development of my flies for dorado has gone on for years, and has led me to produce even more lifelike creations. I believe these flies and poppers, more than anything else, have placed dorado among the easiest of all saltwater gamefish for me to take.

As my flies have grown more lifelike—and smaller—my tippets have grown lighter, and now I've generally ceased using shock tippets altogether, simply tapering my hard nylon leaders down to 15- or 20-pound test. Even when casting poppers for the largest bull dorado, I rarely bother with anything heavier than a 30-pound hard nylon shock that I quickly connect to the class tippet with a surgeon's knot. A dorado has a hard pad of short, needlelike teeth on its tongue and on its palate, and a single row of small teeth on its upper and lower jaws. When a dorado takes a fly or popper deeply, the leader wears directly against these teeth, and as a result I lose a few large fish on the light tippets and shocks. But I hook many more than I would otherwise, a trade-off I'll take anytime.

The single greatest mistake fly fishers make when searching for dorado is casting only one size fly, and that one size large—five inches or longer—on a 4/0 hook. How many times have I seen an angler's stretcher box full of these huge, overly gaudy flies all carefully tied to shock tippets! I only bother with such flies at first light, when big bulls tail boldly on the hunt, because once the sun is hard upon the sea, large flies don't get much attention. I begin down-sizing from midmorning on, usually fishing thinly dressed, three- to four-inch 1/0 and 2/0 flies during midday.

Dorado of both sexes weighing 4 to 12 pounds are often found hunting to-gether in schools of 6 to 30 or more. As they get larger, the bulls especially be-come less social and often swim singly. These dorado, from 15 to over 50 pounds, may be found holding under sargasso by themselves, or with one or two smaller bull or cow dorado. On numerous occasions I have seen a single large bull warily holding below a school of much smaller dorado. Nevertheless, my first-light strategy centers on finding single large bull dorado holding un-der some cover and waiting to pounce on a passing baitfish. For these fish, I'll first cast a popper.

Years ago, a panga captain would drive his boat up on a patch of sargasso, throw a mackerel over the side, and wait for you to cast. This close approach drove the dorado either away or down. If any hung around, the mackerel over the side sent them in pursuit. Either way, the approach was dead wrong for fly fishers. I now ask my panga captain to try to keep the boat about 60 feet from the grass. If I detect a morning breeze—and light winds often blow from land early in the morning—I work to keep the panga upwind, but no so directly that the boat begins drifting down over the sargasso and the dorado. I want the panga to drift by, never getting closer than about 60 feet. This means that

This Mexican "schoolie" bull dorado took a 2/0 Sea Habit Bucktail in the Anchovy Blue pattern. Photograph by Trey Combs.

my initial cast will be more like 80 feet, with subsequent casts shorter until I've drifted past the area.

Usually a dorado takes a popper on the first or second cast. I believe it helps to wait a second after the popper has landed before making the first strip and pop. I've had bulls rocket out the instant the popper landed, only to miss it because I'd already started a strip. For the same reason—and I believe this to be especially important when using flies—once the dorado is streaking for the popper, I give it a final pop *and then stop*. The dorado will come to the popper, pause for a split second to line it up, and then open its mouth and swallow it. As a result, I often find the popper down its throat. I believe this behavior, this confidence, is the direct result of very lifelike poppers.

I use the exact same approach when fishing flies, always working to see the taking dorado, and stopping my strip just before impact.

If I go by the weed cover without a take, and I'm certain that dorado are present but I've had refusals using the popper, I have the captain return to the original starting point, and I repeat the approach using a fly. I've had many dorado, even those obviously distracted by my presence, take the fly after the popper had failed.

Less frequently, I reverse the process, starting with a fly and, if getting refusals, changing to a popper. This works when dorado mill about the boat and see the fly repeatedly. I cast beyond them as far as I'm able, and strip the popper quickly. This technique often sends one of the dorado streaking after the *incoming* "baitfish."

A hooked dorado holds other dorado, a trait with many fly-fishing implications. If a number of schooled-up dorado are being cast to, it prolongs the fishing if one angler keeps his or her fish in the water until another angler has hooked up. Eventually, though, all dorado grow stale, and the strikes become less frequent, even when poppers are exchanged with flies or flies are exchanged with smaller flies in different patterns. Ultimately the fish lose interest altogether, refusing anything cast at them, and disappear. Chum, live or dead, can immediately reverse this, recharging the dorado's interest in your flies.

Often the easiest chum to secure—and surely the most convenient to use—is a chunk of giant squid, or *calamari*. The captain cuts this into small pieces and throws a handful on the water. If the angler immediately casts a fly into the center of the *calamari*, a dorado will take it while the schooled-up fish dash about for the bits of bait. If not overdone, this chumming should extend the fishing for an hour or more. If several pangas are working the same school of dorado, the volume of chum can leave the fish sated, less and less responsive, and swimming ever deeper. At these times I make a long, downwind cast and let the fly sink, either on a complete dead drift, or accompanied by only the occasional twitch on the way down. The take—soft, sometimes nearly imperceptible—occurs after the fly can no longer be seen from the surface. The strike must be made quickly. Long after surface action ends, additional dorado can be hooked in this manner.

Almost any dead fish, if fresh, can be used to chum dorado. On several occasions, when down to one or two live mackerel, I have killed a single bait, chopped it into many small pieces, and used this chum to keep the dorado chasing my flies for a few more minutes.

Live chum works magic on dorado, setting them off into an instant feeding frenzy. Mackerel, if first blinded on one side, will swim on the surface in circles, or dive in a series of spirals. Either behavior slows their descent, and draws dorado to the surface. Sardines often school along a rocky breakwater, and if your panga captain is handy with a throw net, a dozen can be caught quickly. Sardines are worth any delay required to obtain them. A sardine thrown at a cruising bull is immediately consumed. Follow it with a second. The fly or popper goes in on the third go-around. (A friend of mine once likened the sequence to throwing hand grenades.) Unless I've been able to fill the panga's live bait well with dozens of sardines, I use them only to bring in large singles; I don't waste these hard-to-get baits on school dorado.

East Cape lies well to the south of Loreto, where the Sea of Cortez meets the Pacific Ocean. Strong afternoon winds and the resulting wave action prevent the accumulation of a weed line, or even small patches of sargasso. However, a dozen crude buoys, each trailing a large, baited hook for sharks, and spaced a mile or so apart, run from near the Palmas de Cortez resort to Punta Colorado. All are likely to hold dorado (and sometimes 6- to 8-pound yellowfin tuna). A few enterprising panga captains net thousands of sardines on the flats and sell these live baits to captains whose pangas have aerated wells. Knowing this in advance, I only fish from super pangas or cruisers that have wells and dependable pumps to keep the sardines alive. By special arrangement, my fishing begins at first light, or nearly two hours before the rest of the fishing fleet departs. For a couple of hours I'll have my captain run down the coast, stopping at each buoy so that I can cast. If I suspect dorado are present, but none are showing, a couple of sardines thrown at the buoy will provide an answer. Generally, however, I save the sardines until later in the day when they become vital to my continued good fishing. One afternoon, my son, Travis, and I used live chum during several hours of incredible midday fishing. We hooked and released more than thirty dorado, ranging from 6 to 18 pounds, at a single shark buoy. The sardines made all the difference.

In Loreto, when the full heat of the day is on the water, fishing becomes more sporadic, the dorado more difficult to locate. Captains search for places where wind, tide, and currents have produced long drift lines relatively free of wave action. Such breaks afford a good view of flotsam that might hold dorado. Small patches of sargasso, many only the size of pie tins, also hold dorado. They would be very difficult to locate were it not for phalaropes, small sandpipers that migrate from the Arctic across the Sea of Cortez in late July and August. They have already changed into their winter plumage, mostly white and gray, and in this dress they can be seen for hundreds of yards as they paddle about searching the sargasso for flying-fish eggs. Panga captains motor from one group of *pajaros*—"birds"—to another, stopping by each little patch of weeds for a few casts.

At any time of the day, captains watch the sky and the behavior of the ever present frigate birds. These graceful, buoyant, and remarkably agile feathered sailplanes pirate catches from gulls and boobies. Frigate birds are also skilled at using hunting dorado to secure flying fish. When in hot pursuit, dorado send flying fish into the air to glide on their enormous pectoral fins while keeping the wind generally abeam. They gain altitude by turning into the wind, doing so at the expense of flight time. Long, seemingly endless flights from one wave-top to another are completed only by the periodic sculling of the extremely elongated ventral half of their tail fin in the water. During these maneuvers, dorado will track them, racing just below the surface while the flying fish frantically try to stay airborne. At such times, frigate birds will swoop down and snatch the flying fish from the air. Having seen this thousands of times, panga captains watch to see whether the birds are riding thermals and searching, or kiting along, as if following compass coordinates, to keep track of a single—often large—dorado. Captains process this information so skillfully that they are often able to intercept the targeted dorado with live chum.

By late in the morning, dorado may still hold under sargasso paddies, but so far below the surface that an angler standing in a panga presumes the cover to be empty. I have snorkeled around various organic flotsam as far as 30 miles offshore and watched dorado swimming around more than 60 feet below me. Gear fishers know of these dorado, and troll lures by their cover. Each year they catch thousands in this manner. But that is not fly fishing. Several fly-fishing approaches follow.

If chum is not available, I use an extra-fast-sinking shooting taper, such as Scientific Anglers Deep Water Express, that I've connected to monofilament running line. I cast the fly upwind well past the cover. As I drift away from the cover, I strip additional shooting line off the reel while the line sinks. I retrieve with short strips and occasional twitches, bringing the fly right through the dorado's suspected hold.

Another midday method involves trolling by patches of sargasso or other types of cover with small billfish teasers. Dorado are difficult to tease, in part because of their nervous, high-strung temperaments, and in part because of the manner in which they take their prey. Dorado flash in on live chum and teasers and crash them from the side, holding them firmly in their mouths—much as a dog holds a bone—as they race back to the shelter of their cover. A dorado rarely comes back to a teaser after it has been ripped from its mouth. If one tracks a teaser, it does so for only a few seconds before either nailing it, or dashing away to hunt for something else. But with the mate physically on the teaser rod and ready to reel, and the captain acting as lookout from an elevated position, and 30 feet of fly line and a fly or popper trailing behind the boat, a dorado can be cast to so quickly that a hookup is possible. At the very least, a dorado will show itself. This may either hold promise for a go-around later in the day under low light, or promote the immediate use of precious chum, alive or dead.

When I am fly fishing for billfish, and trolling teasers to attract them, I always have a 10- or 11-weight rod with a popper ready to go. Rarely does a day pass without my seeing some sort of *basuro*—"trash"—that might provide cover for lurking dorado. When I do, the captain pulls in the teasers and daisy chain and I get ready to cast. Some of my best dorado fishing has occurred using this technique.

It often happens that a concentration of dorado repeatedly tears into billfish teasers, shredding the carefully stitched mullet or belly strips so relentlessly that in a short time an entire day's supply of baits can be lost. When this occurs, I ask the captain to remove the teasers and troll a skirted lure with a hook. Within a few minutes, the mate has hooked a dorado, and other dorado are nervously following the captive fish back to the boat where I wait with my fly rod. A fly then will get far fewer refusals than a popper, perhaps because the popper relies more on surprise and instant reaction than does the fly. Whatever the reasons, though, these opportunities have provided me with some of the largest dorado and best bluewater fly fishing I've experienced.

Sometimes while searching well offshore for billfish, I have encountered a long drift line that contains all sorts of debris. Unless billfish are evident, I ask my captain to run along this line—which may extend for miles—and search for dorado. I once encountered just such a drift line 70 miles off Cabo Marzo and Bahía de Humboldt on the frontier between Colombia and Panama. High tides had floated entire trees out of the jungle, each a roost for masked boobies, their large size and nearly all white coloration making them visible for great distances. Steve Jensen and I motored from bird to bird, casting flies and poppers to dorado and boating five, from 18 to well over 40 pounds. We also saw larger dorado, losing a bull the captain thought would hit 60 pounds. When I'd fished those waters the year before, a gear fisherman trolling for marlin had hooked a dorado the captain swore would weigh 80 pounds, an estimate very much in keeping with the maximum size that bull dorado are known to reach.

A short run north of Cabo Marzo is Panama's Piñas Bay, where in 1964 Stu Apte took a 58-pound dorado, on 12-pound tippet, that remains the largest ever taken on a fly. Nearly thirty years later, he told me about this dorado when we fished together on the long-range boat, *Royal Star*.

"I saw three dorado holding under this mahogany tree and made a cast with a white 2/0 popper. The smallest of the three got to the popper first. One of the dorado must have weighed over 70 pounds. I think the largest of the three would have weighed at least 90 pounds."

Like Apte's record—the longest standing in saltwater fly fishing—the all-tackle record dorado, Manuel Salazar's 87-pound giant taken in 1976 from Costa Rica's Gulf of Papagayo, may never be beaten. Most other dorado records are equally ancient: 83 pounds, 6 ounces, Mazatlán, Mexico, in 1972; 73 pounds, 11 ounces, Cabo San Lucas, Mexico, in 1962; 77 pounds, 2 ounces, Islamorada, Florida, in 1982; 80 pounds, Walker Cay, Bahamas, in 1989.

I've never read studies that give an age for such dorado. But these record fish likely aren't old, not when a dorado can grow to 20 pounds in only three years. Several years ago, on a November long-range, fly-fishing trip, a crew member, while scooping up baitfish with a fine mesh net, captured some month-old dorado, each about four inches long, heavily barred, already pugnacious, and sexually distinct. They were put in a secure corner of the live bait well and fed bits of mackerel. The baby dorado grew so rapidly I could almost watch it happen.

I have taken dorado on flies and poppers in the Pacific, Atlantic, and Indian Oceans, including both coasts of South America and Africa. Each new experience increases my admiration for the species, and my concern for its future as a fly-rod gamefish. The dorado remains one of the premier food fishes and its commercial importance increases each year everywhere in its range. Despite its extraordinary growth rate, this fishing pressure is bringing its average size down. In Loreto, where it all began for me, I have seen two dorado that I am certain would have weighed 60 pounds, fish over six feet long that on the jump produced the kind of long, low-decibel rush of water I associate with tonnage and broaching whales. Memories of 40-pound dorado, even 30-pound dorado, grow less current each year as local commercial fishermen pirate the Sea of Cortez for its shellfish, sardines, dorado, and bottomfish, and as longliners compete to take the last marlin and sailfish. Many panga captains now smile at the prospect of catch-and-release, wear gloves to assure that they do this properly, cheerfully remind you that the daily limit in Mexico is three dorado, and become disgusted with fishers who believe these dorado belong only to their generation. Hopefully these captains' attitude is not a case of too little too late.

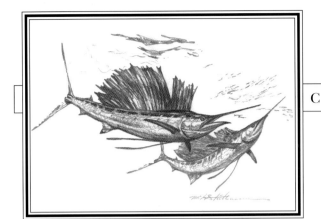

PACIFIC SAILFISH

Gulf of Papagayo, Guanacaste Province, Costa Rica

The Pacific sailfish, *Istiophorus platypterus*, meaning "to bear a sail" and "flat wings," is a fish that, with its immense, cobalt blue dorsal fin, seems to fly as much as to swim.

Certainly any angler who has fought one could only agree. A hooked sailfish cartwheels and somersaults, porpoising gracefully on breakaway runs of 200 yards, and tailwalking in headshaking panic. Some authorities claim its speed is not exceeded by any other billfish; its short bursts are said to approach 60 miles per hour. Whether it is faster than the marlin is arguable. What cannot be argued is that sailfish do not husband their strength by sounding. They stay on top and fight on top with an abandon not equaled by any other pelagic gamefish. In trying to rid a hook, one can exhaust itself on a reel in free spool, and pounds of reel drag become largely meaningless. For the gimballed and harnessed big-game fisher who sits in a fighting chair ready to derrick giant marlin and tuna from the ocean depths, the sail has an abundance of heart, but no staying power. However, this heart is what makes the Pacific sailfish one of the finest of all the bluewater gamefish on a fly rod.

For years, taxonomists divided sailfish into two species, Atlantic (*I. albicans*) and Pacific (*I. greyi*). Sportfishers accepted the separation when they caught Pacific sailfish that were twice the average size of Atlantic sailfish; they most commonly compared sails from Florida and neighboring Caribbean waters with those from the Pacific coasts of mainland Mexico and Baja California. As new areas opened up, the size differences became less marked. For example,

A Costa Rican Pacific sailfish leaps for freedom. Photograph by Linda Rogers.

13

in the Indian Ocean were found sailfish whose size was about midway between the known sizes of Atlantic and Pacific sailfish. While fly fishing in Mozambique's Bazaruto Archipelago, I examined the catch records for Bazaruto Island Lodge and found that the Indian Ocean sailfish—fish that for the purposes of record keeping are considered "Pacific" sailfish by the International Game Fish Association (IGFA)—ranged from 44 to 85 pounds. The East African record was a sail from Milindi, Kenya weighing 145 pounds, well below the all-tackle Pacific record of 221 pounds from Santa Cruz Island, Ecuador, but above the all-tackle Atlantic sail record, a West African fish of 128 pounds from Luanda, Angola.

West African sailfish in particular obscure differences between Atlantic and Pacific sails, for they are twice as large as those in Florida waters, and can average at least as large as those in some Pacific locales. Most of the sailfish I saw in Dakar, Senegal were as large as—or larger than—many sails I've seen caught in Mexico's Sea of Cortez, fish often weighing only 50 pounds. These and other populations of sailfish may be discrete races, but they may also be various age groups—fully mature Senegalese sails to younger Mexican sails, for example.

The whereabouts of spawning Pacific sailfish is little known, and even less is known of their migratory habits. Scientists believe that Pacific sails breed from early spring to summer. When I fished the Cabo Marzo area off Colombia's west coast in February, my fishing companion boated, on conventional gear, a 90-pound sailfish that was very ripe and apparently ready to spawn. When brought aboard, thousands of tiny, pale yellow eggs spewed freely from her vent. But if spawning took place in this vicinity, it would be reasonable to expect some angling record of juvenile sailfish, and there was none.

I always found the scarcity of really small Pacific sailfish, those of several to 20 pounds, most perplexing. A 6-pound sailfish would measure at least four feet long including its bill, might be five to six months old, and would be fully capable of going after teaser baits. But only once have I seen such a Pacific sail, a fish I estimated at 20 pounds that came to my fly while I was fishing off Australia's Cape Bowling Green.

Most often sexually mature Pacific sailfish are caught within sight of land, usually in areas where seamounts and severe drop-offs create cold-water upwellings, a strong mixing of ocean currents, and a rich environment for baitfish. Possibly, for reasons yet to be understood, these sailfish spawn in the open ocean, far from land and beyond the reach of sports boats. We know Pacific sails spawn as free-swimming fish, the eggs left at the mercy of wind, waves, and predators. The young hatch and may remain in that environment until they themselves near sexual maturity. While plausible, this scenario does not yet gain support from the commercial fishing industry, for, regardless of the fishing methods employed, young sailfish remain a rarity wherever they are found. Saltwater fly fishers are left only with the certainty that some areas on the west cost of North America have larger sailfish than other areas, and that the reasons for this are not clear, but involve some combination of migratory movements, age, and discrete populations.

Today, I believe that the largest Pacific sailfish in the world are most often found in the waters off the northern coast of Costa Rica, the West Virginia-sized Central American country bordered by Panama to the south and Nicaragua to the north. I am almost as certain that nowhere else in the Americas are there as many captains and mates skilled at teasing in sailfish for fly fishers.

The Costa Ricans, who live approximately eight to eleven degrees above the equator, call "winter" their cool days of afternoon rain and frequent overcast that persist from May to September. "Summer" is the dry season, October to March. The reason for this is historical: Early colonists were from Spain where summers were hot and dry and winters were wet.

The ocean water warms in "winter," from late March onward. In the waters off Quepos in the south, the water temperature always remains above 80 degrees. At the same time, sailfish are relatively scarce in the country's northwestern Guanacaste Province, where during the "summer" the water temperature may dip to the mid-70s. With the onset of the rainy season in April, the surface temperature rises to 80 degrees, and continues to increase until, in May and June, the daily highs are usually 83 to 86 degrees and Pacific sailfish are concentrated in the Gulf of Papagayo.

Charter boat captains will tell you that these Costa Rican sails are not the same as sails from, say, Panama and Colombia, or Mexico. They believe that the sails from Bahía de Coronado in the Quepos area, which average 85 pounds from December to February, are the same sails that appear in the Gulf of Papagayo in May averaging 100 pounds. More than national pride may be in their convictions. Sails smaller than Quepos sails are not found to the south in neighboring Panama. Nor does Mexico get a run of large sails on any known south-to-north migration from Costa Rica. But no one is certain of the actual movement of Costa Rican sails. From where do those Quepos sails migrate? We know that in late summer and fall, when the Gulf of Papagayo waters cool, some sails will stay there through the months of Papagayo storms; but the whereabouts of the main body of sails remains unknown.

The Pacific sail is very fast growing, reaching 100 pounds in three years. However, in many trips to Costa Rica and during more than 100 days fishing Guanacaste waters, I have yet to see a sail weighing under 80 pounds. Dave Meyers, the former manager of Bahía Pez Vela Lodge, told me that in ten years his captains had released thousands of sails, the smallest about 65 pounds.

Few other areas in the world have such a concentration of angling's most prized saltwater gamefish. Sailfish, blue, striped, and black marlin, wahoo, dorado, bigeye and yellowfin tuna, and a variety of inshore species, including the exotic roosterfish, abound in these waters. This wealth of gamefish was one reason why foreign investment, immigration, tourism, and resort development came with such a rush to Costa Rica in general and to the Guanacaste coast in particular during the 1970s. Contributing factors included the country's peaceful nature—its citizens like to boast they have more teachers than soldiers—and its smooth-ticking democracy, the most stable in Latin America.

Resorts and fishing camps sprang up along the coast, and fleets of locally built Palm Beach 30s were delivered and fitted out to satisfy the most discriminating big-game anglers. Villas Pacifica and Flamingo Beach Resort were built on Guanacaste Province's Flamingo Bay. At the end of the bay, a harbor was

Previous page: Linda Rogers stays with her Costa Rican sailfish. Neal and Linda Rogers are well known among offshore fly fishers for their remarkable gamefish photographs and their beautiful book, The Magic of Saltwater Fly Fishing. *Photograph by Neal Rogers.*

dredged and docks and moorings installed. In the small, remote coastal village of Playa del Coco, Mario Vargas bought three Boston whalers, hired local fishermen including José Canales to captain the boats, and began a charter boat business. A Chicago investment group purchased property between Coco and Flamingo Bay and built a fishing camp just above a beautiful black sand beach. They called their lodge "Bahía Pez Vela," Spanish for "Sailfish Bay." Henry Norton, one of the investors, managed the camp. José Canales's son, Calin, 19 years old, signed on as a mate at the new camp. Within two years he became the youngest game boat captain in Costa Rica. Winston Moore, a wholesale sporting goods dealer from Boise, Idaho, booked Canales, and Curpin Mendez, the mate. The three fished together, often for weeks at a time, aboard *Pez Vela*, a wooden, single screw boat with great fish-attracting harmonics. During the next ten years, the young Tico captain, his mate, and his fly-fishing client combined their talents to catch more than one hundred Pacific sailfish on the fly. While Canales developed into one of the three or four most celebrated captains for fly fishers in the world, Moore became a legend in the sport of bluewater fly fishing.

Winston Moore had, like Billy Pate and Stu Apte, heard how Dr. Web Robinson and his wife teamed up to tease in and hook Pacific sailfish on the fly in Panama's Piñas Bay. Using that information, he traveled to Panama in the mid-1960s and chartered boats out of Club Pacifico to fish the waters off Hannibal Bank. Later, he would book weeks at Tropic Star Lodge and fish Piñas Bay. Moore tried many teaser configurations to determine what was the best number to troll, what colors might make a difference, what were the most effective distances to set them from the boat, whether they fished better with or without bait, and whether trolling teasers with various kinds of attractors made a difference. He came to rely on plastic squid trolled from two teaser rods. Privately, he thought they held sailfish as well as skirted teasers with "meat strips." The crew had far more confidence in teasers with bait, belly strips from either black skipjack or dorado, and he let them have their way. Between the teasers, Moore trolled a Sundance Teaser by the Boone Bait Company. This 16-inch-long cylinder with narrow panels of mirror along its sides produced tremendous bolts of flash when the cylinder rotated. Moore became convinced that this drew sailfish from great distances.

When I visit Costa Rica in May, recent rains have ended the six-month dry season in northwest Guanacaste Province. Only a few days of afternoon showers can transform the tropical deciduous forest from leafless east-Texas-arid to a lush green that fills the hillsides with jungle and frees bands of howler monkeys from their imprisonment in the milk and chicle trees that remain fully foliated throughout the dry season. Cebu, an Indian breed of cattle with bodies of knobs and sticks under loose, pale skins, munch incessantly at the new grass on the *sabanas*. Lowland forests were cut down and burned for these pastures, a terrible bargain, say environmentalists, who claim the sacrilege shortened the rainy season by two months and forever changed the way seeds germinate, trees grow, and rains fall in Costa Rica.

I know the large cebu reserves, the lands of the wealthy rancheros, for they lead me on my drive from San Jose and the coffee *fincas* of the interior highlands to the coastal plains and their miles of white fences, flocks of white-fronted parrots and orange-chinned parakeets, and majestic parasol-shaped guanacaste trees, as characteristic of northern Costa Rica as the baobab is of southern Africa. My journey takes me through Coco, and then to a narrow blacktop road that drops precipitously toward the ocean. When I first view the brick red roofs of Bahía Pez Vela's guest cottages, and see Captain Canales's *Roosterfish* at her mooring buoy, I feel at home.

Canales leaves Bahía Pez Vela Lodge each morning at seven, and by pushing the 31-foot Boston whaler nearly flat out he can make the run to the fishing grounds, the Triente Miles—"30 Miles"—in a little over an hour. In the Gulf of Papagayo, *grounds* most often means an undersea mountain that comes within 300 feet of the surface. Typically, Canales searches this seamount area in close company with a dozen other boats from neighboring resorts.

The seamount's cold-water upwellings ignite a food chain that begins with plankton and ends with the concentrations of billfish for which the area is famous. When I worked with Mako Video Productions in 1992 on getting underwater shots of sailfish, Patrick Guillanton and I snorkeled here and discovered bands of warm and cold water that sometimes flowed only a meter apart. I knew from the boat's thermometer that the warm water was 87 degrees, and I thought the "cold" water was at least 10 degrees less. This experience left us wondering about the dimensions of the displacements happening hundreds of feet below us. Even a conservative estimate involves cubic miles of ocean.

Canales sets a classic half spread. From each port and starboard flat line a teaser bait chugs out and slides down the fifth wave before digging in and disappearing into a blue Pacific swell. On a handline of parachute cord a Boone Bird leads a daisy chain parade of rubber squid down the center of the wake. The bird, a foot-long orange fuselage with stubby supersonic wings, flutters about with its nose in prop wash. For 20 feet behind, the pink squid swim sinuously on the surface.

Sometimes the bait is the belly strip of a black skipjack, locally called "bonito." Dorado belly strips are tougher and last longer. Canales believes they smell better to sailfish. On this May day we'll fish Canales's favorite teaser bait, a mullet with its tail split dorsally, the fish set inside a plastic skirt too short to cover it entirely. When the bait comes out of a wave, the two tails flail about, a convulsive action sailfish can't resist.

More than 10,000 surface-swimming sailfish have taught Canales that they can see this spread laterally from 100 meters. A full spread involving two additional attractors set on outrigger poles gives him a few meters more range for his gear fishers. But then fly fishers must carefully roll cast under one of the poles, wishful thinking when the body grows faint from the rush of adrenaline and the brain is recording the dance between sailfish and teaser one frame at a time.

Mate Curpin Mendez sits on the gunwale. I rest on the cooler where the stitched baits are stored. Canales perches above us both at the engine controls on the flying bridge. We face aft, intensely working on identifying the right kind of shadow, detecting the short length of bill breaking out, or noticing the top few inches of tail cutting the surface. The sailfish may come to any part of the spread and our eyes dart from one teaser to the other, to the bird, and down the line of squid and back to the teasers. When the fishing slows, this tour bores, and I lose my concentration. But on 25-sail days, the search becomes hypnotic, almost hallucinogenic when glare ignites the wake and everything from the bait to an errant jet of water turns into a bill. Once in awhile I see the sailfish when they do. Only a few times have I seen a sail first. Rarely, a half-dozen sails come in at once and latch onto the squid. Occasionally a sail makes everyone crazy by materializing right off the transom and grabbing the lead squid. But generally the raised sail behaves more predictably: It sees the daisy chain of squid, drops back to track them, and comes alongside the baited teasers. If hungry, the sail raises to one of these—not to spear it with its bill, or even to bat it to stun, but to smell it and then eat it. Instinctively, the sailfish tries to take the bait crosswise, for then its raspy jaws can take a hold that prevents any escape. But because the bait keeps trolling along, the fish grabs the teaser from behind, first from one quarter, then from another, each time trying to reposition itself to get a better purchase. If the crew is alert, the mate will be on the teaser rod before the sail can get a death grip on the bait. If not, the mate and the sail begin a tug-of-war. Soft baits like mullet and ballyhoo get shredded, the sail leaving with the remains. Tough baits like dorado belly strips survive, but the sail may be so discouraged by the unexpected struggle that it swims off for less combative prey.

To successfully catch the moving teaser, the sail must keep its tail submerged. This places the fish at an angle: tail down, head up, the bill out of the water. As the fish mauls at the teaser, the captain quickly removes the second teaser, for now it is a distraction. A sail swimming from one teaser to another often loses interest simply out of indecision. Once focused, the sail's frustration over not being able to eat the teaser is exceeded only by its hunger and determination.

Canales has told me that billfish are extraordinarily opportunistic, capable of feeding through a wide range of depths. He isn't so sure from what depths marlin and sailfish will come for his teasers, but common sense suggests a vertical range, from dark depths to brilliantly lit surface, greater than any horizontal range. While fishing with him I have many times observed billfish coming up on a teaser without warning. The previous June, with El Niño in full bloom and surface waters holding at 88 degrees, I was fishing with Canales when he radioed Captain Richard Chellemi on *Gamefisher II* from Flamingo Bay Pacific Charters. I had fished with Chellemi only the month before, and while we chatted about the absence of sailfish, he told us that his fish finder was regularly picking up sails 100 feet down, presumably in cooler water more to their liking. Chellemi's comment prompted me to ask Canales how deep these sails will go to feed.

"Four, five years ago," he said, "the fishing was very good and then no sailfish for three days. Not one. Nothing on the teasers. Didn't even see one. Very unusual. I stopped by some friends on a commercial boat who were fishing for grouper with handlines. They had caught sailfish on handlines, right on the bottom in 600 feet of water. The sailfish were feeding on *calamari* [squid]."

When Canales abruptly changes the boat's course, Curpin and I look over the port bow and see a rapidly expanding, mushroom-shaped cloud moving across the horizon. At its base, a concentration of geysers reaches up from the center and makes the whole business look nuclear. My binoculars turn the smoke into hundreds of birds, and ground zero into spinner dolphin that twist into the air to make the largest splash possible. At any given moment, 1,000 dolphin are in view. Below them are ten times that number, one atop the other, a close-order choreography that corrals baitfish and the small tuna that are alternately feeding and fleeing.

Terns, shearwaters, frigate birds, and boobies wheel and dive. The sharp-eyed terns, both noddy and bridled, track the fleeing baitfish. The huge frigate birds, remarkably agile in any wind, pirate from the other species. Canales tells me that 80% of the time, a frigate bird on the open ocean means a billfish. For all their incredible soaring ability, shearwaters feed on the water. Rarely do they gather in large numbers unless there are concentrations of both small baitfish and the predator fish that mangle them. They remind me of passersby rushing to view an accident.

Canales studies the birds as the distance closes. "Sardines," he says when we are still a mile away. Ten minutes later we motor by a brown circle 100 feet in diameter, a school of sardines driven to the surface by tuna and balled momentarily into the beating heart at the center of this gathering of birds, mammals, and fish. A million more sardines are fleeing, the tuna and dolphin in pursuit. When their mass becomes sufficiently concentrated, these sardines, too, will be balled up and feasted upon. The dynamic is constant, the activity rising and falling like the ocean's tides.

Blue marlin may lurk at the front of a moving school of tuna, while sailfish often hunt along the rear edges. Neither species has anything to fear from the dolphin. Among the species of billfish, I think sailfish are especially willing to pass through schools of dolphin to attack teasers.

I know the drill when the sail comes to the teaser. Canales bolts from his chair and heads for the rod that, for the moment, does not have the sail. Unless he says otherwise, I clear the handline of daisy chain squid, and drop them to the deck, pushing the pile to the right-hand corner of the stern, as far away as possible from my left-handed cast and any running line that might find its way to the deck. Mendez has pulled the bait from the sail's mouth. They hold their rod tips up, Canales waiting a few seconds to make sure the sail gets locked on the other rod, Mendez tensely anticipating the next grab. Sometimes a sail makes an initial grab, loses the bait to the mate, and immediately tries to eat the other teaser bait; Canales and Mendez must make sure they're not clearing the wrong rod. The sail lunges, and as its head comes out of the water, Mendez takes two quick turns on the reel. The sail lunges again, and again it misses. Canales has glimpsed the sail's shoulders. "One-fifteen, one-twenty," he says. He reels in the second teaser, jams the rod in the right gunwale, and returns to the engine controls. I'm in the left-hand corner of the boat with my fly rod in one hand, my Pink Squid popper in the other. Mendez moves to the center of the boat. The sail, with its bill flashing back and forth like a fencer's épée, is on tracks, a hot fish so totally consumed with the split-tail mullet that it could be teased in until I touched it with my rod tip.

Now begins the most exciting thirty seconds in bluewater fly fishing.

My fly line is 55 feet long and the bucket at my feet contains 45 feet of it, stowed from the reel end so that on the cast the line comes out tangle-free. A few turns of fly line remain on the reel; I don't want to strike the fish with backing in my hand. I have a midrange drag setting, four to five pounds, enough to provide some resistance if the running line gets away from me. I toss the popper to my left, away from the boat, and let 15 feet of line slip between my fingers. If I drop it directly over the transom into the turbulence of the wake, the popper bounces around on mini–wave reversals and doesn't go anywhere. With a sail charging in, these lost seconds can be disastrous. I keep the rod tip pointed almost straight up so that the popper skims along with very little drag.

When the sail is about 40 feet away, several actions take place each separated by only a second or two. I drop my rod in preparation for the cast. That is the signal for Canales to take the boat out of gear. That is also the signal for the mate to drop his rod tip to prepare for removal of the teaser. The popper has drifted back a few feet, some line is now on the water, and all is ready for my backcast. The tension from the line and popper on the water—a water-load—gives my backcast the energy needed to keep the big bug moving. I must be sure my backcast is not made straight back, but at an angle, so the popper doesn't foul in the flying bridge, or in the rigging of the folded-up outrigger pole, considerations especially critical when a severe crosswind blows from my left.

During my backcast, Mendez points his rod directly at the teaser, and simultaneously takes a few quick turns on the reel to prevent the sail from catching the bait. As I begin my forward cast, he yanks so hard on the teaser that it flies from the water to land past the bow of the boat and completely out of view of the sailfish, a "clean jerk." Were he to simply reel as fast as possible to clear the teaser, or pull it halfheartedly from the water, the bait would skim along the surface, and the sail would continue after it and overrun the boat.

When I'm fishing with Mendez, I'm with one of the best teaser rod persons in the world; regardless of how exactly I direct my cast to the sail, I know I won't tangle his line. I cast well to my right, across the sailfish, and over Mendez's line as he pulls the teaser free of the water. When my popper hits, line continues to play out until the running line hits the reel. The angle of the cast and the slight movement of the boat combine to put a belly in my fly line. When the line comes under tension, and I make my first strip, the popper begins chugging across the wake to give the sailfish a side view rather than an end view. I keep my eye on the *popper*, not on the sailfish.

The crack-the-whip retrieve sends a foot-high wave cresting before the one-inch-diameter popper. No more than several seconds have passed between the removal of the teaser and the appearance of the popper. To avoid missing the blink-of-an-eye rise, I concentrate on watching only the popper and don't see the neon blues that characterize a lit-up and frantically excited sail. When the fish snaps to its left, its head comes completely out of the water, and in one fluid motion the popper is engulfed. I wait a moment before striking, wait for the line to come taut in my hand, wait as the fish continues to turn, all fractions of one second and three heartbeats, and then with the rod pointed at the fish, and the butt of the rod jammed into my stomach, I strike, once, twice, doing so with the rod horizontal to the water and in the direction opposite from the movement of the sail.

The sailfish stops and shakes its head while panic builds, a very brief time-out that lets me get running line on the reel, back off my drag setting, and collect my senses. When I gain a tight line and the sail feels the tension, it accelerates away for some 75 yards when it breaks out, violently shakes its head, and bounces off its tail through 100 feet of blur and foam before settling down and greyhounding away through 200 yards of backing. The sail then bears left, and goes into a series of berserk headshaking-tailwalking leaps and spins. I have only enough drag to prevent an overrun on the reel, but the huge belly of line increases tension on the leader regardless of what I do. Canales has been backing down the boat, toward not where the sailfish is, but where it has been, so that, with the fish crossing the horizon, he heads for the spot where the fish first changed direction. He does so as rapidly as I can pick up line.

In these few seconds the sailfish, a sprinter in a world of billfish marathoners, has nearly exhausted itself. It will not tailwalk again, and when it does show, its leaps are jumps that no longer possess the kinetic dazzle that marked its first bursts across the water. Copper bars segment its electric-blue-and-white sides, signaling its stress. The sail swims slowly near the surface and must wait for me to catch up.

How fast I do, and increase the stress on this sailfish, determines in large measure how long the struggle lasts. I increase the drag, and reel and reel, as fast as I can, and reel until my arms burn and I think my fingers will fly away, and reel some more. I'm fishing an anti-reverse reel and, with 250 yards of backing out, I can still maintain a decent rate of retrieve, at least as decent as I can expect with a 1:1 gear ratio. Canales watches all this and makes sure we don't create hundreds of feet of slack line and leave the sail with nothing to do but rest and recover.

When I'm again able to go right at the fish with rod pressure and reel drag, the sail is less than one hundred yards out and it reacts and jumps, arching out airborne to only its ventral fin before falling back in. The fish still jumps this way and that way and Canales and I must work toward it carefully for we don't want to pressure it while it thrashes about facing us. Once I've survived the frantic jumps, I figure the sail is mine if I can stay behind it, or can at least have it in this attitude when I apply the maximum pressure my tackle and leader will bear.

When the sail reaches a point of extreme stress, it turns from bronze to copper, takes notice for the first time of our physical presence, and swims down into deeper and cooler water. It clearly identifies the direction of pull, and turns away from it. From this point on, with its head down and huge pectoral fins outstretched, the sail gives me its broad tail.

Canales studies the angle of my line, and complies with my hand signals to continue to back down, stop, or go forward. With the sail holding directly away from me, he spins the boat until I am *beside, above,* and *slightly behind* the fish. As soon as this position is achieved, I lift on the fish with the drag as tight as I can set it, with the fly line pinned against the foregrip with my palm, and with the fly rod pointed down into the water. When I lift, with both hands on the fore-grip, the sail comes up.

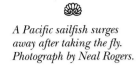

A Pacific sailfish surges away after taking the fly. Photograph by Neal Rogers.

Depending on sail's size and strength, this may be only a few inches, or perhaps a foot or more, but always I am able to lift the fish. I may be able to lift and reel twice from this angle, but if I do the sail invariably turns away, gets its head down, and bores away with its tail. Short of breaking the tippet, I do everything I can to stop it, including putting on the brakes while Canales backs down on the fish. When the sailfish and I have arrived at another stand-off, its tail against my drag, Canales again moves the boat to the side so that I can bring the sail up. Whenever necessary, I move from one side of the boat to the other to complement Canales's efforts and improve my angle on the fish. In a remarkably short time, this constant pressure causes the sail to swim to the surface. I'm not always able to take advantage of this, but today Canales rapidly backs down as I maintain pressure and we're able to keep the sail up. The mate stands ready with the gaff. As we side up to the fish, it goes down several feet, but Mendez quickly lifts its bill up with the gaff and bills the sail with a gloved hand. So complete is the sail's exhaustion that it hardly quivers when Mendez twists the lead hook free.

Years ago sailfish hooked on flies were played until the angler could bring the fish in close enough for the mate to bill. As a result, many were lost beside the boat. When Canales was fishing with Winston Moore he hit upon using the gaff to get the fish's head up and its bill suddenly close enough to grab. This procedure, now routine in Costa Rica, saves a lot of catches and helps prevent the sail from being played to death.

Canales must decide whether the sailfish can be brought aboard for a picture. Almost invariably he agrees to this, but watches the sail intently. A sudden deep bronzing of the fish's gill covers presages death and he orders its immediate release. *Catch-and-release* are more than empty words to Canales. Sailfish keep him employed and Bahía Pez Vela Lodge operating.

Mendez revives the sail by grasping its bill and dorsal fin in his hands and holding its nearly 10-foot length beside the boat. Canales slips the boat in gear and motors slowly along to increase the flow of water through the fish's gills. In several minutes the sail is sufficiently revived to be released safely. With a few feeble strokes of its huge sickle tail, the overheated fish disappears into the darkness of the cool depths.

This is no time to celebrate. I've sometimes had a fresh sailfish on less than a minute after making a release. A second outfit always stands ready to go. While waiting, I check my fly line for any nicks or cuts. If not, I change to a new butt section. The old one has been buffed opaque by the rough skin of the sail's back. I loop on a new class tippet that has been secured to a 100-pound shock and a Pink Squid popper. Canales brings *Roosterfish* to trolling speed, Mendez snaps on freshly stitched teaser baits, and we resume our vigil.

HOOKUPS

I often think that Murphy, whose First Law says, "If something can go wrong, it will," was not an inveterate pessimist but an offshore fly fisherman having a typical day chasing sailfish. Losing sailfish is integral to the sport, part of the mystique and excitement, and one soon adopts a bloody but unbowed philosophy. Losing sailfish? Let me count the ways!

Years ago, I discovered that when a sailfish crushes a piece of ethafoam in its mouth, whether a popper head or a sliding head, it can remain convinced for a remarkably long time that it is something digestible. Once I was fishing with Canales when a sail took the foam sliding head—not the fly—and began a long series of greyhounding leaps. I struck the fish hard and remained convinced it was securely hooked until it opened its mouth and the fly came out. The sail simply turned and ate it again. The entire scene repeated itself. When the sail coughed up the fly again, and again came back to eat it, I was jabbering incoherently and Canales was trying to give me a studious explanation without laughing. Several sailfish later I again hung a fish that was locked only to the sliding head. Since then, I've never been a big fan of sliding heads, but I must add that on at least a dozen occasions I've watched a sail take a popper at the head and hold it so firmly that a hard strike failed to get the hooks into its mouth. These fish, too, ran tailwalking across the ocean while absolutely determined to keep the popper. The sure sign that they were never initially hooked was that when the popper came free, the sail returned to eat it again. After one of these experiences, I found the ⅝-inch-diameter doll eye cut almost in half. That's a lot of compression!

When a sail goes into a full-blown series of panic jumps, it literally bounces off its tail while violently shaking its head. Sometimes the fly comes away and the sail continues jumping. This happened to Bob Harper, a hometown fishing buddy of mine. He got hooked into a sail that jumped away for a couple hundred feet before the popper came free. The sail then fell into the water and repeated all its jumps exactly in reverse. For a moment I wondered if this fish would end up in the boat. Instead Bob and I stood at the transom and watched it go by a few feet away from us, like two kids at a railroad crossing when the noon express roars through.

During a week of fishing I'm likely to experience a severe billwrap either shortly after the initial hookup, or in conjunction with it. I think this most likely occurs when the fish is hooked near the end of its mouth or at the base of its bill. Rather than fleeing in panic, the fish turns and shakes its head. The bill, with its raspy edges, catches the shock and a full wrap is made. Sometimes the hook catches the shock to form a noose. Other times the hook gets a light hold until the shock has a turn or two around the bill. Regardless, the result is a snared rather than hooked sailfish, an irritation that leaves the fish shaking its head and looking down its bill. Otherwise, it will not move. I've had sails hold 25 feet away in this manner for several nerve-racking minutes. Eventually, they free themselves, regardless of any action on my part.

I once had a sail take my popper and greyhound in an absolutely straight line for 250 yards before stopping and fully raising its dorsal fin. "Nerve," said Canales, opening his mouth and putting a forefinger to his palate. He backed *Roosterfish* down as fast as I could reel, and in a couple of minutes we billed the sail, just like that. Canales thought perhaps one sail in ten was affected in this manner by the placement of the hook. I've not observed those kinds of numbers, but I have seen sails begin bronzing up as soon as they began jumping, and virtually quit the fight soon thereafter. Canales would say these fish were "bothered" by the hook. These kinds of hookups have accounted for a few light-tippet records, more than a little bragging about how quickly a sail was brought to the boat, and some complaining about the lack of staying power of the Pacific sailfish.

At the other extreme are the sails hooked in their cheek or shoulder areas, or well outside and above their mouths. No amount of rod pressure can directly interfere with their breathing, and little or nothing in the hook's penetration causes them the kind of duress a hook in the mouth causes. The resulting fight becomes interminable—an hour or more. Several times I have had this occur when the stinger hook swung around and impaled the sail outside its mouth. Eventually the double leverage caused the lead hook to tear out. Usually, however, the hookup happens on the initial grab. Though I often can't see this when I'm fishing, either the captain or mate can. When I'm foul hooked, I play the sail hard, taking liberties that either get the fish to the boat in under an hour, or cause a break in my class tippet.

When a sailfish jumps, a tailwrap sometimes occurs through no fault of the angler. The sail might then swim on the surface in a large circle, or even flip its

The mate removes a Pink Squid popper from a Pacific sailfish that was hooked both in the lower jaw and in the soft spot in the roof of its mouth. Billfish usually react violently to a hook penetrating their palate. Photograph by BJ Meiggs.

tail out of the water in an effort to free itself. If the fish jumps with a tight tail-wrap, something is certain to break. Given the length of an average sailfish in Costa Rican water—9½ to 10 feet—the break often takes place at the end of the fish's tail, in the fly line. This is just one of the reasons I urge fly fishers to set up an extra outfit, and to have several fly lines ready to go—each with butt section, Bimini Twist class tippet, and shock connected and ready to take a fly.

A sailfish has a small head remarkably concentrated in its anatomy. The top and bottom of the concrete-like jaws contain small teeth that form extremely sharp, raspy edges. On the upper jaw, this edge extends without a break for the full length of the bill. Any part of this coming into brief contact with a class tippet separates the angler from the fish. I've found my shock tippets and several inches of my class tippet badly abraded after even a momentary connection to a sail—a rise and a missed strike, for example. On the roof of the sailfish's mouth there is a soft spot, the size of a child's palm, between the forward end of the hard palate and the aft end of the bill. This is the only area that a hook can easily penetrate once its gotten an initial hold. When Dr. Web Robinson fished one of his cork poppers with the hook turned up, he hoped to set the hook into this soft area, and often he did. The rear corner of the jaw is an especially good place to set the hook, for the tissue is very tough, and a needle-sharp hook will penetrate and not easily come out. When I have been able to hook a sail here, and then keep my line and leader behind the fish through its jumps, I've been rewarded with a fairly pristine class tippet even after a long fight. The bony lower jaw can also be a good hookup point if the gap of the hook is sufficient to get around the jaw to penetrate the softer tissue beneath—at least a 4/0 in the case of Pacific sailfish.

I recently read in a magazine article that the phase of the moon makes no difference to the quality of Pacific sailfish fishing. No details were given as to how the survey was conducted, but I suspect much of the information came from a fishing resort trying to fill a full-moon week. I have fished through entire moon phases, sometimes working offshore every day for 15 or more days, and found that the best fishing was the week on either side of the new moon, my preferences being the new moon day, a couple of days after it, and the three or four days preceding it. My last choice was the full moon, including the several days before and after.

When I last fished from a new to a full moon, I experienced a steady decline in the number of sails raised, beginning with 27 fish two days after the new moon, and ending with 4 the day after the full moon. As the full moon approached, my first sail of the day appeared later and later. Then one morning, just before noon, I witnessed a silver projectile on the horizon fly from the water straight up into the air—at least 20 feet. The fish was too far away to see clearly, but the flash of white led me to think *manta* and I gave it no more thought. When this happened several more times, I pointed it out to Canales.

"Sailfish!" he exclaimed.

"Sailfish on the hunt," I said. Canales nodded. Twenty minutes later we had our first sail of the day on the teaser.

Fly fishers theorize that heavy overcast hides the moon and presumably frustrates the sailfish, leaving them ravenous and ready to attack flies at first light. But in reality overcast brings an hour of rain, then breaks up, carrying local showers to other beaches, mountain slopes, and remote jungle valleys. Here and there the moon lights up the sea and the sailfish feed. During the full-moon phase, overcast nights rarely bless my daytime fishing. The silver lining may be the phase's reputation for improving the blue marlin fishing. My first Costa Rican blue ate a Pink Squid popper the day after a full-moon night.

A "lazy" sailfish will appear near one teaser to track it, lightly grab at it; then go to the other teaser; then return to the first, before swimming away. The captain puts the wheel down, runs the teasers through a large circle, and again raises the fish. Perhaps this time the mate can tease the fish in, and it will stay long enough to come to a popper for a delicate "scissorbill" take at the end of its mouth. When you strike, the popper will come free and the sail will not return for it.

The scissorbill rise, so different from the snap roll take of hot sails, is devilishly hard to convert into a hooked sail. With luck—and needle-sharp hooks—I've landed a few that were hooked at the bases of their bills. But generally these too well fed sails must be found on another day when they are hungry and more aggressive.

While on the subject of hookups at the end of a sail's mouth, I should point out that they often occur when trolling a fly or popper for sailfish. I believe that a sail grabs the fly from behind, and before it's able to reposition itself for a crossbill hold, the angler strikes, either pulling the fly free, or gaining such a poor hold at the end of the mouth that the sail tosses the fly during the first series of jumps.

I have faced similar problems when fishing off boats in the 50-foot range. Once taken out of gear, the boat still coasts along like a battleship for a block, and the cast popper becomes a trolled popper. Faced with this dilemma, I make the cast well across the wake and allow additional line from my bucket to belly the retrieve. If the sail takes immediately, the slack line in the cast gives it an opportunity to get a good angle on the fly.

Large boats also produce a wake and afterwake of such size and turbulence that it can put off hot sails. When I was invited to be the guest on ESPN's "Fly Fishing the World," John Barrctt, thc program's producer and host, chartered the largest boat available in Flamingo, Costa Rica, a Bertram 56. Barrett reasoned that the huge boat would give his shooters, Brian Blackburn and Dennis Natalin, a solid two-story platform from which to film. However, to our dismay we found that sails followed the teasers only half the way to the boat and then swam away, far out of range of any cast. After a disappointing day, Blackburn called me to the bridge and we viewed a playback of the last sail. The telephoto lens had captured the sail in close-up, and we could see its bill penetrate the bubbles of the wake. As it continued to chase after the teaser, its head and shoulders were lost from sight. Suddenly the fish turned and swam off. The next day I cast early to the incoming sail and, with the drag backed completely off the reel, I free spooled additional line and then backed off the reel. A long-range teaser removal was made and an instant later the sail had my popper. To strike the fish I kept the rod pointed at it and locked the spool with my hand. After the sailfish was hooked, I adjusted the drag up a shade to avoid an overrun. The fish was hooked and later boated.

Calin Canales estimated this Pacific sailfish (caught by the author) to weigh at least 140 pounds. The sail was caught about thirty miles off Costa Rica's Guanacaste coast. Immediately after the photograph was taken, the fish was revived and released. Photograph by BJ Meiggs.

With little or no wake to contend with, a sailfish can be teased right to the transom. When I worked with Mako Video Productions, Patrick Guillanton and I wanted to get underwater video of a sail taking a fly. We arranged with Canales that, when the sail crashed the teaser, the boat was to immediately be taken out of gear. This would give time for the bubble-congested afterwake to clear out for us. I would then submerge a video camera off the transom, and get a clear view of the sail on the teaser. In the meantime, a popper would be dropped off the transom and not moved. The plan called for the mate to tease the sail right to the popper, then remove the teaser just before Patrick gave the popper a slight "pop." We all held our breath as the sail came in, and when it took the popper—an almost delicate take less than a rod's length away—we got both the video footage we wanted, and a remarkably intimate view of a free-swimming primal hunter.

These efforts to gain underwater video footage of sailfish led Patrick and me to an interesting discovery. Charter boat captains anticipate two sailfish coming in, one on each teaser, and I always keep two rods rigged and ready to go primarily for that reason. Consequently, the boat I'm on is usually good for a double at least once on each trip to Costa Rica. Sometimes when two sails come in only one shows on the teaser, but we're still able to glimpse the second fish. During our time in the water Patrick and I found that two sails came in together far more frequently than even the captains suspected. A second sail sometimes came in low, 20 or 30 feet down, out of view unless one of us was in the water. When the primary sail was hooked, the second fish stayed with it, swimming along while its companion frantically jumped and tried to rid itself of the hook. When the hooked sail was finally brought to the boat to be released, the second sail was there, too, nervously swimming about. Casting then at the second sail with either a fly or a popper proved to be a waste of time. If the hooked sail was brought into the boat for a photograph, the second fish left. We never observed the released sail and its companion swimming together down into cooler water.

The author and Steve Jensen hold a 120-pound Pacific sailfish that the author caught off Bahía Solano. Note the tag. This was the first sailfish tagged for the Billfish Foundation on Colombia's Pacific coast. The author and Jensen provided the various fishing camps on Colombia's west coast with the Billfish Foundation's tag kits.

ATLANTIC SAILFISH

Dakar, Senegal

Cape Verde Peninsula, the westernmost point of land on the African continent, reaches out into the Atlantic Ocean before hooking south and forming the largest sheltered bay

A Senegalese mate bills a fly-caught Atlantic sailfish. Photograph by BJ Meiggs.

off West Africa. Dakar, the capital city of the Republic of Senegal, forms the skyline above the waterfront at the end of the peninsula. Commercial shipping, from fishing boats to huge fuel tankers, fills the many docks and congests the harbor. This great city, a cosmopolitan metropolis with a strong French flavor, and Senegal's cultural hub, looks out over tiny Goree Island, the symbol of the country's past and the link to much of its future.

In 1444, Dinis Dias, a Portuguese navigator, followed the flat, arid West African coastline south from Morocco until he encountered a green lowland that stretched across his horizon. This he named "Cape Verde"; he named the island directly off its tip "Island of Palma." The Portuguese explored the Senegal and Gambia Rivers and used them to bring slaves from the interior to the coast. Coastal forts became collection points and staging areas for the shipment of slaves, first to Caribbean islands to work in the sugar cane fields, and later to Brazil and the United States. When the Portuguese interest in the slave trade declined due to the emergence of the more lucrative trade in Far East spices, the Dutch took over Island de Palma, renaming it "Goede Reede," meaning "good anchorage." Eventually the island passed to the French, who named it "Isle de Goree." Senegal remained a colony of France until it became independent in 1960.

33

Goree is a museum and a memorial to the black holocaust, the slave trade that lasted here for three centuries. However poorly documented the numbers, the overall scope of that misery remains staggering. These few blocks of buildings with terra-cotta walls facing narrow streets became the transatlantic shipping point for an estimated 15 million slaves on their way to the New World. Six million died, either here or in transit. In recent years, Goree has become a pilgrimage destination for those African Americans seeking their roots and coming to terms with their past.

Cape Verde is a fish trap of immense complexity. The finger of land extends to the very edge of the continental shelf, and becomes a feeding stop for the pelagic gamefish that seasonally migrate north and south along the coast. The bottom of the harbor is uneven and so richly vegetated that immense numbers of bottomfish and baitfish reside here permanently. Tuna, marlin, sailfish, and dorado make their way from blue water to these relative shallows to feed on sardines, ballyhoo, and flying fish. The predator fish may stay a week, or a season, but their arrivals and departures proceed continuously.

French-owned, Dakar-based commercial fishing interests, both boats and processing plants, have tapped into this resource. The abundance of fish in the Cape Verde area also supports a coastwide subsistence fishery. But big-game fishing as a tourist attraction was long unknown here, an oversight that ended in the late 1960s due to the efforts of two remarkable men, Leopold Sedar, the first president of an independent Senegal, and Pierre Clostermann, the former president of the International Game Fish Association (IGFA).

Sedar, a poet, writer, and consummate *politique politicien,* was pivotal in peacefully ending French colonial rule while skillfully binding the many ethnic groups into a republic. He sought to broaden Senegal's economic base while fostering worldwide appreciation for African culture. A festival held on Goree Island to celebrate black arts led to an invitation to Clostermann to visit Senegal and sample its fishing.

The choice of Clostermann was eminently logical. He was a national hero of France, a flying ace in World War II, a confidant of Charles de Gaulle, and a deputy for many years in the French National Assembly. His big-game fishing credentials were widely known. Not surprisingly, his success at finding billfish while fishing out of Goree was widely reported in magazines and newspapers, and quite literally jump-started interest in Senegal among big-game fishing enthusiasts. A small fleet of offshore boats soon operated out of Goree. Many huge marlin were boated, and more than a few records for Atlantic sailfish were established.

I came to Senegal to fly fish for Atlantic sailfish. I knew that taxonomically they were now considered the same species as the Pacific sailfish, but for purposes of keeping world records, the IGFA maintained the separation. I knew, too, that the largest Atlantic sailfish were West African, and that many of the most recent records were from Dakar and neighboring Cape Verde waters. Philippe Sleurs, a French citizen and Dakar resident, held the 10 kg record for Atlantic sailfish, an 87-pound, 1-ounce fish caught in 1992, at the time the largest Atlantic ever taken on a fly. (On October 22, 1993, Hugh Vincent landed a 102-pound Atlantic sailfish at the Bom Bom Island Resort on Príncipe

Island. West Africa's São Tomé and Príncipe is the continent's smallest country.) He would be my fishing companion, but before Sleurs was to take over my education on the ways of these gamefish in his home waters, I would put this fishery in perspective by visiting the Lebou fishing village at Yoff on Cape Verde's north coast.

Two hundred years after the Portuguese "discovered" Cape Verde, the Lebou people moved to the peninsula's offshore islands and mainland coast from what is now Mauritania, and became the fishers of Senegal. Their boat, the *loco* (say "locho"), simply crafted, colorfully painted, and driven by a modern outboard, has become one of the most distinct symbols of Senegalese culture. Except on Muslim holy days, the Lebou put to sea each morning and return early in the afternoon with fish to be bartered on the beach and consumed minutes later as *thie-bou-dienne*, "fish and rice," the main meal of the day and the national dish. This internal market maintains the health and vitality of the Senegalese people. Nowhere along the highways did I see a Senegalese male walk unless too old or infirm to run. Senegal may be the jogging capital of the world, less from any addiction to studied principles of whole health than from its people's irrepressible energy.

I walked the beach at Yoff with B. J. Meiggs, our "ship's photographer," and with Patrick Guillanton and Gerard Aulong, two French anglers and video makers I had met the previous winter in Colombia. Along the high tide line, thousands of women in brilliantly colored *boubous*—the beautifully batiked, full-length dresses worn for all occasions—sat shoulder to shoulder, the day's catch assembled before them, each species of fish displayed in its own marketing pattern. Barracuda, grouper, and snapper were the mainstays now, for August was not the month to find tuna. There were a few dorado, some brightly colored exotics, and many small silver perch that children worked over to scrub free of scales. The women talked and called, laughed and exhorted until their voices blended into an orchestra of sounds. Still at the water's edge were sailfish on the wet sand. Each would be butchered, the chunks quickly bartered away. Some of the meat, when lightly smoked and thinly sliced, would become appetizers in swanky hotel restaurants. Nothing was wasted.

The size of the sailfish astounded me. They were, on average, 7½ feet long and weighed between 50 and 60 pounds. Here and there sails topped 80 pounds. I thought one might break 100. I normally do not drive myself crazy with thoughts of world records, but should such a sail come my way, I would be fishing a 16-pound class tippet and taking dead aim at Billy Pate's 75-pound world record. I returned to our beachfront hotel, the Savana, double-checked my stretcher boxes, and fingered through my trove of Bimini Twists. Fishing would begin early the next morning.

Our captain and mate, Youssouf Danfa and Nicolas Mendy, were Wolof, the dominant ethnic group in Senegal, a people tall and lithe, aristocratic in bearing, and handsome or beautiful, depending on your point of view. They spoke French and the Wolof dialect, but hardly a word of English. Guillanton, fluent in four languages, became our interpreter. Philippe Sleurs, who understood Wolof and a little English, would be on the teaser rod. In the morning Danfa ran the *Jessie Why?*, a Bertram 35, to our hotel. Christine Hebert, director of the fishing program at the Savana since 1985, made sure the boat was properly set up for fly fishing, and that sufficient teaser baits were on board.

As we motored out, Mendy skillfully stitched up ballyhoo with cotton twine and a sail needle. He called the gray-and-white baitfish "zoom-zoom," (spelled *soon-soon*), a sound that I thought described perfectly their behavior when being pursued by hungry sails. Sardines received a less complicated treatment: A few turns through the head and gills and they were done. In either case, a single teaser bait on a spinning rod was set on the third wave between two daisy chains of rubber squid, both extending to the fifth wave, an exact reversal from the way I had fished for years in Costa Rica. I noted other differences as well. As soon as a sail showed on a daisy chain—as often happened—the boat would be slowed. The moment the pass-off was completed, when the sail was passed off from the daisy chain to the bait, Danfa would take the boat out of gear while the daisy chains were quickly cleared. Sleurs or the mate would then tease in the sailfish on the spinning rod until I could reach it with a modest cast.

Should a heavy crosswind belly the teaser line and make it difficult to get it and the daisy chain lined up and side by side, the captain could assist the successful pass-off by heading into the wind. Presumably, the sailfish would follow docilely behind.

"All so slow in developing! Do we have that kind of time?" I said. Sleurs assured me this approach would work. He sometimes fished by himself on his Bertram 28, and even found time to get in some false casting before presenting his fly, a few white feathers behind a cone-shaped popper head of a size found on bass lakes. I found him equally casual with regard to his tackle: 9-, 10-, 11-, 12-weight outfits seemed all the same to him. His favorite had been an 11-weight with a Fin-Nor reel, but this had gone over the side, either his or his mate's fault, I never knew which.

I fished a 12-weight Sage, and Billy Pate Marlin reel. For the most part, I gave up the monster one-inch-diameter poppers I sometimes fished for Costa Rican sails and blue marlin, and cast ⅝-inch-diameter ethafoam poppers, usually blue and white, blue, green, and white, or sometimes the Green Machine colors—hot chartreuse and blue, which we soon renamed "Air Afrique" for the way they duplicated the colors of that West African airline.

For two days the sails came in "lazy," at least a dozen fish, none very excited or lit up. If Danfa did not immediately slow the boat from its speed of five to seven knots to a crawl when a sail appeared on the daisy chain, the fish lost interest and left. When Philippe removed the teaser, and I cast, the sail's take was halfhearted, or it ignored the popper and searched for the bait. Philippe then cast the teaser bait at the cruising sail and sometimes brought the fish back to where I could cast to it again. The takes, tentative and scissorbill, prevented solid hookups. The shouts on board, in Wolof, French, and English, did nothing to stimulate the sailfish. "They're not hungry," Sleurs would say in disgust.

Few people anywhere know these and neighboring waters as well as Sleurs. His father owned and managed a fish processing plant in Dakar. The docks, the waterfront, and the commercial tuna boats became his playground while growing up. He worked in the family business until able to afford his own tuna boat, the *Columbia*, a 100-foot, cold-molded boat built in San Diego, California in 1960, at the time the largest of its kind. Sleurs renamed the boat *Irrintzina*, filled its live bait wells with ballyhoo from Cape Verde, put on a crew of Senegalese to jackpole in the fish, and put to sea, following the seasons and the schools of tuna around the bulge of West Africa. He began his year in January and February off Togo and Ghana, moved to the Ivory Coast in March, and to Sierra Leone and Gambia in April and May where the skipjack schools stretched to the horizon and his men worked in the racks until they dropped. He unloaded his catch in Dakar in June and fished off the Senegal coast before spending the summer and fall hunting for albacore and yellowfin in the waters off Mauritania and Morocco. Sleurs worked south in November and December, loading up on bigeye tuna off Senegal before putting into Dakar to market his catch and haul out, remove the marlin bills that were driven through the boat's three-inch-thick hull, paint its bottom, and put to sea again to pursue the tuna to the south and begin his new fishing year.

"It's considered bad luck to change the name of a boat," I said. Sleurs looked at me ruefully.

"Last October a fire in the engine room sank the boat," he said. *Irrintzina* was a way of life. I didn't ask for more details.

Now Sleurs ran a nightclub in Dakar. And he fished. A lot. Both the 1 and 2 kg world-record Atlantic sailfish belonged to him, along with the 10 kg fly record. Other categories had his attention. He said that he could boat nine of every twelve sails on 10 kg class tippet, and three of every twelve on 6 kg. I would see his name again in the IGFA record book.

The next day on *Jessie Why?* the sails were high-strung and nervous. Gone was their lackadaisical mood. Still not so tractable, I thought, nor so easily seduced by the daisy chain as Pacific sails. But in the afternoon a hot sail came in as if it were on tracks. My cast from the left corner of the transom was made exactly as I like to do for Pacific sails, the popper sent over the teaser line and well across the wake to the left side of the sail. When the line formed a belly, the popper began chugging up a spray across the wake. The fish bolted to its left, rolled out with its head and shoulders above the water, and took the popper crosswise, a rise as full of faith and determination as any in fly fishing.

The sail gave me only the briefest moment to strike and get the lead hook into the side of its mouth before it angled away and began a series of greyhounding leaps. Danfa did not overback the boat, and when the sail stopped for a moment some 400 feet away, I immediately had tension on it. I worked the fish hard and could feel it give in to the pressure when it was not boring straight away. As we closed the distance, Danfa caught on that I applied the greatest pressure on the sail when my angle changed from dead aft to a side-and-still-behind position, and though he may not have fully appreciated that the reason had less to do with my tackle than with protecting my class tippet, he began to assist me. As the sail tired, it came in quickly, and when it was beside the boat, mate Mendy reached only for the bill and brought the 60-pound sail aboard for pictures. Ten minutes had passed between hookup and billing.

*Previous page: This
Senegalese Atlantic sailfish
struck an Air Africque
popper and immediately
began greyhounding.*

Captain Danfa said that at the most he and mate Mendy fished but one or two fly fishers each year. Yet their skills at preparing ballyhoo and sardines, at setting teasers on the flat lines, and at managing the boat for fly fishers exceeded those I'd seen anywhere outside of the best camps in Costa Rica and Venezuela. Was Philippe Sleurs responsible for this? And if so, where had *he* learned these skills?

In 1989, an American had chartered *Jessie Why?* and then insisted on fly fishing. Danfa had never seen anything like this before, but out of the experience he learned to tease in sails using ballyhoo. For Mendy, the stitching process was a natural transfer of that used when stitching baits for gear fishers. The following year—or thereabouts—Jerry Dunaway of Houston, Texas brought to West Africa his magnificent ocean fishing tag team; the 110-foot *Madam,* his lavish live-aboard yacht; and his 48-foot custom-built *Hooker,* the ultimate big-game fishing machine. John Cockrane, Dunaway's captain, worked down the coast, fishing Dunaway as they traveled. When they put into Dakar, Captain Danfa got a crash course in setting daisy chains and passing off sails to teaser baits.

After five days of fishing both gear and flies aboard *Jessie Why?,* and getting what I thought must be a mile of underwater footage of hooked sailfish, our party moved to the Ngor Diorama Hotel and the Air Afrique fleet of boats at the Centre de Peche Sportive in Dakar. Pierrette el-Hamoudy, who manages the fleet, had arranged for us to fish aboard *Wahoo II* with Cheichk Fall, her most experienced captain, a boisterous, good-natured man popular in French big-game circles for his skills at night fishing for swordfish. The mate, Sambou Ndong, quiet as a shadow, knew little or nothing of fly fishing. This didn't bother me. Fall could explain the teasing operation. I explained in detail to Ndong how a fly leader was constructed, emphasizing how easily a class tippet could be broken. This explanation was vital to my success.

Fly fishers do not use the doubled line commonplace among gear fishers, and, of course, cannot grab this line and "wire" in a billfish the last 15 feet. However, in third-world countries, where crews have never worked with fly fishers, the subject of line strength centers on the fat, heavy fly line. Common sense suggests that a line of such diameter must be enormously strong. Explaining the rationale for going from a fat fly line to a 100-pound shock and connecting the two with a fragile class tippet gets complicated in a hurry. I brought the subject of line strength back to the class tippet. "Don't touch the leader!" I said. "Don't touch the line! If you do, the thin section of leader will break!" Ndong would be mindful of this, even while wondering why a full-grown man, even a simpleminded one, would fish a weak length of line between two strong lengths of line.

Captain Fall fished Pink Squid in the daisy chain—pink being the universal color for sails—and we found sails regularly. They were as aggressive now as last week's sailfish were desultory. I wasn't certain why, but for the first time we found large schools of sardines, and often teased in sails at their perimeter. Patrick cast to a sail that raced for the popper, but when it was only a few inches from inhaling it, an eight-pound dorado snatched the bug away. Patrick's brooding lasted for only a few minutes. He hooked into the very next fish, a 50-pounder that was brought to the boat and released. I missed two wildly frantic sails, the first hitting the popper on the run and never really getting hooked. The second sail, lit up and mouth agape, rocketed completely out of the water in a wonderful arching leap that carried it to the popper a split second after Ndong removed the teaser. This rise form—if so violent an activity can be described so quaintly—was nearly impossible to time, for the fish never slowed enough to be set on properly without breaking the tippet. The popper disappeared and I tightened to feel for the fish, but the sail was gone and I was left with only badly shaking hands.

Guillanton hired Haider el-Ali, a Lebanese who operates a dive shop on the outskirts of Dakar. He used scuba gear to get deepwater video footage, shooting up toward the surface at a freshly hooked sailfish, and then following the released sail as far as possible down into the cool depths.

I had observed how some sailfish reacted to my sudden appearance beside them, and I wondered now how my class tippet would fare with both Guillanton and Ali chasing after one of these terrified fish. I remembered how in Costa Rica's Gulf of Papagayo my fly line had hooked on Guillanton's regulator while I was fighting a sail. Miraculously, the fish picked that moment not to run and the line was safely cleared. Now, half a world away, the two cameramen chased after the Senegalese sails without incident. When I joined them to shoot underwater stills, a crowded sailfish jumped above the three of us, landed on top of Guillanton, and ran right at me. I tried to grasp its bill, but the fish slipped by under my arm as I pushed away. Months later Aulong faxed me after I'd watched the completed video. "Did you see the sail almost get you in the gut?" he said.

Rick Rosenthal, who has shot dramatic underwater footage of both marlin and sailfish for Flip Pallet's "Walker Cay Chronicles," told me how he had narrowly escaped serious injury when a Costa Rican sailfish calculatingly sized him up and then, with malice and forethought, attacked him. I remembered his story and promised myself I would be more cautious.

Though these sailfish were often half the weight of those I caught in Costa Rica, I know what every fly fisher knows: Size is relative. A sailfish 7½ feet long is only small when compared directly to one 2 feet longer. When I next hooked up using a 16-pound class tippet, Captain Fall estimated the fish at 65 to 70 pounds, close to Billy Pate's record. "A record for Senegal," he said, and indicated that we should take the fish.

I had hooked it in the hinge of its jaw. Because it greyhounded invariably away from me, the shock and class tippet stayed out of harm's way along its right side. Captain Fall proved a clever fellow, keeping line drag to a minimum by always following the backing and not the fish. Despite our coordinated efforts, it took thirty-five minutes for me to work the sail alongside. Remarkable, for I had put down larger Pacific sails in half that time.

Perhaps I had overstimulated Ndong's caution, for now he confessed to having no idea how to gaff the fish. Guillanton gave the dull gaff a try and managed to briefly stick the sail in the tail. Having convinced Fall that the fish must be some sort of world record, Guillanton waved to our companion boat to come

Patrick Guillanton tows an exhausted Atlantic sailfish back to the cruiser. The fish was hooked deeply in the gills. A safe release was made by reaching through its gill cover, removing the hook, and then cutting the monofilament. Photograph by Trey Combs.

alongside, and then called over for a second mate. I waved off Ali, who sat impassively on the fantail platform waiting to go in with his camera. I didn't need a diver in the water to become an additional distraction. When the new mate came aboard I again brought the fish alongside so that the gaffing could be completed. Poor Ndong! He jumped in the fray to club the sail, and passed the wooden baton through the class tippet. As I wondered how to get this illiterate man's explanation onto a notarized affidavit for the IGFA, Captain Fall said "30 kilograms"—about 65 pounds—short of Pate's world record. The scales later confirmed the estimate. Fall, however, was happy, for my catch-and-release ethic had not again robbed the Centre de Peche Sportive of a fish to sell.

LIFE HISTORY NOTES

The American Fisheries Society recognizes only one sailfish species, but continues to develop data that suggest this single species breaks down into separate "biological units," or "stocks." Unfortunately, the stock structures of sailfish, and their degree of isolation from neighboring stocks, whether inhabiting the Atlantic, Pacific, or Indian Oceans, are generally poorly known. Based on worldwide sportfishing and commercial fishing records, and recoveries of tags from Billfish Foundation's tagging program, we know only that sailfish are most concentrated near land, and that they are usually year-round residents with mild to dramatic seasonal variations in their numbers.

The author, Phillipe Sleurs, and mate Nicholas Mendy with a 55-pound Atlantic sailfish.

Previous page: Hader el-Ali, a Lebanese diver, follows an Atlantic sailfish down after its safe release. This photograph was taken during the Mako Video Productions' filming of West African sailfish, which "cooled down" after their release. Nothing definitive was learned. Photograph by Trey Combs.

Certainly some of these biological units define themselves more strongly than others. For example, scientists suspect that sailfish along West Africa, and those from the East Coast of the United States remain separated, even though a few individuals have been caught in mid-ocean. In either area, the movement of sailfish is generally north and south. In the winter the U.S. sailfish are most concentrated off south Florida, while the West African sails concentrate off the Ivory Coast in winter—a time when they're all but absent from Cape Verde and neighboring waters.

Other examples of local, north-and-south sailfish movements have been observed off Mexico's west coast, off Costa Rica, in the Gulf of Panama, and in the Sea of Cortez, where the fish seek isothermic concentrations of water 80 degrees or warmer.

Senegal's sailfish are abundant off Dakar from June through September, with the largest specimens typically found later in the season. Juvenile sailfish of 10 to 20 pounds, fish in their first year, are not common, but they are found. Philippe Sleurs told me of one he caught on gear that weighed 6 kilograms, or about 13 pounds. Guillanton, Aulong, and I fished in late August and the sailfish were large by Atlantic standards, perhaps averaging 55 pounds, slightly larger I think than the sailfish I found on Venezuela's La Guaira Bank when at their most concentrated, September to December.

CHAPTER 4

BLUE MARLIN

Blue marlin hunt the deep waters of the open ocean. Water temperature, ocean currents, and concentrations of squid, tuna, and mackerel influence their migratory

movements, but unless these factors are in alignment, land and structure hold no special attractions for them. Where they are found in this bluewater environment, they are the most sought after and celebrated trophies in the world of big-game fishing. Indeed, their fame is such that for much of the non-fishing public, marlin means only blue marlin. Yet the largest of them, the females encountered on the high seas, are supreme predators living beyond the range of island-based sport boats, and more often seen and caught by commercial interests. Their considerable legend derives both from what is documented and what is rumored.

In Ernest Hemingway's *The Old Man and the Sea*, a fisherman named Santiago fights, on a handline, a blue marlin more than three times as large as any previously caught in sportfishing. Hemingway based his story on a village tale he had heard in Cuba. While critically acclaimed, the story drew smiles from big-game fishers who thought they could separate good literature from a fish story even when they were one and the same. In the years since, handliners who fish the remote margins of our oceans have said that while scarred hands, smashed gear, and lost opportunities are the most compelling evidence of gigantic marlin, not all such encounters are mythical. Some blues are fought to the death and sold to fish buyers who must weigh them to complete the

47

transaction. This documentation, however scant, proves Hemingway's novella less a parable and more a documentary of courage and determination in an arena both primitive and merciless. Santiago was fictitious, but the blue marlin he fought need not have been.

When I fished out of Le Morne, Mauritius with Roland Tyak, he told me of a native fisherman who was handlining in a 90-pound yellowfin tuna when an enormous blue marlin suddenly appeared. The man quickly got the tuna in his skiff, ran a huge hook through its nose, and handlined it back into the ocean. The blue took the bait immediately. The fight ended the next day. The blue was 700 to 800 kilograms, or about 1500 to 1700 pounds. Roland knew I believed his tale, but he told me still another about the Indian Ocean blues that have been his life. A commercial fish buyer in Port Louis, the capital city, phoned him and insisted he come to the icehouse and view the remains of a blue marlin caught commercially. He did so, and found a fish that weighed 950 kilograms after it had been gutted and had its head and tail cut off, a blue that when living would have weighed well over 2,000 pounds. Tyak took pains to explain that he believed clients of his had hooked such blue marlin, fish that made initial runs measured by the mile against 70 pounds of drag, and so physically overwhelmed the fishermen that the outcome of the struggle was never really in doubt.

The last time I fished off Colombia's Pacific coast, local fishermen were abuzz over a monster blue that had recently tangled in a net set for tuna. The fish had been brought to the beach and photographed by everyone who could find a camera. The great fish was then chopped into pieces and weighed; 2,600 pounds was the very rough estimate.

I met Philippe Sleurs in Dakar, Senegal shortly after he had lost his 100-foot, cold-molded commercial fishing trawler to fire. Each year for a decade he had pursued schools of tuna off the west coast of Africa from Mauritania to the Ivory Coast. At the end of the fishing year Sleurs would put into Dakar and pull the boat to effect repairs and clean the bottom. Invariably the three-inch-thick hull would hold the broken-off bills of blue marlin, some completely penetrating it. Though the size of the bills was his sole evidence, Sleurs was confident that some of the Atlantic blue marlin would have weighed over 2,000 pounds.

Stories of marlin (and swordfish) ramming boats with such force that they must break off their bills to escape are among the oldest fish stories told. Why a free-swimming marlin does this remains a mystery. A hooked billfish jumping and thrashing about in terror could be more easily explained, but this rarely happens. During a ten-year period at Costa Rica's Bahía Pez Vela Lodge, thousands of sailfish and marlin were billed and released without serious incident. But several years ago, two of the lodge's boats were rammed by hooked blues, completely penetrating *Swordfish*, a cold-molded wooden boat, and *Roosterfish*, a double-hulled fiberglass boat. In the former case, the bill could not be removed. Both ends were cut off and the bill fiberglassed over.

I had fished off both boats many times, often spending time in the water working to get underwater shots of Pacific sailfish. One day five years ago aboard Captain Calin Canales's *Roosterfish*, a friend fought, on gear, a blue marlin of about 500 pounds. When the fish was close enough to wire, I put on snorkeling equipment, grabbed my underwater camera, and prepared to go over the side. Canales grabbed my shoulder and shook his finger in my face for emphasis. "No! No!" he said. "Not with a blue!"

I was fourteen years old when I began deciphering the mystique of blue marlin. I lived in Pearl Harbor, Hawaii, and I would take the bus to Honolulu on Saturdays to visit the commercial fish docks and warehouses where Japanese longliners unloaded their catches of blue marlin. After the bills were cut off, the fish would be weighed and the weight painted on their sides. I counted marlin from 1,000 to over 1,200 pounds on these visits. Sometimes several of these "granders" would be piled together, each hundreds of pounds larger than any blue that had ever been caught sportfishing.

Greg Trier fights a 170-pound Pacific blue marlin during his stay at Costa Rica's Bahía Pez Vala Lodge. This was the first billfish he ever hooked. Remarkably, the blue marlin was boated and safely released. Photograph by Patricia Beimford.

During this time I crewed on a 100-foot sailing schooner that took tourists for day sails of Waikiki Beach. Long and lazy beam reaches permitted me time to climb the mast and sit in the crow's nest. From this vantage, I saw my first blue marlin in life, a massive, deep-bodied, surface-cruising fish displaying a run of cobalt blue across its back, a fish that I felt synthesized the mystery and power of the ocean itself.

As a fly fisherman, every blue I've sighted since has affected me in the same manner only more so, a *grand mal* of emotions that shuts down coherent

thought and leaves in its stead trembling hands and kneecaps that fibrillate like castanets. If the marlin appears on the teasers, there is also gut-wrenching fear, for now I stand directly in the path of a terrifying violence unlike anything else in fly fishing. Blues don't just attack teasers, they *crash* them, a clear-out-the-bar rush that slows down time and divides a second into many static frames, the kind of slow-motion images that precede a head-on automobile accident.

I remember every blue marlin I ever hooked on a fly, only eleven in all. I haven't seen more than three times that many on fly-fishing teasers. Not a single one of these marlin weighed less than 180 pounds. Two would have weighed 700 pounds. Not one that was hooked was boated. I've hunted for them off Puerto Rico and Papua New Guinea, off Venezuela and Costa Rica, off Mexico, Mauritius, and Hawaii. I've looked in vain for the rare yearling blues of 25 to 75 pounds, but nowhere can they dependably be found, certainly not in the way that black marlin can be found concentrated off Australia's Cape Bowling Green in August and September. I've looked for two-year-old fish of perhaps 50 to 150 pounds, and I know they are often caught during September off the Virgin Islands, and in the Strait of Mayagüez between Puerto Rico and the Dominican Republic; off Mauritius in February; and off Papua New Guinea's north coast in April. I've looked for small male blues of 100 to 150 pounds, and I know they concentrate off Hawaii's Kona Coast in July and August. But looking is not finding, and finding is not catching, and for me, as with other offshore fly fishers, the blue marlin remains the Holy Grail of fly fishing.

Nelson, my Costa Rican captain, estimated the first blue I ever hooked to be about three hundred and fifty pounds, a fly-rod fish if it committed suicide by jumping in the boat. This blue took the popper, ran 50 yards, and spit it out because it had never been hooked. As I reeled back the popper, Nelson called down from the flying bridge, "Pop it! Pop it!" I did, and watched the blue turn around, rush the popper, and inhale it a second time. This time I struck the fish solidly. The blue answered the imposition with a single magnificent jump only 100 feet off the transom. Then it sounded. Seconds later it came out on the opposite horizon at least 500 feet away and dragging up perhaps 700 feet of backing from the depths. Though the reel was in free spool, the 15-pound tippet broke from line drag.

That marlin ended ten days of phenomenal fly fishing for Pacific sailfish. We had raised nearly three hundred sails and on my best day I'd cast to seventeen and hooked twelve. Nelson estimated one sail at 160 pounds, the largest he'd seen in the Gulf of Papagayo in six years, but it had struggled loose from the mate and then broke me off when the rod shattered. No matter. I had blue marlin on the brain. I talked about them wherever I was and I looked for them whatever the ocean. I soon understood that when fly fishing for blues, if something can go wrong, it will. Every time.

One of the best weeks of blue marlin fishing I ever experienced occurred in August at the Palmas de Cortes resort on Baja California's East Cape. Lani Waller and I were teasing for each other on a 30-foot cruiser, and raising two to six blues a day. The fish appeared to be clones of one another, an average of 200 pounds, and so aggressive that the captain sometimes found it necessary, at first, to accelerate away from the marlin to keep them on track, and also to prevent them from munching the teasers for keeps. When a blue came in to my corner of the transom on the teaser run, Waller grabbed the rod, moved to his right, and kept the hard-charging blue coming in as I cast over the teaser line. When he pulled the teaser, the blue whirled to its left, saw my huge Flying Fish popper headed its way, and launched itself into the air, a magnificent leap completely across the boat's afterwake only 15 feet off the transom. The blue came down with its mouth wide open and engulfed the popper in an explosion of spray. Astonishingly, the fish was hooked on the set. Waller, ever the steelhead fly fisher, said, "Now, *that's* what I call a grab!" The marlin immediately sounded. Ten minutes later the popper came free.

At the opposite extreme was a 230-pound blue that came in on the teaser while I was fishing on *Swordfish* with Charley Boillod in Costa Rica's Gulf of Papagayo. The teaser was properly pulled, and the boat taken out of gear, but the blue slowly moved around ten feet down and watched the popper chug back to the boat. The captain motioned for me to cast again. I did, and again began working the huge ethafoam popper back to the boat. The captain saw movement I couldn't and held up his hand, the universal sign for "Wait!" I gave the popper a twitch and then let it bob about on the flat calm ocean. Slowly, ponderously, the blue marlin rose to the surface like a great trout, rolled through a perfect rise, and took the popper down as if it were a dry fly. I could not have struck the fish harder. The blue exploded up on top and kept its head out of the water as it shouldered its way through an almost complete circle before the popper came flying out.

Because my blue marlin flies and poppers are so huge, and I want to be perfectly ready when a blue appears, I often have a rigged-up and ready-to-go 14-weight directly behind me when I'm "up," my primary rod and the bucket holding my fly line in the left corner of the transom. I did this while fishing a 12-weight for Atlantic sails and white marlin off La Guaira Bank, Venezuela. Captain Luis Millan on *Margullia II* saw a surface-basking marlin and changed course to bring the teasers across its path. The blue, however, sounded upon our approach. Seconds later it appeared on the left teaser and charged in, slamming it from first one quarter and then the other, trying to gain a firm purchase, and immediately lighting up in its frustration. The mate couldn't reel fast enough, Millan couldn't clear the other teasers fast enough, and the daisy chain of squid was still attached to a stern cleat when the boat was taken out of gear. Into this mess I made a spastic heave of a cast, stripping line off the reel to carry the popper back to the marlin. As the popper drifted away from the coasting boat, and the teaser came in with the marlin, the three parts arrived together only 25 feet off the transom. The mate cleanly jerked away the teaser and the marlin instantly took the popper. Not even ten seconds had passed since the blue first appeared on the teaser. I hammered home the hook without the slightest reaction from the blue. Like a submarine, the fish slid beneath the waves with scarcely a ripple and began a sound that carried it more than 500 feet down. After a pause, it continued on down again until I thought 800 feet of backing and fly line had left the reel.

When a marlin moves up from such an extreme depth, it is at first impossible to determine from the slack whether the fish is moving away or toward the angler. If the fish is moving away, and the boat doesn't overrun it, the shock tippet can still be kept alongside the marlin's head and the class tippet away from its bill. However, if the marlin starts up directly toward the source of the line, the class tippet will get at least chafed. At the worst, a billwrap will occur. When this happens, even when the marlin holds a deep sound, the angler can feel the difference, for headshakes are telegraphed from the bill. I felt this twenty minutes into the fight, and said as much to Steve Jensen, my fishing partner. A moment later the marlin was free. The class tippet had worn through two feet above the hook, indicating that the billwrap had taken place beyond the end of the marlin's mouth.

I've never stayed hooked to a blue marlin that didn't sound. If the sound didn't ultimately free the fish, its incredible strength and endurance did. A marlin cruising around five hundred feet down isn't the same fish as the one wearing itself out by going ballistic on top. Given enough time, something bad happens. The degree of difficulty is such that Jim Gray allegedly made a small fortune out of a large one hunting Costa Rican blues. After losing more than ninety, a hooked blue jumped into his boat and was killed. This 203-pound, 8-ounce fish became a world record for the 8 kg (16-pound) tippet class. To demonstrate that he was not just lucky, but a world class big-game fly fisherman, Gray came back six months later and boated a 260-pound blue on 10 kg tippet, an extraordinary feat.

Billy Pate has never boated a Pacific blue. Lord knows he's tried. More than thirty times he's tried. Several years ago he called me and recounted an epic tale, of a 400-pound Costa Rican blue he had fought for seven-and-a-half hours. Extra mates were loaned to make the gaffing. Pate lost the use of his fingers and had to reel with his palm. At times, the clearly laboring fish was only 30 feet away. Night fell and the fight continued on in the dark. Eventually, Pate broke the fish off.

Luck plays a major part in any effort to take a blue on a fly legal by the rules of the International Game Fish Association (IGFA). Anyone who has taken more than a few billfish on a fly recognizes that individuals of the same species act differently when hooked. Some sulk, some jump themselves silly, some seem impossibly strong, and some run out of energy quickly. Hook placement has a bearing on this behavior. A hook taking hold outside the mouth hardly bothers a billfish at all. A marlin hooked in this manner can seem to go on forever. A hook in the corner of the jaw gains the angler a secure hold if it fully penetrates, but again this is not a hookup that particularly bothers a billfish, and from some angles it can put the fly and most of the shock tippet in the fish's mouth. A hookup toward the bony end of the lower jaw is a tough one to keep, but can interfere with the fish's breathing and help to shut it down. A hookup in which the hook penetrates the soft part of the palate provides a secure hold, and keeps most of the shock tippet out of the fish's mouth. More importantly, this hookup hits nerves and so bothers a billfish that it sets off in a series of frantic jumps that soon causes exhaustion. (I like to use a bait hook with a flat, rolled point that won't cut its way across the roof of the fish's mouth and ultimately fall out. For this reason, regardless of what I use as a lead hook, I prefer to use an Owner bait hook for the stinger hook.)

No matter where the hook takes a hold, some billfish immediately become sluggish, possibly the result of having just pursued baitfish. I recall a blue marlin of about 180 pounds that appeared on the teaser when I was fishing with Ray Beadle out of Costa Rica's Bahía Pez Vela Lodge. The fish came in hot enough, but when Beadle cast and hooked the blue, it could get no more than its shoulders out of the water on the first jumps, much like a marlin would behave an hour or more into a fight. Unfortunately, the fish almost immediately got its bill on the class tippet and broke off. But we both exclaimed how this was the perfectly behaved blue, one that appeared already tired at the moment of hookup.

Some years ago I began noticing that the kind of fly or popper could affect both my hookup success and the behavior of the billfish once it was hooked. When fishing a highly buoyant, ethafoam-type popper, the billfish often moved the popper away in an effort to get it. Using a fast-sinking sink tip or shooting taper rather than a floating or slow-sinking line helped prevent this. A billfish, regardless of how it takes the popper, often gets too much of the popper head between its jaws for me to cleanly drive the hook into its mouth. I think this to be especially true with marlin because of the immense pressure their jaws can bring to bear on the popper head. Also, when using tube-style poppers—in which the fly comes free and slides up the shock tippet—or when using a sliding ethafoam head in front of the fly, the billfish can see what is causing them all the aggravation and become distracted by it. Once they focus on this *thing* hanging in front of their faces, they'll stop, shake their heads, and bat at it. When this happens with the billfish facing the anglers, it becomes difficult to protect the class tippet from getting either severely chafed or billwrapped. I've watched blue marlin do this, getting free even before the fight really started. For these reasons, I fish tandem hook flies without a sliding head when fishing for marlin.

TACKLE NOTES

If the marlin is over 100 pounds, whether striped, blue, or black, I want every advantage possible. My class tippet leader of hard nylon will test as close as possible to 22 pounds without testing over 10 kg—usually 22.4 pounds, the maximum class tippet category allowed by the IGFA. My shock of 150-pound soft monofilament, including all knots, will run 11⅞ inches, and I'll max out my Bimini closures so that no slippage occurs. At least 300 yards of the backing, *connecting directly to the fly line*, will be one of the new superthin gel-spun polyethylene lines in 50-pound test. My reel will be huge and provide me with the best possible rate of retrieve. *The cork drag on my reel will be cleaned and freshly lubricated.* I'll hope for a captain experienced with fly fishers, and I'll pray that the boat has twin screws so that it is nimble and quick when backing down or spinning suddenly around. If fishing for blues which I expect to run in the 200-pound range, I'll use a 14/15-weight rod so that I can muscle up a deep-sounding fish.

Because I have usually encountered blue marlin incidentally, they have come in on teasers set for sailfish. However, I believe that size, rather than color, does make a difference, and I'll run foot-long teasers when blue marlin are anticipated in a billfish mix. Some captains will run a huge skirted lure on parachute cord close to the boat specifically to bring up a blue, even when other flat line teasers are intended for sailfish. I personally like blue over white, and hot greens and blues—the Green Machine colors—when searching for blue marlin.

Mention blue marlin to fly tiers and they'll knock out the largest possible fly or popper, sometimes producing something that when wet can't be picked up and cast. "Large" is important to bring in a blue, and the fly and popper must be large enough for the blue to quickly find amid the after-wake's turbulence, but eight-inch flies and poppers that can be properly cast will do the trick.

BLUE MARLIN *(Makaira nigricans)*

Some taxonomists separate blue marlin into two species: the Pacific blue (*Nakaira mazara*), inhabiting the Pacific Ocean from 48 degrees north to 48 degrees south; and the Atlantic blue (*Makaira indica*), inhabiting the Atlantic Ocean from 45 degrees north to 35 degrees south. Those Indian Ocean blues found off the east coast of Africa and island nations such as Mauritius are considered Pacific blue marlin, though scientists suspect that a few "Pacifics" pass around the Cape of Good Hope into Atlantic waters. Other taxonomists treat the Atlantic and Pacific populations of blue marlin as subspecies. Currently, for the purposes of record keeping, the IGFA lists the Atlantic and Pacific blue marlin separately, but considers them to be closely related subspecies, *Makaira nigricans nigracans*, and *Makaira nigricans mazara*.

Jim Gray holds the Atlantic blue marlin fly-fishing record for 16-pound class tippet, a 159-pound blue from St. Thomas, Virgin Islands in 1990. To my knowledge, he is the only person to be recognized by the IGFA as having established world records for both Atlantic and Pacific blue marlin.

*Dave Linkiewicz poses with his shortbilled spearfish (*Tetrapturus angustirostris*), a 37-pound, 78-inch-long specimen caught off Kona, Hawaii, in March 1995. This was the first shortbilled spearfish ever taken on a fly. Thus far, this exotic and rare gamefish is found only in Hawaii in numbers sufficient to attract fly fishers. Charles Owen caught the equally rare longbill spearfish (*Tetrapturus pfuegeri*) on a fly in 1991, off Cozumel, Mexico. Little information is available about the life history of either spearfish. Photograph by Rick Azevedo.*

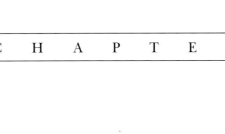

CHAPTER 5

BLACK MARLIN

Cape Bowling Green, Australia

The Great Barrier Reef, a natural wonder on such a colossal scale that astronauts can view it from space, fans across the northern coast of Australia like an inland sea, more a

continental shelf of coral than a wall. Visible strips of coral, the "ribbons," mark its ocean edge. The most celebrated of these are named and numbered, from Cairns to Lizard Island, "one" to "ten." Pelagic baitfish raft outside the ribbons and draw many species of gamefish to the area. Among these gamefish are dorado, Pacific sailfish, wahoo, yellowfin tuna, and black marlin.

Mature male black marlin, fish of 100 to 350 pounds, arrive at the ribbons early each September to spawn. The much larger females join them days or weeks later. By the middle of the month a big-game fisher catches the first "grander," a female black of 1,000 pounds or more. During the three-month season, about a hundred granders will be boated, and most released. Experienced captains tell stories of granders fought and never beaten, near-mythical blacks pushing the 2,000-pound mark. Some captains underestimate the size of a client's black, calling a grander 950 pounds to assure that it will be released. Regardless of the true number of granders, no other area in the world has such a wealth of huge marlin as do the ribbons during Australia's spring.

The black marlin newly hatched from the September spawning are not found in any local fishery until late the following May, when yearling blacks of 20 to 30 pounds begin appearing in the shallows of the Great Barrier Reef to the south of Townsville. Here rivers flush nutrients into the ocean, the start of

A mate bills Ed Rice's 56-pound black marlin. Photograph by Rod Harrison.

57

a food chain that supports immense concentrations of pilchard and yellowtail scad, locally called "yakka." These small marlin build in numbers and, by July and August, game boats may raise two dozen blacks from 20 to 50 pounds in a single day. For twenty years, anglers seeking to take a black marlin on a fly have come to Townsville, for nowhere else are they so abundant and so small.

I have long dreamed of traveling to Australia and fly fishing for black marlin. Ed Rice and I have each landed the same four species of billfish on a fly, all legal by the rules of the International Game Fish Association (IGFA). Both of us want a black and a blue to get all six, to do a "slam." We also have, in Ray Beadle, a fishing companion in common. He traveled to Townsville in 1987 and, under the guidance of Captain Frank Thompson, caught two blacks on flies, an 85-pound, 15-ounce marlin on 12-pound tippet, and another of 94 pounds, 3 ounces on 16-pound tippet. Both marlin were fly-rod world records, and both records still stand seven years later because the fish were atypically large. Black marlin of that size, fish at least two years old, haven't been seen in the Townsville area since.

Dean Butler, of Dean Butler's Sportfishing Adventures, in Cairns, put two game boats under charter for our party of five. Ed Rice and Harm Seville will fish on Captain Bobby Jones's 48-foot *Diamond Girl*, while Charley Boillod and I fish on Captain Craig "Sparrow" Denham's 40-foot *Spirit of Brisbane*. Wendy Hanvold will alternate between the two boats. Three of Australia's most experienced bluewater fly fishers will be our deckies: Dean Butler and Alan "Fish" Philliskirk for Denham, and Rod Harrison for Jones. To maximize our fishing time we'll anchor at night on the fishing grounds.

When we pull out of Townsville early in August and begin a run 40 miles to the south, we know that our 1994 will be like Beadle's 1987. Water temperatures hold at a frigid 71 degrees (our captains consider 74 degrees about the minimum for blacks), ocean currents off Cairns are still running south at a time they should be running north, and the yearling blacks are nowhere to be found. We aren't completely glum about this; the few reports we've heard of black marlin tell of fish in the 50- to 150-pound range, always singles, two-year-old fish larger than any black in the typical run of yearlings.

Our general destination is Cape Bowling Green, a long spit of sand and mangrove that provides such quiet anchorages in its lee that fishers liken the flat water to a bowling green. The ocean remains extremely shallow in the area, 100 feet or less, and will prevent the marlin from making deep sounds. As we run, Sparrow's depth sounder continuously flashes on huge rafts of yakka, while Fish and Butler begin setting up the teasers.

Australian mates divide teasers into those that swim and those that skip. Whole fish, as small as eight-inch mullet and as large as yard-long narrow barred mackerel, fill either role. Regardless of the size of the bait, a mate runs a rigging needle down through the fish's head and out below its mouth, following this with heavy monofilament. An egg sinker is then slipped on the monofilament and kept tucked under the fish's mouth by crimping the monofilament directly in front of the fish. This weight keeps the bait down and swimming. The monofilament is run out a couple of feet and gets crimped again to a swivel.

Instead of a large, brightly colored, skirted lure set as the primary attractor, Butler and Philliskirk rig a single, swimming queenfish on a short line and set it off one corner of the boat. I find the attractor's action astonishingly lifelike, its extremely tough skin giving it a trolling life of a day or more. They then set daisy chains using either five-spot garfish or mullet, four to the group, each weighted to swim on a short lead. They cover the garfish skip teasers with a squid "hoochie," or "skirt" as the Australians call it. This provides some extra protection and gives the garfish additional color and flash. Eight miles from Cape Bowling Green, Sparrow slows the boat to seven knots, and studies the depth sounder for concentrations of yakka. Fish and Butler set the teasers. Swimmers and skip teasers light up our wake with tracers of silver, and our vigil begins.

The marlin are scarce and the boats split courses, work different water, and barely remain in visual contact. Sparrow soon tells us that a lazy black, which Jones estimates at 100 pounds and change, pursued their teasers for ten minutes and gave Rice several shots. For us, the seas look so empty that the few boobies about repeatedly dive on our teaser baits. I've seen this before on other oceans, and I always think it's the worst of all bad signs. The yakka may be plentiful down deep, the marlin may be somewhere down deep too, but the boobies act as if they're half starved.

The next day Sparrow receives a radio message saying that a game boat has raised two blacks on a nearby reefy seamount. We troll our way there, find nothing, and debate whether to quit the area and make a night run 100 miles down the coast. Both captains discuss the situation and decide to stay.

On Day Three a juvenile Pacific sailfish, so small that Butler describes its bill as a radio antenna, "crashes" the teasers as hard as its 20-pound body can bring to the task. Sparrow takes the boat out of gear, I cast to the fish, it attacks the fly and can't get its mouth around the hook. I cast to it a second time, and the fish again takes the fly. Nothing. I will gladly trade it for nearly all of the eighty or so sailfish I've hooked on flies. By at least 25 pounds, this is the smallest sail I've ever seen. We raise a black early in the afternoon, but the fish is mostly passing through. A nod at our teasers and it's gone. *Diamond Girl* reports raising three blacks, with a shot at one. No grabs. We anchor with *Diamond Girl* on the Great Barrier Reef and, while Harrison bottom fishes for sharks and emperors, we drink beer, put on some tunes, and party.

To change our luck, Hanvold comes aboard the *Spirit of Brisbane* and we all change hats. This works. A black comes in on our queenfish, chases the teaser to the transom, and then bails out. I cast to it, but the marlin has already slipped away. I'm shaking all over, my legs jelly from the overrich mixture of oxygen and adrenaline.

Hanvold quickly settles me down. "God, Trey, I can hear your knees knocking from up here on the flying bridge!"

An hour later Sparrow calls down. Rice has hooked up. We pull in the teasers and motor close enough to watch the marlin dance off the transom. Harrison soon bills it, and we see blood run down one side; the fish has sucked the 7/0 fly deeply into one gill. Harrison makes a well-intentioned release, but the fish floats near dead on the surface. They bill the marlin again. Butler's soon-to-be-held Cairns barbecue of crocodile cheeks, tiger prawns, and kangaroo steaks now will offer black marlin kabobs as well.

Not thirty minutes pass before our first hot black shows on the daisy chain of swimming garfish. Sparrow winds in the bridge teaser as the marlin darts about trying to eat anything that swims or skips. Fish tries to tease in the black, but it crosses over to the skipping baits, changes its mind, and crosses back for the swimming daisy chain, chasing the baits nearly to the transom. As Fish pulls the baits into the air, Sparrow takes the boat out of gear, and I cast at least 30 feet beyond the black. It turns, sees the fly and immediately races for it. As the marlin makes a perfect rise, its head and big shoulders rolling out of the water, it engulfs the fly going away. I strike the black and it stops, and I hit it twice more, hard each time. Sparrow sees an opportunity to hot gaff the black and backs the boat. Not a chance. What takes place next is a blur.

The marlin jumps, comes out twice again 100 feet off the transom, and goes down. Sparrow hits full reverse and I lose the black in a cloud of engine exhaust. I barely keep my balance and begin to protest, then glimpse the marlin on top again, off the bow, and know that the streaking fish nearly caught the fly line on the propeller. It continues to race about, frantically jumping and shaking its head. Sparrow stays close to the fish, and maneuvers the boat to give me a clear playing field. After five minutes, the fish makes a shallow sound, and I turn up the lightly set drag and wonder about my 20-pound class tippet. I think the marlin will go 90 to 100 pounds.

The black remains so explosive I can never tether it to a big drag, and I simply palm on the rim control and hang on as the fish exhausts itself. When I feel a sharp headshake 20 feet down I'm certain the marlin is billwrapped. As I work it toward the surface, I can see that this is so, the leader emerging from a point about even with its lower jaw, the marlin's short, raspy upper bill wearing directly on the class tippet. The fish is nearly to the surface when it sounds again, a movement that frees the billwrap. I play the fish with steady pressure, leaning really hard on it, and the next time up Butler makes the gaff, taking the fish low. Incredibly, the fish twists and tears out the gaff. It goes down 20 feet, and is again pumped up, gaffed, and brought aboard.

The fly's stinger hook had taken hold in the fish's palate, almost certainly the reason it reacted so violently after the strike. The class tippet was so severely abraded that I marveled the fish had been landed.

To submit the marlin to the IGFA for world record consideration, I will need to weigh the fish on land with a certified scales. We cover the fish with towels, keep the saltwater hose running over it, and return to our fishing. Late in the afternoon both boats pull in their lines and begin running for Cape Bowling Green. Once at anchor, we put over an inflatable and motor to the sand-flea-infested beach. Hanvold carries the scales and acts as weighmaster. Butler witnesses the weighing. The setting sun bathes the spit in hot orange as Butler climbs a casuarina tree, throws a rope over a branch, and ties the scales in place. We boost the marlin up: 81 pounds, 40 pounds over the existing record. Rice's fish hits 56 pounds.

I have no illusions about the durability of this record. Saltwater fly fishing has taken hold in Australia. Butler says I should fax in the record application,

The author and Dean Butler hold the author's 81-pound world-record black marlin. Photograph by Wendy Hanvold.

a tease with a thread of seriousness. He explains that in September he and Fish will charter the *Spirit of Brisbane* for a week of fishing off Cairns. They'll be looking for those midsized male blacks.

"With Sparrow at the controls, a 200-pound black would be possible," I say to Butler.

"We think 300 is possible," he replies.

A 300-pound marlin of any species, IGFA legal, would be an incredible catch, involving both a perfectly behaved fish and a good deal of luck. Billy Pate nearly got a Pacific blue that size. Les Eichhorn, in Australia, and Stu Apte, in Panama, each nearly got blacks of over 300.

I leave Butler with my best saltwater reel backed with superthin 50-pound backing, and wish the two men luck. Their good fortune will be the best possible reason for my returning to fish outside the ribbons.

BLACK MARLIN (*Makaira indica*)

Black marlin range throughout the tropic and subtropic areas in the Pacific and Indian Oceans. They favor islands, seamounts, and the outer edges of reefs, and in this regard may be most structure-oriented of all the marlin. (In Australia's Jervis Bay, about two hundred miles south of Sydney, small blacks

Alan "Fish" Philliskirk hooks a 300-pound black marlin on a fly off Cairns, Australia. After several jumps, the marlin was free. Large adult black marlin are found off, not on, the Great Barrier Reef. Here the fly fisher faces the challenge of a deep-sounding marlin.

are sometimes caught from shore.) With their short dorsal fins, extremely short and fixed pectoral fins, short, massive bills, and great body depth, blacks appear to be the most compact of all the billfish. The body is slate blue dorsally, and silvery white ventrally, the silver color more dramatic in the tropics. (For years, silvery blacks caught in the Hawaiian Islands were called "silver marlin" and thought to be a separate species. The "species" appears frequently in the writings of Zane Grey.)

During the early 1950s, wealthy American big-game fishers began catching ever-larger granders off Cabo Blanco, Peru. Today, Alfred Glassell, Jr.'s 1,560-pounder, taken August 4, 1953, and Mrs. Charles E. Hughes's 1,523-pounder, taken April 22, 1954, are, respectively, the men's and women's records and the two largest blacks ever taken. (Footage shot of Glassell's fish was spliced into the movie version of Hemingway's *Old Man and the Sea*. In the film, Santiago's great marlin was neither a "he" nor a blue.) When the currents running off Peru changed, the baitfish left, and so, too, did the great female blacks. Since the 1950s the world's largest black marlin have come from the vicinity of Cairns, Australia. Many light-tackle records, both fly and gear, have come from the

neighboring area of Cape Bowling Green.

I fish a tandem hook Sea Habit Billfish fly, 7/0 Gamakatsu and 5/0 Owner bait hooks opened up a shade and connected with 150-pound Jinkai monofilament. *I keep the fly soaking in water all day so that when it hits the water it will immediately right itself and begin swimming.* If I don't drop the fly on the nose of the billfish, I immediately want a swimming profile; I don't want the fly lying on its side. Rice used a 7/0 Mylar Minnow tied by Ralph Kanz, an eight-inch-long FisHair and Flashabou fly that has proven very effective on other billfish as well. My Sage 13-weight rod will again be my choice for blacks of 100 pounds or less in the shallows of the Great Barrier Reef.

Australian game boat captains I meet in Cairns and Townsville, besides Bobby Jones and Craig Dunham, include Laurie Woodbridge and Barry Cross. Collectively, they are among the very best in the world. If fishing 10 kg tippets with one of these captains in September for 200- and 300-pound blacks off the ribbons, where blacks have plenty of bottom beneath them for humongous sounds, I will switch to a 14/15-weight rod and the finest large reel on the market, topped off with 500 yards of 50-pound superthin backing.

STRIPED MARLIN

"The ridge," Baja California Sur, Mexico

Bluewater fly fishers had never witnessed such a scene: Striped marlin tailing to the horizon in every direction, schools of thirty marlin so frantically crashing balled-up sardines that seagulls were struck by their bills; free jumpers connecting these pods of violence with series after series of flashing leaps; less than a minute passing before another dorsal fin broke the surface and a marlin was storming after one of the two teasers trolled behind *Royal Star*, a luxurious, 92-foot, long-range fishing boat out of San Diego, California, chartered for Ed Rice's 1993 Blue Water Fly Rod Invitational.

When I visited Captain Tim Eckstrom on the bridge for an explanation of this concentration of marlin, so remarkable in scope and dynamics, he ran his index finger down the chart before him. "This is 'the ridge,'" he said of the string of banks 40 miles off the Baja California coastline. "I've watched bait building up here for several weeks now during *Royal Star*'s last two trips."

I could guess the rest. "And the striped marlin migrating south out of California's cooling waters have run right into it?"

"Yes," said Eckstrom, "but here's where the marlin are concentrated." He stabbed at the chart for emphasis. "They are in kind of a no-man's land, not directly over a bank or a ridge, or anything."

The marlin, now gorging on baitfish in surface water of 71 to 73 degrees, would shortly be found off Cabo San Lucas, the resort city on Baja's southern tip, more than 100 miles south of us. In the meantime, the marlin had sixteen

A fly-hooked striped marlin begins a series of jumps off "the ridge." Photograph by Marty Downey.

fly fishers gasping with wonderment—and questioning our collective wisdom.

These reactions were hardly atypical of long-range fly fishers, regardless of the species of gamefish they encountered. The LoPreste-Dunn sportfishing fleet had, in only four charters over three years, become the leader in exploring the frontiers of bluewater fly fishing. I had participated in three of those ten-day, long-range fly-fishing trips and had seen records broken for skipjack, black skipjack, yellowfin tuna, Pacific bonito, and wahoo. During the first two trips we had seen few billfish and had hooked none. When I sailed on *Shogun* on the third charter, I observed the start of the immense buildup of billfish now being experienced by *Royal Star*'s fly fishers. We found many striped marlin, and a few Pacific sailfish, the mates using either live chum or chunk bait to draw the billfish within casting range. I was fortunate enough to boat a 90-pound Pacific sailfish, the first billfish boated on a long-range fly-fishing trip. I sailed on *Royal Star* a week later.

I came aboard *Royal Star* doubting that billfish could be teased in to such a huge boat, one that generated a wake of foamy turbulence hundreds of yards long. But with Ray Beadle and Mike Wolverton running the teasers out well past the traditional fifth wave, and Eckstrom taking *Royal Star* out of gear the moment a striper showed, the long tease proceeded on a coasting boat and a clearing wake. The marlin arrived lit up and nearly berserk with frustration.

The fact that the boat was still moving at the time of the cast initially proved troublesome, for invariably anglers set too early, pulling the fly from the marlin's mouth before it had fully turned. At first, only Rice proved deft enough to manage a solid hookup, doing so by keeping the rod straight up and then dropping it and slipping line as the marlin turned. As the fly was drawn back into the corner of the marlin's mouth, he would strike, and hit the fish several times more when the running line was on the reel. As Rice demonstrated it, the approach looked straightforward enough, but after a violent take from a huge fish, striking at precisely the right moment with badly shaking hands required intense concentration.

In just two days, we successfully teased in more than 100 marlin, always with the boat out of gear so that our casts conformed to the rules of the International Game Fish Association (IGFA). The 60 marlin hooked became a clinic in big-game fly fishing and what can go wrong: billwraps, class tippets breaking on the strike, fly lines breaking, backing parting at connecting loops, rods breaking, reel drags failing, side plates collapsing, and much, much more. While reviewing the wreckage and witnessing the schools, pods, and shoals of marlin, I thought that this was a *calamity of marlin*, one promoting an incredibly steep learning curve, and one as empirical as bluewater fly fishing ever gets.

Landing a striped marlin on a fly rod is always the result of skill and luck; by the end of the second day, only Ray Beadle had successfully brought a marlin to gaff. But hour by hour and day by day, through dozens of fish, we learned from our mistakes, and studied our few successes, and our hookup rates increased.

Royal Star came equipped with four 16-foot Avon rubber skiffs, each with a 30-horsepower outboard, an experienced mate to operate it, and a radio telephone for communication with Eckstrom on *Royal Star*. The crew held two of

A striped marlin engulfs a white ethafoam popper. Note the pale, neon-blue pectoral fin and hot blue streak down the dorsal fin, indicating a lit-up, very excited striped marlin. Look carefully, and the marlin's eye can be seen just below the surface. Photograph by Trey Combs.

these skiffs in reserve to enable anglers to follow their hooked marlin more efficiently. Additional skiffs were used by pairs of anglers to troll teasers and to hunt for marlin independently of the mothership.

Finding marlin by skiff proved just as easy as finding them with *Royal Star*, even without her wealth of sophisticated fish-finding electronics. When I teamed up with Rod Harrison, Australia's premier bluewater fly fisherman, and mate David Wolfson, we trolled for no more than a minute before a striped marlin, its pectoral fins neon blue, its vertical bars hot blue lightning bolts, crashed the teaser and sent spray smoking off its dorsal fin as it rushed the raft. As I pulled the teaser, Harrison dropped his fly directly in the path of the oncoming fish. He got in a clean strike on the take, but as the fish accelerated away, the backing broke near the fly line.

"Okay, mate," Harrison said, as he grabbed the teaser rod and Wolfson slipped the skiff back in gear. Only seconds later it was my turn. I missed the strike, the marlin never really getting stuck, but when I cast again, one of several other free-swimming marlin schooled near the teased-in fish stopped the fly. I hit the marlin hard three times, noticing that on the third strike the fish's fully erect dorsal fin dropped halfway down and then raised again. The striper, perfectly casual in its forbearance, swam off with our little skiff in pursuit. At nearly that exact moment, Ed Rice struck his fourth marlin of the trip, safely

Marty Downey works an exhausted striped marlin close to the inflatable skiff. Photograph by Janet Downey.

transferred himself to a waiting skiff, and began running down the fish, a "fatty" of well over 150 pounds, the mate would claim.

Wolfson followed our marlin, staying on its right rear quarter to keep its bill away from the class tippet, and tried to keep within 200 feet. I maintained heavy pressure on the marlin, forcing it at times to tow the raft while the 50-pound ultrathin backing stretched as tight as a banjo string. At the end of an hour, the marlin launched itself out of a swell, wide pectorals balancing huge shoulders through a flight that carried it into the next swell 25 feet away. The marlin's flanks still ran clean, blue and white; no dorsal bronzing signaled fatigue or stress.

"That marlin is huge," I said. "It's a blue?"

"Na! A striper. A real fatty!" said Wolfson.

I continued to extract as much grief as possible from the marlin's spirit. When my fatigue granted the fish renewed energy, Harrison urged me to gang up on its faltering powers and beat it with the last of my strength. This I tried to do even as the marlin, still looking baleful and contemptuous, shot out of yet another wave. When the sun went down after four hours on the fish, I was certain that the marlin, not I, would be the survivor of this encounter. The skiff, a "rubber ducky," in Harrison's Aussie lingo, was, over the long haul, a killer of a fish-fighting environment, for I could find nothing against which to brace my body. Without respite, all leverage worked against my arms and back. And then, in the dark, I could no longer make the subtle changes necessary to keep the 12 inches of shock tippet on the right side of the marlin's head.

Wolfson maintained radio contact with *Royal Star*, and for the first time I heard that Ed Rice was also in the fish fight of his life. He would tell me that after nearly five hours, compression from his backing spread the side plates of his reel. He eventually retrieved line by twisting the rim control. At one point, the marlin was no more than 20 feet from the two mates and their 8-foot gaffs. When the reel finally locked up, the marlin broke off.

Eckstrom had stayed in visual contact with Rice, and now took the exhausted angler and crew aboard. After tethering the raft, Eckstrom radioed Wolfson. *Royal Star* was at least five miles from us. To give the mothership a bearing, he asked Wolfson to light off a flare. Several minutes later, *Royal Star* appeared on the horizon, her port and starboard running lights twinkling in the distance. When either the red or green light disappeared, Wolfson called in the correction. In a half hour, with the marlin still on, we were illuminated in *Royal Star*'s floodlights and I transferred from the raft without anyone touching my rod.

Now able to brace myself against *Royal Star*'s waist-high bulwark, I worked furiously on the marlin while Eckstrom slipped the boat into gear and followed

Walt Jennings bills an 80-pound striped marlin from one of Royal Star's *four inflatable skiffs. Photograph by Ray Beadle.*

❦

The author hangs on as an enormous striped marlin begins a series of jumps. The marlin was hooked from the long-range ship Royal Star *and pursued from a 16-foot inflatable skiff. Photograph by Janet Downey.*

my line. In only a few minutes we could see the fish ghosting along off the bow. Several times the three mates who assembled for the gaffing almost reached the marlin. To end the standoff, Eckstrom suggested I lead the fish to the transom area where it could be reached more easily. As if reading Eckstrom's mind, the huge striper started down the side of the boat while I raced along the side deck, locked up the drag, and tried to keep its head up. When the marlin came to a stop 20 feet from the transom, the three mates were waiting and immediately reached out to strike the fish. The marlin suddenly leaped half out of the water, directly at the boat. One gaff went in; the other two did not. The marlin slipped free, broke the 17-pound tippet, and disappeared into the darkness beneath *Royal Star*, free, finally, after five hours.

Besides the two stripers described, two additional marlin were brought to gaff on Day Three, one that Tony Sarp released, and one that Bryan Peterson

elected to gaff and submit to the IGFA for world record consideration. Collectively, the fly fishers aboard *Royal Star* had now hooked more than eighty striped marlin on flies and poppers.

When we first encountered the run of marlin, many began debating the relative effectiveness of flies, flies with sliding heads, and poppers. Normally, such debates go nowhere, each angler a slave only to his or her own limited experiences. But the incredible volume of encounters with hot striped marlin on *Royal Star* granted anglers some distinct impressions, and confirmed for me my firmly held ranking of the various approaches.

Over the years I have alternately used all three setups for both Atlantic and Pacific sailfish, and white, blue, and striped marlin. Nothing in my experience makes a better commotion and draws billfish through dense afterwake turbulence so readily as one-inch-diameter foam poppers with a feather-duster pile of saddle hackles behind. But this arrangement also has its downside. The superbuoyant popper, when taken from directly behind, can float away from the billfish's most aggressive efforts to inhale it. The large foam head can get crushed in the billfish's mouth on a side take, preventing the angler from obtaining a good hook set. For both Atlantic and Pacific blues, and Venezuelan whites, I've had more marlin throw the popper than break the tippet.

I experience more refusals when fishing only a fly, simply because the billfish have a harder time finding it, *and this fact puts a premium on initial placement.* I want the fly close to the billfish, to one side or the other. Failing that, I want it immediately behind the billfish. Least of all I want it short, and directly in front of the fish. Regardless of how the take proceeds, the billfish must be given time to turn and, if possible, have the fly drawn back to the corner of its mouth. But wherever the fly finds a hold, the hookup is more secure when I strike with the fish turning and going away.

During the second day on *Royal Star*, most of the fly fishers had made a run at the striped marlin with poppers. A few anglers tried flies with sliding heads, while fewer still fished with the flies only. As expected, the marlin had no trouble finding the poppers and crushing them on some monster takes, and this generated a lot of popper babble in the rerigging areas. By the end of the day, anglers had gotten nearly fifty shots, but no one fishing the poppers or the sliding head flies had been able to hold the fish. The only marlin that provided long fights, and the only marlin boated, were hooked on flies. (It must be admitted that the most of the experienced bluewater fly fishers were casting only flies.) Soon nearly everyone was scrambling, borrowing, and trading for the billfish flies on board, and hoping to hold a marlin until it could be billed.

By the fourth day I was out of flies. Stiff and sore from the five-hour fight the night before, I cast a ⅝-inch-diameter Green Machine popper early the next morning, and solidly hooked into a striper that took the popper down so quickly that reconstructing what happened became impossible. After I transferred to a skiff, mates David Wolfson and Jason Sweeny chased after the fish for twenty minutes before it suddenly reversed itself, angrily shook its head, and managed a billwrap. A minute later the marlin was free.

That should have ended the trip for me. But Ray Beadle gave me the very last of his billfish flies. After I tied up a new leader and shock, the fates delivered to me one last shot. A few seconds later I was again in the skiff and racing after a marlin with Wolfson and Sweeny, the fish first wildly greyhounding at the raft and spreading slack line across the ocean. By all that is reasonable, the fish should have caught my leader in a billwrap, but it did not, and the mates soon had the skiff riding on the marlin's right shoulder.

Typically, once striped marlin finish their initial series of headshaking tailwalks and have settled down, they alternate long sounds with steady surface runs, each action seeming to promote the other. This marlin's first sound was neither long nor deep, and when it surfaced it had bronzed up and showed signs of fatigue. Only ten minutes had passed since the hookup. Five minutes later, it made a second sound, but heavy pressure soon brought it up. The mates and I were then able to maneuver to within 25 feet of the marlin, now clearly laboring. I dared not believe what I was seeing, and said as much to the mates, suggesting that we go for the marlin as soon as possible before it got its second wind. When the marlin came up from the next sound, we were nearly beside it. I put tremendous pressure on the fish, and was able to hold its head up as Wolfson motored alongside. First Sweeny, and then Wolfson drove in his gaff and snugged the fish to the raft. A moment later they flipped the marlin into the raft and the three of us were on top of it trying to prevent its bill from holing the forward flotation chamber.

Bryan Peterson, Ray Beadle, Wendy Hanvold, and I all submitted our marlin to the IGFA for record consideration in the 10 kg class tippet category. Hanvold won this marlin sweepstakes going away with a magnificent 136-pound striper that took her into the night and nearly three hours to beat.

For the most part, the striped marlin appeared to be clones of one another, fish from 110 to 120 pounds. We occasionally saw a marlin that clearly would not break the 100-pound mark, while out of the more than 300 teased in and 110 hooked on flies and poppers, we were certain of close encounters with a dozen fatties of over 150 pounds—all in all, staggering numbers for such edge-of-the-envelope stuff as fly fishing for striped marlin.

Taking a striped marlin by the IGFA rules, whereby the boat must be out of gear before the cast is made, and the shock tippet can be no more than 12

A 110-pound striped marlin is safely released.

inches long including all knots, has been an extremely rare event in fly fishing. Those bluewater fly fishers aboard *Royal Star*—among the most experienced in the world—considered the total number and realized that until this December trip the number of striped marlin successfully taken on the fly could be counted on both hands. Everyone was convinced that *Royal Star*, and the other LoPreste-Dunn long-range fishing boats operating out of San Diego, had radically altered the dimensions of bluewater fly fishing for this gamefish.

EPILOGUE

During the 1994 Blue Water Fly Rod Invitational, our party hooked sixty and boated twenty-eight striped marlin in four days. All but one of these fish were released. Almost all the marlin were fought from the skiffs. Three women, Wendy Hanvold, Janet Downey, and Nanci Morris, boated marlin and made safe releases. I believe the dramatic increase in the ratio of hooked to boated striped marlin was the result of better anglers; better swimming flies; skiff crews who understood how to keep the marlin off balance and stressed; and the use of 14/15-weight rods, and reels loaded with ultrathin backing.

I was tying all my 8- to 10-inch Sea Habit Billfish tandem hook flies on 7/0 Gamakatsu (lead) and 6/0 Owner or Gamakatsu (rear). Using my flies tied on these hooks, Steve Jensen, Nanci Morris, and I hooked ten striped marlin, lost one when the hook came out, lost two due to broken class tippets, and boated seven, from 80 to 125 pounds.

A month after the completion of this trip, from January 5 to 14, 1995, Nanci Morris and I co-hosted a long-range trip for LoPreste-Dunn aboard *Royal Star*. We again located striped marlin on "the ridge," finding them in sizes never before encountered: 100 to 200 pounds. Our party hooked and fought sixty-seven stripers, and boated twelve. I think the average was around 130 pounds.

While casting from *Royal Star*, Morris and I hooked huge marlin, back to back, then pursued them in skiffs. The marlin eventually came so close together that we could yell back and forth to each other. Both marlin were landed in about an hour and twenty minutes. At the time they were boated, Morris's marlin weighed approximately 186 pounds, mine about 170. A week later in San Diego, the fish weighed 173 and 157. These striped marlin, the largest ever caught IGFA legal, were submitted to the IGFA for world record consideration.

TACKLE AND FLIES

Fishing for striped marlin on *Royal Star*, I used direct drive reels holding 500 to 1,000 yards of backing that included 250 to 500 yards of superthin 50-pound gel-spun polyethylene line.

Because of the rather slow reaction time of these large long-range boats when following runaway billfish, and because of the time it takes to transfer an

Wendy Hanvold poses with her 136-pound striped marlin, a world record for the 10-kilogram class tippet category at the time of its capture in 1993.

angler to a skiff, striped marlin sometimes got a lot of backing on the water. I believe the vastly reduced line drag of the ultrathin backing then became a tremendous advantage.

I connected this backing directly to the fly line. Every angler on *Royal Star* who placed monofilament between fly line and backing experienced a break in the monofilament backing while fighting a striped marlin.

I used Sage's Graphite III RPL-X 13- and 14-weight rods and Loomis 13/15 Mega Taper Saltwater for this fishing. Striped marlin are an up-and-down fish similar in my experience to white marlin, but not nearly so prone to long and deep sounds as blue marlin. The angler's fighting platform, whether on the mothership or in one of the skiffs, is very much up and down, too. I felt that the rods possessed enough backbone to lift a deep-running striper, and still provided some cushion for fighting these unpredictable gamefish in a seaway.

Trying to fight striped marlin close in proved to be a mistake. The not-yet-exhausted fish got breathers as we tried to run them down, and then sounded when we got really close. A better method involved staying 100 to 150 yards

The author holds a freshly billed striped marlin. The marlin was estimated to have weighed 170 to 175 pounds at the time. Weighed after storage for a week in Royal Star's spray brine hold, the marlin officially weighed 157.3 pounds. This fish is currently a pending world record with the International Game Fish Association.

from them. They then motored along very near the surface, towed the skiffs, and were unable to get up enough speed to sweep sufficient water through their gills. Not until the marlin were clearly out of gas did we rapidly approach them to bill and revive for a safe release. In this manner, some marlin in the 80- to 100-pound range were boated in thirty minutes or less.

I make up most of my bluewater fly-fishing lines. For billfish, I use the running line from a Scientific Anglers Mastery Series Tarpon Taper. Using braided monocore loop-to-loop connections, I loop this running line to a 550-grain, 30-foot Deep Water Express shooting taper cut back to 26 feet. The four feet that I cut off comes unequally from both tapers, 30 inches from the back taper, 18 inches from the front taper. If purchasing a stock line for this fishing, I use a Teeny 500, or one of the Teeny saltwater lines in 550 or 650 grains. I do not cut these lines back, because being able to cast (or strip off, for additional sink) the entire fly line is helpful when fishing for either billfish or wahoo on the long-range trips.

My 8- to 10-inch Sea Habit Billfish tandem hook flies proved large enough to attract and hold, yet were small enough to cast to free-swimming marlin, even from a skiff. If spending a lot of time casting to free-swimming marlin, I prefer the single hook fly for its better swimming action. I caught my largest striped marlin (described above) on a Sea Habit Bucktail tied on a single 7/0 Gamakatsu bait hook. The fish nearly swallowed the fly and only a few inches of shock tippet remained outside of its mouth. Incredibly, the class tippet survived with only minor abrasion.

STRIPED MARLIN (*Tetrapturus audax*)

Striped marlin are distributed throughout tropical and subtropical waters in the Pacific and Indian Oceans. Worldwide, they are most concentrated in the eastern and central Pacific areas, approximately thirty degrees above and below the equator. Striped marlin are especially abundant off southern California and Baja California between June and November, with strong winter populations found between Baja's Magdalena Bay and the Revillagigedo islands.

The marlin's principal spawning area lies in the central north Pacific, especially the Hawaiian chain of islands. Spawning takes place in the spring and summer months, April to July. I recall a story Captain Del Dykes told me several years ago when we were fly fishing for yellowfin tuna during a July night off Kailua-Kona. He said that only the week before he had hand netted some tiny needlefish drawn in by the boat's light, and upon examination of the catch had discovered a perfectly formed 11-inch-long striped marlin. He promptly released the rare find. During the winter, Hawaiian fishers often encounter juvenile striped marlin weighing 10 to 40 pounds. This run offers fly fishers the best opportunity for taking a striped marlin on either 3 kg (6.6-pound) or 4 kg (8.8-pound) class tippets, categories currently vacant for the species.

At the opposite extreme are striped marlin from New Zealand's northwest coast, fish that are known to sometimes top 400 pounds, and that are the largest in the world for the species. The all-tackle record, a striped marlin of 494 pounds, came from Tutukaka, New Zealand. Occasionally, striped marlin over 300 pounds are caught from neighboring Australian waters off the country's northeast, Great Barrier Reef, coast. Though a 406½-pound striped marlin was caught off La Jolla, California, in 1955, and a 483-pounder was once taken from Chilean waters, striped marlin in North America of over 150 pounds are uncommon. The few records of Baja stripers of over 200 pounds are now twenty years old. This is almost certainly due to the impact of commercial fishing interests.

Until Nanci Morris and I took our Baja stripers, the largest fly-rod striped marlin—and among the longest standing records in the sport—were caught from waters off Salinas, Ecuador by two legendary anglers. Lee Wulff took a 148-pound striper in 1967 on a 12-pound class tippet, then the maximum allowed, while Billy Pate followed three years later with a 146-pounder on a 15-pound class tippet.

FISHING NOTES

I am most familiar with striped marlin in Baja waters, having fished for them out of Cabo San Lucas, East Cape (Palmas de Cortez), La Paz, and off Loreto well up the Sea of Cortez. I believe that Cabo San Lucas in January and February is the best striped marlin fishing area in the world. During a single day of fishing there in January 1994, on Captain Roberto Olascoaga's *Marea II*, a companion and I saw several dozen marlin balling up bait while mate Poly Perez teased in six for a couple of hookups. The downside to Cabo's fishing is the methods locally used. Stripers are invariably first seen chasing bait on the surface, the soaring frigate birds telegraphing their every movement to boat captains. When a frigate bird suddenly begins to swoop to the water, a striped marlin is certain to appear at the nadir of its dive. All Cabo captains know this and race to the spot where the bird is diving. When they and competing boats arrive, live mackerel are cast over the side, the baits landing in the center of the melee and then swimming down toward the waiting marlin. In the face of such competition, it's very difficult to troll teasers, and impossible to effectively cast a fly to the free-swimming marlin.

Striped marlin can be found off Cabo year round, but late each spring many migrate northward into southern California waters on the West Coast, and around to East Cape and north well into the Sea of Cortez on the east side of the Baja California peninsula. At East Cape's Palmas de Cortez, stripers can be found in the winter, but the heavy winds then make fishing difficult. By May, the winds have subsided, charter boat traffic remains light, and the marlin are much in evidence. Save for a long-range fly-fishing charter, this is where I'd go to take a striped marlin on a fly. Even in August, when blue marlin and sailfish are sometimes abundant, stripers at East Cape normally outnumber both of these species combined.

Because Mexican captains are generally not familiar with fly fishers—particularly where billfish are concerned—I am convinced that the most successful strategy is for two fly fishers to charter a boat, bringing their own teaser rods and teasers, and alternate between teasing and fishing. The captain need then only know where to find fish, when to slow ("*despacio*"), and when to take the boat out of gear ("*alto*"). Half measures in which fly fishers depend on a Mexican mate to tease and the captain to supply teasing outfits usually come to grief, for long practice has convinced the mates and captains to pursue angling methods fly fishers find frustratingly counterproductive.

Each Mexican captain favors certain color combinations in his rubber skirted billfish lures. Time and again I've seen a captain go below, take out a battered teaser only slightly different from the one I put on, and watch the next half-dozen stripers come only to this lure. Here are some of the favorites among Mexican captains: green/yellow (the "dorado," and a Cabo favorite); green/white/silver (for mackerel); orange/yellow (an East Cape favorite); light green/yellow/pale orange (the "zucchini" combination); and red in any combination (a favorite when stripers are feeding on the huge, brick red Baja *calamari* [squid]), or in an all-red teaser (when the fish are feeding on red pelagic crabs). Other worthwhile combinations: black/green/silver, and purple/red.

WHITE MARLIN

La Guaira Bank, Venezuela

With a couple of *cuba libres* made barely flame retardant by melting ice, Steve Jensen and I stand on the quay, sip our drinks, and watch with satisfaction as Captain Luis Millan sends the two mates scurrying about with duct tape, plastic bags, and newspaper. We've seen the drill before. We're fly fishermen, and while that counts for only a blank stare in many big-game fishing circles, it counts for a lot with Millan. His boat, *Margullia II*, a Bertram 35 looking tired after seventeen years of regular charter work off Venezuela's La Guaira coast, will not have a cleat, hook, vent, or lock in the transom area that can catch a fly line. That's his promise and half of the bargain. Millan himself is the other half.

I have fished with Millan many times out of Casa Margullia, the little dockside fishing resort in the port of La Guaira some 10 miles downcoast from Venezuela's Caracas International Airport. I've found him in all ways to be the consummate fly-fishing captain. He can hold a dorado belly in one hand, needle and waxed thread in the other, and, after carefully studying the operation before him, stitch up a bait using procedures surgeons employ when closing wounds. He does this with such speed and economy of motion that even after watching him closely I will never duplicate the results. When mullet are not commercially available—and Millan favors these, the *lisas*, above all other baits for white marlin—he will row a dinghy across the channel from *Margullia*'s berth and secure some with a throw net. After arriving at La Guaira Bank late each morning, Millan never leaves his perch on the flying bridge, and rarely

A fly-caught white marlin of approximately 50 pounds caught off La Guaira Bank. Photograph by Trey Combs.

lets his concentration wander from the three teaser baits, two on flat lines and one close in on an outrigger pole. He can sight dozens of billfish in a week of fishing and only once can I recall a mate ever seeing a tailing fish before Millan did. But his ultimate value as a captain remains his uncanny ability to know exactly what a hooked billfish means to me as a fly fisherman. Always, as I begin to signal that the boat should now be in reverse, or moving forward and away from a billfish greyhounding at the boat, or spun this way or that way with the engines reversed, Millan has already done so and my hand signal turns into a wave.

Millan does all these things and more. But for the behavior of the white marlin (*Tetrapturus albidus*), he can do nothing.

The white, at 50 to 60 pounds the smallest of the marlin, is no pocket blue. A blue marlin, regardless of its size, carries an aura of ponderous majesty, a kind of big-shouldered, in-your-face nonchalance seen in whales and 500-pound gorillas. This marlin, a phantasm of silvery white and pale greenish blue, with a tall, uniquely rounded dorsal fin, lives on a high voltage, flank speed setting that keeps it dashing unpredictably, at times aggressively, at times curiously, but never timidly or casually. Its extremely long pectoral fins communicate this excitement by turning a pale neon blue. Head on, a white charging a teaser looks like a great bird gliding through waves without any apparent effort. Its lack of predictability is the one consistent characteristic of its behavior: When you've experienced the behavior of one white, you've experienced one white. Any conclusions drawn from the encounter and pontificated upon will only make you look foolish if you ever go back for seconds, for the same fish will not be there.

I've watched whites lock on teaser baits and attack them with a fanatic persistence no other marlin can match. I once had a white frantically try to eat a teaser bait that was running from the outrigger. When Millan, like a puppeteer, reeled in the bait from the flying bridge, took the boat out of gear, and hauled the teaser up into the air, the marlin parked under the dangling bait like an outfielder waiting for a fly ball to come down. No amount of pop-pop-pop from my popper could persuade the marlin to give up its vigil. Millan put the boat in gear and dropped the teaser back in the water. The white again crashed the bait, and again the boat was taken out of gear. This entire sequence was repeated four times before the marlin tired of the game and disappeared.

I have seen whites track teasers for half a mile, and never once touch them with their bills. At such times Millan's staccato Spanish would rain down on the hapless mates, who tried desperately to follow directions and fire up the marlin. As I waited to cast, the mate would speed up the retrieve, then drop the teaser back. More shouting would follow. The marlin ultimately would leave. Millan never disguised his disgust. What was wrong? I would ask. Size or color of the teaser? The bait itself? A lazy fish? "*No hambre,*" he would say. Not hungry.

Many times I've seen a white race to the teasers, and charge from one to the other like a child checking out a dessert tray. Then, in a flash, it would be gone. Lots of screaming on board when that happened. I tell Jensen that three of these madcap sequences back-to-back and I would need to wear a straitjacket to attend my own sanity hearing.

I have seen the rare white so pathologically aggressive—I call them suicide fish—that they cannot be discouraged from eating a fly-rod popper no matter how many wheels come off in the process. Once, I was fishing with Patrick Guillanton, the owner of Mako Video Productions, Paris, France, when a white came storming in, madly trying to get its mouth around the split-tailed *lisa*. When the teaser was removed, the white jumped on Guillanton's popper, a ⅝-inch-diameter, six-inch-long Green Machine. The marlin started to turn away, but Guillanton was faster and pulled the popper free. The marlin ate it a second time and again the popper came out. Back and forth they went, each grimly determined to get their way, until finally on the fifth take the marlin got hooked. It then left like a rifle shot.

Just as individual fish can run hot or cold, so too can La Guaira Bank's entire white marlin fishery. I have seen this happen so dramatically that I'd rather hear that the fishing is poor upon my arrival, for then I'd at least know that given a week the fishing will likely get better. If I arrive and the fishing for the past couple of days has been scorching hot, I am confident only that I'm about to see the downside of all that fun.

Millan leaves punctually at 9, late by most fishing standards, but it is an hour run to La Guaira Bank and he says that rarely does the fishing turn on before 11. It will be six and nearly dark before we return.

Along Venezuela's north coast, the Atlantic Ocean crashes against the base of the Coastal Mountains, a towering velvet green ridgeline with 9,072-foot Pico Naiguata the barely noticeable high point. White stucco houses with red tile roofs rise above the hotels, fill the foothills, and cling precariously to the mountainsides. The natural beaches, boulder strewn and dangerous, remain tourist-free. A few hundred yards offshore, the bottom falls away to 30 fathoms and Millan slows to inspect a quivering brown slick, *carnada*, "bait," one pod of sardines among the thousands that white marlin, blue marlin, sailfish, yellowfin and blackfin tuna, and dorado have been feeding on heavily for the past week. *Carnada* so close to the coast is a good omen. Millan assures us that our flies will find all of these gamefish during the next week.

La Guaira Bank rises from an ocean floor hundreds of fathoms deep, an undersea mountain range reaching to within 300 feet of the surface, practically a shallows by pelagic gamefish standards. Given protection against commercial exploitation by the Venezuelan government, La Guaira Bank remains at the center of the area's year-round sportfishing. While white marlin are found throughout Atlantic, Caribbean, and Gulf of Mexico waters, from 35 degrees south to 45 degrees north, there is no better place in the world to fish for white marlin than on La Guaira Bank in September when they are tailing on top and feeding on rafts of *carnada*. Young captains in the waterfront bars tell me stories of wealthy owners flying in and raising fifty marlin in a single day. Transoms on their seven-figure big-game fishing machines include the United States East and Gulf Coasts, Puerto Rico, and many Caribbean vacation islands.

These La Guaira waters, almost as famous for their mountainous seas as for their marlin, run true to form, for the surf is up, and waves break over and pass through *Margullia II*'s cockpit. Knowing that we will be playing Pinball Wizard with these big seas during every hookup, Jensen and I rig up 12-weights in hopes the lighter-weight rods will protect the tippets. He fishes foam poppers. I fish Sea Habit Billfish flies, *las plumas,* for I have seen a lot of marlin cough up poppers during the past year and I think the choice will change my fortunes.

The first marlin to come streaking in doesn't bear out my new faith in flies. It takes aggressively enough, but after only 100 feet of berserk pyrotechnics the fly sails free. I do a better job striking the second white, but it, too, throws the fly. Then, in an effort to make me crazy, it darts back to the transom and gobbles up Jensen's popper, tosses that on a jump, comes back to take a whack at the teaser the mate is swinging about, again goes after the popper, and finally runs down my fly only to reject it at the last second. All these frantic marlin activities are attended by English curses and Millan's "coaching," Spanish curses and withering denouncements that leave each mate in an emotional shambles.

I change to an identical fly, but one tied on Owner offset bait hooks with rolled-in points, 5/0 to 4/0, not at all big-game hooks, but hooks with a reputation for digging in and holding. When the third white crashes the *lisa,* and the mate successfully teases it to 30 feet from the transom, I hook it securely.

When I cast flies for whites, I use either a Teeny 500 with the full 28 feet of sink tip, or 26 feet of 550-grain Deep Water Express looped to monocore running line cut from a Scientific Anglers Mastery Series Tarpon or Bonefish Taper, any weight from 7 to 12. In either case, the fly is cast to one side and past the marlin, the sinking portion taking the fly quickly down. If the out-of-gear boat is coasting, I may strip off some additional line to get the fly down while preventing it from trolling behind the boat. I find it very hard to set on a white marlin—or any marlin for that matter—that has doubled back to find the missing teaser and takes the fly going away while the out-of-gear boat coasts along. If I hit the fish hard enough to get proper hook penetration, I run the risk of breaking the fish off. However, if I don't set sufficiently hard, the fly usually comes free on the first series of jumps. The best solution I've found is to have as little slack running line as possible so that after an initial strike, additional sets on the fish can be made directly from the reel—*with the free hand not clamped to the rim control, the reel's drag preventing a broken class tippet.* To accomplish this, I keep the drag set very tight—7 or 8 pounds—and then remember to quickly back it off once the marlin starts running.

Millan begins backing down the boat as the white races away, its leaps blowing out the side of one wave and exploding into the next, a dazzling rhythm punctuated by headshaking tailwalks that sometimes remain partially hidden behind the steep seas. This activity take a heavy toll on the fish's energy and often leads to a damaged class tippet, but if the tippet survives these first few minutes, I become confident that I'll get the fish to the boat. Millan and I know which side of the marlin's jaw carries the hook, and once the fish slows and settles on a course a dozen feet down, we close the distance, carefully watch the angle of the fly line to the fish, and ride its right shoulder.

Whites do not immediately sound as blues so often do. A marlin coming up from a deep sound will, at best, put a huge strain on the tippet even with the reel nearly drag-free. At worst, the fish will come straight at the angler, the slack resulting in a billwrap. I have seen a fly-hooked white twenty minutes into the fight go down 500 feet. But that fish was not this one; Millan and I keep the fish pinned to the surface. In less than thirty minutes we have the fish beside the boat.

Luis Millan and Luis Suarez, Casa Margullia's two remarkable captains, compete annually with one another for world supremacy in the number of billfish they tag and release for the Billfish Foundation. One or the other usually receives the organization's national award for these conservation efforts. More importantly, for years they have maintained a strong conservation influence on the entire La Guaira sport fishery. Indeed, one can hardly find a Venezuelan boat along the cost without a Billfish Foundation sticker reading SUELTEME, "Release Me," below a drawing of a marlin.

When I bring the fish to the mates, and ask them to guess its weight, they say 50 to 60 pounds, and I elect to kill the marlin and submit it for the 10 kg class world record, a new category and one still vacant in 1992. Because billfish are so rarely taken, its size has been badly misjudged. Later that day I find the marlin weighs only 43 pounds, small, even for a white. Nevertheless, I am determined to submit the fish for record consideration, and just as determined not to kill another, regardless of its weight.

Only a few minutes pass before white number five charges in on the teaser. The mate does not remove the teaser cleanly, but instead allows it to dap across the water. The marlin pursues it to the transom as Jensen makes his cast. When the lit-up and thoroughly frustrated marlin cannot locate the teaser, it

The author holds a tagged and just-billed 70-pound white marlin. Immediately after the picture was taken, the fly was removed and the fish released. Photograph by Steve Jensen.

does a quick 180, spots the popper, and changes from a search to a destroy mode. With the popper dead in its sights, the white flies like an arrow, barely breaking the surface with its head as it engulfs the good-to-eat but elusive popper. Jensen has practiced for this moment. After pointing the rod directly at the fish, and holding the running line tightly, he strikes the marlin. Following the sharp report of the tippet breaking, the fly line recoils, flies out of the water, and lands in the cockpit with most of its length draped over my shoulders. I scarcely know what to say. At that moment, had there been a loaded pistol on board, Jensen would have worked his way through the captain, crew, and me before shooting himself. Instead, he screams.

Another white brings his fit to an end. The fish takes my fly, and turns and slows for me to make a good hookup. A half hour later the marlin, estimated at more than 10 pounds heavier than the one killed, is successfully tagged and released. (In January 1995, I received a letter from the National Marine Fisheries Service confirming that the 50-pound white marlin I tagged and released on September 21, 1993, was recaptured on June 10, 1994, by long line from high-sea-fishery Captain Justo Adrian. The fish was 262 days at large between my tag and release and its recapture.)

The next morning, Jensen and I, after each losing a white, boat very large white marlin we estimate at around seventy pounds apiece. They are tagged, brought aboard for pictures, and safely released. The other marlin raised, including a blue of about two hundred pounds, are showing signs of the blahs, a dash-about, *lisa*-munching, you-can't-catch-me attitude I am only too familiar with. I know in my bones that the fishing is shutting down, the peak well behind us. Predictably, the next day is slower, and the day after slower still. Jensen has a white take the popper, get seriously hooked, and make a run and a jump before the popper comes away. The marlin returns, more lit up than ever. Jensen casts to it again, and again has the white take. A missed strike, and the fish is gone. I hook into a 230-pound blue that gets billwrapped 800 feet below *Margullia II* and breaks me off precisely twenty minutes into the fight. When Millan locates slicks of *carnada* and diving *bobas*, Spanish for "dummies"—a nickname for boobies—we find yellowfin and blackfin tuna and dorado feeding together. Some of the dorado are over 40 pounds, some yellowfin over 80. Thirty-pound dorado, 20-pound yellowfin, and 12-pound blackfin tear our bucktail flies to pieces. The white marlin, for the most part, remain scouting the hinterlands of La Guaira Bank. Still, I count the first couple of days a success: three whites boated and at least a dozen hooked. If the marlin get picky after that, I stop to smell the roses.

NOTES

I fished my Sea Habit Billfish flies in both the Flying Fish (blue and white) and Ballyhoo (blue/gray and white) with equal success. Jensen fished ⅝-inch foam poppers in the Green Machine and Flying Fish patterns. When the whites really turned on, they crashed just about any dressing seven to eight inches long, either a fly or popper. Millan urges the single angler to fish two outfits and have both flies and poppers rigged. If a white rejects the fly, it will often jump all over

Steve Jensen strikes and the white marlin begins a series of jumps. Photograph by Trey Combs.

a popper. The reverse can also be true, especially when trying to hook the more tentative and less aggressive white.

Because of the mercurial nature of this fishery, an angler hoping to take a Venezuelan white on a fly would do well to schedule at least a week of fishing almost anytime from September through November. Whites are still on La Guaira Bank in March. Some captains believe that large numbers of blue marlin in the spring drive off the whites. More likely, the whites are migrating north. By May they are locally abundant off Puerto Rico and the nearby Dominican Republic. By summer, they have followed the Gulf Stream as far north as New York, and are the target of major sport fisheries off Virginia and Maryland. Other whites have migrated west and are commonly taken off Mexico's Yucatán Peninsula.

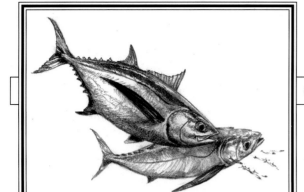

CHAPTER 8

ALBACORE

Westport, Washington

T he albacore tuna (*Thunnus alalunga*), a pelagic, highly migratory species, has a worldwide distribution throughout tropical and temperate oceans 40 degrees above and below the equator. Nicknamed "longfin" for its long, graceful pectoral fins, which reach a point beyond its anal fin, the albacore is widely pursued commercially and represents approximately 10 percent of the world's total tuna catch. In the United States, only albacore and blackfin tuna can be canned and marketed as "white meat tuna," and as such have a higher market value than other "light meat" tuna.

Albacore make extremely long seasonal migrations. During summer months they may be found as far north as New England on the Atlantic coast, and British Columbia and Washington on the Pacific coast. During the El Niño summers of 1992 and 1993, when West Coast ocean temperatures were uncommonly warm, albacore ranged to British Columbia's Queen Charlotte Islands and southeastern Alaska.

Albacore at the end of their first year reach 10 to 12 pounds, and they may double that weight their second year. According to Ray Beadle, a longtime salt-water fly-fishing companion who commercially jackpoled tuna during college summers, albacore eat their way north from California and continue to grow rapidly, the 12- to 15-pound spring fish hitting 20 to 25 pounds by midsummer and 25 to 28 pounds by fall. Record albacore have been caught in California waters late in the fall in Catalina Channel: 71 pounds, 12 ounces, and 75 pounds, both in November, 1984. The all-tackle angling record fish of 88 pounds, 2 ounces was caught off the Canary Islands in 1977. In more recent years, some of the world's largest albacore, fish in the 70-pound range, have come from Cape Point and neighboring Hout Bay in South Africa's Cape of Good Hope waters, where they are abundant from November to May.

At the time Ray Beadle was working in the "rack," jackpoling albacore on the tuna clippers, and bringing catches back to the canneries on Terminal Island, California, I was working inside one of the canneries and helping process the tuna he caught. That was thirty years ago and in the twilight of California's commercial albacore fishing industry. Down at San Pedro's docks, row after row of wooden tuna boats was up for sale. The reasons for the decline were in part a cyclical downturn in the fishery, and in part the downside of overharvesting, but I was also witnessing the dawn of the huge corporate tuna boats that could range at sea for months, until their holds were bursting with frozen tuna. And I knew which albacore were which when I had to unload the catches. I typically carried four locally caught albacore to a cooking basket, the fish running from "peanuts" or "footballs" of 10 pounds to tuna topping 20 pounds. The South Pacific fish taken well off the coast of Peru often filled a basket singly, enormous albacore well over the rod-and-reel record that at the time stood at 66 pounds.

Albacore feed on numerous marine organisms, including squid, crab larvae, amphipods, and fish such as anchovies. They travel in deeper, cooler water than other tuna, but may feed from the surface to depths of hundreds of feet. Shoals of these tuna usually are of the same age and size, and, for reasons not yet understood, older and larger albacore generally prefer more tropical regions.

When I first went aboard Captain Del Dykes's *Reel Action* for the *iki-shibi* fishery (literally, "night handline"), the albacore being caught off Hawaii's Kona Coast were running 50 to 70 pounds. Locals called them "penguins," and claimed that a few of these tuna weighed 100 pounds. They did not catch them with the eagerness that attended their pursuit of the yellowfin, the *ahi* that commanded two or three times the price of albacore and was consumed raw in the Japanese community as *sashimi* or *sushi*, or cured in sea salt and seasonings and served as *poki*, a traditional Hawaiian dish. We chummed all night with chopped-up anchovies, hopeful of bringing either species to the waterproof lightbulb that hung 25 feet below the boat. While I cast a fly into the anchovy slick, my companion fished a handline, the single hook baited with a fresh *akule*, the Hawaiian bigeye scad. Only once during the night did the albacore come close, and then it was to rip off the *akule* 20 feet down and miss the hook. We had lost "Charlie." "You have to get a Charlie," say the locals; "he'll hold the school long enough to get them going on the chum." I reasoned that once the fish were eating the chum, I could get one to the fly. I still feel that the *iki-shibi* fishery's methods hold promise for fly fishers who want a crack at giant albacore. I intend to try for albacore again, *iki-shibi* style, for I don't believe any other method in Hawaii will bring up these deep-running, thermocline-hugging tuna.

Westport guards the south entrance to Grays Harbor, Washington's most protected and commercially important Pacific coast port. Salmon built this "Salmon Capital" town, a single strip of restaurants and gift shops facing a boat haven and enough wharf fingers to moor hundreds of commercial, charter, and recreational boats. The huge Chehalis River, the main arterial for a host of salmon-rich tributaries, turns the harbor brackish on the slack tide. On any tide, during the spring and fall, a million shorebirds blanket intertidal shore-lines and provide an unexpected boost to the tourism industries of Aberdeen and Hoquiam—sister cities no longer prospering from a healthy timber industry.

For two generations, owners of commercial salmon boats saw in the late summer run of albacore a chance at a few extra bucks. The area had no can-neries that would turn their catches into "Chicken of the Sea," and the owners had to be content with marketing their catches fresh, whole and frozen, or sim-ply iced down. Often a catch was sold right off the boat to housewives who prac-ticed home canning. I bought albacore this way twenty years ago when the boats bothered to beat their way north, around the Olympic Peninsula, and ran east into Puget Sound to sell their catches dockside in Port Townsend. Some-times their albacore was sold out of the backs of pickup trucks. More rarely I found the tuna in fish markets. Regardless, back then the white meat tuna was something of a pickup game, cash the IRS never heard about when salmon fish-ery shutdowns grew increasingly long and families for the first time com-plained about the hardships of making bank payments on their boats.

Sportfishers are never far behind commercial fishers, and it wasn't long before anglers began negotiating two-day charters out of Westport and chasing after Washington's annual run of longfin tuna. At first this was no more com-plicated than trolling jigs in areas where the albacore had been seen last. Later, live chum was stored aboard in 50-gallon drums. Casting anchovies with light-weight gear soon made albacore a popular alternative to Westport's traditional late summer run of silver salmon.

This was not yet a Washington fishery that attracted fly fishers. A few an-glers bucktailed for silver salmon on the Washington coast of the Strait of Juan de Fuca, and for these salmon—British Columbia's "coho"—on the Vancouver Island coast. Fly fishing in these northern latitudes meant trout, steelhead, and salmon in rivers and lakes. Offshore fly fishing for salmon and albacore was unknown.

When Dick Thrasher and I contacted Bill and Sue Hoffman at Westport's Neptune Charters and requested a "fly-fishing only" boat for albacore, we knew that the key to our angling success was first finding the gamefish, and then be-ing able to hold them with live bait. Whereas a single anchovy could bring an albacore to a hook, dozens of these live baitfish would be necessary to set up a successful fly presentation. The quantity of bait we wanted was beyond the ca-pacity of any Westport boat save for one, the *Deluxe*, and that led us to Cliff and Sharon Beatty. They had purchased the boat from the San Diego long-range fleet and then had her completely refurbished. If Beatty could get the "new" boat Coast Guard approved, our fly-fishing charter would be his first.

The whereabouts of albacore off the Washington and Oregon coasts in Au-gust and September can be predictable, the tuna holding for weeks off Westport, often only 30 miles from the coast. But this can change overnight, the fast-traveling schools suddenly following food and the warm Japanese Current north for hundreds of miles.

Westport's albacore charters depart late in the afternoon for all-night runs and begin the search for tuna at first light. Beatty warned me that albacore had not been seen recently off Westport. His last confirmed report placed schools off the Oregon coast at the latitude of Depot Bay. Ocean surface currents were running 62 degrees and cooling fast, and this could be driving the albacore south. Mid-September was on the cusp, and I wondered if we could catch the fish in time, and if we did, where. Beatty fed a course west and then southwest into the ship's computerized autopilot. After dinner, I turned in, felt the surge of the ship as it plowed through the huge ocean swells, and thought about stories I'd heard of Washington albacore, caught on conventional gear, that had topped 50 pounds, larger than the Hout Bay, South African record of 39 pounds, 10 ounces on a 16-pound class tippet, larger even than the 47-pounder on 20-pound tippet taken by Robert Lubarsky from the tuna-rich Hudson Canyon off New Jersey.

At dawn, Beatty orders the mates to troll four rubber skirted, chrome headed, double hook jigs on 50-pound trolling rods. Only a few minutes pass before the first click breaks out and line rachets noisily off the reel. Beatty takes *Deluxe* out of gear while mates begin chumming live anchovies off the downwind corner of the transom. Wind sets the boat drifting over the bait, giving the two anglers holding down the transom, port and starboard, an equal shot. At first nothing comes to the chum except greedy fulmars, and black-footed albatross drawn out of curiosity to the feeding birds. A flash of silver well down, then another, then four or five, and then a single geyser of activity off the transom, an almost insignificant boil considering the number of live anchovies now fleeing for their lives. "Boil!" cries the mate. The anglers begin casting their flies. "Fish up!" the mate calls out. Looking straight down into the dark water, I can see high speed, foil-bright fish flashing two stories below. These deep-running albacore are the most alien and secretive of all the bluewater tuna I've encountered. The expected scenario, a feast of strikes and joyous exclamations, receives a reality check.

Ed Rice hooks up with an albacore of over 20 pounds, a potential record for his 12-pound class tippet. Ray Beadle casts and immediately has an albacore take his fly, a second up-from-the-depths and down-to-the-depths furtive take, not at all like the take received when casting into a maelstrom of well-chummed yellowfin. The rotation continues. At the net, Rice's big longfin cuts through the 12-pound tippet. Beadle's albacore hits the deck, and I run to study it in life, for this is surely one of the world's most beautiful gamefish, with its formal dress of blue-black and pearlescent white, and fins and finlets cast in gold. More live anchovies are chummed. The flashes of silver disappear, the bite over in five minutes. Beatty puts *Deluxe* in gear, the mates set the jib rods, and the fly fishermen, still pumped from the close encounter, pray for more albacore.

These albacore don't stop piling out of the depths in ones and twos for the jigs, but our ability to slow down the main body of fast-traveling tuna, and then bring some to the surface, declines with every degree the sun climbs off the

Previous page: Ed Rice works up an albacore in dawn's first light.

horizon. I get a shot midmorning and break the albacore off on the strike. These tuna are incredibly strong and carry more body mass aft than any other member of *Thunnus*, for their greatest girth is near their *second* dorsal fin. After that loss, the fishing becomes very spotty, the tuna hitting the jigs, getting some of the chum, but not coming close enough to the surface to nail our flies. By late in the morning no one is getting a shot, and the rotation stops.

A captain from a neighboring charter boat radios Beatty to say that his gear fishermen have taken several dozen albacore to 47 pounds. This news only underscores our disappointment.

The low light of late afternoon should have ushered up the tuna, but not until the next morning does the fishing really resume. Several more albacore, all running about 15 to 20 pounds, come aboard before I again get a mid-morning shot. With Ray Beadle chumming, I cast a 4/0 Sea Habit Deceiver, Anchovy pattern, making four or five quick, darting strips before casting it back. This continues for five minutes and I'm ready to quit when Beadle calls, "Flash!" In perfect light, I see a single albacore come up from a dozen feet below to take my fly from the side.

The tuna sprints 100 yards upwind, slows for a moment, and continues on under the medium drag setting before I palm the rim control and bring it to a stop more than 500 feet away. The albacore doesn't sound, as I would have expected from such a deep-running species, but holds within 20 feet of the surface and gives me plenty of lateral resistance to work against. With the boat drifting away from the tuna, I'm glad for the 12-weight rod and 20-pound test tippet. I work the tuna closer, foot by foot, a minute per pound, until the fly line shows and the fish sounds. As I short stroke the albacore up to be netted, I know that no 24-pound tuna has ever fought me harder.

As the day wears on, the fish boxes on the ship's afterdeck fill with jig-caught albacore, the live anchovies and our frantic casts unable to move the schools of tuna to the surface. Our frustration doubles when we can actually see the tracers of albacore flash by 30 to 40 feet down. Late in the morning when Beatty turns *Deluxe* north for Westport, we have hooked a dozen albacore on flies, landed but half that number, and made plans to repeat the trip next year.

I feel we would have been more successful had we found the albacore in late August or early September, when they were feeding for weeks at a time off Westport. I would also have liked to investigate whether fishing my Sea Habit Anchovy patterns on an extra-fast-sinking shooting head (V or VI) would result in more strikes when these tuna are so reluctant to come to the surface. I only know with certainty that in the years ahead more and more fly fishers will be searching for these hard-fighting gamefish off the coasts of Oregon, Washington, and British Columbia.

The author holds a 23-pound albacore taken off the Oregon coast. The fish hit a Sea Habit Deceiver in the Anchovy Blue pattern. Note the fish's extremely long pectoral fin, thus the name "longfin tuna." Photograph by Ray Beadle.

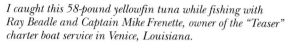

I caught this 58-pound yellowfin tuna while fishing with Ray Beadle and Captain Mike Frenette, owner of the "Teaser" charter boat service in Venice, Louisiana.

Venice, a small Mississippi Delta town literally at the end of the road, supports both a huge commercial fishing and shrimping fleet and the ships that supply the workers on the numerous offshore oil rigs.

The Mississippi River deposits nutrient-rich sediments into the Delta, a huge and immensely rich nursery for shellfish and baitfish. Inshore gamefish such as spotted weakfish (locally called speckled trout), drum, and redfish are abundant in the shallows. Offshore, the oil rigs (each the size of a city block) hold gamefish like a magnet.

Mike Frenette has been a leader in developing the sports fishing in this area. He took Beadle and me to flats that held redfish weighing up to 20 pounds and speckled trout in the 5- to 8-pound range. My first "trout," at a little over 7 pounds, was a world record in the International Game Fish Association's 10 kg class tippet category.

Beadle and I sampled some of the world's best offshore fly fishing when Frenette left Venice's Cypress Point Marina in the afternoon and drove his 41-foot cruiser for four hours to reach a floating drilling rig anchored 50 miles offshore in bluewater 3,000 feet deep. Here we took skipjack tuna weighing from 8 to 10 pounds on flies, and learned that 20-pound skipjack aren't uncommon. After the sun went down, we found blackfin tuna in the 8- to 15-pound range. (Frenette told us he had taken six blackfin tuna over 30 pounds.) By dawn the yellowfin were averaging 50 to 80 pounds, and bluefin tuna, too large to believe, were hitting trolled plugs and spooling the two mates on Mike's heaviest stand-up gear. One bluefin tuna ran off 800 yards of line against a drag set at 26 pounds. Frenette said many of the bluefin would weigh over 500 pounds—not exactly fly-rod gamefish.

The yellowfin tuna made leaps ten feet or more out of the water—behavior I'd never observed before in tuna so large. As soon as a tuna hit one of the trolled plugs, Frenette would take the boat out of gear, throw chum over the side, and Beadle and I would cast. We both hooked large tuna in this manner. Beadle had the unfortunate luck of hooking a tuna that simply couldn't be stopped. The yellowfin I hooked hit a Sea Habit Deceiver in the Anchovy Green pattern tied on a single 7/0 Gamakatsu hook. Using a Sage 14-weight rod and an Abel 5 reel, I needed a little more that an hour to land the fish.

This area has tremendous potential for the inshore and offshore fly fishers. Wahoo are regularly taken in the 80- to 90-pound range. White and blue marlin are the principal billfish. Other "oil rig" gamefish include cobia, kingfish, and jack crevalle.

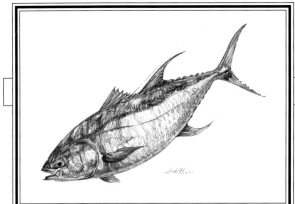

YELLOWFIN TUNA

Baja California, Mexico

The yellowfin tuna swim in furious pursuit, thousands of superheated metabolisms that race past as *Royal Star* motors over Thetis Bank for the dawn bite. I join a dozen other fly fishers at the ship's transom to view the spectacle. We do not know where the yellowfin are bound for, where they have come from, or even what baitfish now drive them. But this immense concert of energy has put miles of Pacific under the extraordinary kind of tension described as a "breezer." Here off Mexico's Baja California coastline, the ocean surface simmers with geysers of water, each a circle of spray holding, for a blink of time, a dark back and a flash of chrome yellow in its center.

When Captain Tim Eckstrom orders the mates to begin chumming, Larry Kida scoops sardines from one of the ship's five aft live bait tanks and begins tossing them off the stern. Less than a minute passes before the first boil appears. *Royal Star* is taken out of gear so that every cast conforms to the fly-fishing rules of the International Game Fish Association (IGFA). In a few seconds dozens of yellowfin rocket through the afterwake. I think the tuna will average 30 pounds, twice what we found on Potato Bank, and my hands begin to shake. Team Two is up and four fly fishers move to the rail with 13- and 14-weight rods. On this morning Team Three will fish from the skiffs, Avon's 16-foot inflatables with 30-horsepower outboards. Ray Beadle and I run for our rods and tackle boxes. As we load our gear into the skiff, members of Team Two grunt exclamations, muscles and rods strain, and four hot tuna streak away. Mates give

97

advice and anglers begin clearing their lines by weaving among each other along the gunwale. Already, hot green backing stretches more than 500 feet on either side of *Royal Star* and Team One is heading for the rail. Another day has begun in the 1992 Blue Water Fly Rod Invitational.

Steve Abel, now at the rail with a rod full of deep-sounding fish, put together the first such bluewater trip only the year before. Stories of that adventure percolated through the fly-fishing fraternity for months. Ed Rice, president of International Sportsman's Expositions, then put the 92-foot *Royal Star* under charter, and invited many top saltwater fly fishers for a second trip. The ship would depart from San Diego, California and travel south to offshore banks as fabled in gear-fishing circles as any river in fly fishing: Potato, Uncle Sam, Thetis, and 23 Fathom. Our party would return by clearing customs in San Carlos, and then take a chartered bus across the Baja Peninsula to La Paz and to our scheduled Aero California flight to Los Angeles. The invitation promised a ship that contained the most advanced fish-locating electronics, air-conditioning, comfortable staterooms, an endless supply of hot water for showers (the ship boasts a fresh watermaker), a spray brine system to keep fish at 18 degrees Fahrenheit and in "just caught" condition for the duration of the trip, and five meals a day to satisfy the most discriminating gourmand. I was not a hard sell, but Rice's letter added, "The yellowfin run from 15 pounds to you don't want to know." Those who accepted the invitation, my shipmates during the 10-day trip, made an impressive list. Besides Abel, Rice, and Ray Beadle— my roommate—the group included such fly-fishing luminaries as Stu Apte, Dan Byford, Nick Curcione, Terry Gunn, Wendy Hanvold, Tony Oswald, Dave Whitlock, and Mike Wolverton. An added bonus was John Barrett, the producer and host of the top-rated ESPN show, "Fly Fishing the World." His entire production crew was on hand, and at times the aft deck resembled a sound-stage.

Mate Chris Garcia motored us away to rejoin what I decided must be the Mother of all Breezers. Never before had he chased after tuna from a skiff. Normally his clients were gear fishermen who, as they liked to claim, "do it standing up" at the rail, live baiting gamefish while harnessed and belted to short, powerful rods. Fly fishers, of course, need more space, if only to cast. Three skiffs would ease the angling pressure on *Royal Star*, provide individuals with some breathing room, and give us boats in which to pursue gamefish that refused to slow down for any drag system regardless of the amount of backing.

To know that a "breezer" is to a "foamer" as a fuse is to a bomb helps one appreciate what Garcia was seeking. As we motored along, whorls of violent surface currents signaled the passage of tuna. Pomerine jaegers and northern fulmars swooped down to catch panic-stricken baitfish. Frigate birds soared in great circles above where the tuna were most concentrated, where they might break out, where for a moment of frenzy the normally sharp-eyed and discriminating tuna would take this angler's fly without hesitation. "The birds don't lie," said Garcia. As we skimmed off the wavetops to where we hoped the foamer would occur, *Royal Star* became a dot on the horizon.

Garcia saw the developing edge of the breakout and changed course to intercept it. Catching a foamer is part luck; a thousand tuna gorging on sardines can change direction in a heartbeat, for these fish may be traveling at *40 feet per second.* It is also part strategy; almost any boat run through a school of feeding tuna will put the fish down. To my disappointment, I've seen this happen on the forward cast on all three of the world's tropical oceans for five species of tuna. Though I have likened a school of feeding tuna to a traveling Cuisinart, they more often seem as skittish and pattern conscious as any brown trout you can name. None of these concerns mattered, for Garcia had incredible instincts. At just the right moment, he stopped the boat and shut off the engine.

The phalanx of huge tuna porpoised toward us, first a wave, then a crescendo of waves, one upon the other, until the spray reached above our heads and the sound deafened our ears. The water turned from an oxygen-rich pale blue to foam white, a combination of air and water whipped into a lather by the beating tails of a thousand tuna. As the edge neared us, I reached over it with a cast and dropped my fly in the middle of the cauldron. Our skiff was bouncing about at the epicenter by the time I made my first strip. I wondered if my small tube fly would be found amid those incredible hydraulics, but a tuna immediately took it, paused for an instant as I struck, and continued past me, still part of the living wave.

"I'm on!" I shouted as the running line snaked through the skiff and broke out the drag.

The author and BJ Meiggs hold a 16-pound yellowfin tuna that Meiggs took off Mozambique's Bazaruto Island.

"Me too!" called back Beadle. "A fish hit my line! Another! Ah! I'm off!"

The foamer was settling out, the wave now deep with only a single row of tuna, and in 200 feet these fish, too, had slipped beneath the surface. We were left with the sounds of our thumping hearts and the Billy Pate Marlin paying out line, for 100 yards before I began to breathe again, for 200 yards before Garcia started the engine, and for 300 yards before I felt the tuna falter and leave the hunt.

The skiff proved an ideal fighting platform. Garcia never overran my ability to retrieve line and I kept the fish working. When the yellowfin sounded, I knew that I was drawing on its reserves and that the final struggle would be waged directly below. I pointed my rod straight down, and put a nearly complete lock on the reel by using both hands on the foregrip and pinning the line. Then, using both arms and legs, I lifted the fish while calculating the precise strain I was exerting. When the rod was on the horizontal, I dropped it very quickly and reeled again until it pointed down at the fish.

The long run exhausted the yellowfin more than I expected, for when I first braced myself and lifted, I felt the fish give in to the pressure, moving up a foot even though it was nearly on its side and swimming in tight circles. Gear fishers call this a "death spiral," the final labors of the tuna, and they "short stroke" the fish to keep its head up and prevent it from boring down, regaining leverage, and prolonging the struggle. But fly rods, even 13-weight fly rods, were designed to be cast and then to fight fish, the rod absorbing those sudden strains that prevent broken class tippets. A big yellowfin exploits any pause in the fight, and however quickly you short stroke the deeply flexed fly rod, the tuna often gets its head back down and you again fight the strength of its tail.

Beadle sat patiently and encouraged me not to push things too much, for we both knew the fish could be a record, a yellowfin larger than Dave Inks's 38-pound pending record for the 10 kg class tippet. Just about everyone on board had been near this record. I could point to a 35-pound fish I'd boated only the day before. As I worked the fish, new foamers appeared and disappeared; I didn't want this remarkable morning to end without Beadle again intercepting a school of feeding yellowfin.

"I see color!" said Garcia when the tuna appeared 20 feet below. He estimated its weight at 40 to 42 pounds, and chose the net instead of the gaff so that no blood would be lost.

With the fish safely in the skiff we were off again to find another foamer. Beadle was soon fast to a tuna that nearly emptied his huge reel before the fly came away. This yellowfin had rejoined the school, and as Beadle reeled in the quarter mile of backing, we wondered whether the hooked fish had in fact continued feeding. We thought this entirely likely and that made us crazy to try it again.

When weighed, back on *Royal Star*, my fish bounced around in the high 30s on one of three scales that never quite agreed. A mate told me that a larger fish had come aboard from Nick Curcione, and then stapled my tag number to the yellowfin's gill cover before consigning the fish to the spray brine hold. After losing about eight percent of their body weight, both Curcione's and my yellowfin were within a pound or so of Dave Inks's 38-pound record.

After listening again and again to my description of the foamer line, Frank LoPreste began referring to it as my "religious experience," a view that Kevin Shelley, *Royal Star*'s first mate, fully appreciated. On that day, he had been running fly fishers in a skiff in tandem with Garcia. "I went to sea when I was 13. Now I'm 47," he said. "Only seven or eight times in my life have I seen a foamer like that." Like what? The perfect wave of yellowfin: form, size, and synchronization of purpose coming together to produce a spectacle of breathtaking power.

I have fly fished over less perfect foamers, schools of feeding yellowfin in the Atlantic, Pacific, and Indian Oceans whose dynamics have nevertheless awed and excited me like few other events in saltwater fly fishing. Gulls and terns dive and scream on panic-stricken baitfish while the dark backs of porpoise and tuna froth the water until I can feel the collective energy through the soles of my feet.

Yellowfin of like size and age travel at like speeds. A "school" of these tuna can be anything from thousands of tuna of nearly the same size, to several or more sizes temporarily drawn together by a school of bait. The smaller the yellowfin, the more likely they are to leap in pursuit of baitfish, and thus be more visible to the angler. Fish one to two years old and 8 to 15 pounds make wonderful arching leaps. Yellowfin weighing 30 to 80 pounds jump less frequently and on the same school of baitfish may show only their backs as they race down waves after the bait. The large yellowfin, those fish around the 100-pound mark or higher, come less commonly to the surface of all in mixed schools. The reason for this is not certain for all oceans and degrees of latitude, but relates to the greater concentrations of oxygen in the deeper and colder water, and the increased oxygen demands of the larger tuna.

Several years ago I worked with Patrick Guillanton and Gerard Aulong of Mako Video Productions in Costa Rica's Gulf of Payagayo. We were on Captain Calin Canales's *Roosterfish* when we encountered a vast school of spinner dolphin running with yellowfin tuna of 10 to 20 pounds. When we were able to get in front of the dolphin, Guillanton went over the side with scuba gear to film their passage. The fast-moving dolphin, stacked back-to-belly seven or more animals deep, formed a living barrier. The school tuna passed by Guillanton in hot pursuit of the sardines that had the dolphin packed up, but then, well down and visible enough to be clearly picked up on film, came a parade of huge tuna hunting clean-up. I soon found the smaller yellowfin with my flies. Had I not viewed the replay of the video footage, I would never have known about these large yellowfin. Their presence was not even suspected by Captain Canales. How to reach these deep-running monsters? And if I could, what would happen then? A lot like swatting an elephant in the butt with a flyswatter?

One evening during the 1992 Blue Water Fly Rod Invitational on *Royal Star*, John Barrett asked whether I thought a 100-pound yellowfin could be landed on a fly rod. Perhaps because my body ached from a day spent heaving on 13-weights against nine yellowfin tuna in the 30- to 40-pound range, my initial reaction was negative. But the question intrigued me and I thought hard on the matter. First and foremost, success would depend on what mode the tuna were in. For example, if the fish were in hot pursuit of baitfish, I was dead certain a 100-pound yellowfin couldn't be stopped. If a school of such tuna was

Previous page: Yellowfin tuna often travel in tightly packed schools containing nearly identical-size individuals. Photograph by Tony Oswald.

held close with live chum, and if the tuna in question was held with this group long enough, then possibly enough energy could be sapped from it to give the angler the upper hand. A half-dozen other factors, including the fitness of the angler, were admitted into the question. I said to Barrett, "Probably not."

My answer was tested six months later. Captain Del Dykes took *Reel Action* to the fish aggregation device, the FAD buoy, south of Hawaii's Kailua-Kona harbor. As we began slowly motoring upcurrent, I began tossing crushed anchovies over the side. A quarter mile later we had disposed of one 25-pound box. We returned to the buoy and had begun dumping off a second box when three enormous yellowfin—or "*ahi*" as they're known in Hawaii—suddenly appeared on the chum line. Dykes estimated them at about 140 pounds each. Without any apparent movement from tail or pectoral fins, they glided about picking up the slow-sinking chum, their dramatically extended second dorsal and anal fins marking them as adults. From the bow I made cast after cast, stripping back a 4/0 Sea Habit Deceiver at various speeds. The tuna wouldn't so much as look at the fly. Without much hope, I made another cast and walked along the side deck to the transom. I hadn't taken three steps before one of the *ahi* casually picked up the dead-drifted fly. Its behavior didn't change much when I struck. Without concern, the fish and its two companions just headed down at cruising speed. When the fly line and 1,000 feet of backing ran out, the fish leveled off and began swimming around.

At such a depth, it was critical that we remain directly over the fish. If my fish then changed levels it wouldn't create so much line drag that the 20-pound tippet would break. If the tuna streaked away from me, regardless of the depth, drag from that much backing would break the class tippet even with the reel in free spool. I bent the 12-weight rod double and, by using hand signals, kept us over the fish. Nothing changed for two hours.

When a tuna begins to tire and starts laboring, its tail swings in a wider arc, a throbbing that is readily telegraphed to the angler. Early into the third hour, my rod tip began bobbing up and down. I was elated, sweating hard, and taking all the water Dykes could find on *Reel Action*. The tuna wasn't remotely exhausted, for I couldn't yet move the giant, but it had blinked first.

As I began hour four, I noticed my own fatigue. The angle never changes; the back, arms, and shoulders hold the same painful embrace. Periodically I put the rod over my shoulder, but then I think the tuna, too, got rested. I turned up the drag, put the rod straight down, and pulled up on the fish. It moved up an inch or two, backing came back onto the reel, and I braced myself for another try. Sometimes the yellowfin came easily, swimming up on the pump, and I gained 50 feet. After forty-five minutes the tuna was down only 200 feet. For another ten minutes it resisted my every effort to bring it up. My body played tricks on me. The forefinger of my right hand, my reel handle finger, suddenly locked tight against my palm and would not open. Dykes forced it open. My left arm cramped badly, and became useless. Dykes grabbed the arm and literally beat out the cramp. I pumped, the fish came up, and after four hours the monocore loop of my fly line appeared. When the fish got its head down and took out 100 feet of backing, I thought my body would fall apart. As I started the tuna up again, my right arm went into spasm, the muscles jumping around at will, my mind unable to force them to work together. Dykes slapped and pounded, the fish moved up, I turned up the drag, pumped and pumped, and again reached the fly line. Dykes yelled out, "Color!" I could yell, too, the fish now in death spirals, ponderously spinning its way up, a beat fish. Dykes moved the boat out of the fish's way, and it broke the surface 15 feet behind Reel Action. I could barely make the reel work, hardly hold the rod, nothing functioned as it should have. Dykes backed down as I reeled in with my palm. The tuna snapped its head and the tippet broke. Slowly the yellowfin righted itself and began its descent.

I knew that a 100-pound tuna could be taken fly fishing. The equipment was up to the task. I had not been. Since then, I've fought larger billfish for longer periods of time and taken a far less severe beating. The constant angle made the four hours especially punishing. I was months recovering. Several weeks later I was throwing live sardines to some immense yellowfin off Baja's East Cape. I saw an 80-pound tuna break from the pack and come down a wave straight at my fly. When only inches away from the Deceiver, I said to the fish, "Don't eat it!" It didn't. That was the first time I could remember wishing that a record fish wouldn't eat my fly.

Bill Hayes, a friend and fishing companion of mine on Rice's 1993 and 1994 Blue Water Fly Rod Invitationals, broke Inks's 10 kg 38-pound yellowfin record in 1993 with a 52-pound yellowfin taken while fishing the Hudson Canyon off New Jersey. He then broke his own record the following year with a 68-pound, 2-ounce yellowfin. Hayes accomplished this while fishing at night aboard Eugene Burger's *On A Fly*, a 38-foot Harris on charter out of Brielle, New Jersey.

Hayes and his companions made an afternoon run of nearly 100 miles off the coast until reaching the East Wall of the Hudson Canyon. Using a chum of chunked-up butterfish, they cast and soaked their flies in the slick. Hayes fished an 850-grain Deep Water Express connected to a 150-foot running line of 25-pound Berkley Big Game monofilament, and then packed 1,700 yards of 35-pound Spectra on his Abel 5. The fly, an eight-inch-long all-white Deceiver, could be taken as a live bait when stripped, or as a chunk of butterfish when drifted and "soaked." Fully 70% of tuna come on a 4 A.M. bite. Hayes says these night fish don't seem leader shy; he uses 50-pound Maxima shocks.

Hayes's catches are all the more remarkable for the time he needed to beat these huge tuna: 15 minutes flat on the 52-pounder, 20 minutes on the 68-pound, 2-ounce yellowfin. Hayes does set a huge drag, 15 pounds at the start, 20 pounds when the tuna starts coming up, and he uses a Loomis 15/17-weight Mega Taper Saltwater fly rod to do the heavy lifting.

I asked Hayes if fishing at night was key, if the tuna grew disoriented in the darkness and could be beaten more quickly. He didn't know, having never fought tuna this size in daylight. Both of us thought these questions about really large yellowfin tuna on a fly would be answered in 1994 during Rice's invitational: *Royal Star* was scheduled to leave from Cabo San Lucas and motor directly to "The Islands," the Revillagigedo Islands of Clarion, Roca Partida, San Benedicto, and Soccoro. But just before departure, the Mexican government closed the area to American sports boats. Hopefully, soon, a charter that will include the Revillagigedo Islands, home of the world's largest yellowfin tuna, will provide answers to these questions.

YELLOWFIN TUNA (*Thunnus albacares*)

Jim Allen and Dean Butler hold a fly-caught longtail tuna (Thunnus tonggol) taken off Australia's Great Barrier Reef. Australians, who call this superb game-fish the northern bluefin tuna, have thus far accounted for all the International Game Fish Association's gear-fishing records and the very few fly-rod records. In Australian waters, the fish typically ranges from 10 to 50 pounds. The largest long-tail taken in sports fishing weighed 70 pounds 2 ounces and was caught off New South Wales, Australia.

The longfin tuna is found in the central Pacific and eastern Indian Oceans. Because of its coastal mi-gratory nature, and its great strength—some anglers consider it more powerful than the yellowfin—the longfin has great potential as a fly-rod gamefish. Photograph by Tim Leary.

This remarkably powerful and beautiful gamefish is found worldwide, often abundantly so, in tropical and warm temperate oceans. Fortunately for American anglers, the largest yellowfin are found first in "The Islands" off Baja California, where they reach nearly 400 pounds, and then in the Hawaiian Islands where they have been caught weighing as much as 250 pounds.

Frank LoPreste, co-owner of the LoPreste-Dunn long-range fishing fleet in San Diego, describes the yellowfin tuna as an eating machine with such a high metabolism that after reaching 300 pounds or so the fish experiences more and more difficulty taking in as many calories as its body burns each day; it ultimately starves to death. Four hundred pounds seems to be a metabolic barrier for the Baja populations.

On the Pacific coast, bluefin tuna (*Thunnus thynnus*) prove a far more difficult species to chum in close, remain deeper running, and are only cyclically abundant. Rarely have fly fishers encountered them. Gear fishers found them off Baja in 1994 to about 150 pounds. However, captains on the LoPreste-Dunn boats believe the populations of Pacific bluefin reach at least 200 pounds off California and Mexico. Nowhere in the Pacific do the bluefin tuna reach the colossal sizes found in the Atlantic off the Canadian Maritimes—the Nova Scotia and Prince Edward Island fish of 1,000 pounds or more. Every mate I spoke with at San Diego's Fisherman's Landing who had caught both species on live bait said that the yellowfin, pound for pound, was much the stronger of the two. I would be delighted to determine their relative strengths for myself, but I have yet to encounter bluefin tuna in my offshore fly fishing.

BIGEYE TUNA

Bahía Tebada, Choco, Colombia

ver the beat of the *vallenato* blaring from a boom box, I order the best cup of coffee in the world for 70 pesos, about ten cents, at Cafe de Colombia, half of Bahía Solano's

open-air Aeropuerto Jose Calestino Mustis, a tiny jungle airstrip honoring Colombia's foremost botanist. Steve Jensen and I will soon transfer our bags and rod tubes to a waiting launch for the 18-mile run up the Pacific coast to Bahía Tebada Lodge. I have thought of our return a hundred times since I first came here during an El Niño February and found the movements of billfish, dorado, and tuna unpredictable. To locate our fish on that visit, Jensen and I had to depend on blind luck, not to choices calculated upon currents, tides, moon phases, or water temperatures. The resulting frustrations were due almost entirely to our inability to develop a coherent strategy. Ten days of fishing, first light to last, now promised to change that.

Thumbtacked to the wall at the end of the counter are yellowing front pages of *El Espectador*, carrying an article by Fernando Caño, editor of the Bogotá newspaper, about the first big-game fishing tournament held off Colombia's Pacific coast. I study the faded color pictures of Patrick Guillanton and me cooking *lomo* steaks we'd cut from Steve Jensen's prizewinning 51-pound yellowfin tuna, and of Gerard Aulong with a huge blue marlin, both fish caught on gear. I had fished *la mosca*, "the fly," and showed Pipa, the mate, how to stitch baits and tease in sails, and we had hooked one that way, probably the first on this coast. Aulong owned most of the fly-rod records for bigeye tuna, all caught

107

from these waters. His bigeye had chased baitfish in waves of frantic pursuit, very different from my experience with nervous water, a few boobies, and then nothing to the fly as the tuna flashed away before our captain's hurried approach. When I finally managed a bigeye on a fly, I was certain the fish was a record, and warned Pipa of dire consequence should he botch the gaffing. Pip stood ready to strike the fish but then choked on his astonishment and stood transfixed. I leaned over the gunwale to see my leader disappearing into the mouth of a 300-pound blue marlin, the tuna safely in its stomach, the great fish looking positively dour. The marlin had come up on the last few pumps of the 10-weight, and we could almost reach it with the gaff. The eight-pound tippet broke when the marlin shook its head to rid itself of the minor irritant, but the fish had brazenly held its position, waiting for another handout. The chorus of bilingual expletives in the cockpit became a din and Caño had begun his story with one of mine.

"'Mierda!' *said the American fly fisherman.*"

Caño clearly had enjoyed this lighthearted respite from his crushing responsibilities as editor of the huge Bogotá daily.

I knew something of Caño before we fished together. Mutual friends had told me that he was "the bravest man in Colombia," and called his family "the most famous in Latin America," claims made without the benefit of an explanation. When I pursued the matter, Caño told me an epochal tale in a simple, self-effacing manner. Despite repeated warnings, his father, Fernando Caño Sr., the editor of *El Espectador*, had written editorials critical of the *mafia*—the Cartel de Cali and the Cartel de Medellín, the two giant multinationals dominating the production and distribution of cocaine. When he was kidnapped and murdered, young Caño became editor and took up the cause. Eventually bombs destroyed his newspaper's offices and presses. Borrowed presses kept the paper going. Repeated death threats forced Caño and his brother to live in exile for two years in Spain. But Colombia was his home, and when we fished together Caño had only recently returned. He was 28 years old.

On the run up the coast to the lodge, we watch the seas crash against rocky cliffs, the hillsides rising nearly straight up, one behind the other, each higher than the one before, until the highest Andean peaks disappear into the clouds. This rain forest, the Choco, as remote as any part of Amazonia, and the largest such coastal forest on earth, stretches from Panama to Ecuador along the weather side of the Andes Mountains. The area gained its name from *chocoes*, the original name given to the Native Americans of the region by the Spanish. Only here and there have beachfront squatters nibbled away at the virgin stands of balsa, guino, and jigua negro. The jungle reclaims any shack abandoned, the clearing soon covered with tree-sized antheriams and platanillos, and the long trails of blind army ants—the *hormiga ciega*—carting off every molecule of agriculture. The Envera Indian village closest to the coast is at least four days into the mountains on nearly impassable footpaths. Anthropologists describe many of the villages as "stone age," so complete is their privacy.

Offshore, the cold Humboldt Current (also called the Peru Current) collides with the warmer Equatorial Counter Current to generate an upwelling of nutrient-rich waters that feed immense schools of sardines, which in turn attract various pelagic gamefish. On the ocean floor, the Nazca, Cocos, and Caribbean tectonic plates have produced dramatic drop-offs starting several hundred feet from a coastline characterized by a wealth of bays and headlands, the *bahías* and *puntas* of the nautical charts. Bluewater fishing begins nearly on the beach.

Bahía Tebada Lodge, a series of lovely palm-thatched, hardwood-sided structures, each with a private terrace, sunken shower, and hot and cold running water, has electrical outlets functional when the huge diesel generator is running. Construction crews built these luxurious quarters and the nearby dining facility on stilts; I sleep with a high tide surf running under my cabin during my first night here. Morning and evening the clearing becomes an amphitheater of birds: parrots, toucans, tanagers, warblers, kingfishers. While sipping a Poker beer one evening, I count twenty species of birds in a single tree beside my terrace.

Enrique García-Reyes, the camp manager, advises Jensen and me to head north where many sailfish have been sighted recently. We discuss the plan with Victor, our captain, and Pipa, who will again be mating for us. We'll be near the frontier, the waters along the Panamanian border, and Victor ties a large Colombian flag to the radio antenna of *Sabalo*, our 28-foot cruiser.

The previous year, as we ran south from the frontier, a Colombian gunboat had opened fire on us with 40-mm cannons, nearly blowing *Sabalo* out of the water. Later, Jensen and I laughed about the incident, but only some fast talking by Antonio Uribe, one of the lodge owners, had saved us from being boarded and becoming guests of the Colombian navy. The sailors may have looked like something out of *Terry and the Pirates*, but they were taking their responsibilities for drug interdictions *very seriously*.

The days form a pattern. We work out from the little islands, *los islotes*, that guard Bahía Tebada, and troll teasers up the coast, first by Bahía Chirichiri, then off the Golfo de Cupica, and, by late in the morning, off a headland, islands that look like pineapples, Punta Piñas, or Pineapple Point. Here we stop to put away the teaser rods to chase after three- and four-pound black skipjack with 8-weight outfits, a hunt we've been eagerly anticipating, for it relieves us from the boredom of watching the stern wake for billfish. Pipa cuts belly strips from our catch to stitch up for billfish teasers and saves the little tuna to later grill over charcoal. Unlike Mexicans and Costa Ricans, Colombians find the fish delicious.

Our flies also find small amberjack, rainbow runners, and many green jacks (*Caranx caballus*), the "blue runners" that the locals call "*buricas*."

Our hunt for billfish continues up to Cabo Marzo and the fish-rich islands that guard it, the Rocas Octavia, or 21 Sentinels. We find only striped marlin here, 200-pound surface-lolling fish that swing by our carefully stitched Panama baits only for a heart-stopping look.

Each morning we find sailfish off Bahía Chirichiri; rarely as singles, often as double and triples, and sometimes as a school of as many as ten. Invariably, they are on the surface. So sure are they of seeing the free-swimming sails first, the captain and mate never bother checking the teasers. We tease the fish by trolling the baited lures across their path and watch the sails surge forward and disappear. After a moment, one or two reappear to grab the bait. Jensen has never caught a sail on a fly, and he can think of nothing else. The sails prove temperamental, for they won't come in close and never really get excited. A single grab at the bait is often all we see before they swim off. Steve does hook his first sail, and the hook breaks. When a school of seven sailfish sounds rather than attacking our teasers we begin to think we're jinxed.

On the fourth day we motor north in a cold drizzle to find the waters all the way to Cabo Marzo swept clean of every living thing save the deadly poisonous brown-and-orange sea snakes (*Pelamis platurus*) that swarm on the surface by the thousands. I think that the thin layer of warm surface water that holds the billfish has disappeared. Victor is perplexed, a condition that often plagues him. Without saying a word, Pipa takes the controls and drives the boat south for an hour until we're off Punta Solano. From a mile away, we can see that brown boobies and frigate birds fill the air. The bay, the point, and the seas are for miles filled with sardines, scattered pods of feeding black skipjack, schools of gentle rainbow runners flashing broad yellow tails, rafts of bold little *buricas* so concentrated they flatten the seas, and waves of rampaging schools of bigeye tuna averaging 8 to 12 pounds. We watch the occasional sailfish race about in tight circles corralling baitfish by fully extending its dorsal fin. We are so weary of trolling teasers that we do not give billfish another try for four days, and then only because we run out of bigeye tuna.

I find the bigeye tuna (*Thunnus obessus*) a somewhat mysterious fly-rod gamefish. The tuna grows to immense weights throughout the tropical and temperate regions of the Pacific, Atlantic, and Indian Oceans. Examples over 100 pounds have been caught off California, Hawaii, and the Baja Peninsula; East Coast bigeye have topped 300 pounds, and the 435-pound all-tackle record came from Cabo Blanco, Peru in 1957. But the fly records are juvenile, one-year-old fish of around 8 to 14 pounds. I have caught bigeye in this size range off Colombia's west coast, Hawaii's Kona Coast, and around the coastal islands off Costa Rica's Gulf of Papagayo. Nowhere have my flies found bigeye larger than 15 pounds.

As juveniles, bigeye and yellowfin tuna are nearly indistinguishable, the white striations and two equal lobes of the bigeye's liver the one absolutely reliable test acceptable to the International Game Fish Association (IGFA). It is easy to imagine that some caught fish that were larger than existing bigeye records were erroneously identified as yellowfin. But I think this scenario unlikely. More likely the reason that the records remark only on juvenile populations lies with the larger bigeye's habit of running at the colder, oxygen-rich depths our flies don't reach.

I believe that the long-range fly-fishing charters running out of San Diego, California will eventually change this situation. Their lavish use of live chum can bring tuna up from great depths and make bigeye as large as 40 pounds available to fly fishers. Within a few years, the current records may seem ancient.

Seeing schools of bigeye, regardless of the fish's size, should never be confused with catching the fish, even when they are porpoising over waves and sar-

The author holds an 11-pound tuna taken off Colombia's Pacific Choco coast. Note the Andean foothills in the background.

dines are flying before them. My captains have run up on feeding schools more times than I care to remember, and invariably the tuna sound, only to reappear seconds later 100 yards away. The captain becomes doubly confused when he can actually see the tuna right off the bow. But when he puts the boat in neutral, several things are wrong at once. The still-moving boat forces me to cast at the tuna directly into the wind created by the boat. The tuna are already fleeing and temporarily out of their feeding mode. In this attitude, they'll not come racing back to my fly. Whether I trail my fly beside the boat, or hold on to the fly, at least one false cast is necessary to get the fly going in the direction of the tuna. Because of the speed the bigeye are traveling, the fly lands in water empty of fish. What at first seems logical to the captain becomes the worst approach possible.

Jensen and I want to be casting downwind whenever possible. This is not so simple as it sounds, for in the early morning, with the ocean warmer than the land, light breezes come off the land. By midmorning, winds often cease altogether. But soon thereafter, onshore breezes build and continue all afternoon. By keeping this wind at our backs, we increase our casting distances, a vital advantage when hunting gamefish as wary as bigeye tuna. This downwind casting has secondary advantages as well. It takes tuna about one millisecond to either accept or reject a fly. Casting into the wind creates a small amount of slack that requires a strip to remove, and to get the fly swimming. In that brief second or two, tuna have seen enough and are on their way. If casting downwind, the angler starts the fly swimming on a tight line as it hits the water. The final advantage is less obvious. Flies, regardless of the type, are less prone to foul when cast downwind.

Brown boobies track the fleeing schools of sardines and reliably indicate where the bigeye tuna will appear. When the tuna have driven the sardines into a ball only a dozen feet across and are feeding on them, the boobies dive into the concentration to snatch a fish, then stay and paddle about to pick up the cripples. This bombing of the school scatters the sardines, the tuna pursuing them in all directions. If we position the drifting boat within 100 feet of this activity, we find that the tuna are still in hot pursuit when they race by, and that they will take our flies.

The searching boobies soon join together to fly in a single direction and again begin plummeting from the sky when the tuna have balled up the sardines. These brief convulsions of activity repeat themselves for hours.

Less frequently, the bigeye force the fleeing sardines to the surface and pursue them with wonderful arching leaps that can be seen from a great distance. We try to anticipate this activity by getting in front of the boobies, stopping the boat, and, as the tuna break out and turn the water into a froth, *shutting the engine off.* This is key. At least half the time, the bait and tuna do not come our way, but veer off and leave us momentarily at loose ends. However, when the bigeye continue to feed toward us the boat does not alarm them, and we often have dozens of tuna coursing after the fleeing bait only 20 feet from the boat.

The native fishermen, mostly African-Colombians in the area we are fishing, paddle among us and the schools of tuna in tiny dugouts they gracefully sculpted from the abarco tree. They trace their ancestry to runaway slaves who escaped from interior ranches and made their way over the Andes until they could follow west-flowing streams down through the Choco jungle to the coast. The streams just above tidewater abounded with silvery little fish, the *sabaleta,* or little tarpon, and enormous shrimp the Native Americans called "*pichimara.*" Many settled near the mouth of the largest of the rivers, the Gella, and lived in isolation for generations on fish and fried bananas, *patacones,* literally "bananas that have been stepped on," a dish now served for all meals in western Colombia. Their settlement became Bahía Solano, and because they never mixed with Native Americans, their African ancestry remained pure.

If the tuna disappear, and we hunt for them up the coast without luck, Pipa motors back to the waters off Bahía Solano and asks these fishermen about the tuna. If any have recently been sighted, we stay and concentrate on finding them. If they have not been seen for an hour or more, Pipa thinks it unlikely they will return that day, and we search for them elsewhere. Never is our request for information denied. In the days to come, these seafaring people prove invaluable.

Jensen and I set up our rods, 8- to 10-weights, with class tippets testing 8, 12, and 15 pounds that satisfy the IGFA's 4, 6, and 8 kg category rules. I believe that for school tuna in the 5- to 15-pound range, the best all-around tippet size is eight-pound, and that taking these leader shy fish becomes progressively harder as the tippet size increases. I have rarely experienced difficulty with tuna in this size range wearing through eight-pound leader if it was the hard nylon type. I change to heavier tippets only if I'm looking for a record fish in a heavier tippet category. And unless the fish are in a feeding frenzy, or unless the angler is trolling, 20-pound test hard nylon leader can look like rope to juvenile bigeye.

The previous year, after a discouraging day of chasing bigeye off Bahía Tebada, Gerard Aulong examined my carefully tied Sea Habit Tubes with their bright little black eyes. "What you need," he announced, "is a chicken!" The flies he showed me were hardly more than that, a couple of white chicken feathers tied on a hook with some sewing thread. *Crude* doesn't begin to give an accurate picture. How, I wondered, did this Frenchman take his three bigeye records with such a fly? I ultimately saw video footage of Gerard casting to an acre of bigeye gone absolutely bonkers over millions of sardines. I have also experienced such periods of fly-fishing nirvana; any fly will then work so long as it is primarily or totally white.

Such dramatic conditions represent but a small fraction of the opportunities encountered when fly fishing for tuna. I am convinced that the more closely the fly represents what tuna are feeding on, the more likely it will trigger a strike. Also, if one errs in the particulars of the dressing, a fly smaller than the baitfish is a much better choice than one larger.

Regardless of the fly cast, it must not foul itself on the cast. This is the single most important characteristic of any fly intended for school tuna, because you'll most often get only one all-too-brief shot at these fish. A fly with the wing fouled around the hook is worthless. Tuna simply will not take it.

I begin my search for school tuna with one pattern, a Sea Habit Anchovy

Blue, tied as a 1/0 or 2/0 Tube, Bucktail, or Deceiver, and about four inches long. If the tuna reject the fly, I drop down to a smaller size in the same pattern, a fly no more than three inches long. Failing that, I'll fish the original size, but change patterns, usually to Sea Habit Anchovy Green, or Sardine. I especially like these dressings when the green is pale, resulting in semi-transparent flies. One of the least effective school tuna patterns for me has been one with dark blue over white, especially if the blue carries a load of bright, metallic blue tinsel.

A bigeye will—as will all tuna, in my experience—pause at the moment of the strike to flare its gills to suck in the fly or baitfish. This action can take the fly down into its throat, and even into its stomach. More often, as the fish turns to rejoin the rest of the school, the fly is pulled to the corner of its mouth and the hinge of its jaw, where a very secure hold is gained. Regardless of where the hook takes hold, this pause provides the angler time to strike the fish and set the hook.

The initial run of the bigeye is directly away from the source of resistance. Not until it has tired and slowed down does that change. As a result, a full-length fly line is suitable for all class tippets down to eight-pound. (If fishing two- and four-pound tippets I switch to mini-heads and thin monofilament running line. See chapter 20 for a complete description.) This initial run is likely to be 50 to 75 yards, rarely more. At that point, the fish usually sounds, and one must fight it to the surface. When a bigeye is on top again, it digs down into its reserves and the last 20 feet of line can be a third of the fight, especially if the fly fisher is trying to tail the fish for a safe release.

The stories told by some writers of 14-pound bigeye tearing 300 yards off saltwater reels attached to 12-weights are absolute nonsense. Something remotely like that occurs when trolling for bigeye. In such a case, the fish pretty much hooks itself, and runs directly away from the boat's heading, giving the impression of a strike on the run. When the captain slips the engine out of gear, the boat still coasts along while the bigeye continues on in the opposite direction. The result can be a 150-yard run instead of one of 75 yards. But 300 yards? Not hardly!

On an 8-weight outfit and an 8-pound class tippet, an 8- to 10-pound bigeye takes fifteen minutes or less to land. This time does not change much when fishing a 10-weight and heavier class tippets. My concern here is not about breaking the rod or the tippet, but about tearing the hook out. The tough hinge of the tuna's jaw provides a very secure hold, but elsewhere the hook can tear a hole, and fall out the first time the fish gains some slack line. I play these tuna hard, but I do not try to break their necks regardless of the rod I use.

I generally line my school tuna rods 1 weight heavier than the manufacturer's recommendation. This helps me load the rod with a minimum of effort, and get off a quick delivery. While I find an 8-weight an ideal choice for the three- to five-pound black skipjack, a 10-weight is just about ideal for school-sized bigeye. Casts are longer, always less at the mercy of the wind, and more efficient when larger, 3/0 and 4/0, flies must be cast.

Using these strategies, fine-diameter tippets, and Sea Habit flies, Jensen and I take numerous bigeye tuna, including a couple of record fish that nick away at Aulong's fly-rod dominance of the species.

I have caught bigeye tuna using several other methods, all somewhat unorthodox. Bigeye and yellowfin commonly feed on squid. I've seen both species in Colombian and Costa Rican waters attack the billfish daisy chain of rubber squid. If I remembered to keep a 10-weight at the ready, the tuna were easily hooked. This has happened frequently enough that when trolling teasers in areas frequented by these tuna, I'll make sure that a daisy chain of rubber squid is snaking its way through the whitewater wake between the teasers on the two flat lines.

Captain Richard Chellemi of *Gamefisher II* put me on a school of bigeye tuna when we were fishing Costa Rica's Gulf of Papagayo for sailfish. Thousands of spinner dolphin provided evidence of tuna; distant leaping bigeye confirmed it. Chellemi drove near the fast-moving school of tuna while I trailed a fly 35 feet behind the boat. When his fish finder indicated tuna below us and 30 feet down, he took the boat out of gear and I cast downwind. The coasting boat, combined with a fast-stripped retrieve, brought up a tuna. In this manner, we hooked four or five bigeye tuna in an hour.

I have fished these same waters out of Bahía Pez Vela Lodge with Captain Calin Canales of *Roosterfish*. At the end of a day chasing after billfish, Canales would take a swing around nearby islands that often held bigeye tuna. As I trailed a fly 35 feet behind the boat, Canales would take the boat out of gear, I would make long cast at nearly a right angle to the course of the boat, make a fast, 50-foot, "crack-the-whip" retrieve, and signal him to again put the boat in gear. Though tedious, we did manage to hook bigeye tuna in this manner, all caught IGFA legal.

The blackfin tuna was struck by a Sailfish Tube popper (not pictured). Photograph by Trey Combs.

BLACKFIN TUNA *and* LITTLE TUNNY

Key West, Florida

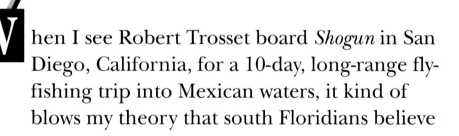

When I see Robert Trosset board *Shogun* in San Diego, California, for a 10-day, long-range fly-fishing trip into Mexican waters, it kind of blows my theory that south Floridians believe that the world is flat, and that anyone fishing other than off their hallowed shores does so in the netherworld of oblivion. My thinking, itself a metaphor for their center-of-the-world smugness, gets an additional comeuppance when I see that the famous Key West charter boat captain has a retinue of admirers with him that includes Carlos Solos and Teddy Lund, anglers who, by their own admission, are players in the south Florida fly-fishing scene. Right away I know that the complement of sixteen anglers aboard *Shogun* will break down into an East Coast–West Coast, Atlantic-Pacific, friendly sort of show-me thing. This will be illuminating if the boys from Florida don't view the rest of us as riding around on turnip trucks and occasionally falling off.

As *Shogun* motors south for "the ridge," those banks off Magdalena Bay holding tuna, billfish, wahoo, and dorado, I learn that among us are Phil Caputo and Stu Dunn, former clients of Trosset who hold him in awe and call him "RT." Caputo, a Pulitzer Prize–winning writer, gives me RT, chapter and verse, explaining that fishing with him is to be *trossetized*, past tense of a verb in the *Dictionary of South Florida Slang* that means "trauma in a libertine sort of way," the result of being so overstimulated with alcohol, fishing stories, and good times while hanging out with RT that a dreamy exhaustion sets in, the kind usually experienced only in opium dens.

RT proves to be a compelling storyteller during the ride down the Baja coast, though some of us don't know what to make of his tale of using penguins as teasers for killer whales. "Put 'em in little harnesses and line 'em up in a neat row," he explains.

When we arrive at Uncle Sam Bank and begin to "rip some lips," as one blood-lust aficionado of the "gentle art" put it, I see RT work his craft; the man's a world-class fisherman. He most assuredly has his own way of doing things, and this is often foreign to how some of us proceed. While I work my meticulously crafted baitfish-imitating flies on tuna and billfish that *Shogun*'s crew have chummed up with live anchovies, RT and his minions take big knives and convert school tuna into buckets of gore: Chop, chop, whack, whack, and over the side. RT's arsenal of two different fly patterns reflects this approach. He calls one, made on the spot, a "Bump Fly" because it consists of a few inches of white wire-cored bump chenille twisted on a bare hook. RT ties the other fly with red marabou, coats the result with silicone, and calls it a "Chunk Fly" because it looks like a chunk of something that once had been living. Both flies catch fish, the Bump Fly especially effective, and either sets saltwater fly tying back a century. RT, a free spirit, could care less. I tie flies only to fish, but I cannot tie so pragmatically.

Conversations with RT invariably lead to Key West and its flats fishing for tarpon, permit, and bonefish. He guides for everything, including a variety of inshore gamefish on various wreck sites. When the subject turns to offshore fly fishing for little tunny and blackfin tuna, I know that meeting RT is serendipitous; he has practically invented the sport.

I have long wanted to fish Key West specifically for these gamefish; an examination of the International Game Fish Association (IGFA) *World Record Game Fishes* explains why: Both species are found off Key West in record sizes, little tunny to 20 pounds and blackfin tuna to 30. RT assures me that finding these fish with a fly wouldn't be a problem; he had to first find anchored shrimp boats, and his loran would sort that out. A single day would be more than enough. He explains that the shrimpers work at night, their nets scouring the bottom when the shrimp are out of their burrows. The resulting harvest contain prawns to die for, and a by-catch that in volume and variety would gladden the heart of any budding marine biologist. Everything from snails, to crabs, to small fish of every description comes aboard. The crew picks out the prawns and tosses the by-catch overboard. That's where the tuna come in. In the late spring, when the shrimp fleet works the enormous shallows on Florida's Gulf Coast, the tuna key on the by-catch, quite literally growing fat on these easy pickings. Even after the tuna consume the by-catch from a night's fishing, they hang around the boats, ready to turn and feed on top the moment more food appears.

RT was the first charter boat captain to make the association between the appearance of tuna and the dumping of the by-catch; for a couple of years in the early 1980s his "luck" at finding blackfin tuna was thought to border on the mystical. Eventually, of course, word got around, and the shrimp boats started saving some of their by-catch to sell or trade for beer to the sportfishing boats that tagged along after them.

I make plans to fish with RT the following May. Two fly-fishing companions who are aboard *Shogun,* and who also delight in RT's company, will join me: Nanci Morris, the head fishing guide and manager at the Quinnat Landing Hotel in King Salmon, Alaska, and Steve Jensen, an American businessman who lives in Bogotá, Colombia.

Blackfin tuna (*Thunnus atlanticus*) are distributed throughout the Caribbean and the Gulf of Mexico, and range in the Atlantic from North Carolina to Brazil. My first encounter with the species occurred when Steve Jensen and I were fly fishing for white marlin off Venezuela's La Guaira Bank. One afternoon in seas typically rough we encountered immense shoals of sardines and pods of surface-feeding yellowfin tuna from 10 pounds to at least 80. (At the time, gear fishers were hanging yellowfin of over 150 pounds, but we didn't see tuna of this size on the surface.) I fought a tuna of about twelve pounds to the boat, and when it was gaffed I noticed that instead of the chrome yellow dorsal and anal finlets that characterize a yellowfin's tail, the finlets were black. This blackfin tuna was otherwise identical, down to the lateral wash of yellow that typifies yellowfin and bigeye tuna.

My experience with little tunny (*Euthynnus alletteratus*) was limited to chasing after them on a series of relatively shallow banks in the Strait of Mayagüez between Puerto Rico and the Dominican Republic. My captain would run at each loose surface commotion as fast as his dead-slow boat would go, invariably putting the fish down before cursing his misfortune at having a fly fisherman on board who would not troll. At the time, I was more familiar with the other members of the *Euthynnus* family, the black skipjack of the Pacific coast, and the kawakawa with its huge Indo-Pacific distribution. I knew that they and the little tunny were offshore, as well as inshore, species, and that at times all three could be caught from the beach. I was certain my lack of success with little tunny off Puerto Rico was due simply to how idiotically the captain and I were fishing.

RT stores his sleek 25-foot offshore boat at tiny Stock Island, a five-minute, across-the-bridge drive from Key West. Morris, Jensen, and I meet him each morning and, after buying a case of Budweiser to trade with the shrimpers, a forklift drops RT's boat in the harbor and we roar off, quickly leaving the tarpon-rich Marquesas in our wake. RT radios ahead to make sure mates hold sufficient chum for us, and then gets a bearing on their whereabouts. In an hour or two—on some days we are closer to Havana, Cuba than to Key West—the loose colony of shrimp boats at anchor appears on the horizon. When we motor alongside one, the work-weary mates pass us a laundry basket of by-catch for the six-pack of Bud we pass back. After a couple of baskets are dumped into the forward hold, and with the shrimp boat's supply of by-catch exhausted, RT jets to the next shrimper and we repeat the exchange. Two boats and their by-catch are all we need for our day of fly fishing to begin.

RT motors upwind to another shrimp boat and begins tossing over small fish from the by-catch. He smashes a few crabs with a knife handle to cloud up the slick. We slowly drift away from the boat; RT doesn't want our fly lines to tangle up in the shrimper's anchor ropes. In a couple of minutes we see dark forms 30 feet down racing through the rain of chum. A moment later little geysers of water erupt around us. Little tunny, their backs of electric blue breaking the surface, surround us and take down anything thrown at them. They hit our Sea Habit Bucktails when they land.

"Bonito," says RT of the tuna. He doesn't mean Atlantic bonito (*Sarda sarda*) but little tunny, the false albacore—or albacore—of the east coast of the United States, called the "bonito" in south Florida. By any name, they are a load on our 10-weight rods, tuna of 8 to 12 pounds that take our flies on the run and strip off 200 feet of backing in less than five seconds. A second and third equally shallow run follows. Not until the tuna tire do they bore down and circle, giving us their entire bodies to work against. As Morris, Jensen, and I try to keep our lines clear of one another, RT stares intently into the water for the dark, almost black, back of a blackfin tuna. He finally spots a single tuna in the group. The fish holds deeper than the "bonito," and is more reluctant to come to the surface for the chum. When it does come up, the blackfin flashes through the chum for a second before streaking down and disappearing into the depths.

After we bring in our fish and release them, RT moves us to the next shrimp boat down the line. Little tunny immediately show in the chum line. Not a single blackfin appears. We investigate another shrimp boat with identical results.

The ocean remains shallow here, 100 feet or so, and the late morning sun penetrates right to the sea floor. This is not typical tuna habitat, for members of *Thunnus*, the yellowfin, bluefin, bigeye, albacore, and blackfin tuna, cruise at cool depths far greater than 100 feet. The shrimp fleet's by-catch holds blackfin in water uncommonly shallow for the species. Regardless of ocean depth, I've always done far better on *Thunnus* early and late in the day. RT says that the next day we should be ready to leave the dock at seven when he wants to make a beeline for the shrimp boats. In the meantime, his Key West menu includes other à la cartes, a stop at a wreck site for permit and African pompano, and an afternoon of tarpon fishing in a deepwater channel near Stock Island.

Less than an hour later RT anchors on a midocean pinnacle and begins smashing crabs. The tide runs strongly and carries the chum to deeper water. Not 10 minutes pass before a phalanx of at least 50 permit moves upcurrent into the chum line and within casting range.

We fish a crab imitation I've made by joining together pale tan Velcro patches with epoxy, tying in some variant hackles at the tail and lead barbell eyes at the head, and sandwiching rubber bands between the Velcro to simulate six legs. Using marking pens, I've stippled the crab with a few spots of brown, and then tipped the legs in red. I find the whole business close to the color of the crabs now floating downtide in the chum line. The permit must think so, too. RT says my first permit will hit 30 pounds. After 15 minutes it goes over the edge of the shallows and breaks me off on coral. Morris gets hers up and scores with a permit of 18 pounds. (Had this permit not been weighed, it would have topped 25 pounds, easy. Like dorado, estimates of permit weights are often outrageously generous.) Jensen and I follow with permit of 8 and 12 pounds, respectively.

When African pompano show in the chum line, Morris switches to one of RT's bump chenille flies. She immediately hangs an "African," a fish that RT

A little tunny rushes away after striking a 2/0 Sea Habit Bucktail in the Sardine pattern.

says is more difficult to take on a fly—any fly—than permit. After twenty minutes we can see it ghosting along 10 feet below, a strobe of silver flashing up at us, the tendrils of its dorsal and ventral fins now visible. I think, 20 pounds and change, and then the hook pulls out.

True to his word, RT has us on a school of tarpon that afternoon, time enough for Morris to beat one of 125 pounds before a freaky tailwrap prevents her from being a Kodak moment, and for Jensen to have a 90-pounder within gaffing range before the leader parts. Their misfortune is not contagious; I don't even jump a tarpon.

We return to Key West to get further trossetized: beachside drinks with RT, dinners of stone crab, and some downtown gawking. Key West is a scene: Seams of artistic wellness in a matrix of garish artsy-craftsy commercialism. Called the Conch Republic of the Florida Keys by the chamber of commerce, it is also the T-Shirt Capital of the Americas, and the place where Ernest Hemingway lived and wrote during the most productive years of his life. The image of Papa, in a dozen bad taste media, all versions of the famous Karsh portrait, are numbingly omnipresent. His memory deserves better. Fortunately, the Ernest Hemingway House Museum hints at what attracted Hemingway to Key West more than sixty years ago.

At the turn of the century Key West was a fishing village and a destination for bohemian vacationers willing to book passage on a ship to reach this remote destination. Henry Flagler changed all that by overseeing the construction of a

Key-hopping railroad track from the mainland to Key West. Considered an engineering marvel when completed in 1912, the train line opened up the Keys to the outside world; Key Largo, Islamorada, Marathon, Big Pine, Sugarloaf Key, and Key West became part of the American vacationer's vocabulary. In 1935, when a hurricane destroyed many of the bridges in the system, the Florida legislature created the Overseas Road and Toll Bridge District. (The classic Humphrey Bogart-Lauren Bacall film, *Key Largo*, in which the protagonists match wits with Edward G. Robinson and a hurricane, became one of Hollywood's classic examples of art imitating life.) Bonds were sold to raise the money needed to purchase what was left of the defunct railroad line, and for the construction of the future highway project that would, in large part, be built on Flagler's work. When U.S. Highway 1 was completed in 1944, it became possible to drive the entire length of the Keys, a bonanza seized upon by post–World War II businesses and vacationing sportfishers. If one were to write a definitive history of saltwater fly fishing that calls into account those factors

Nanci Morris holds a 15-pound little tunny taken while fly fishing beside Florida's Gulf Coast shrimp boats. Photograph by Trey Combs.

that most influenced the development of the sport, the completion of Highway 1 would, in my view, take its place beside the people, rod, reels, and fly lines.

RT leaves the dock at seven and runs hard for the shrimp boats, covering more than 50 miles in under two hours. The little tunny are again everywhere, but larger than we have previously found, fish of 10 pounds or more. Morris boats one of 15 pounds that I photograph. Jensen takes one still larger that we kill, for RT believes the fish could be a record. (At 16 pounds on a certified scales, it ties the world record for the 10 kg class tippet. Unfortunately, the IGFA finds that the leader overtests.) When I hook up, I'm thinking blackfin, for the fish makes a straight-line surface run of over 100 yards before slowing. But this fish, too, is a little tunny, one well into the teens, and all my 10-weight can handle. As more chum hits the water, and with dozens of little tunny racing about, several blackfin tuna show. When we cast to a blackfin flashing by, a little tunny finds the fly first. How do we separate out the tuna?

RT and Morris plot a strategy. She ties on one of my ⁹⁄₁₆-inch-diameter, 6-inch-long, ethafoam sailfish poppers, casts it a short distance off the transom, and leaves it motionless. All of her concentration is given to the popper as it rocks gently on the swells. When RT throws chum at the popper, little tunny instantly turn the water into a froth. Morris remains motionless, continuing to stare into the water. More chum is thrown and the water again turns to froth. As the little tunny race away and the water begins to clear, she gives her rod tip a twitch, and sets the popper in motion. A 25-pound blackfin engulfs the popper, she times the strike perfectly, and lets out a primal scream, "Eeeeahaaa!"

This Alaska woman, who hunts big game and wears fur coats when not guiding fly fishers to trophy trout, exhibits the kind of total pleasure only another predator living atop the food chain could understand.

Morris spares no effort, and soon works the blackfin to the boat for in-the-water pictures, and an in-the-water release. We both know that getting a shot of an angler with a live tuna *in or out of the water* is extremely difficult, the fish so immediately stressed by the hands-on treatment that it usually dies.

A day later Jensen and I hook blackfin, more a case of blind luck than of picking out the millisecond when a tuna, and not the wealth of little tunny, has the best shot at the fly. These are tremendously strong fish, their fight made more interesting because they can take out 100 yards of backing on their initial runs, but can never sound deeper than the bottom, 90 to 100 feet down.

The blackfin remain uncommonly scarce regardless of the shrimp boat we investigate, but the little tunny remain in the teens and I can't get enough of them. The 10-weight rods are an ideal choice. Given the use of by-catch for chum, probably almost any fly works. When Morris switches to RT's Bump Fly, she continues to catch little tunny on command.

I don't appreciate RT's bump chenille concoction until I get in the water to take underwater photographs of little tunny. To keep the fish in camera range, RT tosses chum on the water. Small fish, pieces of crab, chunks of larger fish rain down. In this environment, the salient feature of the Bump Fly is obvious: It doesn't particularly represent anything except something to eat.

RT says that though we are a couple months late for king mackerel, a few are still hunting the wreck sites and we should give the fish a try. Like a magician pulling one more rabbit out of his hat, he finds them for us, our first experience with the gamefish we liken to wahoo and other visions of lightning incarnated. We find barracuda, too, or they soon find us. One afternoon I lose two Mylar poppers and three Sea Habit Bucktails to a pack of them while hunting for other species. When my flies and poppers do find a fish, the barracuda munches them in half. At one point 'cudas run like railroad ties across 200 feet of wreck site.

When a school of 15- to 20-pound jack crevalle cruises by, RT casts a natural wooden chugger at them with a spinning rod, reeling the hookless plug back as fast as possible with a half-dozen jacks in hot pursuit every time. If one of us has a popper in the air, and can land it exactly where and when RT pulls the chugger, the popper is nailed. We cast poppers with a lot of different finishes, but the Silver Bullets I'm so crazy about for tuna really have the jacks' numbers. These prove to be incredibly tough fish. During a couple hours of hot fishing, I manage to break both of my 10-weight rods, while Morris straightens out the hooks on a couple of poppers.

Each day that begins with offshore gamefish leads to lunch at a wreck site, and a go at tarpon in the afternoon. My most vivid recollection of our time with RT is the struggle that occurred when Morris stuck a tarpon so large that it simply rejoined the school and tooled around the bay on cruise control for over two hours, a journey that RT watched on the screen of his fish finder. His coaching, and a drag set as tight as Morris dared, could not slow, speed up, or otherwise disturb this fish. RT would say only that the tarpon was "over 150," and that no one should touch Morris's rod. Well, into the third hour, the fly—a Bump Fly, of course—simply pulled out.

Key West offers the most diversified saltwater fly fishing I have experienced anywhere in the world. Just a few days of fishing in this area leaves so many scores unsettled that a lifetime of returns couldn't wipe the slate clean. When Morris, Jensen, and I leave Key West for a run at bonefish and permit on Mexico's Ascensión Bay, I still do not think the earth is flat. Not yet, at least. I am, however, feeling uneasy, sensing that traveling to another fishing destination is bound to be reductive. I have RT pencil in ten days for me the following year. I tell him I'd like to spend more time on tarpon, including some sight casting in the Marquesas.

"Will ten days be enough?" I ask.

"Enough for what?" says RT.

KAWAKAWA TUNA

Bazaruto Archipelago, Mozambique

T he five islands, arks of endemic life looking peacefully adrift in the Indian Ocean, come into view three miles below. Tony West, the pilot of the Beechcraft King Air on charter from Durban,

South Africa, begins a long descent that carries us toward Bazaruto, the largest in the archipelago and the island cleaved most recently from East Africa, a creation that began only 7,000 years ago. To the north are Magaruque and Benguerra, islands making up a national park, the designation suggesting greater protection for their flora and fauna than could be enforced in Mozambique's unsettled political climate. The archipelago, including Paradise and Bengué, has for centuries supported native subsistence fishermen who learned to trap mullet, herring, and bonefish on the flats using weirs of natural vegetation and, when hooks became available, to take the wealth of inshore gamefish such as giant trevally, pompano, and ladyfish. Their way of life is now threatened by refugees fleeing the mainland's civil war and interminable drought, co-sponsors of misery that seems without end. Two thousand have crossed the 20-mile strait by dhow to build temporary encampments on Bazaruto, the thinly vegetated island suffering egregiously from their hurried slash-and-burn agriculture. The returns on this labor are harvests so meager that only corn donated by the United Nations prevents starvation.

Modern facilities for anglers, divers, and ecotourists come one to an island, the manager on each promoting its own fishing for marlin, sailfish, and other pelagic gamefish while remaining sensitive to the extreme vulnerability of the

125

island's flora and fauna to human assaults. Hotel developers eye these "African Galapagos" with more ambitious visions and see big-game fishing fleets, marinas, and tourist dollars.

Our flight low over the flats of Bazaruto's leeward coast raises clouds of lesser flamingos, a gift the island shares with Kenya's Great Rift Valley. West points down as we pass Paul Dutton's Piper Super Cub, which has been pulled up on the marly flats to the high tide line. As executant of the Bazaruto Archipelago Master Plan for the World Wildlife Fund for Nature, and the Southern Africa Nature Foundation, Dutton must develop a strategy to include all five islands in a national park complex that can address the needs of tourists and natives, while ensuring the preservation of the archipelago's rare wildlife. An hour later over ice-cold Impala beers, Dutton details for me the staggering difficulties he faces in implementing the Plan.

Bruce Theunissen, director of African Rod & Rifle Safaris in Durban, South Africa, and my partner on many fly-fishing trips, stares out the window during the island flyover. "You'll feel like Robinson Crusoe!" he calls to me, a promise I have heard many times from him, and one I now want badly to experience.

"More like a fly fisherman in Eden," I say. Save for Belize, I have never before viewed such a concentration of different fishing environments. On the windward end of the island, blue water reaches to the edge of the surf line, where anglers catch pelagic gamefish, including tuna and sailfish, casting from the beach. The flats extend for miles, and hold bonefish averaging 11 pounds that have never seen a fly. Between the islands, in narrow straits knotted with aquamarine shallows, live barracuda, wahoo, king mackerel, and queenfish. I feel like a child with too many desserts to choose from, happy for the first time in days with the mountain of fly-fishing tackle I've dragged out of one baggage claim after another across three continents.

A sward of grass at the center of Bazaruto serves as a landing strip. Louis and Pauline Erasmus, managers of Bazaruto Island Lodge, stand by with two Land Rovers, and Trash, their Irish wolfhound. Some bulk supplies can be ferried over by dhow from Vilanculos on the mainland, but everything else must be brought in by plane from South Africa. These unscheduled charters have become their lifeline, and this day the flight brings them everything from yogurt to engine parts. Counting the thirty minutes needed to clear customs in Maputo, the capital of Mozambique, the flight has taken nearly five hours from Durban. B. J. Meiggs and I arrived in Durban that same morning after an overnight, thirteen-hour flight from London. She and Rhonda Klevansky, a photojournalist from Durban on assignment for *Salt Water Sportsman*, immediately buddy up to do some of the offshore photography I will need for *Bluewater Fly Fishing*.

Fly fishers do not often visit these islands. Other than Theunissen, Mel Krieger is the only fly fisher I know personally who has been here. He caught giant trevally, or "ignobilis," as they are sometimes called (from the Latin name, *Caranx ignobilis*) to distinguish them from the wealth of smaller, less esteemed species of trevally. South Africans, who have a mania for the fish much as Pacific Northwest anglers have for chinook salmon, more frequently call them "giant kingfish," or "kingfish," or "kingies," the latter a reflection of the country's fetish for the diminutive. While pursuing these and other gamefish, I will hear "bakkie," "tackie," "airie," "mossie," "sami," "deckie," and "sailie," for "truck," "tennis shoe," "airplane," "mosquito," "sandwich," "mate," and "sailfish," the latter the ostensible focal point of our fishing.

Alfy, our captain, and David, our deckie, speak a Xitswa dialect, and enough Fanagalo' for Theunissen to make our wishes known. This pidgin language, a combination of Zulu, Afrikaans (Dutch), Xhosa, and a sprinkling of English, came out of South Africa's gold mines, filling the need for a common language in a country where whites spoke two languages, and blacks spoke dozens of dialects. Theunissen, a professional hunter, learned Fanagalo' as a child in Bechuanaland, one of four languages he speaks fluently.

We launch on the incoming tide, carefully following the serpentine channel through the flats for a mile before breaking through the surf line and reaching blue water. The tides typically range more than 10 feet, the incoming tide covering the miles of flats with such a rush that the first bonefish taken on a fly here will not come to a wading angler.

Bruce and I set teasers for Indian Ocean sails that, according to the lodge's catch records, typically weigh 40 to 90 pounds, with 60 to 70 pounds the average. The rough seas and uncommonly cold weather have driven the sails elsewhere, and soon have us hunting on the calmer water in the lee of bights, or hugging the deepwater coastline in Sailfish Bay. Rafts of baitfish, or "sprats,"— a generic name South Africans casually apply to any silversided baitfish, including sardines and roundherring—periodically shower into the air before a wave of feeding tuna. Alfy calls them "bonito," a name with many faces worldwide, often any tuna used to live bait a marlin. I want a few belly strips, or "belly shines" as the South Africans say, to run inside the teaser skirts, and I make up any excuse to chase after school tuna with a fly rod to secure them. Not having a clue as to the color of the sprats, we set up 8-weight outfits and begin trolling two different Sea Habit Tube flies alongside the sailfish teasers, a moss-green-and-white fly and a gray-blue-and-white fly. The strikes are immediate, the tuna racing away from the boat with 50 yards of backing as David frantically works to clear the teaser lines. In ten minutes we have the fish to a point off the transom where David can reach them with a gaff.

With the breezy air of an expert witness, I identify the twin five-pound tuna as black skipjack: They generally possess the right markings, though the stripes are somewhat wavy, more like vermiculations, and different from the stripes of any black skipjack I've caught in the Americas. But they are equally relentless in their struggles, and more powerful than yellowfin for their weight. Also, I think the manner in which they run close to the surface, and remain less prone to sounding than either yellowfin or bigeye, provides further evidence for my identification. I later learn I have only the genus right, not the species. A more thorough examination of the fish in camp, and a careful reading of Rudy Van Der Elst's *A Guide to Common Sea Fishes of Southern Africa*, tells me that these "bonito" are kawakawa tuna, *Euthynnus affinis*, a close relative of both the black skipjack, *Euthynnus lineatus*, and the little tunny, *Euthynnus alletteratus*. Whereas the little tunny is an Atlantic species, and the black skipjack a Pacific species

along the coast of the Americas from California to Peru, the kawakawa has an enormous tropical and subtropical Indo-Pacific range, approximately thirty degrees above and below the equator. They are uncommon or incidental only along the Pacific coast, though regularly found around the Revillagigedo Islands—a yellowfin tuna stronghold well off Mexico's Baja Peninsula—and abundant off the Hawaiian Islands in winter.

All three species share an attraction to headlands, banks, rocky islets, and islands. As a family, they are generally more pelagic than true bonito, and less pelagic—less the open-ocean tuna—than skipjack, *Katsuwonus pelamis*. According to the International Game Fish Association's *World Record Game Fishes*, the principal current difference *may be* one of size; the little tunny and kawakawa tuna fly-rod records approach 20 pounds, specimens considerably larger than the record black skipjack, which have been in the 8- to 16-pound range. The all-tackle record kawakawa of 29 pounds came from Clarion Island, Mexico in 1986. However, most kawakawa records, both fly and gear, have come from Australian waters.

We return to our fishing, again trolling to determine the kawakawa's preference for color, and soon determine that the small, three-inch-long, gray-blue-over-white tube is the most effective. By early afternoon we have several more belly shines and head for cover before a strong offshore wind that has set up whitecapped seas so steep that standing to cast is impossible.

The next day Sailfish Bay belongs to the kawakawa. For several hours we troll teasers around acres of the feeding tuna in a vain hunt for billfish. I have seen cold weather shut down sails many times, and as pods of tuna blow sprats into the air, I grow more and more disheartened with our prospects for a sail. I begin explaining tuna strategies to Bruce, who in turn explains them to Alfy. Running straight at the fish is a waste of time, for they will only sound before our approach. Better to anticipate by moving in front of where the fish are generally moving, and then stop the boat and wait. Free casting for the tuna becomes a tricky business for even experienced captains. For the moment, Alfy cannot imagine what we are about, and runs at the tuna a few times before comprehending Bruce's instructions.

These acres of kawakawa remind me of acres of black skipjack, pods here and there of feeding activity, the individual schools sometimes of different sizes and age groups. The first fish are in the five-pound range, handfuls to beat on the 8-weight rods. When the seas calm, I go forward and keep 30 feet of line trailing behind the boat while Bruce trolls a fly. The moment a tuna hits Theunissen's fly, Alfy takes the boat out of gear and I cast at a 60-degree angle from the boat. Usually several kawakawa have come up at once to intercept the trolled tube, and one will usually then go after mine, always the same pattern and size as the trolled fly. Sometimes I am able to spot the tuna coming up from the depths and turning to intercept the fly. I stop stripping to watch the take, a very deliberate eating of the fly, the tuna stopping, opening its mouth, and taking it in.

We begin finding the pods of larger kawakawa, extraordinary gamefish averaging 10 pounds that have us tearing into the rod tubes for 10-weight sticks. I can see rafts of still-larger tuna, dark backs a yard long cutting through the

Previous page: The author casts a fly for trevally on Bazaruto Island's north coast. At some points along the coast, the drop-offs were so severe that kawakawa tuna could be taken by fly casting from the beach.

A small kawakawa tuna caught in Bazaruto Island's Sailfish Bay. The tuna struck a Sea Habit Tube Fly in the Ballyhoo pattern. Photograph by BJ Meiggs.

surface before waves of silver sprats. When we drift with the wind and find these tuna with our flies, two show no sign of stopping, sprinting away until over 200 yards of backing is gone and my bonefish reel is nearly emptied. With only 50 feet of backing left, I palm down on the reel until the eight-pound tippet parts. Theunissen fares no better, for eventually his 2/0 fly tears out. I do not doubt that we have both lost 20-pound kawakawa, larger than Jeffrey Grist's Australian record of 18 pounds, 15 ounces, the 8 kg class record and the largest ever taken on a fly rod.

When one of the ancient outboards coughs and dies, Alfy's eyes begin rolling about. Tuna are everywhere, rafts of huge kawakawa only 70 feet up-wind of us, continuing to plunder the sprats. East of us is Madagascar, a week away by drifting boat should the second engine quit. With the wind picking up, and the seas building, Alfy begins limping half throttle down the coast to the safety of the flats. We find more kawakawa in the days to come, sometimes only a dozen feet off the windward shore where *a à* lava has formed rough cliffs that plunge into the blue water's abyssal depths. Never again do we find kawakawa the size we hooked off Sailfish Bay.

On one wall at Bazaruto Lodge hang several groups of black-and-white pictures, each vintage framed and dated. The photographs, all yellowed with age, begin with BAZARUTO 1954. First, seven anglers are pictured sitting in front of a picket fence of ignobilis trevally; a second picture shows 100-pound yellowfin tuna massed together with a compact car-sized grouper in the foreground; a rather dour-looking angler poses with a small marlin and a king mackerel in the third picture, while an angler sitting in a chair beside a stack of pre–World War II wooden rods and reels completes the series. The pictures could be subtitled, PORTUGUESE COLONIALISTS ENJOYING THEIR LEISURE. The more recent photographs celebrate only marlin and big-game tournaments, the winning anglers South African: 1967, Mervyn Thompson, 1,067-pound blue marlin; 1971, Basil Hill, 860-pound blue marlin. This pictorial history of the islands' angling history ends here; no photographs are more current than these.

In the early 1950s a ferry began running twice weekly between Vilanculos, on Mozambique's mainland, and the archipelago. For the first time, bulk foods, East African tourists, and building materials could be inexpensively freighted to the islands. Joachim Alves, a hotel owner from Vilanculos, saw in this development an opportunity to build a rustic "self-catering" fishing camp on Paradise Island, or "Santa Carolina," as it was known at the time. The D'Anna Hotel, named for his wife, remained in business on Paradise from 1952 until 1971, when operations were moved to a new facility on Bazaruto Island.

Alves was Portuguese, as were nearly all Mozambicans of Euro-African descent. The Portuguese, who had established trading stations on the coast as early as 1505, and organized Mozambique as a colony within its current boundaries in 1885, continued to economically develop—and exploit—the country as more and more Portuguese immigrants settled here permanently in the late 19th century. The Mozambican struggle for independence lasted from 1961 until 1975, when a Marxist government gained power. The period of political upheaval that followed saw the exodus of thousands of Portuguese to Portugal and the nearly complete loss of the country's administrative infrastructure. Soviet military personnel and advisers poured into the country, replaced the Portuguese, and precipitated a period remarkable for its mismanagement of people and natural resources. One of the new government's first orders of business was to toss the South Africans out of the country. The fishing camps in the Bazaruto Archipelago shut down.

When Mozambique signed a cooperation agreement with South Africa in 1989, camps reopened and South Africans began returning to the Bazaruto Archipelago to troll again for marlin and to surf cast for trevally. The civil unrest that had plagued the country through its years of independence also showed signs of ending, for the government and insurgents signed a cease-fire several weeks before my arrival in 1992. The countryside, however, remains armed, dangerous, desperately poor, and in the grips of such a drought that the feeding of nearly 2 million of the country's people remains the responsibility of international relief agencies. Little evidence remains of the Soviet occupation save for the endless cases of Moskovskaya vodka in Maputo's duty-free store.

The Bazaruto Archipelago survives in relatively unspoiled splendor amid all this grief. In the evening, on its great flats, I watch native fishermen take bonefish from their nets, which are really too large to believe, and drag them ashore, and carry them a mile downcoast to Peter Taylor's Crocodiles de

Mozambique, where they are dumped into a brackish lake to feed future shoes and handbags. I watch the flats come alive with greenshanks, turnstones, and sacred ibises, and listen at night to the unearthly sounds of thousands of flamingos straining the mud for blue-green algae and diatoms. The day I watch a rare samango monkey race down a giant sand dune for the safety of a tangle of maroela trees I feel as though I am witnessing the dawn of primate history. I experience these and many other natural history dramas, but I best remember the spindrifts of silver sprats and the kawakawa tuna of Sailfish Bay. I see in them my return to these African Galapagos.

NOTE: Since first taking kawakawa tuna off Mozambique, I've caught them off Mauritius and Papua New Guinea. Neither destination produced kawakawa remotely the size of those encountered in Bazaruto Island's Sailfish Bay.

BLACK SKIPJACK

Thetis Bank, Mexico

"*A tun?*" I would say, and point to the sardines roiling the ocean brown and the boobies dropping from the sky like so many winged javelins. Sometimes Victor nodded, and then I would see bigeye tuna in a hundred arching leaps, their flanks of gold glinting in the day's first rays of Andean sun, the silver streamers of baitfish radiating away. But more frequently my Colombian captain shook his head, and wondered why I did not know better. "*Pati seca,*" he would reply and give me a laugh. I did not know what fish he meant, if in fact he meant a fish at all, for his answer to my question was "dry tail." Perhaps he was telling me the tuna were gone, like a dry well, or something like that, and that they had been replaced by some other fish that did not leap but could still shred their way through a school of sardines.

My confusion ended when one of the tuna, smaller and more easily managed on the 10-weight rod, turned out to be a four-pound black skipjack.

"*Pati seca,*" said Victor, pointing to the fish.

"Because the meat is dry to eat?"

"No! No!" He grabbed the fish and held it up, the very-much-alive tuna beating its tail in the air. Victor passed the fish up and down his face like an electric razor and I understood.

"The tail moves so fast you can dry yourself with it!"

"Of course!" said Victor. I soon learned that all the captains and mates along Colombia's west coast called the black skipjack *pati seca*, though if pressed on

Dan Blanton holds up a 15-pound black skipjack taken on "the ridge" off Baja California. Photograph by Janet Downey.

135

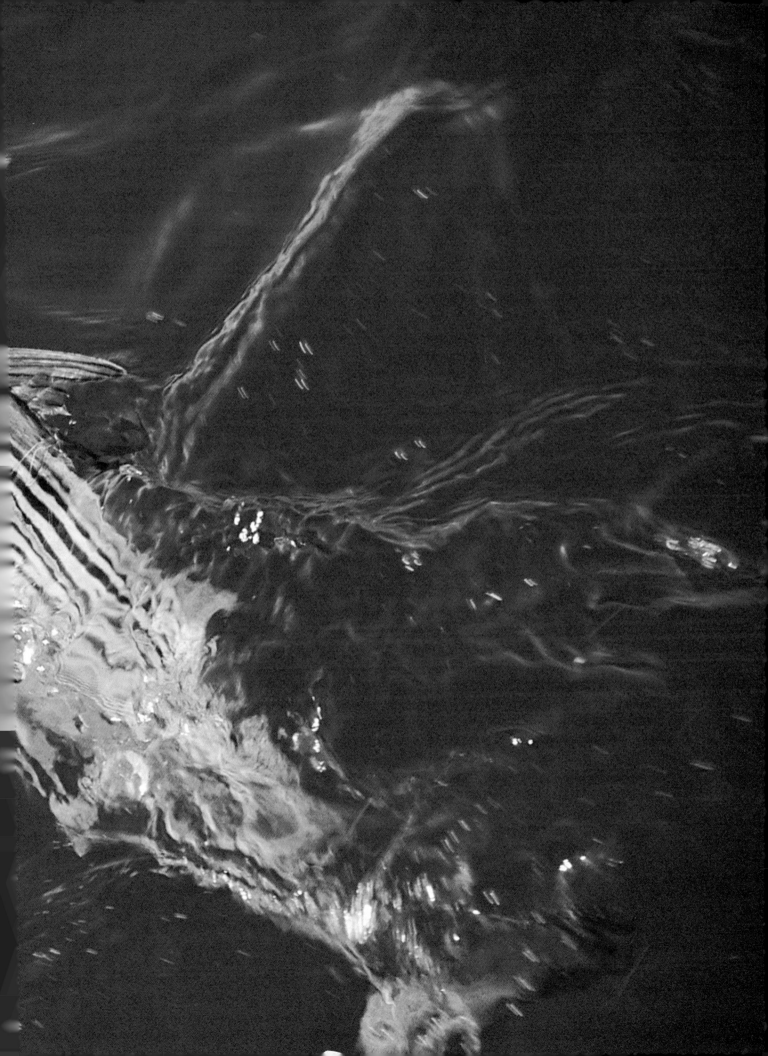

the matter, and asked to give its real name, most would have said, "bonito."

"*Pati seca!*" I said to Steve Jensen, my Colombian connection when fishing the country's gamefish-rich Pacific coast. "A perfect description of the black skipjack!"

Jensen and I were dividing our days, chasing bigeye tuna and billfish each morning from Bahía Solano to Cabo Marzo, the great cape that led us around to the frontier waters between Colombia and Panama. We would break for lunch at noon, munching first on buttered *arepes*, the corn pancakes that begin each Colombian's day, and draining the first of the several thermoses of coffee put aboard each morning. As we ate, Victor began picking his way through the myriad of rocky islets, *los islotes*, sometimes at Punta Piñas, but more often at Cabo Marzo's Rocas Octavia, and we would troll little Sea Habit Bucktails with 7-weight rods for black skipjack. We usually located them off the headlands or between the islands, where the waves surged and exploded on the hidden reefs. Often the four- to five-pound tuna schooled in water only 50 feet deep. When we found them so concentrated, we cast for them with bonefish lines that kept the flies no more than a foot below the surface, stripping the bucktails back easily a foot at a time. Sometimes a school could be seen milling about, not actively feeding, but giving the ocean currents and eddies where there should have been none, and it was necessary to shut off the engine and drift until the school moved down on us and we could reach the fish with our flies.

The black skipjack took the flies eagerly, quick grabs made before racing away on runs that took us 50 yards into our backing. The sprints changed to determined borings down, up, and out, never just down. We killed the first few fish for Victor and the mate to charcoal broil whole, and for belly strips, the "Panama baits" we ran inside our billfish teasers. Then we fished on for the intense enjoyment the "skippies" provided, even as we knew that this was time subtracted from the hunt for sailfish and striped marlin.

My introduction to black skipjack had begun one morning years before in Baja California. As my panga captain motored along searching for patches of sargasso and the dorado that might lurk beneath them, the water erupted several hundred yards in front of us into pockets of foam, dark backs, and sardines that scattered frantically into the air. He dashed for the commotion at high speed while I balanced in the bow and prepared to cast, my running line streaming back into the boat. When we came upon the school of fish, he cast a small live mackerel over the side and the water literally went flat on my backcast. Nothing came to my fly, but the captain suddenly struck, his shoulders bunched up to take the load, and the heavy boat rod bent double. The fish proved tremendously strong and, unlike a dorado, would not jump. The captain soon pumped up a greenish silver, football-fat 12-pound tuna, swept it out of the water and into the boat, and clubbed it twice. He told me that it was a bonito, and that it was not good to eat. While unable to take my eyes off the fish, I was left wondering why he had just killed something he found so worthless. I had caught bonito when I lived in southern California, and this tuna did not fit that memory. I didn't know what to call it, but I knew what it was, a beautiful and powerful gamefish, and I thought, oh, to catch such a fish on a fly rod!

That day began my love affair with black skipjack (*Euthynnus lineatus*), the

The black skipjack took an Abel Anchovy on Thetis Bank. Photograph by Trey Combs.

"bonito" of North America's Pacific coast from California to Peru. The *Euthynnus* family of tuna includes the closely related kawakawa tuna (*Euthynnus affinis*), the "mackerel bonito" of the Indian and Pacific Oceans (its range rarely overlapping that of the black skipjack), and the little tunny (*Euthynnus alletteratus*) of the Atlantic Ocean.

Over the years, I've spent as much time searching for black skipjack along the Pacific coast of the Americas, from Mexico to Colombia, as I have for any other species of saltwater gamefish. This tuna relieves me from the burden of pool cue fighting sticks while stretching the limitations of my single digit outfits. And once a black skipjack tops 10 pounds, it is a load on any size outfit. I know that a few bluewater gamefish are faster, and that many are larger, but few are more available to fly fishers within their range, struggle with more muscle-bound determination, or so commonly fight the rod until they die. Whereas I once thought black skipjack nearly impossible to hook on a cast fly, I now find them challenging to pursue without the benefit of live bait. This keen hunter is forever being hunted, and it remains as trip-wire nervous and ready to take flight as any permit. Black skipjack also possess the aesthetic component we so value in fly fishing; the species is remarkably handsome, so much so that it was the first gamefish of any species that I had duplicated in fiberglass and gel coat, an astonishingly lifelike, museum quality 13-pound trophy by Lyons & O'Haver that swims in midturn above my fly-tying bench.

For many years big-game fishers trolled feather jigs for black skipjack and then used the fish to bait blue and black marlin. Until very recently few fly fishers were even aware of the gamefish, and among these only a handful pursued them singularly. I have viewed the growing interest in this gamefish as a fly-fishing trophy with great satisfaction. It has taken me years to develop effective techniques and flies for the gamefish. For the first time, I can visit with other anglers such as Terry Gunn and Wendy Hanvold and exchange ideas for fly lines, fly patterns, and methods of presentation for black skipjack.

Species of tuna do not all exhibit the same behavior when schooling and feeding. Yellowfin and bigeye tuna, for example, may compress themselves into a single wave several tuna deep, each fish trying to leap over the one before it to get at the fleeing baitfish, and in this feeding frenzy they'll practically run over a waiting fly fisher. Conversely, black skipjack prefer to spread out into pods of feeding activity, boiling the surface, getting their backs out, but not making arching leaps for their prey, or for a fly or popper. The largest black skipjack, and those most wary, are often fish running at the edges of the school. Even when a school is moving rapidly on baitfish, this behavior makes an approach to dense concentrations of black skipjack nearly impossible. Unnoticed fish at the edges of the school panic, immediately scattering with them those fish feeding actively at the center.

Any boat run up to or over a school of black skipjack immediately puts the fish down. This skipjack trait becomes doubly frustrating because the school disappears when the boat is only one good cast away. The "one good cast" occurs when you're standing in the bow of a boat moving toward the fish, casting into the very wind the boat creates. This shortens up the cast, forcing you to get even closer. Typically, the skipjack are already fleeing from the approach before your fly touches the water, giving you a quick view of a lot of tails and green backs. Panga captains throwing live chum to an edge of the same school do not appreciate your difficulties, for black skipjack will reverse themselves and come immediately to a sardine or mackerel swimming for its life.

A more successful strategy involves running ahead of a moving school of black skipjack, stopping the boat, and shutting off the engine. I prefer to be at an edge of the school rather than directly in its path. Ideally, I'll be upwind, too. I believe the lower the boat's profile, the better. If I'm fishing from a cruiser and directly in the path of a fast-moving school of black skipjack, the fish will sound before the boat and then reappear a couple hundred feet away.

Casting downwind doesn't produce just longer casts, but casts in which the fly hits on a tight leader and immediately can be stripped to suggest a fleeing baitfish. This is extremely important. Black skipjack decide to strike or not strike in a fraction of a second. I have experienced much less success casting into the wind, when the fly falls on a slack leader, for a single strip is then necessary just to get a tight line to the fly. Cruising fish get a very clear view of the fly and reject it; black skipjack take the fly reflexively, not calculatingly.

The initial run of a black skipjack is automatic transmission fast, a smooth, standing-start acceleration that takes it from 0 to 40 mph in a couple of seconds. No headshaking jumps mar this exhibition of pure strength. Often, when the fish stops fighting, it is either dying or already dead. Only strong pressure gets the fish in quickly enough for a lifesaving release.

While yellowfin do not school like black skipjack, and neither do the two species fight the same when hooked, a fact that makes comparing their relative strengths more difficult. But I believe that pound for pound the black skipjack is the stronger of the two. Certainly it is the more interesting and less punishing fish to fight on a fly rod. While the yellowfin often makes one run before sounding, the black skipjack is far more up and down—an initial run, a sound, a second run followed by a sound, and so on. This behavior puts great strain on the terminal tackle, for the fish is suddenly up and moving laterally, dragging fly line and 100 yards of backing through the water. It is worth noting that on Frank LoPreste's long-range fly-fishing charters out of San Diego, more fly lines are permanently fixed to the bottom of his boats by black skipjack than by any other gamefish.

I cast Sea Habit flies and those Gaines cork-bodied poppers covered with Mylar piping for black skipjack. When I tie the Sea Habit flies, I'm concerned with contour, length, and color combination. I tie the Sea Habit Tubes so sparsely with Flashabou, Krystal Flash, and bucktail or FisHair that they seem semi-transparent. For the Deceivers, I try to find pencil-thin and perfectly straight saddles. I use short bucktail in the bellies, then finish the flies with longer portions of Krystal Flash and bucktail, but kept very thin. I always tie the Sea Habit Bucktails thinly when I intend them for black skipjack. Length and color are largely determined by what the fish are feeding on, but generally I tie these flies in lengths of three to five inches. I usually like a few strands of peacock herl as a topping, and tie the flies in the Sardine, Anchovy, and Ballyhoo patterns.

I normally tie leaders tapered to an 8- or 12-pound hard nylon tippet for black skipjack. I lose a few double digit skippies this way, but I hook a lot more as a result of the small-diameter tippets. When fishing heavier class tippets for record fish, I go to a brand of fine-diameter, soft monofilament such as Jinkai in 16- and 20-pound.

Loreto, Mexico, on Baja California's Sea of Cortez, has long been a favorite summer destination for saltwater fly fishers seeking trophy dorado and the occasional sailfish or striped marlin. Typical of many such Mexican villages, Loreto has many shallows edged by sudden drop-offs, areas that hold black skipjack like magnets. When the more celebrated dorado and sailfish are absent—and often that is the case—black skipjack become a reliable drag flying alternative for those in the know. I like an area favored by commercial fisherman just north of Coronado Island; Punta Lobos, off Carman Island; and a seamount south of Carman off Danzante Island. The latter is especially interesting, for the bottom is easily visible from a boat. I first searched this area for dorado, but so frequently observed black skipjack streaking out of the depths and flashing over the top of the seamount in pursuit of baitfish that I came to specifically fish the area for these fish. But even when no tuna were showing, all was not lost. I found them from 4 to 7 pounds in just a few minutes by trolling a fly around the edges of the islands and headlands, and over the connecting shallows, by using the entire length of my 100-foot fly line. When I had a companion, I'd make sure that we were not both fishing the same pattern. I'd fish a green and white to his blue-green and white, for example. Usually the fish struck one or the other, their preference changing from one day to the next. When I was over fish, and confident that they had a decided preference for one pattern, we would both fish it, but change the routine. One of us would troll off the back, while the other went forward and trailed 35 feet of line in the water. When a skipjack hit the trolled fly, we knew others would follow. The panga captain needed only take the boat out of gear for the forward fly fisher to make a cast absolutely legal by the rules of the International Game Fish Association (IGFA).

I have been unable to tease in black skipjack to a daisy chain of squid, as I have often been able to do with yellowfin and bigeye tuna. I suspect the reason for this is dietary.

The most successful way to fly fish for black skipjack—or any species of tuna, for that matter—involves chumming the fish into a feeding frenzy with live bait. In Loreto, panga captains sometimes catch sardines by casting a throw net along the breakwaters early in the morning. The baits are expensive and they're often sold individually. I haven't found that setting up a chum slick works unless live bait has been used to light the fuse. At least, I've never been able to hold black skipjack using chunk bait. Currently, only Frank LoPreste's long-range fly-fishing boats, ranging south from San Diego, California into Mexican waters, possess the huge live bait tanks and sophisticated fish-finding electronics needed to consistently find black skipjack in both large numbers and record sizes.

I was part of Ed Rice's 1992 Blue Water Fly Rod Invitational aboard Frank LoPreste's *Royal Star*. When working over Uncle Sam and Thetis Banks, several dozen live anchovies tossed off the transom were sure to bring in dozens of yellowfin and a few wahoo. The yellowfin tuna frequently averaged over 30 pounds, while some wahoo were twice that weight. When black skipjack joined the feeding melee, they averaged larger than fly fishers had ever encountered before—fish of over 10 pounds. Small black skipjack were about, but avoided the heavy feeding traffic off the transom, presumably for fear of being seen as more live bait. At the time, the world records for fly-rod black skipjack ranged from 5 pounds to 11 pounds, 4 ounces, the latter Wendy Hanvold's 6 kg record. These black skipjack records were soon broken on Thetis Bank, and then the new records began to fall. When a crew member pointed to a black skipjack racing by that he thought would go 17 pounds, I rigged a 10-weight with a 4 kg class tippet and immediately hooked a 13-pound fish that took me around the boat for thirty minutes before it could be netted. Ray Beadle and Mike Wolverton, fishing 2 kg (4-pound) and 6 kg (12-pound) tippets, boated black skipjack weighing 13 to 14 pounds. Beadle went back and nailed one more skippie on a 20-pound tippet, a fish of 13 pounds, 4 ounces. These skipjack were all recognized as world records by the IGFA.

The records didn't stand. No one expected that they would. I saw most fall the following year while fishing aboard *Shogun*, another of LoPreste-Dunn's San Diego–based long-range boats. Stu Dunn of Deerfield, Illinois led the way with a 16-pound fish on 20-pound tippet. Phil Caputo followed with world records in the 6 and 8 kg categories. Many black skipjack came aboard in the 13- to 15-pound range, serious loads on 10-weight rods. Twelve-pounders, larger than any black skipjack ever taken on the fly only two years before, hardly warranted a glance.

On the long-range charters, black skipjack were usually part of a mixed bag, the yellowfin, black skipjack, skipjack, wahoo, bonito, and even striped marlin and Pacific sailfish drawn to the live chum while the boats drifted over banks 30 to 40 fathoms down. But I often experienced better fishing specifically for black skipjack near the end of a day, when the boat was anchored and live sardines or anchovies were tossed over. Invariably, only a few minutes would pass before the first of the black skipjack showed. More and more tuna would pour in, often joined by skipjack, becoming bolder and more aggressive as the light grew low. At this time, conditions were ideal for fishing one of the Mylar-covered, cork-bodied Gaines poppers.

Any of these poppers, regardless of its original color, would be, when covered with pearlescent Mylar piping, run down and gobbled up by the black skipjack. Several years ago, I covered the poppers with silver Mylar piping, spray painting the backs a brilliant metallic blue. When I cast one of these Silver Bullet poppers in the last light of day, I watched in amazement as a dozen tuna raced for it. Was it possible to cast the popper and get it back to the boat *without* hooking a fish, no matter how radically fast I stripped it back? Not a chance! A black skipjack of over 10 pounds would get it every time.

The mates aboard the long-range boats told me that each season black skipjack close to 20 pounds were caught by gear fishers. The largest black skipjack on record was a 20-pound, 2-ounce fish caught on 30-pound gear off Mexico's Clarion Island on May 6, 1982 by Whitney Patterson. I've read that the maximum weight may be 25 pounds. But Kevin Shelley, former first mate on *Royal Star,* scoffs at that. He once worked on a tuna boat that ran from San Diego to Tahiti. During the days of searching for albacore, he claims that they occasionally found black skipjack of up to 30 pounds. Maybe so, or maybe they were finding the larger and nearly identical kawakawa tuna.

Fly fishers still have much to learn about black skipjack. Each year old records fall, we fill a few more gaps in our understanding, and we gain a greater appreciation for this remarkable gamefish. Fortunately, the fish has little commercial importance. Few gear fishers consider it much of a food fish, and they tend to take it only incidentally. Perhaps just fly fishers will continue to hunt for black skipjack, simply to experience the fish's strength, spirit, and beauty.

SKIPJACK TUNA

Le Morne, Mauritius
Kona Coast, Hawaii

Mine the imagination of any westerner for a vision of an island paradise and certain images, vivid and romantic, leap into the consciousness: Black volcanic mountains rise above white sand beaches, palm trees rim blue lagoons, hard bodies surf down waves that thunder over tropical reefs, soft bodies in leis of perfumed plumaria dance by moonlight to the beat of jungle drums. Add the trade wind strains of Paul Francis Webster's *Return to Paradise* and the scene is complete.

Faith in this stereotypical dreamscape lives forever in the heart of our culture. Those contemporary elements of paradise, the fields of pineapple and sugar cane, the rum drinks, the luxurious resorts, and the big-game fishing, have done little to dilute this heady spiritual brew we drink between toasts to the memory of the HMS *Bounty*'s Lieutenant Fletcher Christian, patron saint of would-be adventurers who dream of escaping forever to the South Seas.

For millions of American tourists, these images complete a remarkably balanced picture of Hawaii. But at almost the exact opposite side of the earth, in the Indian Ocean, lies Mauritius, a volcanic mountaintop African republic, 38 by 28 miles, remarkably similar to Hawaii, and filling an identical role for the many tourists who escape from Europe and South Africa to its unhurried tropical ambience. This multicultural, English-speaking country enjoys many claims to fame, perhaps most notably the dodo bird, long extinct thanks to 17th-century Dutch settlers; and blue marlin, very much alive here, and among the largest on earth.

The author casts a Mylar popper on Thetis Bank for this skipjack tuna. Photograph by Trey Combs.

145

Hawaii and Mauritius are also the foremost destinations in the world for anglers seeking record-sized skipjack tuna, *Katsuwonus pelamis*, a tropical and subtropical deepwater species found worldwide in the Atlantic, Pacific, and Indian Oceans, and one that has tremendous commercial value. In the United States it is canned with both yellowfin and bluefin tuna and sold as "light meat" tuna.

Roland Tyak, an eighth-generation Mauritian of French and English descent, is my friend in Le Morne, the resort village in the Black River District at the southwest corner of the country. He has fished professionally all his adult life and owns the Challenger fleet of six 36-foot big-game fishing boats. Blue marlin are his life. Photographs of anglers with their "granders," blues of over 1,000 pounds, line the walls of his beachfront office in the Paradis Hotel. Tyak assures everyone that these fish are at the frontier of what modern tackle and the human spirit can endure. I believe him, for the marlin look two stories high and dwarf the anglers. Tyak's stories of much larger marlin, fought and lost, leave much to the imagination.

I am not stirred by these tales, not as Tyak probably believes I should be, for I have come to Mauritius with Bruce Theunissen to fly fish for skipjack, the tuna Tyak likes to use to live bait giant blues. He is curious over my single-minded interest in the skipjack as a fly-rod gamefish, and does not disparage the fact that I've come halfway around the world seeking a fish he considers bait. I tell him that I have fished for skipjack in many places, especially off Hawaii's Kona Coast, where commercial fishers have taken specimens weighing over 30 pounds. I explain that any skipjack over 15 pounds will be a fly-rod record. I appeal to his business sense, and say that saltwater fly fishing is the fastest growing sport in North America, and that one day the skipjack will have a devoted following. "Ah," he says and slaps his desktop, "we have many, many skipjack over 30 pounds. Do you know about the skipjack caught at Black River that weighed 41 pounds? I think that is the record. Last year a Frenchman came in with 28 skipjack that weighed 31 to 39½ pounds."

"I would be a king for one such fish on a fly rod!" I say.

The strength of gamefish is relative to the tackle used to catch them, and with his marlin frame of reference I find it difficult to impress upon Tyak the reasons I find the skipjack tuna such a remarkable gamefish. I rework the pound-for-pound, ounce-for-ounce claim of gamefish primacy Dr. James A. Henshall bestowed upon the smallmouth bass a century ago. "For its size," I begin, "the skipjack tuna may be the strongest gamefish in the world. Their runs are incredibly fast, long, and take place just below the surface. They are the bonefish of blue water," I say, "really superb fly-rod gamefish. A 10-pound skipjack can run off 100 yards in a blink. To catch one of 20 pounds on a 10-weight? Well! That would be incredible! Thirty pounds? I think you would have to go at them with a billfish outfit!"

Bruce Theunissen, director of African Rod & Rifle Safaris in Durban, South Africa, believes we can rewrite the International Game Fish Association (IGFA) record book for skipjack tuna. Tyak isn't so sure. "The big skipjack," he says, his tone a serious rebuttal of our enthusiasm, "come in April and May, even June. Now in September, they're not so big. This can be a time of anticyclone, bad weather. Always it moves from South Africa to here. When the weather is nice, we get bites. Twenty-nine degrees is perfect for blue marlin. Twenty-five degrees is normal. Now we have 19 to 20 degrees."

Down from the mid-80s to the high 60s. Frigid!

"We'll hunt for skipjack. What else can we expect to find?" I say.

Tyak runs down the gamefish and seasons for us, ticking them off on his fingers as he speaks. March and April are the best months for yellowfin tuna, November to March for blue marlin, October to March for dogtooth tuna. One of 224 pounds came from Le Morne, the second largest dogtooth ever taken, he explains. "Mackerel bonito," the local name for kawakawa tuna, which is also caught and immediately trolled live for blue marlin, can be found during all months. September and October, March and April are good periods for black marlin. They will tolerate colder water. Big marlin, the females, can be found during any month, but especially November and December. During several weeks in January, Le Morne gets a strong run of very small marlin, many fish of around a hundred pounds, about thirty percent black, and seventy percent blue.

"Perfect for the fly rod!" I say, and glance at Bruce.

"I was here then!" Tyak says. "The marlin weren't even large enough to take in one of the live mackerel bonito. Just managed to ruin them. They were a pest!"

Bruce, a somewhat recent convert to fly fishing, laughs at his remark. "And what of sailfish?" he says.

"No one comes here to fish for sailfish," says Tyak. "They are often found close in, just to the other side of the reef. We don't fish there when we look for marlin."

"We'll look for your sailfish, too," I say.

We do, each morning motoring across the huge lagoon and picking our way through the narrow opening in the reef to meet the blue water and Indian Ocean seas that sometimes make fly casting a high-wire act. We look for loose flocks of noddy terns, for they lead us to schools of bait and to, first, the more inshore kawakawa tuna; then dorado (locally called "mahimahi," the Hawaiian name for the gamefish); and, ultimately, the mixed schools of yellowfin and skipjack tuna.

The sailfish are elsewhere, lost so persistently to the cold weather and high winds of the anticyclone that Tyak offers to get us a branch of the pionden tree so that we might beat the devil out of the rods. "This is a Mauritian custom," he says. "The blacks, especially, believe this." I look at my slender fly rods and demur.

Our luck changes the next day. Bruce and I have been working with a video crew to shoot a hotel promo. We team up and fight to the flying gaff, on 130-pound gear, an 870-pound blue marlin, a magnificent colossus of a fish that we can barely winch through the transom door. I nearly drive Tyak crazy when I show more excitement over the 8- to 10-pound skipjack on fly rods than over the 870-pound marlin.

Tyak, of course, was right: The immense 30- to 40-pound skipjack that heat up the schools of sprat off Black River are months away. I know these fish would burn dry the oil from the cork drag in my reels and I badly want to experience such skipjack on the fly, pearlescent bullets perhaps faster for their size than anything in fins save a wahoo or barracuda, but with far more endurance.

The smaller skipjack we do find, mixed so evenly with 12- to 15-pound yellowfin tuna that a fair comparison between the two fish is possible. Side by side, the physical differences become quite evident, the yellowfin all shoulders and wide tails, the skipjack possessing more muscle mass aft, the tails themselves not so wide, all in all more supersonic profiles. I think this difference is immediately reflected in the fish's incredible initial runs. Only when skipjack tire do they get their heads down to bore away.

When chasing baitfish, yellowfin and bigeye frequently make arching leaps, a trait often duplicated when they're trying to nail fast-trolled skirted lures or flies. Skipjack slash at lures and flies, turning on their sides to take poppers in the surface film. Never have I seen skipjack leap out of the water in pursuit of a fly.

When removed from the water, a yellowfin can be turned upside down to stop its struggles, and then righted for a quick picture and safe release. The manic, high-strung skipjack never stops beating its tail, and falls still for a picture only when it dies.

Upon my return home from Mauritius, Del Dykes, a longtime friend and light-tackle charter boat captain in Kailua-Kona, Hawaii, calls to say that a client caught a skipjack tuna of 28 pounds, almost twice the weight of any previous fly-caught skipjack. July, says Dykes, is *otaru* heaven, and I should come out and fish with him. I attended high school in Hawaii, and know that locally the skipjack is called *aku*, or sometimes *otaru* (say the "r" as a "d"), Japanese for *aku* weighing over 10 pounds. *Aku* and *ahi*, the yellowfin tuna, are highly esteemed food fish in Hawaii, and command a premium price when sold fresh.

I have fly fished for *aku* off Big Island in both winter and spring. They reside in the Hawaiian Islands year-round in water ranging from 64 to 86 degrees. Typically the *aku* average from three to six pounds.

One April I hitched a ride aboard a Japanese commercial fishing boat, Ray Shirakawa's *Lori Lei II*. He had trailered the beefy 25-foot boat with twin Volvo Penta engines from his home in Naalehu and launched it at South Point, the southernmost point in the United States, and an area famous for its violent seas. Here there is no lee, just a collision of trade wind seas driven down both Hawaii's coastlines, a violent mixing and an area more gamefish-rich than any other in the islands. "You are lucky," he told me. "This is the calmest day we have had here in a year." I watched as reefs and volcanic islets appeared and disappeared under the battering of 20-foot waves.

"You call this calm!" I said.

Shirakawa fished the two largest Penn Internationals made, each loaded with 180-pound monofilament, gear that can take a blue marlin—the *a'u*—or a 100-pound *ahi* down in short order. "That's pretty heavy stuff for five-pound skipjack," I observed. He looked over my pencil-thin Sage 11-weight and should have laughed but didn't.

The loose school of *aku* feeding on Hawaiian anchovies was several miles across, moving quickly first one way, then another, some pods of fish larger than others, the wolf packs of wahoo, or *ono*, working the edges, the occasional porpoise cutting through the activity. When the feeding activity slowed, noddy, bridled, and fairy terns kept the *aku* located. Shirakawa trolled a red-feathered, double hook King King jig off each rod, reeling in the little tuna as fast as possible. When two *ono* came aboard, he said they would pay for his gas with a little left over. We set out to intercept part of the school of *aku* and try to take one on a fly.

As the frantically feeding *aku* raced by, I would cast downwind and hook the little tuna on both flies and poppers. After chasing the fish for an hour, I hooked a larger *aku* that immediately took me 200 feet into my backing. As I began to muscle the fish to the boat, three porpoise from three different directions made a beeline to where it struggled. Suddenly I couldn't move the *aku* and then it began a long, powerful run straight down. I tightened up the drag and watched the handle turn into a blur as several hundred feet of backing melted away. Shirakawa ran into the pilothouse and studied the big screen of his depth sounder. A huge blip appeared at 50 fathoms, 300 feet down.

"A porpoise has your fish!"

"No way! Maybe a big *ahi* ate the skipjack! Maybe a shark! Porpoise don't sound like this!" I insisted. Whatever I had on continued down, a smooth overdrive without headshakes or pumping tail. I counted off the distance: "Four hundred, 500, 600, 700 feet!" Another pause.

"He's playin' wit' you!" Shirakawa was laughing, obviously enjoying my "expert" commentary. I backed the drag entirely off and put the reel into free spool. The line went limp. I could still feel some weight. The *aku*? I waited. After a minute, I tightened up the drag and reeled as fast as I could, the rate of retrieve now down to a few inches per turn. The fish hadn't moved six feet before it stopped, the rod bent double, and the line again plunged toward the bottom of the ocean. I tightened up the drag and broke the leader. Shirakawa watched the big screen plot out the entire sequence.

"A porpoise, and he's playing. Right?"

"Right!" he said.

We continued after the skipjack, knowing that the larger fish would become toys for the porpoise. "How did such a thing come to pass, porpoise that drive fishermen crazy for the pleasure it gives them?"

Shirakawa told me a story of how the U.S. Navy had trained porpoise at a facility just down the coast from where we were now fishing. Eco-terrorists broke open the pens and released the porpoise into the open ocean. The hand-fed porpoise soon began seeking the attention of humans by tugging at their hooked fish. One generation taught the next and so on until the commercial fishing pretty much went to hell. Huge reels and heavy monofilament were Shirakawa's answer to the problem.

Shirakawa had never before seen a fly fisher, which made his gift to me of a day off South Point all the more remarkable. Out of gratitude, I sent him a 10-weight outfit and a few flies. Despite Shirakawa's best efforts, skipjack over 10 pounds had eluded me. I hoped Del Dykes's invitation would change that.

Dykes, a paramedic with the Kailua-Kona fire department, skippers the 30-foot *Reel Action* as a second line of work. In July, Dykes falls ill again and again, as do hundreds of other employees of the state, and everyone prays that fires don't start, banks don't get robbed, and no one requires emergency medical attention. Coincidentally, during July a tremendous run of *aku, ahi,* and *a'u*—both blue and striped marlin—occurs on the Kona Coast, this in a state where anyone with a fishing license can sell his or her catch commercially, and a single big *ahi* can fetch $300. A few people have been rude enough to suggest that perhaps everyone is out fishing, but they are considered harmless eccentrics and ignored. It is generally understood that the strange malady affecting the state's civil infrastructure will begin to pass as the run of *aku* and *ahi* declines.

After leaving the Kailua-Kona marina, Dykes begins his fishing day at a FAD buoy, the acronym standing for "fish aggregating device," a large metal buoy tethered to a cable that is permanently anchored to the sea floor. Several dozen of these buoys have been placed off the islands by the Division of Aquatic Resources of Hawaii's Department of Land and Natural Resources. The buoys draw and hold pelagic gamefish like magnets, the *aku* usually holding upcurrent, the *ahi* downcurrent, from the cable, and the mahimahi, or dorado, immediately around and under the buoy.

Though July is the season of the *otaru,* the surface-feeding *aku* we find around the buoys are small, nothing much over four pounds, and Dykes strikes out well offshore. We sometimes see a flurry of surface-feeding *otaru,* but it does not persist long enough to intercept the fish with flies. Dykes hooks a skipjack of 14 pounds, by trolling a red-feathered King King. I'm able to get the

The author holds a 13-pound skipjack tuna caught off Hawaii's Kona Coast.

same result when I troll a 4/0 Sea Habit Deceiver, a 13-pound skipjack, and a record, had I been able to cast to the fish with the boat out of gear.

This pattern persists, the larger skipjack never holding near the surface long enough to reach with cast flies. We try chumming them up with dead anchovies, sometimes setting up a ¼-mile slick with 50 pounds of the bait, and while this brings up porpoise-sized *ahi*, the large skipjack don't show. The reason for this may be found in U.S. Fisheries Bulletin 76, an article by Richard Barkley, William H. Neill, and Reginald M. Gooding that describes the oxygen needs of *aku* captured and placed in tanks. The writers conclude that small *aku* can survive in a temperature range of 64 to 86 degrees, but that larger *aku*, those of 10 pounds or more, the very *otaru* I am hunting for, prefer water no warmer than 68 degrees. This colder water, 100 to 200 feet down in Hawaii, contains the more dissolved levels of oxygen that the larger *aku* require. If this is the case, it helps explain why the smaller *aku* are routinely abundant on the surface, while the *otaru* are only found at this level intermittently.

My search for record-sized skipjack has led me to the San Diego-based long-range boats that search Baja California waters as far south as Cabo San Lucas. The mates on these trips call the skipjack "blue skipjack," both for their electric blue dorsal slashes, and to distinguish them from the black skipjack, which carry a greenish hue across their backs. Frank LoPreste, part-owner of the long-range fleet and a pioneer in the field, tells me that blue skipjack reach 20 pounds in those Baja waters, and uncommonly top 15 pounds, sizes large enough to rewrite the IGFA fly-rod records but still far short of those skipjack reach in Hawaiian and Mauritian waters. Yet for two reasons the *otaru*-sized skipjack may be more consistently caught on flies here than elsewhere: They are abundant off the Baja coastline in the winter when surface temperatures hover at about seventy degrees, and the long-range boats carry sufficient bait to bring the fish up to the surface and hold them in a feeding frenzy for hours.

During a four-year period covering six of these 10-day, long-range fly-fishing trips, I caught many skipjack in the 8- to 12-pound range, and several a pound or so larger, using a Sage 10-weight rod and a shooting head system that connected a slow-sinking monocore running line to a 26-foot head with a sink rate of III or IV. This was some of the most enjoyable saltwater fishing I ever experienced, particularly when the skipjack were chummed up as the early evening and the setting sun were starting to turn the horizon orange. As the ocean grew darker, and the skipjack held more boldly just below the surface, I would switch from flies to silver Mylar poppers. The results were dazzling, the skipjack and black skipjack coming at the poppers in packs and throwing themselves at their chugging progress in a maelstrom of aggression. So eager were they to get at the poppers that simply dangling one over the side of the boat with its tail brushing the water brought an immediate strike.

Previous page, top: The author snorkels off Hawaii's Kona Coast. Fly fishers associate brightly colored fish of the coral reefs with Hawaii. But Hawaii offers some of the best big-game offshore fly fishing in the world. The rare short-billed spearfish is a legitimate fly-rod game-fish during the spring months. Small blue marlin are often abundant in July and August. Yellowfin tuna average 100 pounds in July. Hawaiian albacore are among the world's largest. Bigeye tuna are often abundant. Huge schools of kawakawa can sometimes be found in the islands during winter months. Juvenile striped marlin, fish under 50 pounds, give fly fishers an opportunity for record fish in 3 kilogram- and 4 kilogram-class tippet categories.

Previous page, bottom: Dave Linkiewicz and Captain Gene VanderHoek pose with Linkiewicz's 40-pound striped marlin.

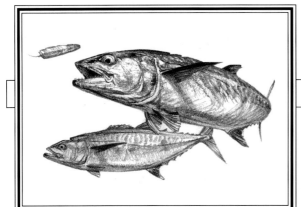

DOGTOOTH TUNA

Hangkow Reef, Bismarck Archipelago,
Papua New Guinea

T he dogtooth tuna surely had 19th-century taxonomists scratching their heads. The fish was clearly a predacious killing machine of the highest order, but it was also such a strange patchwork of physical characteristics foreign to other tuna that evolutionary lines were obscured. It possessed huge eyes, possibly an advantage when gathering in light at great depths, or when feeding at night, but the dogtooth could be observed hunting by day, terrorizing reef fish living in 50 feet of water. Its large head and huge mouth filled with long conical teeth suggested a lineage more barracuda than tuna. Its remarkably broad crescent-shaped tail was unlike the V-shaped tails of other tuna. Nor did the almost scaleless fish display the dramatic dorsal-ventral separation of colors seen on other tuna. Its silver color held from top to bottom, with only a tinge of blue on top. Morphologically the fish reminded taxonomists of a bonito—albeit a colossal one—genus *Sarda*, but unlike a bonito, or any other tuna, the dogtooth had an air bladder. This didn't sit well in terms of sorting out its taxonomy, but spoke volumes about the fish's residential habits. An air bladder would prevent a migratory, deepwater tuna from passing rapidly from great depths to the surface and back again. Because there was no related species to suggest how this particular species might have evolved, the dogtooth tuna, *Gymnosarda unicolor*, became the lone species in its own genus.

The fish's history in angling is recent and the dogtooth is well documented as a gear-caught gamefish. But a search of the fly-fishing section of the 1994

153

International Game Fish Association's record book reveals "Vacant" beside every tippet category. One reason for this is the fish's distribution off remote reefs in the Indian and western Pacific Oceans, often areas where offshore game boats are rare and fly fishing is virtually unknown. Just a few of the countries involved are Comoros, Seychelles, Mauritius, Australia, Papua New Guinea, and South Korea—where the largest dogtooth tuna, a 288-pounder, was taken on rod and reel.

The case of Mauritius illustrates the problem. When I fished off this bustling Indian Ocean country in 1992, I found that dogtooth tuna were sometimes caught off the reef at Le Morne. But I was told that they were deepwater fish, usually found singly and incidentally, and that nothing about them suggested fly fishing. I caught many dorado, plus yellowfin, skipjack, and kawakawa tuna, and some rainbow runners, directly off the reef. I never glimpsed a dogtooth, dead or alive, and I didn't realize that the capture of the rainbow runners might have gotten me a shot at the species with the fly.

A couple of years later Ed Rice, president of International Sportsman's Expositions (ISE), told me a story about some Australians who had found a way to take dogtooth tuna on flies off the north coast of Papua New Guinea. Rice soon found a copy of an unedited video that documented their experiences. In March, 1994, at ISE's San Mateo outdoors show, I met Dean Butler, one of the principals in that dogtooth video.

Butler and Alan Philliskirk operated Dean Butler's Sportfishing Adventures in Cairns, Australia, their programs catering to the adventure minded, regardless of angling convictions. Their "New Frontier" was Papua New Guinea, a country of unimaginable wildness to westerners. Butler marketed 12-day expeditions 300 kilometers up the Aramia River on the 82-foot *Golden Dawn* for New Guinea bass and ironing board–sized barramundi, and trips through the exotic Bismarck Archipelago aboard the 36-foot *Talio* for billfish and dogtooth tuna. Not surprisingly, Rice opted to take both trips and invited a few friends to join him.

After being flown out of headwaters of the Aramia and returning to Port Moresby, Rice, Wendy Hanvold, Charley Boillod, and I said good-byes to Nick Curcione and Harm Seville and booked a flight across the country to Madang on the Bismarck Sea. Brett Middleton, skipper of *Talio*, was on hand to greet us and describe our upcoming itinerary. Rod Harrison, one of Australia's premier fly fishermen, had joined us to get in some fishing and be our deckie aboard *Talio*. He would be assisted by two New Guinea mates.

Brett and Viki Middleton own Dylup Plantation, an hour's drive up the coast from Madang. He is a third-generation New Guinean, his grandfather immigrating from Australia in 1914. Six huge copra and cocoa producing plantations, the Kulili Estates, make up the family holdings. All but Dylup are sited in the volcanic mountaintop islands comprising the Bismarck Archipelago. During the five-day charter, we would stay first at Dylup Plantation on the mainland, then spend several nights at the guest house at Derek and Joel Middleton's Wadau Plantation on Karkar Island before fishing Hangkow Reef, and anchoring the final night in a small bay off deserted Crown Island.

Brett Middleton, an experienced big-game fisherman and a vigilant and considerate skipper, bought *Talio* in 1992, equipped it with sophisticated navigational and fish-finding electronics, and put it under charter for Kulili Estates. It was the first commercially available offshore game boat on the coast. Middleton found that blue and black marlin of up to 500 pounds arrived in October and November to hunt down the yellowfin tuna that were then seasonally abundant. Small, fly-rod marlin, both blues and blacks, were an April proposition, while Pacific sailfish filled the island chain from December through March. The Bismarck Archipelago, a set of volcanic islands both active and ancient, rising thousands of feet from the ocean floor and rimmed with coral reefs, proved to be an incredible stronghold for dogtooth tuna. Divers swore they had seen them to 500 pounds. Hundred-pound fish were routine. The tuna were joined by giant trevally, bluefin trevally, narrow barred mackerel (close relatives of the king mackerel the Australians call "Spanish mackerel" or simply "Spaniards"), kawakawa tuna, and an enormous variety of reef fish including rainbow runners.

We were only Middleton's third charter for dogtooth tuna, the "doggies," or "dogs," as the Australians called them. The impetus for previous trips, involving both Butler and Philliskirk, was the discovery, while gear fishing, that doggies would come on top to smash a live bait. If the bait could be removed quickly enough, and a fly substituted, would the doggie take the fly? The answer was a resounding "yes," and that led to a number of secondary discoveries.

Butler said that even when using 60-pound single strand wire the fish was difficult to hook securely, its mouth so hard that a fly might rattle around inside and never take a hold. Also, when the fish took the fly, it flared its gills to suck it down, lying on its side almost motionless for a second or two before making a warp speed run for the bottom. This initial movement often resulted in a pectoral fin catching the class tippet. The fin does not contain any razor edges, but some combination of body action, line tension, and roughness of the fin combined to cut the leader. If that didn't free the fish, the coral certainly would when the fish streaked a path through the labyrinth of coral formations that forested the edges and slopes of the mountaintop reefs. Dogtooth tuna of 40 pounds and more had been hooked; one, by Philliskirk, of nearly 20 pounds was the largest landed. None had been submitted for world record consideration.

As we motored for our first doggie destination, the reefs of Bagabaga Island, Middleton explained how the teasing would proceed. The tuna naturally targeted rainbow runners. We would catch these baits by trolling small bucktails, and store them alive in a 50-gallon drum of seawater. A mate prepared a rainbow runner by running a rigging needle with waxed thread through the very top of its eye sockets, and tying off the bridle to a swivel. The bait was snapped to a 10-foot teasing rod and to its high speed, 6-1 reel filed with 80-pound monofilament. To keep the bait from finding sanctuary under the boat, the teasing line was led to a block attached to the base of an outrigger pole. By yarding the block to the end of the pole, the rainbow runner was kept swimming 10 to 15 feet away from *Talio*, deep on one roll, shallow or sometimes pulled free of the water on the next. Middleton believed that when excited, rainbow runners emit a grunting sound that carries a great distance. For doggies lurking in the depths, this is the sound of a dinner bell going off.

Alan "Fish" Philliskirk holds up a 20-pound fly-caught dogtooth tuna taken from New Guinea's Bismark Archipelago. Photograph by Dean Butler.

A second teasing method involved casting a large wooden chugger from a spinning rod. When Harrison put his broad back into the cast, the chugger flew nearly out of sight. As he began a jerky, high speed retrieve, the chugger plowed through and flew off waves, geysers of water erupting off its face, the commotion bringing in doggies, giant trevally, and red bass.

Off Bagabaga, small wahoo of 12 to 15 pounds were easily secured by trolling skirted lures. We chopped up these fish and used the chum to hold doggies that had followed in the chugger.

Hanvold, Boillod, and I fished identical 13-weight rods; Rice stuck with his favorite 14-weight. I had backed my big saltwater reel with 350 yards of 30-pound Dacron and topped this off with 200 yards of 50-pound ultrathin Spectra backing. My custom-built fly line consisted of 100 feet of sinking monocore running line and 26 feet of Scientific Anglers 550-grain Deep Water Express. The line made long casts a breeze and permitted me to hook tuna at a variety of depths. Other lines we used included the Teeny 500, and the Teeny saltwater lines in 550 and 650 grains.

Late in the day off Bagabaga, Harrison's chugger brought in several doggies at once, fish of 10 to over 30 pounds. We all noticed that the largest tuna in any group—the alpha member—led the primary attack, the smaller fish opportunistically dashing in to get the chum. While the chugger and chum had the tuna going bonkers just off the transom, I cast to a small tuna, which missed the fly on the strip. I paused, let the eight-inch-long 6/0 Sea Habit Deceiver sink headfirst a foot, and stripped again. A tuna took the fly, was solidly hooked on the strike, and headed for the bottom, going into overdrive against a very heavy drag. Thirty pounds, easy, I thought. Middleton backed the boat away from the reef in hopes that the tuna would come with him, giving me an ever greater depth into which to carry the fight. When the fish reached the sloping bottom about three hundred and fifty feet down it slowed, then stopped. Middleton continued to pull away and I soon could move the fish. The line then went dead. When I reeled in Harrison examined the cleanly cut class tippet, and noted the lack of abrasion.

He said, "You were 'pected,' mate!"

The next morning, in perfect light and over extremely clear water, Harrison and I teased for Hanvold. For the first time I could see the tuna—blue, seal-sized torpedoes in an attack mode containing more pure violence than I had ever observed in tuna, one I'd rarely observed in any gamefish, including blue and black marlin. They tracked the bridled rainbow runner 30 or 40 feet down, telegraphed their excitement by displaying hot blue lines across their backs, and then in a fury rushed the bait. This took less than a second, a blur often beyond our reaction time. I'd be looking at the fish and then the bait would be gone in a heaving wash of spray. One doggie of around 80 pounds swallowed Harrison's rainbow runner. He tugged back and the bait flew back up out of the fish's throat, and again began swimming for its life.

Hanvold's first shot was at a doggie of at least 40 pounds, a berserk tuna that turned on the fly when it couldn't get the bait. Somehow, on the strike, the leader and wire trace flew out of the water and got wrapped around the rod. Clearing the line, and with the wire a corkscrewed mess, she cast a second time. The high speed take was savage. Hanvold struck perfectly. I saw the rod take a deep set, watched in horror as the running line jumped off the deck and collected in a huge ball just above the reel, saw her desperately shake it out to get the line cleanly hitting the reel and the cork drag humming away, the whole business lasting a single second in time divided into stop action frames of panic and deliverance.

Hanvold, one of the finest saltwater fly fishers on the scene today, set up a big drag and then palmed the reel. No one on board was so dim as to offer advice; Rice, Boillod, and I had all watched her ice one of the largest striped marlin ever taken on a fly. But even with Middleton helping her work the tuna into deeper water, she got cut off by the fish's pectoral fin.

We alternated between casting the chugger while setting up a chum slick of chopped-up wahoo, and trolling a bridled rainbow runner. The chugger brought in fish especially well during first and last light. One morning when I was working a chugger for Hanvold, the plug landed and a doggie of over 100 pounds simultaneously made a long arching leap, the plug locked in its mouth. When I was able to get the chugger free, it looked as if a maniac had tried to destroy it with an ice pick.

Late in the afternoon we raced for distant Karkar Island and our accommodations at Derek and Joel Middleton's Wadau Plantation. The circular island, some 20 miles in diameter, has at its center 6,014-foot-high Mount

Kamagio. Carefully manicured lawns and gardens surround the Middletons' palatial beachfront home. Its secluded setting gives no hint that 40,000 people reside on the island. As we dined by candlelight on the beach with the Middleton brothers, we felt like castaways in paradise. We overnighted here twice and made plans to end the trip on Hangkow Reef.

The mountain holding Hangkow Reef was once a volcano that rose from the ocean floor to barely break through the surface. As the cauldron cooled and filled with seawater, coral ringed the mountain, eventually forming a reef three miles in diameter. Middleton reasoned that if we could pull the doggies off the mountain's steep slopes, we could fight them in water so deep that they could never reach the bottom and cut us off on the coral.

Rough seas on Hangkow made teasing with live bait difficult and nerve-racking. Even when I was alternately reeling and free-spooling line from the teaser rod to keep the bait swimming near the surface, the heavy rolling of the boat invariably gave the live bait too much slack, putting it a yard down and dead in the sights of the stalking doggie. I could see both tuna and live bait but often I couldn't prevent the take. Whether the rainbow runner resided in the doggie's mouth or its stomach, the tuna wouldn't cough it up. The rod bent double and the reel paid out the 80-pound line with the drag at the maximum setting. I was in danger of being vaulted out of the boat as Hanvold and Boillod cheered at my monkey-humping-a-coconut stance. Astonishingly, and unlike the case of billfish, this experience only served to give the doggie's voraciousness an additional edge; it often came right back to see what else the boat had to offer.

Because the tuna stalked the bridled live bait from behind, the rush often passed alongside the boat, the cast fly landing behind the fish and remaining unseen. It became obvious that a second angler should be up on the bow, casting at the same fish. When we tried this, it led to some interesting discoveries. Those smaller doggies, fish of 10 to 15 pounds, that came in sniffing around the large doggie tracking the bait, often nailed the flies cast from the bow. Hanvold and I both hooked and boated dogtooth in this manner. The one I took leaped completely out of the water as the fly hit, and took the fly on its way down. I've never seen any other species of tuna do this, even when I cast poppers at them.

Rod Harrison led us to another discovery. Knowing that the chugger, the chum, and the bridled rainbow runner attracted unseen tuna to the boat, Harrison suggested that I cast off the bow, strip off additional running line to get a deep sink, and, with the fly down 50 to 60 feet, begin a slow strip retrieve. The Sea Habit Deceiver, with its heavy epoxy head, proved especially well suited to this approach. Between each strip, the fly tipped head down and the long saddle hackles undulated like something very alive. I was soon fast to a big doggie that had me running down the boat toward the transom as Middleton pivoted the boat around and began trying to pull the streaking fish off the reef. Certain that the tuna would be lost if it reached the coral, I kept turning up the drag until I reached the last setting, very near the breaking point of my 22-pound tippet. As the knot connecting my 30-pound green Dacron backing to the white, 50-pound ultrathin backing came up through the stripping guide, I

This 10-pound dogtooth tuna nearly swallowed the author's billfish-sized Green Machine Sea Habit Deceiver.

knew the fish was at least 600 feet down. Then it stopped and held. Ten minutes later, when I pumped as hard as I dared, the tuna came up a foot. Applying more constant pressure than I'd ever put on a fish, I began working the doggie up. After a half hour, I was fighting the fish on my fly line. When only about seventy feet down, it again ran, taking down all the fly line and 50 feet of backing. Quite suddenly the fight went out of the fish and I could move it at will. Middleton called from the flying bridge, "Color!"

I saw a white shape, larger than I dared hope. Middleton called out again. "Been hit by a shark!"

So it had, a dogtooth tuna of about seventy-five pounds, its graceful symmetry now marred by horrible wounds behind its dorsal fin. Such a mutilated fish couldn't be submitted for world record consideration, but would still be delicious eating. The two New Guinea mates began butchering up the huge fish, steaks to be broiled over a fire of coconut shells.

The bow, I decided, was where it was at. From this casting station, Hanvold and I went on to hook two very large doggies. We struck both fish again and again on the take, but each eventually spit the hook. Sometimes we took turns, casting alternately. She boated a small doggie from the bow, and had numerous tuna chasing after her flies. I came to feel that an additional angler casting from the transom would have worked, too. At least when the postmortem of our hookups on Hangkow Reef revealed more doggies hooked randomly than were hooked when teased up with a bridled live rainbow runner, I became convinced that only one angler fishing at a time didn't remotely make use of our opportunities.

The color of the fly used mattered less than its size. The bigger the better. When Boillod got refusals on his 4/0 Abel Anchovy, I rigged him up with one of Bill Howe's 8/0, 10-inch-long hot green rainbow runner flies. A few minutes later a 10-pound doggie took the fly and was boated. Rice got a half-dozen hookups with Ralph Kanz's billfish-sized silver Mylar flies. Hanvold fished both large Abel Anchovies and some of my Sea Habit Deceivers. Besides Howe's giant ALF flies, the Sea Habit Deceivers I fished included the hot-green-and-blue Green Machine colors (my first choice), Flying Fish (blue and white), and Anchovy (blue, green, and white). These flies were all tied on single offset bait hooks. I felt that the single hook, as opposed to a tandem hook setup, provided a far superior action when I was running a fly deep. I regret we didn't rig up some tandem hook billfish flies with foam heads tied down in front. Having 100-pound doggies (we called them "good-bye fish") crashing these flies on top would have been an incredible experience.

Rice lost his largest doggie when it wrapped his fly line around the boat's propeller. Hanvold released her doggie after some pictures. After more pictures, Boillod sacrificed his doggie for *sashimi* served aboard *Talio.* (Middleton wouldn't think of putting to sea without soy sauce and wasabi.) My doggie was still intact. I told my friends I would submit it for world record consideration. After all, I pointed out, every class tippet category was still vacant.

"You can't," said Boillod, "it's too small."

"Small? Ten pounds, maybe even fifteen!"

"Just a baby," replied Hanvold.

"Just hatched, hardly more than an egg," added Boillod.

The author straddles a dogtooth tuna estimated at 75 pounds. Note the huge shark bites at the rear of the fish.

Alan Philliskirk makes his cast.

Previous page: The bridled rainbow runner is removed from the water before the onrushing dogtooth tuna.

The ribbing persisted as we ran for Middleton's Dylup Plantation on the mainland. The next morning my friends relented. Hanvold greeted me and held up her certified scales. Boillod was holding a measuring tape.

"Come on, we'll help you get your fish weighed and measured," he said. The two walked me over to the big freezer by the guest house. With great fanfare, Boillod opened it up. There was my fish, its sides cleanly removed.

"Last night's *sashimi*?"

They were laughing too hard to answer.

Two days later we met Dean Butler and Alan Philliskirk in Cairns, Australia and told them of our adventures—and failures—on Hangkow.

Butler said, "There are a thousand Hangkows." He believed that remote areas like Hangkow Reef will be much a part of the future of fly fishing for the species. The tuna's residential nature is both a blessing and its downfall. Fly fishers can visit Hangkow with the assurance that the tuna will be there. But the kind of pressure gear fishing can put on a dogtooth population can bring about a swift and permanent decline in their numbers. After heavy angling pressure, the species does not recover but rather disappears altogether.

Butler, Philliskirk, and our party barely touched the surface of the fabulous fly-fishing potential of the Bismarck Archipelago and its dogtooth tuna. Rod Harrison had taken some small doggies on flies in the neighboring

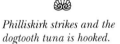
*Philliskirk strikes and the
dogtooth tuna is hooked.*

Solomon Islands. Richard Stoll, a fishing buddy of mine who owns Northwest Angler in Poulsbo, Washington, had caught small doggies on flies in Tonga. These are just the beginnings of an angling history destined to grow and flourish as fly fishers find the means to search the remote corners of the Pacific and Indian Oceans for these remarkable gamefish.

WAHOO

Alijos Rocks, Mexico

Captain Tim Eckstrom has driven *Royal Star* from the marlin-rich waters along "the ridge" to Alijos Rocks, 170 miles west of Baja California's Magdalena Bay, timing the night run for a dawn arrival at a scene of frightening power and utter desolation. Twenty-foot seas crash and seethe about the three stark pinnacles, the magma cores of mountains birthed on the sea floor eons ago. As gusting winds send Laysan and black-footed albatross soaring skyward off the waves, *Royal Star*, the luxurious, 92-foot, San Diego-based long-range boat, rolls on her beam ends and keeps fifteen fly fishers walking from one handhold to the next. I think, *this wild place, this sailor's worst nightmare, is the ultimate wahoo lair.* And I wonder, *what great wahoo had been spawned in this cauldron of ocean and seamounts and grown to record sizes?* Mate Larry Kida, wise and taciturn, says, "Maybe not many wahoo, but here they could be large."

The crew and anglers returning to *Royal Star* in 1993 following the 1992 Blue Water Fly Rod Invitational know the drill to come. Before that November in 1992, wahoo had almost invariably been an incidental fly-rod catch. But that changed dramatically when my companions and I intentionally hooked more than seventy wahoo on flies, boated fifteen, and rewrote the International Game Fish Association (IGFA) record book, facts that speak both for the methods we developed and for the gamefish itself.

Wahoo (*Acanthocybium solanderi*) possess the stuff of legend. That reputation is built first on their speed—nothing in fins is as fast—and then on their razor-

A free-jumping wahoo on open ocean. Photograph by Tony Oswald.

165

Bill Hayes holds up Ed Rice's remarkable world record for 4-kilogram (8.8 pound) tippet, a wahoo of nearly 40 pounds. Rice took more than an hour to wear down the 'hoo. Photograph by Marty Downey.

sharp teeth, set in jaws that overlap and shear through their prey rather than grabbing and tearing it as do barracuda and shark jaws. A decent-sized wahoo can cut a 5-pound tuna in half without the angler even feeling the attack. It can also cut through almost anything else. Once, while I was fishing with Lani Waller at Palmas de Cortez, a Mexican resort on Baja California's East Cape, a wahoo cut our plastic billfish teaser in half. Lani grabbed a 13-weight rod and cast a billfish popper with a 100-pound shock tippet. It was to laugh. Good-bye popper. Good-bye wahoo.

That had always been my experience, too. While casting for tuna or dorado, I sometimes hooked into a wahoo for a short time. This happened to me so frequently in Costa Rica's Gulf of Papagayo, and off Hawaii's South Point, that I tied on a wire trace five or six inches long. No matter. Wahoo mauled their way up the wire far enough to bite through the monofilament class tippet.

Thus when I boarded *Royal Star* in 1992, I had never boated a fly-hooked wahoo. I had lots of company. Among the anglers aboard, only Stu Apte could claim a wahoo on a fly, and two of Apte's wahoo were world records. Neither was big, or even average, insofar as Mexican wahoo went—each was something like 16 or 17 pounds—but the records had stood since 1975. Les Eichhorn, a pioneering saltwater fly fisherman and, before his death in 1992, a close friend of many on this trip, took a wahoo on a fly, a 46-pound, 4-ounce fish, while fly fishing for black marlin off Cairns, Australia in 1988. He saw a huge swirl on his teaser, could not identify the fish, and cast his fly. The wahoo was hooked at the very end of its mouth and Eichhorn was able to land the fish on an 8 kg class tippet without a wire leader. Four years later that wahoo remained the largest ever taken fly fishing.

The scarcity of wahoo records relates directly to the fish's well-deserved lone wolf reputation, the single fish so often opportunistically coming out of nowhere to buzz saw through its prey. Few anglers normally fish flies with wire traces on the off chance of finding a wahoo, because tuna in particular will reject a fly on a wire leader unless they are boiling on baitfish. But despite their reputation, wahoo throughout their worldwide tropical and subtropical range will just as often travel in twos and threes, or sometimes in packs of a dozen or more. These packs were the wahoo that *Royal Star* had set out to find in 1992.

Royal Star's mates trolled two bright orange Marauder wahoo plugs on heavy duty 80-pound rods. While the ship motored over the banks, sophisticated electronics searched the depths for telltale blips. When a wahoo hit, others were usually present. As one mate brought in the fish and a second mate cleared the unused rod, live chum was thrown into the ship's wake. Two fly fishers waited, one at each corner of the transom. The captain searched for the boil that marked a feeding wahoo. When wahoo showed, the boat was taken out of gear, the crew chummed still more bait into the water, and the anglers cast their flies. Often by this time wahoo could be seen racing, cruising, even parked and glaring.

Common sense suggests a two-handed strip retrieve will generate the kind of speed a wahoo can respect. Not so. This predator remains so confident of its ability to commit mayhem without breathing hard that it darts from bait to bait, mangling, cutting in half, and swallowing as it goes. A fly five to eight inches long, if larded up with silver tinsel and allowed to sink with only a twitch or two, gets a wahoo. The Abel Anchovy, Kanz's Mylar Minnow, and my Sea Habit Bucktails and Sea Habit Deceivers have worked well when connected to a wire shock of single strand wire. I like Mason #6 wire testing 58 pounds. Regardless of their size, wahoo usually will not bite through this.

Using a Haywire Twist, I secure a wire loop to the fly at one end, and to a small black swivel or black ring at the other end. I keep the total length of the wire to about ten inches. A Palomar Knot secures the single strand of class tippet directly to the swivel or ring. (An Albright Knot can also be used to secure the Bimini Loop of a class tippet to the wire loop. Use an Improved Blood Knot to secure the Bimini Loop to 30-pound hard nylon. Use this same hard nylon to make the Albright in the Haywire Loop. This isn't very clean, and I won't bother with it unless I'm out of swivels or rings.)

The strike can be a jolt, but more often the wahoo just stops the fly and you must immediately set the hook. If you're still striking as the wahoo accelerates away—something like 0 to 60 mph in a couple of body lengths—the class tippet will break. Strike once or twice between heartbeats and clear your line. A wahoo's first run covers several hundred feet in the fastest five seconds in fly fishing. I keep a drag set just light enough to prevent an overrun. Survive this initial run, and the odds favor you, for what the wahoo gains in pure speed, it gives up in stamina. Nevertheless, a 40-pound wahoo can keep a fly fisher very busy for twenty minutes or more.

Wahoo leap to remarkable heights, sometimes, perhaps, out of shock when first hooked on a trolled plug; sometimes in the pursuit of baitfish; and sometimes, it seems, for the sheer hell of it. I heard one story of a six-foot wahoo coming through the window of a long-range fishing boat and landing on a table where a half-dozen anglers were enjoying a poker game. When I was fishing for blue marlin in Puerto Rico's Strait of Mayagüez, a wahoo came straight up, like a missile, 25 feet into the air. Kevin Shelley, first mate aboard *Royal Star*, told me that once a wahoo leaped across *Royal Star*'s 25-foot beam at a point above the aft bait wells—a leap of at least 40 feet. Terry Gunn's experience aboard *Royal Star* reminded me a bit of this incident. He hung his fly over the transom and began stripping off line in preparation for a cast. A wahoo full of teeth and hunger pangs launched itself into the air and, with astonishing precision, hit the fly before smashing into the stern of the boat an inch below the gunwale. Terry jumped back in ashen astonishment as his running line formed a big ball at the stripping guide. The wahoo fell back into the ocean.

Tony Oswald had begun the parade of wahoo records that November on *Royal Star*. The two of us were called to the transom to cast to the boils, my fish breaking off my entire shooting head and Tony's coming aboard, a 51-pounder. At that moment, everyone felt his record would stand for the ages. But records on this trip stood mostly for hours, and only a sign-up sheet in the companionway kept us sorted out. Dan Byford and then Wendy Hanvold broke Stu Apte's 6 kg record, with Hanvold's 42-pound, 9-ounce wahoo going into the record book. (Apte's subsequent wahoo of 38 pounds came close to taking the record back.) Ed Rice broke Eichhorn's 8 kg record with a 51-pound fish. Steve Abel followed with two "fatty hoos" or 54 pounds, 11 ounces, and 64 pounds. The 10 kg class tippet Abel used for the 64-pound wahoo overtested, preventing the fish from being accepted by the IGFA as a world record. His smaller wahoo, however, became the new 10 kg class tippet record.

My first wahoo topped 30 pounds, and then on 6 kg I broke off four fish, one of which looked like a tiger-striped submarine. Mike Wolverton landed one of 40 pounds with ease, then broke off five in a row and sheared off a fly reel handle along the way. By one means or another, Ray Beadle lost a half dozen. Dave Whitlock hooked a wahoo that looked seven feet long, an example, I thought, of the tail wagging the dog. Ultimately, he lost the huge fish to an attack by a bull sea lion.

Wahoo, the fast-draw wonders of the bluewater world, had made some of the best saltwater fly fishers in the world look accident-prone.

Now in early December, a year and a week later, *Royal Star* is at Alijos Rocks and Ray Beadle and I, right- and left-handed, stand ready at the transom. The big orange Maurader plugs go in as the ship's fish-finding sonar begins pinging the depths for signs of fish.

In a few minutes, a wahoo strikes one of the plugs, the mate standing atop the aft bait well sounds a primal scream to the bridge, and another mate begins horsing the fish to the boat. "Out of gear," comes back Eckstrom's laconic reply from the bridge's loudspeaker. He adds, "Let's try some bait. There seems

Terry Gunn, Wendy Hanvold, and Stu Apte hold up Hanvold's wahoo that broke Apte's long-standing wahoo record in the 6-kilogram class-tippet category.

to be a few fish around." The mate blinds a sardine in one eye to keep it swimming on the surface, and tosses it high into the air. *Royal Star* coasts along, leaving a trail of sardines in its clearing wake as frigate birds swoop down to carry off any bait not able to quickly orient itself.

"A boil!" calls the mate. I see the boil too, not the quick little geyser of a skipjack or small yellowfin, but a swirl six feet across, a wahoo for sure. I cast a 4/0 Sea Habit Deceiver, my sink tip line carrying the fly well past where the bait has been landing, the fly swimming down, white saddles and silver Flashabou fluttering behind, until it levels off below the frantically swimming bait. I wait. I begin retrieving the fly with short, very slow strips. I feel a light pluck and tighten. A wahoo, but then nothing. Quickly pulling a yard of line off the reel, I send the fly into a free fall. Nothing. Another strip and the fly stops. I strike hard, once.

A wahoo's reaction to a hook being driven into its jaw is instantaneous. I look only at my running line and stumble toward the direction of pull, a movement that I hope gives me a fraction of a second. The handle is a blur as I lead the sizzling running line around it. As the line snaps clean to the reel, my knuckles get a rap from the direct drive reel. I raise the rod, notice that half of the back of my free hand is turning purple, and feel the rod bucking for a second until the reel pays out line at warp speed and sounds like a blender. In seconds 100 yards of ultrathin 50-pound backing is cutting through the water.

A few more seconds pass before the wahoo slows, 200 yards out, and begins circling the boat and leading me to the bow.

The fishing doesn't stop. More bait is thrown, more wahoo are hooked, and the rotation continues. Beadle races forward, passes under me, goes around the bow, and returns to the transom. When a cheer goes up, I know he has landed his first wahoo. *Royal Star* drifts before the wind and strong currents. With the boat rising and falling, I'm careful to keep my hand off the rim control, and depend on the reel's smooth drag to give line on the elevatorlike surges. I am unable to move the surface-holding wahoo toward me, and then with wind on our beam I begin to lose ground. Eckstrom sees this, shuts down the fishing, and slips the boat into gear to begin running down my fish. In ten minutes, we have the wahoo beside the boat for Kevin Shelley to gaff.

The wahoo easily tops 50 pounds on a scales. I call it 54 and change, and I discover that it has been hooked outside its mouth: Shutting down a fish hooked in this manner is always hard. Shelley staples my boat number to the gill cover of this potential world record and tosses it into the brine hold.

Eckstrom says that when wahoo are caught in a particular area, they quickly grow suspicious of plugs, flies, even live bait, and the water must be rested. To that end, he periodically anchors *Royal Star* and orders mates to chum live bait to bring in yellowfin, skipjack, and black skipjack. This fishing continues at a furious pace and frees us from the drudgery of taking a number and waiting to get a shot at a wahoo. After a couple hours of this, Eckstrom pulls anchor and resumes the hunt for wahoo.

Ed Rice limits his Blue Water Fly Rod Invitational to twelve rods, and as a "half rod" I have a shot once every twenty-four times. It takes a lot of wahoo bit-

The author took this 54-pound very-much-alive wahoo on a Sea Habit Deceiver in the Anchovy Blue pattern. Note the fish's overlapping scissor-like bite and small razor-sharp teeth. Photograph by Trey Combs.

ing a lot of flies to get me up more than once in a day, but late in the afternoon Eckstrom calls my number a second time. I've been so certain of not fishing again that the same fly and wire leader remain on my rod. Because the IGFA requires that the entire leader plus an inch or so of fly line be sent in with a record application, fishing a record leader a second time makes no sense. Should a wahoo break off the fly—and that is usually what happens—no application for a record can be made. With these misgivings, I cast, and do not feel the wahoo until the 26-foot sink tip portion of the line is in the guides and the fly swimming straight up as if crawling up a rope. From this unusual angle, I can use only the rod—not a tight line straight at the fish *and* the rod—to strike. I hit the wahoo as hard as I can and hope the 13-weight rod will provide sufficient stiffness to drive the hook in.

The first run is extraordinary, several dashes that string 300 yards together, the speed flailing the reel and blowing the ultrathin backing up into a fluffy mess that somehow remains tangle-free. Then, with remarkable suddenness, the wahoo runs out of gas. On each pump, I can feel the fish move. I call out to Larry Kida and Kevin Shelley, the mates who stand ready with long-handled gaffs. "Not a big fish. No problem moving this guy."

"Color!" calls back Shelley, who can see a chrome bar of white and electric blue 30 feet down. "Don't be too sure about its size. This wahoo is bigger than you think."

When the wahoo is on the surface I stop breathing. It looks huge, 70 pounds, maybe more. No one says anything as I work it around in ever tighter circles. "One more time," says Shelley. Both gaffs go in, the mates holding the fish half out of the water and making sure it's secure. I strip off two long pulls of fly line to avoid being broken off should the fish free itself as the mates hoist it aboard.

"The wahoo had a heart attack," says Shelley. "That sometimes happens."

After a week in the supercold salt brine hold the wahoo is officially weighed on a certified scales at Fisherman's Landing in San Diego: 66.4 pounds and the largest wahoo ever taken on a fly rod. Since fish lose about eight percent of their body weight in salt brine, my wahoo weighed well over 70 pounds when first brought aboard.

How long will this record stand? I think not long. Each season on Lo-Preste-Dunn's long-range boats, gear fishers catch wahoo that push the 100-pound mark. The largest wahoo caught on these trips is 136 pounds. Scotty Shintaku, a woman who works for LoPreste-Dunn at Fisherman's Landing, and who once caught a 107-pound wahoo off Baja, says that while 80-pound wahoo surprise no one on these trips, "anything over 60 pounds is considered a good fish." A lot of "good fish" come aboard these charters. I know that areas in the Caribbean, especially Bermuda and the Bahamas, produce some huge wahoo, fish of 150 pounds. And I have heard undocumented stories of commercially caught wahoo of over 200 pounds. Nevertheless, I believe that most, if not all, of the wahoo fly-rod records in the years to come will occur from San Diego's long-range fishing fleet. Live bait, sophisticated fish-finding electronics, and these boats' ability to reach remote wahoo strongholds makes it almost a sure bet.

Kevin Shelley helps the author hold up his wahoo estimated at over 70 pounds, the largest ever taken on a fly. Officially weighed a week later, the wahoo was 66.4 pounds. It was recognized in 1994 by the International Game Fish Association as the world record in the 10-kilogram class-tippet category.

NOTES

The shorter the wire trace, the easier it is to cast—and the less likely to land a respectable wahoo. Short or long matters not at all to wahoo turned on to flies with live bait. Short matters a lot to the angler, though, when a huge wahoo is able to reach the class tippet. I tie all my wire traces 9½ to 10 inches long and experience no problems casting 4/0 flies on wire traces of this length. However, I do not false cast. I roll out my line until the 24 to 28 feet of fast-sinking line is outside the rod. I then pick up my line off the water, and make my forward cast after a single backcast. This helps reduce the chance of kinking the long wire trace as a result of repeated false casts.

Wahoo have jaws like concrete, and hooks must be as sharp as possible to penetrate. Some anglers on the first *Royal Star* trip fished extra-large flies with massive 7/0 hooks. Most experienced no problems hooking up, but they did experience difficulty holding the fish. Those who fished smaller flies—some as small as 3/0—hit just as many fish and had a much easier time getting the finer diameter hooks to penetrate and hold. My own preference is for 5/0 or 6/0 in Gamakatsu and Owner bait hooks.

One need not labor over the choice of fly patterns; wahoo hit just about anything. I do feel that a head-heavy fly helps, for the fly dives on a slack line. I don't feel that the traditional wahoo colors—purple, deep orange, or black, for example—make flies any more effective than the conventional baitfish colors, the combinations of blues and greens over white. I have hooked wahoo on tube flies, Sea Habit Bucktails, and Sea Habit Deceivers all tied to suggest real fish. Given a choice of one fly, I would take a 6/0 Sea Habit Deceiver, because of its action on a dead drop, and I would fish it in Anchovy patterns with considerable silver Flashabou incorporated into the tie, especially along the shoulders. But many other flies work well, especially the Abel Anchovy and Ralph Kanz's Mylar Minnow.

If the wahoo are typically running 30 pounds or more, I choose my tippet and rod combinations as follows: 4 kg—10-weight; 6 kg—11-weight; 8 kg—12- or 13-weight; 10 kg—13-weight. For most of my Baja wahoo fishing, I relied on a Sage 13-weight RPL-X rod, and an Abel 4.5 reel. Wahoo weighing 10 to 25 pounds can be handled easily on rods of one less weight for each of the above IGFA class tippet designations.

Wahoo are typically found around structure: seamounts, banks, undersea canyons, and the severe drop-offs beside offshore islands. In this regard, they are often accessible to fly fishers. But without live bait and a single-minded determination to search only for wahoo, one rarely has an opportunity to free cast to a wahoo. Knowing this, I still keep a 12-weight rigged with a wire leader when I'm trolling teasers for billfish. Hopefully, one day my patience will pay off. In the meantime, if I'm trying to run down a single wahoo for the lodge's dinner table, I'll troll either a fly filled with silver Flashabou or a Mylar-covered pencil popper.

Troll-caught wahoo can never be submitted to the IGFA for record consideration, but if trolling is the only option, here is a suggestion: Connect 30- or 40-pound hard nylon to 80-pound wire. Even that may not be enough. A wahoo slamming a fast-trolled fly puts much more stress on a tippet and a wire trace than a fly fisher will ever experience when free casting. While Charley Boillod and I were trolling around Coronado Island off Costa Rica's Flamingo Beach Resort, he hit two wahoo in short order and was broken off by both. I told him that I would rig a "take-no-prisoners" combo of 80-pound wire and 40-pound hard nylon leader. We saw the spray from the oncoming wahoo 20 feet before the monster hit the fly and kept on going, the 80-pound wire cut neatly in half. Charley still laughs about it.

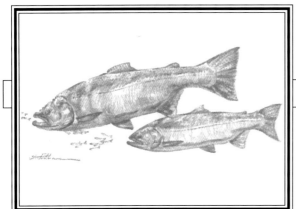

PACIFIC SALMON

Langara Island, British Columbia, Canada

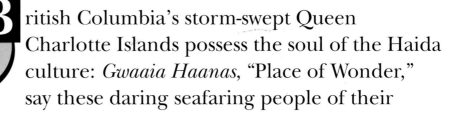

ritish Columbia's storm-swept Queen Charlotte Islands possess the soul of the Haida culture: *Gwaaia Haanas*, "Place of Wonder," say these daring seafaring people of their

archipelago. Biologists, with no less wonderment, call the 138 islands the "Canadian Galapagos" for the wealth of endemic plants and animals that evolved here during their long isolation from the mainland. Backpackers, too, embrace the Misty Isles, losing themselves in the silence of moss-carpeted trails that deer and bear have tunneled deep into the ancient forests of Sitka spruce, hemlock, and red cedar. But the Charlottes reserve their greatest riches for anglers. Five species of Pacific salmon, high-seas fish in the prime of life, salmon from nearly every watershed between northern Oregon and southeastern Alaska, stop during the last summer of their lives at tiny Langara, the Charlottes' northernmost island. For those anglers who cast a fly, Langara is paradise.

The dynamics that create this remarkable high-seas rendezvous are several. The Queen Charlottes perch on the very edge of the continental shelf, where massive cold-water upwellings bring to the surface dissolved nutrient salts, mainly nitrates and phosphates. These are energized by the sun and absorbed by phytoplankton, the foundation of the marine food chain. The phytoplankton bloom that occurs during long hours of spring and summer daylight feeds copepods and other crustaceans, which support immense schools of Pacific sand lance (*Ammodytes hexapterus*) and Pacific herring (*Clupea harengus pallasi*),

As a high-seas salmon, the pink or humpback salmon is a beautiful fine-scaled gamefish. Photograph by Trey Combs.

175

which in turn feed the vast numbers of migrating salmon. Anglers familiar with these baitfish on home waters are astonished when encountering great rafts of them at Langara. Sand lances, known as "needlefish" along the Canadian coast, and "candlefish" in Washington's Puget Sound, may be so tightly balled by feeding salmon and rhinoceros auklets that gulls can stand on the tumult. At such times, bald eagles swoop down to snatch up dozens of the fish in their talons and carry them to waiting young.

The second reason for Langara's concentration of salmon is the way these high-seas fish close with land in preparation for a final migration to their spawning rivers. Dixon Entrance, a deepwater passage between the Queen Charlotte Islands and Alaska's Dall and Prince of Wales islands to the north, lies at the right latitude to draw salmon, in summer, from the high seas to its fjord-rich coastline, and to its many reaches and channels that comprise the Inside Passage between Washington and Alaska. Directly east of the Queen Charlottes is Hecate Strait, where the water is so shallow that if the ocean level were to drop 50 feet, one could walk, at low tide, the 40 miles from the mainland to the islands. Storms here cause seas so steep that boats have collided with the ocean floor. "Horrible Hecate," say the commercial fishers who cross it at their peril for the richer fishing grounds beyond. But the shallow strait concentrates salmon at Dixon Entrance and the northwest Charlottes in general, and at Langara in particular.

Once salmon have reached Langara, the abundant food supply holds them for weeks, until sexual maturation moves them toward their spawning rivers. Ultimately, the shorter days of fall cause declines in the herring and sand lance populations. By winter, only small, immature silver and chinook salmon remain to pursue remnant baitfish.

Steve Shelly, a steelhead fly-fishing companion of mine from our days together at Chick and Marilyn Stewart's Babine Steelhead Lodge, manages the guide program at Langara Island's North Island Lodge. This has traditionally been a gear-fishing program for chinook salmon, known in Canada as the "spring" or "tyee," the latter name reserved for chinook salmon weighing 30 pounds or more. Shelly and lodge owner Fred Edworthy had long been interested in building a fly-fishing clientele at North Island. To this end, Edworthy asked if I would be interested in coming to his lodge and sampling the fishing.

I first visited the Charlottes fifteen years ago, sailing with my wife and two children aboard *Shearwater*, our 38-foot cutter. We wandered for more than a month along the coasts of Graham and Moresby Islands, diving for abalone and rock scallops with sea lions, visiting deserted Haida villages, fishing the bays for salmon and yelloweye rockfish, and finding sea-run cutthroat in the little streams that ran off the Queen Charlotte Mountains. The experience left me with an abiding fascination with the islands, and a determination to one day return.

I asked Les Johnson from Seattle, Washington to join me. He had co-authored *Fly Fishing for Pacific Salmon* (Frank Amato Publications, 1985) with Bruce Ferguson and Pat Trotter.

I was confident of finding the "northern coho"—silver salmon weighing in the teens—that crowd Langara late each summer for a final feeding binge.

Shelly had told me to expect ocean-bright pink and chum salmon, too. Edworthy's interest naturally centered on the huge chinooks. Neither Shelly, Johnson, nor I had ever caught them in deep water. The Charlottes' huge tides could further complicate our efforts. Rick Steen, an extremely knowledgeable Canadian saltwater fly fisher who guided on the *Charlotte Explorer,* and who had caught many ocean chinooks on a fly, had once described large chinooks to me as "the hardest fish to take in salt water, worse than permit."

Johnson and I flew on the lodge's charter flight from Vancouver, British Columbia, to Masset on Graham Island. While waiting for our amphibian shuttle flight to the lodge, a Museum of Flight–perfect Grumman Goose, we asked a departing angler for an update on the fishing.

"Well, in four days my partner and I boated seventy-two springs that averaged 25 pounds. The largest weighed 56." The man's laconic answer contrasted to my wide-eyed, open-mouthed look of disbelief. Where I come from, in Washington's salmon-rich Puget Sound, a single 25-pound chinook in a year is reason to buy the house a round.

Shortly after our arrival, Edworthy and I reviewed the lodge's current catch records and confirmed these remarkable figures. The possession limit on springs is four. Guides at North Island and neighboring Langara Lodge encourage anglers to kill salmon injured by the hook, "bleeders," regardless of their weight. Nevertheless, for the previous eight weeks, the average chinook killed and packed for shipment home weighed exactly 30 pounds.

Iced-down chinook, many over 40 pounds, filled tubs on the dock. These were remarkably handsome fish, so sexually immature that no kyping (hooking) of their jaws disfigured their sleek, hog-fat lines. Colors remained high-seas silver and gunmetal gray, a dress I had associated only with winter-caught chinooks, Washington's blackmouth salmon, and the feeder springs of lower mainland British Columbia.

Could these salmon be taken on the fly? Edworthy told us that the previous year a Canadian fly fisher had watched a spring of 40 pounds crashing bait; he had cast to it, hooked it, and successfully landed it, the only chinook thus far caught while fly fishing at North Island Lodge. One salmon does not a strategy make, but that was our only lead, a fish Johnson and I searched for in vain. In the meantime, other salmon found our flies, an embarrassment of incredible riches.

Langara Island is somewhat shaped like a frying pan, the handle fitting deep into Parry Passage, the narrows that separates huge Graham Island from tiny Langara. North Island Lodge, a luxurious condominium built on an ocean barge, floats in a tiny bay at the end of the handle. Headlands, rocky islets, bays, and reefs characterize Langara's convoluted coast. Boats remain in radio contact with each other and guides readily communicate news of a chinook bite. Within a few minutes of such news, anglers from North Island, neighboring Langara Lodge, and the *Charlotte Princess* mothership are racing toward the action. Boats pile up, the congestion forgivable; chinooks are on the cutplug herring before anglers can get a dozen pulls off their reels. Everyone hooks up, the boats drift apart, 50-pound tyee sometimes taking anglers a mile away.

Amid this action are the other salmon, the pinks, chums, and coho, mag-

This Langara Island chum salmon hit a Sea Habit Bucktail in the Herring pattern. Photograph by Trey Combs.

nificent 4- to 15-pound fish slashing through the ever present schools of bait. This goes on before the chinook bite begins and continues long after the deep-running chinook have slipped away for other headlands to plunder their herring and sand lance.

TACKLE AND FLIES

I fished a 9-foot 8-weight rod lined with a 30-foot shooting head, sink rate IV, and a .030 medium-sinking monocore running line for pink, coho, and chum salmon. My 9-foot leader tapered to 15-pound test. If there had been really large coho about, or if I'd located chinook crashing baitfish near the surface, I would have changed to a 9-weight. My saltwater reel held 250 yards of 20-pound backing. For chinook salmon, I fished a forward taper, experimental Scientific Anglers Bluewater line with a sink rate the same as that of the 550-grain Deep Water Express. (This line, not yet in production, can be reasonably duplicated with a forward taper full-sinking line in a sink rate of V.)

I fished Sea Habit Bucktails and Sea Habit Deceivers in the Herring and Sardine patterns. A single fly—basically a Sea Habit Deceiver in the Sardine pattern tied long and extremely thin to imitate a sand lance—took four species of salmon. Johnson successfully fished tube flies of his own design.

PINK SALMON (*Oncorhynchus gorbuscha*)

Pink salmon, named for the color of their flesh, and called "humpback" salmon, or "humpies," for the disfigurement that characterizes their sexual maturity, are fine-scaled, remarkably handsome fish of four to six pounds at Langara. With a range in both the Pacific and Arctic Oceans and the Bering and Okhotsk Seas, and a distribution in North American rivers from California's Sacramento to the McKenzie in Canada's Northwest Territories, they number among our most abundant salmon.

Pinks have a characteristic way of leaping out of the water on their flanks when they pursue crustaceans and small baitfish, a kind of skipping action that marks them at a considerable distance. They showed a decided preference for open water; rarely did we find them around the dense forests of kelp that filled the shore and small bays. I thought them the most surface-oriented of the salmon, often taking our flies as we stripped them back only a foot below the surface. I didn't observe them balling up bait, and I didn't notice them joining coho or chum salmon that did so. For this reason, we often took pinks incidentally while casting for the larger coho and chums that were charging around tightly packed schools of herring and sand lance.

Fly selection was for me simple and straightforward: Sea Habit Bucktails, sizes 4 to 1/0, in the Sand Lance and Herring patterns.

No special retrieve was necessary. I generally cast the fly blind to where pinks were feeding, gave the fly a few seconds to sink, and began stripping it back. The shooting head allowed me to cover a lot of water with ease.

Pinks took the fly solidly and fought well enough to take me into my backing. I wasn't thinking of world records, and hadn't bothered checking the International Game Fish Association's *1993 World Record Game Fishes*. Therein, all Pacific salmon are listed as "freshwater species." For pink salmon, the 10 kg category, added in 1992, was vacant. Records in the 8 kg and 6 kg categories were 5 and 6 pounds—pinks Johnson and I found ourselves releasing.

CHUM SALMON (*Oncorhynchus keta*)
and
COHO SALMON (*Oncorhynchus kisutch*)

Anglers searching for chum salmon in fresh water or on saltwater flats near the mouths of spawning rivers find green-backed fish with deep red vertical markings. Their hooked jaws are grotesquely bared with long caninelike teeth, a physical characteristic that some say was the inspiration for their common name, "dog salmon." (Alaskan natives feed their sled dogs chum salmon. I believe the common name "dog salmon" actually derived from this custom.) Such aesthetically unappealing fish would be hard to love were it not for their in-

The author holds an ocean-bright 10-pound chum salmon. Photograph by Les Johnson.

credible strength. First-time chum fishers immediately subscribe to the widely held belief that, pound for pound, they are the strongest of all Pacific salmon.

The same species, when a high-seas, fly-caught salmon, is a revelation. No salmon is more dramatically handsome, with indescribable shades of blue and grass green over the eyes that give way to dorsal runs of traditional salmon colors, gray and silver, but overlaid with traces of green. When hooked, an ocean chum shakes and twists before exploding into a series of long runs interspersed with leaps that can make a coho look lame. As the fish tires, it remains bull-tough, turning on its side and resisting the rod every inch of the way.

Though chum salmon are widely distributed throughout the Pacific and Arctic Oceans, the Bering Sea, and the Sea of Japan, and ascend rivers from California's San Lorenzo to at least as far east as the McKenzie in the Northwest Territories, the Queen Charlottes offer the best opportunity to take them as sexually immature ocean fish. I often found myself casting for chums in water 80 feet deep, while behind me, only 300 feet away, Pacific white-sided dolphin had schooled up in water that was hundreds of fathoms deep.

We regularly observed coho and chum salmon ball sand lance and herring into pulsating masses 30 or more feet across, and 10 feet deep. We could not separate the species as the salmon streaked through, under, and around the bait. If we cast on the bait and immediately began our retrieves, we invariably hooked baitfish. Letting a fly sink until it had fallen below the bait avoided fouling the fly, and gave it the appearance of a cripple.

Under these conditions, I fished my Sea Habit flies, either Bucktails or Deceivers, tying the fly onto the tippet with a fixed loop knot. The epoxy-soaked head tipped the fly head down on the sink, leaving the narrow fly to flutter helplessly downward. The chums and coho often took the fly when it was in this attitude. If they didn't, a few strips—casual, so the fly worked properly—were all that was necessary to get a strike.

While on the subject of coho flies, I must add that the tandem hook coho fly, with the forward hook down, and the rear or "stinger" hook up, is an outgrowth of "bucktailing," the fine art of trolling a fly in the wake of the boat that pioneering Canadian angler Jimmy Gilbert perfected two generations ago. Many Pacific salmon fly fishers have assumed this tying habit. But fly casting is not trolling. When casting, I believe the tandem hook arrangement both unnecessary and unwise. Coho and chum salmon attack flies from many different angles and invariably find the single hook. More importantly, tandem hooks detract from the action of the fly, which never dives as effectively as does one tied on a single hook. Also, the stinger hook can foul the material in the fly, especially if FisHair is used, creating on each false cast an ever greater mess. I believe that using a traditional 3X or 4X long streamer–type hook is equally unnecessary. It fouls too readily on the cast and adds absolutely nothing to the fish-catching attractiveness of the fly. I go to the opposite extreme, tying my Sea Habit salmon flies on short shank bait hooks by Gamakatsu and Owner.

We often located chum and coho lurking at the edges of the thick kelp forests that filled the shoreline. These fishing areas were especially productive

This silver (coho) salmon hit the Bucktail so hard that the fly passed completely through its jaw. The fly had to be cut off to make a safe release. Photograph by Trey Combs.

where the kelp clung precariously to severe, wave-pounded drop-offs. The salmon either pinned baitfish against the walls, or dashed out from the cover to attack cruising schools of baitfish. In either case we simply cast at the shore, gave the flies ten seconds to sink, and began strip retrieves. The retrieve could be a mixed bag: long, short, quick, and slow. Regardless, angling success remained constant.

　　After a couple of days casting along these edges, I felt that the chum salmon required a deeper sink than did the coho. When I gave the fly a half minute to sink before stripping it back, the chum might immediately pounce on it, or track it nearly to the surface before grabbing it only a rod's length away.

Steve Shelly casts a fly for coho salmon off Langara Island.

CHINOOK SALMON (*Oncorhynchus tshawyscha*)

Finding ways to take chinook, the springs and great tyee, in deep water when the bite was on became our challenge. Rick Steen likens them to "sumo wrestlers waiting to be fed," fish that suck in baitfish from a foot away, and take deep-running flies as lightly as any trout picking up a nymph. I had jigged for chinooks in deep water on gear and remembered how they often took lures that were fluttering down on the drop between upstrokes of the rod. I decided to duplicate, as closely as possible, this approach while using flies.

Johnson and I fished full-sinking forward taper lines, a IV and an experimental VI respectively. The considerable weight in the running lines made long shoots impossible, but the sink rate allowed us to reach the level where chinooks were feeding, *and then keep the flies swimming at this level.* To accomplish this, we found it necessary to fish on, or nearly on, the slack tide, and to do so where there was very little wind. We began the presentations by casting the flies in the direction the boat was drifting, paying out additional line as we floated over the fast-sinking lines. We would then pass the lines around the bow or stern of the boat and begin the retrieves as the lines assumed a slight angle away from the boat. At this point our flies were down 50 feet or more, and the 25-meter fly lines entirely off the reels. We retrieved the flies in slow, short strips while giving the rod tips slight twitches.

The fly I found most effective was a Sea Habit Deceiver tied to imitate the sand lance—an especially thin, primarily white dressing. It would swim nearly straight up on the short strip and rod twitch, and then turn head down on the slack created when the rod tip was dropped. Sometimes a chinook would follow the fly right to the surface, but usually it crushed the fly while on its feeding level, 30 to 50 feet down. If the wind remained light, I could release retrieved line when the fly was halfway to the surface and then repeat the retrieve. Wind blowing more than a couple of miles per hour on the slack tide dragged

The author releases a fly-caught chinook salmon. The fish took a Sea Habit Deceiver tied to suggest a Pacific sand lance. Photograph by Les Johnson.

The author took this chinook salmon on a Sea Habit Deceiver in the Sand Lance pattern.

up the line to above the desired level, and prevented a superslow, jiglike retrieve. At such times it was necessary to move to a headland situated in the lee of the wind.

Not until our last morning at Langara did we finally hook chinook salmon using this approach. At Coho Point, Johnson got one in the teens while I got one in the twenties. Shelly and I both had door-sized chinook follow flies up from the depths. When a chinook snapped my fly off on the strike, I changed from a 15- to a 20-pound tippet. While these fish are not known to be leader shy when anglers troll cutplug herring, I felt that my flies sank and fished better on a fine-diameter, soft monofilament leader.

Other refinements will surely follow. I left Langara Island convinced that the full-sinking line approach (rather than the use of shooting heads), the method of presentation, and the flies fished would ultimately lead me to Langara's great tyee, chinook salmon of 30 pounds or more.

INSHORE GAMEFISH

Permit, a highly prized gamefish of the flats, more commonly inhabits inshore waters. Photograph by Trey Combs.

he distinction between "offshore" and "inshore" gamefish cannot be made succinctly because fly fishers often encounter both species hunting over the same sliver of marine geography. I recall trolling teasers for blue and black marlin along Papua New Guinea's volcanic north coast on Brett Middleton's *Talio*. So severe was the drop-off from the beach to the blue-black depths that I could have thrown a coconut and hit the shore. We looked for marlin—and anticipated giant trevally. Mountainous islands of volcanic origin, such as Hawaii and Mauritius, similarly exhibit the kind of dramatically precipitous undersea topography that can have classic deepwater gamefish like blue marlin hunting just behind the surf line. Barrier reefs carry shallow continental shelves of coral to the edge of ocean abysses. When I was fishing for black marlin on Australia's Great Barrier Reef in the area of Cape Bowling Green, my captain rarely had us in more than 100 feet of water, and it was no trick to take bottomfish in the same area. Several years ago, while hunting for permit on Belize's Dangriga Reef, my guide ran the panga across open water toward another ribbon of coral. When the water boiled in front of us, I cast the only bucktail I could find, a tarpon Cockroach, and was fast to a skipjack tuna, a true deepwater species. The structure-oriented little tunny, black skipjack, and kawakawa tuna—the family of *Euthynnus* tuna—are caught fly casting from the beach, off headlands and islets, but also many miles offshore over banks. I have alternately caught dorado, an "offshore" species, with Pacific jack crevalle, more of a beach-hugging "inshore"

The author holds an Atlantic jack crevalle that hit a Mylar popper. Photograph by Robert Trosset.

gamefish, in Costa Rica's Gulf of Papagayo. Pelagic deepwater species such as yellowfin tuna often come onto ocean flats to feed on concentrations of bait and inadvertently mingle with inshore gamefish such as barracuda and king-fish. Conversely, I have caught barracuda offshore in water several thousand feet deep. Pacific salmon grow and mature for years on the high seas, but they spawn in fresh water, a practice that holds them inshore for many weeks, where they are most commonly caught by sportfishers. When I fished with Robert "RT" Trosset out of Key West, Florida, we used shrimpers' by-catch to chum the Gulf of Mexico's relative shallows for blackfin tuna and little tunny. But then, after a short run to a wreck site, we caught permit on crab patterns and Atlantic jack crevalle on poppers.

Most of the fly patterns described in the following chapter are equally effective on inshore gamefish. Lefty's Deceiver in its many sizes and forms attracts just about anything that swims. The Mylar-covered Gaines poppers I so like for dorado and school tuna are deadly on a host of inshore gamefish. I've seen deepwater bonefish, flats tarpon, and river salmon taken on my Sea Habit Bucktails.

Because of this frequent mixing of inshore and offshore species, I carry a few additional patterns in my offshore tackle bag. I always have a box holding crab patterns and a few bonefish flies. I wouldn't get in a boat without Dan Blanton's Whistler flies. Weighted with lead barbell eyes, and fished with loop connections, they have tremendous action on inshore gamefish. I'll also throw in some nylon-coated braided wire, a few floating lines, a couple of feet of bump chenille, and some of Popovics's barracuda flies, and be quite satisfied that I'll have every advantage when I visit "inshore" waters in the process of get-ting "offshore."

On the next several pages, I've pictured a few of the inshore gamefish commonly encountered by offshore fly fishers.

The Pacific bonito, a superb inshore gamefish for single-digit rods, strikes a great variety of Bucktails and Deceivers.

Hawaiians call the giant trevally ulua. *East Africans call it "kingfish" or "kingie." In other areas, anglers nickname it "GT." By any name they are superb fly-rod gamefish. Randall Kaufmann took this 50-pound-plus giant trevally off Christmas Island.*

The pargo snapper, found off Central America's Pacific coast, is an enormously strong gamefish. Despite the fly fisher's best efforts, many pargo are able to swim under ledges or into holes and no amount of rod pressure can dislodge them.

Because of the sierra mackerel's razor-sharp teeth, a light, braided wire leader is necessary.

The mackerel scan is often abundant on the offshore banks of Baja California.

Australia's and New Guinea's narrow-barred mackerel is similar in habit and size to the king mackerel. The fish are capable of prodigeous arching leaps, sometimes soaring 25 feet above the water where, with mouth agape, they come down on a school of baitfish.

This bluefin trevally, one of several that struck a Silver Mylar Ralph Kanz Fly off New Guinea's Hankow Reef, has a widespread distribution in the Indian and Pacific Oceans.

The beautiful rainbow runner is a fine fly-rod gamefish. The author used these fish as live, bridled teaser bait to bring dogtooth tuna within casting range.

The red bass, a common inshore gamefish of Australia and New Guinea, will strike a variety of baitfish imitating flies.

The Pacific yellowtail, an incredibly powerful inshore gamefish, eagerly takes Bucktails and Deceivers.

Pacific coast fly fishers often encounter the green jack in large schools. The author carries a 3-piece 6-weight for such times.

BLUEWATER

Methods

PART 2

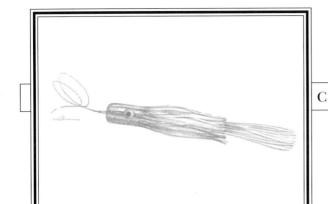

TEASING

Anglers call "teasing" the sport of attracting a gamefish to a trolled or cast lure without hooks, then maintaining the fish's attention until a lure with hooks can be substituted.

The teaser can be a whole fish; a belly strip from a dorado or tuna that has been sewn up (sometimes called a "Panama bait"); any such sewn bait set inside a skirted, Konahead-type trolled lure; or any of a myriad of lures by itself. As most frequently practiced, teasing gives big-game fishers an opportunity to select the billfish they wish to bait and catch. If dorado, small marlin, and sailfish are not the targets, then whole tuna—carefully stitched and rigged with hooks—need only be sacrificed after a large marlin has been raised. Dorado, especially, can tear trolled baits to pieces and become expensive pests.

For fly fishers, trolling teasers raises fish that otherwise could not be located. Once a billfish has been raised, once it has "crashed the bait" and the person on the teaser rod has the fish's attention, the "sport" part of the teasing comes into play. A billfish will lunge at the teaser, and try to get a secure hold on it from one rear quarter or the other. The person on the teaser rod must anticipate this and, by moving the rod tip and taking turns on the reel, keep the teaser just barely out of reach.

If the teaser is pulled away too rapidly, the billfish can get discouraged and leave. If the teaser is not pulled away rapidly enough, the billfish may get a firm purchase on it nearly crosswise in its mouth and stubbornly refuse to give it up. Often, when the teaser is then ripped from the billfish's mouth, the fish leaves in disgust—or with the bait. The successful tease becomes a cat-and-mouse ballet, the billfish drawn in until well within casting range, 25 to 40 feet.

For the cast to be legal by the rules of the International Game Fish Association (IGFA), the boat must first be out of gear. Trolling is a no-no. I can't begin to count the number of anglers who have told me, "I'm not fishing for records," and thus kept the boat in gear—a decision many captains not familiar with fly fishing likely will support. After all, gear fishers troll, and when a billfish shows up and crashes a gear fisher's bait, the captains don't have to take the boat out of gear. But fly fishing is not gear fishing. Fly rods were not designed for trolling, and do not have the backbone to successfully drive a hook through a billfish's mouth. A high proportion of fly fishers' hookups take place at the end of the fish's mouth; if the fly fishers are fortunate, they may get a run and jump out of the fish. More often, the fish will not be hooked at all. Having the boat stopped actually helps fly fishers, for then they only have to contend with the movement of the fish. The billfish has time to turn and get the fly crosswise in its mouth, a movement critical to a successful hookup. With the fish either broadside, or turning away from the angler, a really hard set can be made without the tippet breaking, and with a good chance of the hook penetrating in either the side or the corner of the jaw.

If I'm on a cruiser and trolling teasers downwind, I know the boat will coast along after the engine is out of gear. When I make my cast, I'll keep my rod tip high, and drop it on the take. I may even slip some slack line to give the billfish an opportunity to get fully turned. Above all else, I want to avoid the fish frantically chasing the fly and grabbing it from behind.

NOTES ON TEASING

A good teaser person is invaluable and deserves at least half the credit for any fly-caught billfish. Teasing is also extremely exciting, and it gets both of the anglers who are paying for the charter working as a team.

Teasers run directly from rods are said to be on "flat lines." Usually two flat lines are run off the transom, one from each other.

Captains and mates describe the position of teasers behind a boat as being on a wave from the wake, each wave numbered from the transom, the "first wave" being directly off the transom, followed by the "second wave," and so on. The port and starboard teasers on the flat lines are typically set, from mid-sized cruisers, at the fifth wave, particularly in the middle of the day. Early and late in the day, under low light, these teasers may be set closer—at the third wave, for example. Obviously, the closer a teaser is set, the less time an angler, the teaser rod companion, the captain, and the mate will have to react to a raised billfish.

When the billfish first appears on the teaser, the boat should not be slowed, as the change in engine rpms can throw the fish off. The captain should wait a moment until the billfish has "locked on" the teaser before slowing the boat. Once a hot billfish has been locked on, it telegraphs its excitement by lighting up, its fins turning neon, its stripes glowing hot blues. In this state, it will follow the teaser to the transom of the boat, literally overrunning the fly fisher. I remember one such berserk sailfish that took a popper at my feet; only the leader was outside my rod tip.

A teaser must be removed with a "clean jerk" by reeling and dropping the rod until the tip is pointing at the teaser. Then, with a single swing, the teaser is pulled free of the water and tossed toward the bow of the boat. If the teaser isn't pulled cleanly, but instead bounces along on top, the billfish will pursue it until it leaves the water. With the cast already made, the angler runs the risk of the billfish not seeing the fly or popper and swimming away.

Not all species of billfish act the same. Sailfish are far more docile than marlin. In my experience, no marlin comes in so quickly or aggressively as a blue. Sometimes you can't reel the teaser in fast enough; I've seen blues come in so suddenly that the captain had to accelerate away from them just to keep the tease going and prevent the marlin from getting death grips on the teasers.

Individuals of the same species also act differently, some "hot" and aggressive, others passive and "lazy." A lazy fish is prone to follow a teaser without taking it in its mouth, or to take the teaser at the end of its mouth, a "scissorbill" take. A fly taken in this manner rarely results in a hookup that lasts.

A billfish can only concentrate on one teaser at a time. Two teasers left in the water, or a teaser and a fly side by side in the water, can leave the billfish with a choice it can't make. It may then leave simply out of indecision.

When the captain runs two teasers on flat lines, and a billfish rises behind one teaser and grabs it, the second teaser must immediately be removed. If it's not, the billfish, out of frustration over not being able to get a secure hold on the primary teaser, may streak across and nail the second teaser from the side. This puts the teaser crosswise on the rasplike, bony ridge of the billfish's mouth. Held in this position, the teaser becomes very hard to pull free. I have lost teasers to blue marlin in exactly this manner.

The captain often sets a daisy chain of soft rubber squid amidships between the two flat lines. He runs a "bird" at the front of the daisy chain. This torpedo-shaped lure has short wings that flutter back and forth on the surface, a disturbance that helps draw billfish up to where they can see—and eventually smell—the baited teasers. The bird motors along at the very edge of the turbulent wake, where the water is still filled with bubbles. The squid trail is behind, running out to the third wave. Sometimes a billfish will grab the squid first. The teaser person must then reel in the baited teaser and complete a "pass off," whereby the teaser is drawn alongside the billfish, the daisy chain of squid is pulled in, and the billfish is passed off to the baited teaser. I have watched even blue marlin get passed from one teaser to another. It takes a nervy teaser person to pull this off!

The "spread" of teasers, the distance between them, can be increased by running a teaser from a rod to an outrigger pole. If this is done, normally only one outrigger pole is set, that being opposite the angler's casting hand. Fly fishers do not want to find themselves trying to cast under an outrigger pole with a lit-up billfish storming around! I'm left-handed. When my turn is done, and my right-handed companion is up, I must alert the crew that the outrigger pole must be changed.

The captain often runs the outrigger teaser line to a reel mounted on the flying bridge. On this line, the captain will likely troll a very large skirted lure (15 to 18 inches is typical) that does not contain bait. This teaser will be close in, on the third wave, or even closer. A billfish can see this lure for a considerable distance, and it's used solely to bring a billfish up on top. From his elevated position, the captain can see the fish clearly and note its every movement. Normally, the mate will reel the baited teaser from the fifth to the third wave, and pass off the fish from the large teaser to the smaller baited teaser on the flat line.

TEASER RODS AND REELS

More than a little debate attends the subject of what makes for a perfect teaser rod. All the successful teasing I've seen by mates has been accomplished with stiff rods of under six feet, invariably the same 30- or 50-pound outfits clients use when trolling. The reels have usually been Penn Internationals with retrieve rates of 3:1.

When I put together my first teasing outfits, I purchased lighter, longer rods that weren't so stiff, and I put high speed, 6:1 reels on them. The outfits didn't perform well for a number of reason. When trolled, the rods took such a deep set that the guides were soon damaged. The butts weren't gimballed and could not be seated in place in the holder set in the gunwale. The strain on the reels soon blew out the pawls. (I locked the reels by setting up the drag as tightly as possible.) When the teaser dug into a swell and a fish was grabbing at it, the high speed retrieve became a disadvantage, for the teaser resisted the high rate of retrieve until it suddenly flew into the air. A couple of quick turns on the reel, and the teaser was pulled away too abruptly. Also, I'd loaded the reels with 50-pound monofilament. This was too light; a couple of Mexican blues took off with $50 teasers. After two seasons, I scrapped what was left of the outfits.

I purchased two-piece rods a bit over six feet long that, when broken down, would fit into my 40-inch-long, 6-inch-diameter carry-on tube. The rods had gimballed butts. The upper guides were roller-type. The grips were rubber. (Cork grips get chewed up by the rod holders.) The reels I chose were old-fashioned, inexpensive, and rugged Penn 66s, reels with a 2.5:1 gear ratio. (You can get this reel in wider models, the Penn 67 and 68. But why bother? You only need to have 100 or so feet of line out.) I completely filled each reel with 80-pound Ande. They worked well for me for both sailfish and marlin. On long-range boats, I found I would have preferred a higher rate of retrieve when working a long tease for striped marlin.

Ed Rice and Ray Beadle tease with rods twelve feet long. I'm a head shorter than either man, and I find their rods slow and clumsy to use, especially when pulling the teaser for the cast. Other anglers, equally world class, choose rods eight feet long.

LURES FOR TEASING

Catalogues present a bewildering variety of rubber skirted trolling lures with names like "Konahead," "Doorknob," "Big Eye Rocket," "Kona Clone Hacksaw," and "Green Machine." Before getting into sizes, actions, and colors, let me simplify the whole business by breaking down all the lures into two categories: soft-type heads in which the entire lure is rubber, and hard-type heads in which the head is plastic and only the skirt is rubber.

Soft heads are less prone to damage from billfish, and are likely to be held in the mouth longer, especially by sailfish. Lures with hard, plastic heads can be damaged by a marlin's bill, or shattered on a clean jerk if they hit some part of the boat. The hard head does not necessarily discourage an especially aggressive billfish; I've watched both blue and striped marlin grab this type of lure and leave with it despite a lot of tugging on my part.

Regardless of whether the lure is hard or soft, the shape of the head determines the lure's action, the depth it works, and the speed at which it can be trolled. Additionally, holes are often drilled in heads of both types, soft and hard, that leave fine trails of bubbles, the "smoke" that becomes an additional factor in attracting billfish.

The reason for trolling a teaser is, of course, to get the fish's attention. For this reason, I usually pick chugger-style trolling lures that make a lot of commotion but track well at the speed I'm trolling, five to seven knots. *I don't want a lure with an action so erratic that I can't control its movements when working in a hot billfish.*

Several factors determine the most desirable size for a teaser. If belly strips of dorado and tuna are sewn up and run inside the teaser, the size of these baits decides what size lure can be used. Really large lures—anything over 12 inches with a diameter of 1½ to 2 inches—should be avoided on flat line teasers run to rods. They offer so much resistance that they become difficult to work away quickly and smoothly from hard-charging billfish. Sailfish and white marlin seem especially willing to crash small teasers, chuggers sometimes only seven to eight inches long.

Here are some combinations that have worked for me. This is meant only as a general guide. Fly fishers should seek the advice of gear anglers and charter boat captains familiar with the area they intend to fish, and then experiment for themselves.

George Parker, Del Dykes, and the author (left to right) discuss offshore flies used for ahi, Hawaii's yellowfin tuna. George Parker and Henry Chee were famous pre–World War II charter-boat captains in Hawaii. Parker pioneered the use of skirted lures for marlin. He took a short length of chrome pipe, painted a large eye on each side, and filled the pipe with a wood dowel containing a center hole for the fishing line to pass through. A rubber skirt was made by cutting strips from automobile inner tubes. At the time, they came in three colors: red, black, and white. Using these primitive lures, one could accomplish a fast troll and search a much larger area for marlin. This was a dramatic departure from previous methods that involved a slow troll with a bridled live tuna. In the mid-fifties, the automobile industry produced vinyl seat covers in a variety of colors, and Parker switched to this lighter, more supple material. Lure manufacturers around the world were soon marketing skirted lures for offshore fishermen in endless variety. Parker, now in his eighties, still runs daily charters from Kailua-Kona on his big-game boat, Playboy. His son, Marlin Parker, operates his own big-game boat Marlin Magic. Both men have seen granders, blue marlin over 1,000 pounds, come aboard their boats.

SOFT HEADS

Pink and white is a favorite sailfish color combination the world over. I like a Mold Craft Hooker Softhead—the eight-inch "Standard Hooker" in Pink/White. If I run a stitched belly strip inside, I can only get by with using black skipjack in the three- to four-pound range, or school dorado in the three- to six-pound range. I've raised many sails on this teaser, a size that's a delight to work on the teaser rod. The next size up, the 10½-inch "Senior Hooker," would be my choice if striped and blue marlin are mixed with sailfish, as they are off Baja's East Cape in July and August. I've raised these fish on many color combinations, including the Blue/White,

Black/Green, Purple/Silver/Black, and Black/Red. Belly strips from tuna and dorado of up to 10 pounds (larger if you cut away some of the meat from the inside of the belly strip) fit nicely into these lures. If a lot of blue marlin are showing, and the belly strips are running especially large, I often go to Mold Craft's "Wide Range," the 12½-inch "Senior" model in Blue/White.

These soft head teasers, regardless of size or color, come with a double skirt: A loose skirt fits inside an integrally molded one. This loose skirt must be removed to accommodate a belly strip. Don't throw this extra skirt away! It can be slipped over the end of a long belly strip of dorado, or fit over the head of a baitfish, to give these baits extra color and provide some protection while trolling.

HARD HEADS

I've fished a lot of hard head teasers for striped and blue marlin, preferring lures 11 to 12 inches long with heads that taper a bit. This configuration produces a lot of commotion, has good size, and still retrieves well on the tease. As with the soft heads, I generally avoid lures in this size that have especially large chugger heads. I fish these skirted lures with and without belly strips; I find little need for belly strips if the billfish are aggressive. Also, a badly stitched or incorrectly sized belly strip can ruin the action of the lure.

I have not found billfish to be sensitive to changes in size and color from the teaser to the fly or popper. If a teased-in billfish is excited and lit up when the cast is made, it will eat just about anything it can find that resembles food.

STITCHING BAITS FOR TEASING

Baits for teasing can be either belly strips cut from tuna or dorado or whole ballyhoo, mullet, sardines, and mackerel. All these baits can be trolled by themselves, trolled with short skirts over the leading ends, or set inside the rubber skirts of trolling lures. Many anglers feel that when a billfish first grabs a teaser and gets a "taste" (i.e., smell), the addition of a bait to the lure helps keep the fish turned on as the tease progresses.

Whenever I fish Baja waters, I visit the resort's fish-cleaning station at the end of the day. Here, fillets are cut from both tuna and dorado without gutting the fish. As a result, these stations are a wonderful source for teaser bait belly strips. For a few dollars, one of the workers will likely follow your instructions so that the belly strips are cut from the fish correctly.

Whether you catch the source for belly strips yourself, or make arrangements with gear fishers, or visit a fish-cleaning station, the belly strips should be cut from the fish as follows: Lay the fish on its back and cut across and straight down just forward of the pectoral fins. Cut completely through the bones and cartilage that hold these fins together. (Try to avoid cutting into the stomach area.) Using the point of the knife, cut down each side to the anal opening and lift the strip free. Wash it in salt water, place it in a plastic sack, and stow it in the cooler until you have enough belly strips to stitch up at one sitting.

The materials needed for stitching baits are quite simple: a cooler; a cutting board; a butcher knife with a five- to nine-inch blade; a sharpening stone; large plastic bags that can be sealed; six-inch rigging needles; dental floss (wide) or heavy, waxed string; a scrub brush; and an assortment of swivels. To complete the initial rigging of the teasers, you'll need crimping pliers, sleeves, and stainless thimbles sized for monofilament from 150- (minimum) to 300-pound test. Billfish are not leader shy!

I like to cut a piece of ½-inch plywood into approximately the shape of the cooler top, coat it with a marine bedding compound, and screw it to the cooler. This gives me a portable work station where I can cut, stitch, and then stow the results.

Needles specifically designed for stitching bait, along with heavy, waxed string, can be purchased through Offshore Angler, 1935 S. Campbell, Springfield, MO 96898 -0400. Phone: 1-800-633-9131. Order the rigging needles that are also known as mortician's needles.

At the end of my 80-pound reel line, I use a sleeve, and crimp on a high quality, heavy duty snap swivel in a black finish. This will prevent the teaser from twisting the line. Because this connection is a wear point, I cut off the swivel along with a few inches of monofilament every couple of days, and crimp on the swivel again using a new sleeve. I like to rig my teasers on six feet of 250-pound monofilament. At the end that connects to the line on the reel, I use a sleeve, and crimp in a loop of monofilament that is protected with a stainless thimble. I then lead the 250-pound monofilament through the teaser and, using another sleeve, crimp in a loop of monofilament that holds a heavy swivel, or a loop protected with a second thimble.

The basic procedure for stitching belly strips is simple if you start correctly. I begin by laying the swivel against the cartilage that holds the pectoral fins together, and running the rigging needle through the swivel and the belly strip several times before tying off the waxed string. As extra insurance against the stitching coming loose, I repeat this procedure using the next opening up in the swivel. (This cartilage is the one point in a belly strip that won't tear and will support the entire strip through hours of trolling.) The belly strip is closed by stitching down in one direction at ½-inch intervals, then cross-stitching back up to the original point using the same holes. The final tie-off is key. Wind the waxed rigging string several times around the head of the bait, run the needle through the bait, and repeat. I like to have at least a dozen wraps completely around the very head of the bait. This will help prevent the strip from mushrooming out at its end. If this happens, the bait must be replaced, for it will get partially outside the skirt of the lure and ruin the lure's action. If I've done everything right, all the swivel and any sleeve will be inside the belly strip. To finish the job, I angle the needle so that it comes out from the center of the bait, near the monofilament leader. I make four or five half-hitches around the line and trim off the extra. The result fits snugly up inside of the skirt of the lure.

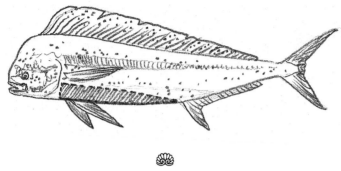

Standard Dorado Bait

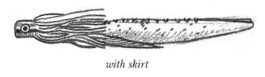

with skirt

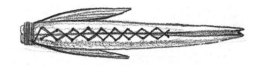

dorsal view

It's fine for the bait to extend well beyond the skirt. If this happens, I often stitch up only the upper three-quarters of the strip, and split the balance, the two halves that extend beyond the skirt giving the strip a flailing action. The single biggest mistake people make is initially cutting the strips too wide, and then stitching up a bait that does not properly fit the teaser. Long and thin is better.

Belly strips can be cut from dorado well into the teens if the strips are cut thin. Some of the flesh on the inside must be cut away in order to properly close the sides and stitch up the strip. The long pectoral fins on a larger dorado extend beyond the lure's skirt and produce an incredible swimming action.

Worldwide, one of the whole fish most commonly used to tease and bait billfish is the balao, or ballyhoo—"garfish," as it is known in Australia—a beaked fish on which the lower jaw extends out as far as does the upper jaw of a billfish. I stitch up these fish in two steps. After crimping a swivel to the end of my line, I force the swivel *entirely* into the fish's mouth, and run my rigging needle down through the top of the head, through the swivel, and through the lower jaw—in order to later tie off the rigged bait, I run the string 180 degrees around the fish's head and repeat, twice. The third time the string comes out the bottom of the jaw, I continue it around on the other side of the fish, repeat twice, and tie off both pieces at the top of the head. At this point, if the mouth were tied shut with soft copper wire, and the beak broken off, the ballyhoo could be cast or trolled. But for added insurance, I take my rigging needle and run it through the fish, eye to eye—again, leaving six inches extra to use for tying off—and stitch down the side, the stitches alternating from above to just below the fish's backbone. I return to the head using the same holes, and tie off at the top of the head. This additional stitching can help keep a billfish from immediately pulling the bait free. Other whole fish rigged in this manner include large sardines, mullet, and mackerel.

A mullet can be given additional action by taking a razor-sharp knife and splitting the last third of fish dorsally, right to the end of the tail. The two halves fly about when the bait rolls out on a wave, an action billfish find irresistible.

The unweighted teasers described thus far are called *skipping baits*, teasers that make a commotion on top, often popping out of waves amid a shower of water. Whole fish, when weighted, are called *swimming baits*. These can be as small as a ballyhoo or as large as a 10-pound narrow barred mackerel rigged for "grander" black marlin. The swimming baits usually used by fly fishers for teasing are ballyhoo, mullet, and, in Australia, queenfish and leatherbacks.

To rig a fish to swim, run a rigging needle down through the top of its head and out the bottom, behind the mouth. Pass the end of a foot-long length of 100-pound monofilament through the hole, and slip an egg sinker onto the monofilament under the mouth. Take the tag end of monofilament immediately in front of the mouth and crimp tight to the standing monofilament. Crimp a loop in the longer piece and you're ready to snap the bait to the teasing rod. To keep the fish swimming properly, its mouth should be wired shut and its beak either broken off (ballyhoo), or sewn shut (mullet).

TEASING

A Mexican panga, complete with a captain who probably hasn't worked much with fly fishers, can still be chartered for as little as $100 per day. This remains the best bargain in the world of offshore fly fishing. If the anglers are prepared—and this means they must bring their own teaser rods and teasers—the offshore experience can include a shot at a billfish. If the captain speaks little English, and they speak no Spanish, they need not despair. By drawing some pictures, using a bit of pantomime, and going through some mock drills, the essence of what they're trying to accomplish can be made clear. (Even after the captain understands, he'll think they're *loco* for trolling around a lure with no hooks.) No matter what, the anglers shouldn't wait until a billfish shows to discover that they and the captain cannot communicate.

Mexican Panga
(or any small, single-engine skiff)

At its most basic, teasing from a panga involves the captain at the engine, one person responsible for the single flat line/teaser rod, and the fly fisher who's "up." If the angler does not have a companion who will operate the teaser rod, the captain—or whoever is at the engine controls—must do the teasing. However, if going after billfish, I would do it with a companion other than the captain, who is almost certainly not familiar with teasing.

Even when running through this very basic scenario, the angler has responsibilities. Fly line must be stowed in a bucket—please, no handle or hooks—beginning from the reel, so that nothing tangles on the cast. (I don't travel with a bucket. I generally purchase one at my destination, and give it to the captain before leaving. Sometimes this is more dishpan than bucket. Something collapsible in canvas can also be used, such as a stripping basket.) The standard routine calls for water to be put in the bucket to slow things down and provide an additional safeguard against line tangles. I don't know how this practice got started. In a rough seaway, the water sloshing back and forth actually *causes* the line to tangle. Also, the water causes line drag and shortens up the distance you can cast. On rough days, I leave the bucket empty and use it to keep the fly line tangle-free and away from the wind. If the ocean is relatively calm, I put in a bit of seawater—just enough to cover the fly line. I do this to dampen the recoil of the running line after the strike. I have seen running line fly off the deck and tangle at the reel as a result of suddenly released tension. A little water in the bucket may help to prevent this.

I try very hard to keep my cast from falling in front of a billfish, especially if the boat is still coasting. If a billfish takes the fly before turning, even the most steadfast angler will feel the *big grab*, react, and strike before the fish has had an opportunity to turn fully and begin swimming away. Almost invariably, the fly or popper flies away on the strike, leaving the angler, teaser person, and captain in a disheartened daze.

I'm left-handed. If the person on the teaser is experienced, and I have discussed the cast I'm going to make ahead of time, I'll make my forward cast well to my right and over the top of the teaser line. As my fly or popper goes forward, he will pull the teaser out from under my line with his rod horizontal to the water. The fly line flies out better than the wind-resistant fly and creates a belly on the water. As I begin stripping, the bug is passing across in front of the billfish. The fish needs to turn very little to get it crosswise in its mouth. The result of such a take is a fish solidly hooked in the side or corner of its jaw.

The tease and cast, step by step, proceed as follows:

1. The billfish crashes the teaser. The teaser person grabs the flat line teaser rod and takes a couple of turns on the reel.

2. The billfish keeps coming after the teaser. (I often say a hot fish is now "on tracks.") The boat is slowed.

3. At the same moment, the angler tosses his fly or popper to the side of the boat and lets 15 feet of fly line escape. (If a popper is tossed directly into the wake, it can ride wave reversals and actually follow the boat.) The rod tip is kept straight up so that the bug skips along with little drag.

4. When the fish is well within casting range the angler drops his rod tip. This will lay enough line on the water to load the rod for the cast. The fly rod's downward movement signals the person on the teaser rod to drop his own rod in preparation for removing the teaser. He'll need to take several quick turns when he does this to prevent slack from dropping the teaser back into the billfish's mouth. As the angler lifts the rod to cast, the boat is taken out of gear, and the teaser is pulled—one, two, three, just like that. The angler's backcast must be at an angle, too, or the fly could tangle in the boat's console, railing, or stowed outrigger poles. (On a cruiser, this list can include the flying bridge and the captain. Hooking the captain with a huge billfish fly is considered extremely bad form. Don't laugh; it's happened more than once.)

5. The angler makes his forward cast at an angle and begins stripping back the fly. The rise of a billfish is incredibly fast; it took me years with motor drive cameras to finally get a decent photograph of it. *The angler must concentrate on the fly, not on the fish.* On the take, the angler holds the running line, turns his hand to get a good grip on the running line, and strikes the fish in the opposite direction from that of the take. How many times? Two or three if the fish permits it, but a billfish really rolling along may give an angler only one good shot.

6. If the hook is needle sharp and doesn't go into the roof of the fish's mouth—this hookup can really set a billfish off—the angler will have a few seconds to collect himself, get the running line on the reel, and get a tight line to the fish. When the billfish feels this resistance, the fireworks begin.

A Mexican panga, or a like-sized skiff, can also troll a daisy chain of squid on a short line from the other corner of the transom. With three people in the boat, this addition automatically becomes the "up" angler's responsibility. This is a great attractor of billfish, especially sailfish, but one that can also pull in yellowfin and bigeye tuna. Usually a billfish will see the daisy chain, swing by it, come up alongside the teaser, and eat the teaser first.

The artist sized this illustration to apply to large game boats and to long-range fly-fishing boats, such as the 92-foot Royal Star. If facing aft, the right-handed fly fisher stands besides the flatline in the right corner of the transom. If the billfish appears on the right-hand teaser, the teaser person must move to the left to make it possible for the fly fisher to cast. The fly fisher casts over the teaser line—and across the wake—as the teaser person pulls the teaser from under the cast fly. The marlin, as shown, turns to take the stripped-in fly crosswise in its mouth. An alternative to this presentation, possible if there is no right-to-left crosswind, would be a cast to the right of the marlin. With a coasting boat, avoid casting at the marlin, as the fish will at first take the fly from directly behind, and the fly fisher will likely react too quickly and pull the fly out before the hooks can take a hold.

However, the occasional sailfish will initially munch one of the squid. It that happens, the person on the teaser rod must quickly reel in the teaser and try to pass off the sailfish to the baited teaser. You shouldn't automatically retrieve the daisy chain when a billfish first shows, for it may be the daisy chain that's holding the fish's interest. Wait until the fish makes a grab at the teaser before retrieving the daisy chain.

Some pangas, the so-called "Super Pangas," are fitted out like little cruisers: live bait wells built into the transom, Bimini tops, integral gas tanks, fish finders, and outrigger poles. Such a boat will generally have the same narrow beam as a regular panga, but by using the outrigger pole, sufficient spread can be gained to run an extra teaser. If this is done, and the captain is to stay at the engine controls, it becomes necessary for the fly fishers to assist the teaser person by clearing the line not holding the billfish. If billfish show up on both teasers at the same time, one line still must be cleared to free up the single angler so that the cast can be made.

STANDARD CRUISER

The classic billfish setup for cruisers in the 25- to 40-foot range consists of a flat line at each corner of the transom, and a daisy chain of squid running down the center. Each teaser rides on the fifth wave, while the daisy chain extends back to the third wave. If the angler is

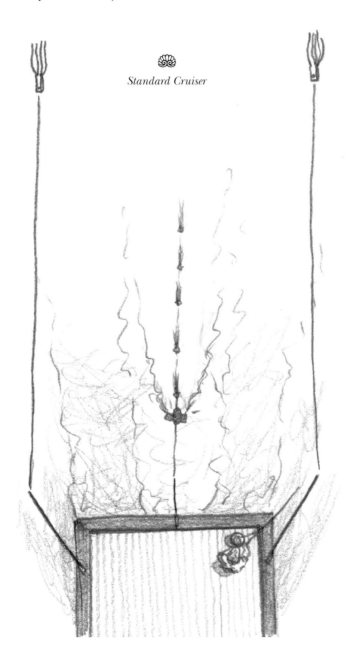

Standard Cruiser

right-handed, a bucket is set in the right corner (facing aft) of the transom. If the boat has a captain, a mate, and two fly fishers, the tease and cast to a billfish on one of the teasers proceed as follows:

1. The fish shows and the primary teaser person takes the teaser rod.

2. The captain leaves the console, makes sure the fish is locked on the teaser, clears the spare teaser, and *sets the rod in the gunwale opposite the angler.* (If the captain stows the rod on the wrong side, it will prevent the angler from casting.) The captain returns to the console and slows the boat.

3. The non-teaser person has already cleared the daisy chain of squid. This pile of line and squid must be placed in the corner of the boat opposite the bucket. The angler doesn't want his running line tangling up in the daisy chain.

4. The tease and cast proceed as described above.

VARIATIONS ON THE STANDARD CRUISER

1. When I fished Cape Verde Peninsula waters off Dakar, Senegal, we trolled two daisy chains of rubber squid at the fifth wave and ran a single ballyhoo off a spinning rod down the center to the third wave. Invariably the Atlantic sailfish came to the daisy chain of squid first. The boat was then taken out of gear, and the fish passed off from the daisy chain to the ballyhoo. The tease continued until the fly cast was made.

2. As I previously pointed out, many captains like to fish two flat lines and a daisy chain, but add in a very large trolling lure or swimming fish that leads first to the outrigger pole opposite the angler, and then to a reel mounted on the flying bridge beside the captain. Normally sailfish will come upon one of the two teasers on the flat lines. But really large blue marlin are more likely to crash this big teaser. Because the teaser is so close to the boat, the sudden appearance of a blue is dramatic. Twice I've had blues of over 700 pounds crash this teaser. Regardless of the size of the marlin, little chance exists to hook it on a fly until the baited teaser is brought in and the marlin is passed off. While the mate and captain orchestrate this, the "up" angler clears the daisy chain and his companion clears the other flat line.

Using essentially this same setup, a captain may run another baited teaser from the outrigger pole, three in all. A daisy chain of squid may or may not be set. If it is, the four lines get everyone's attention in a hurry when a billfish shows. Again, the "up" angler must then be responsible for managing the daisy chain. However, the captain may elect to call for the cast immediately if the marlin goes megaviolent. In that event, the mates must first give the angler room to cast, and then drop their rods down so that the backcast doesn't foul their lines. In such close quarters, the "up" angler may wish to simply roll cast his fly or popper at the marlin. In any event, it becomes the responsibility of the fly fisher to survey the playing field and quietly call out his needs.

3. A few captains will troll a "full speed"—two teasers on flat lines, and two teasers on outrigger poles, four teasers in all. Regardless of how this is managed, the angler must keep a clear head and roll cast his fly under one of the outrigger poles. With four people on board, including the angler, the captain and mate must do a lot of clearing while the person doing the teasing keeps the fish coming. However, this can work, as long as the lines are set well aft and everyone knows what is expected of them when a billfish first crashes the teaser.

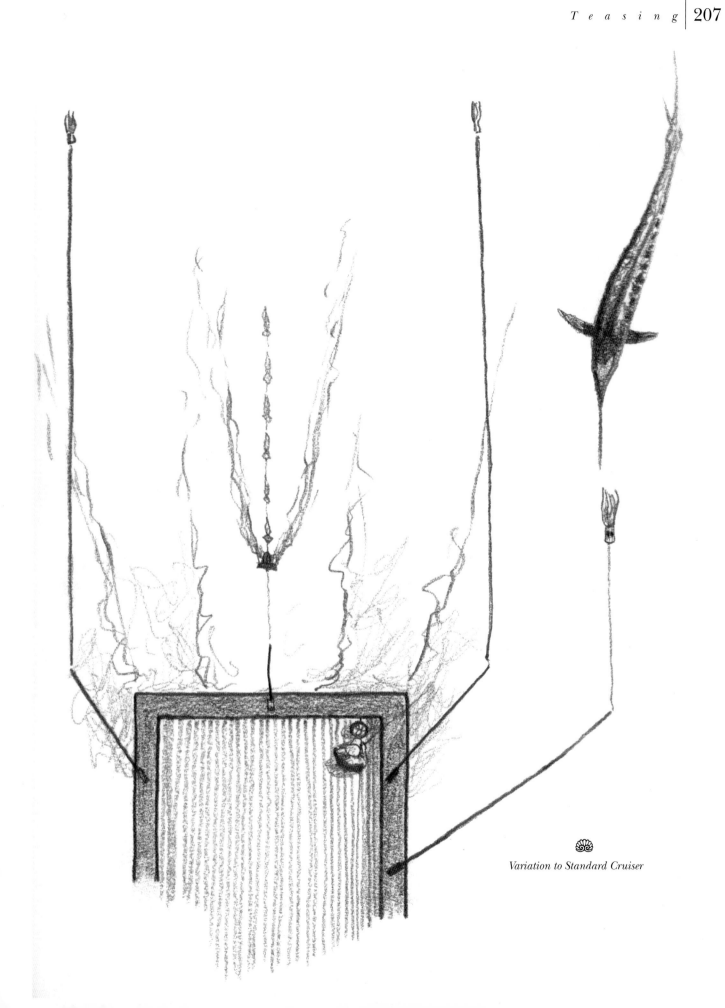

Variation to Standard Cruiser

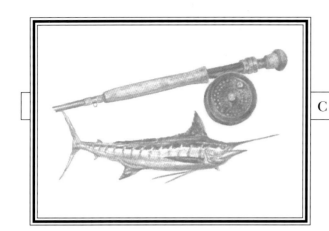

CHAPTER 20

RODS AND REELS

W hile writing *Bluewater Fly Fishing*, I was part of the Team Sage Advisory of the Sage Rod Company in Bainbridge Island, Washington. As a member of their pro staff, I was under

contract to endorse and use Sage rods. This arrangement never proved compromising. Sage had long been recognized as the leader in the production of high quality saltwater rods, doing so in a wider selection than any other manufacturer in the world. As a result, I was able to fish a number of different Sage rods, compare their actions, and see how they performed when I was fighting large and extremely strong offshore gamefish.

Sage never prevented me from fishing rods manufactured by other companies, and I did so whenever possible. Some of my companions on offshore fishing trips, superb anglers in every way, professionally represented other rod manufacturers: Ray Beadle for G. Loomis; Bryan Peterson for Thomas and Thomas; Nick Curcione, Jim Lepage, and Steve Huff for Orvis; and Kate and Bill Howe for Graphite USA. Fishing with these anglers, and other fly fishers associated with Sage such as Dave Whitlock, Lani Waller, and Mike Wolverton, I was able to compare rods, actions, and experiences "off the record." Working from the axiom that you're only as good as the company you keep, I developed a critical eye

for what really worked in the field, not what was just claimed to work in ridiculously overblown press releases.

RODS

Saltwater rods have come a long way since Joe Brooks sang the praises of a slow action 9½-foot Orvis Battenkill cane rod for his saltwater fishing. Brooks lived to see fiberglass replace cane, and to see the lighter and stronger graphite begin replacing fiberglass. During this progression, some wonderfully tough, fine-casting, fish-fighting glass rods, and a few simply awful boron rods, became part of a bluewater fly-fishing history. Today, graphite dominates saltwater fly fishing. Rods of this material have been made ever lighter, thinner walled, stronger, easier to cast, and, in most cases, fragile. Gone are the days when fly rods could spend a season bouncing around in the bottom of a Florida flats skiff and still be used to whip a 100-pound tarpon the next year. I now take care to never let my rods even touch the gunwale when the captain runs to a new destination.

Fiberglass-graphite composite rods show particular promise, both as casting and as fish-fighting rods. A few manufacturers are also discreetly looking into developing a modern line of fiberglass rods.

Manufacturers have always had tremendous latitude in designing fly rods. The International Game Fish Association (IGFA), the governing body that determines what is, and what is not, a world record gamefish based on the tackle and strength of leaders used, says only the following on the matter: "Regardless of material used or number of sections, rods must conform to generally accepted fly fishing customs and practices. A rod shall not measure less than 6 feet (1.82 meters) in overall length. Any rod that gives the angler an unsporting advantage will be disqualified. Extension butts are limited to 6 inches (15.24 cm)."

That's it. Nevertheless, somewhat out of tradition, at least 95% of all saltwater rods are 9 feet long. The remaining 5% are those longer—the 5-weights for fishing ultralight 1 and 2 kg class tippets; and those shorter—the brutish 14- to 18-weight big-game fighting sticks.

But beyond length, what should a fly fisher look for?

Action is difficult to describe because terms like "strong," "stiff," and "fast" are relative to the entire line of rods by a single manufacturer, and relative to the experiences of the fly fisher. Certainly a tarpon fisher and an angler whose principal fly-fishing experiences had been confined to spring creeks would view a "powerful" 7-weight from opposite ends of the barrel. Though not qualifying these terms, I still must say that I look for rods with stiff, powerful butt sections and fast tips for their ability to both lift and generate high line speed on the cast. Sages's Graphite III RPL-X Saltwater Series, rods from 7-weight to 14-weight, possess these and other attributes as well: high quality oversized guides that enable the caster to shoot line farther; a heavy duty saltwater reel seat with two locking rings that do not come loose; built-in fighting butts; a full wells grip; and, for rods from the 11-weight up, a large-diameter foregrip.

I'll discuss these assets one by one, for each is key to trouble-free offshore fly fishing.

GUIDES

Salt water corrodes guides unless they are of the very highest quality. Under heavy stress, the abrasion-resistant rings in stripping guides may blow out. If the guides themselves, including the snake guides, are not hard as well as resistant to corrosion, they will be grooved by the new superthin, ultrahard, gel-spun polyethylene backings now in use.

REEL SEATS

Reel seats should be massively strong, nonmetallic, up-

locking, with two locking rings separated by an O-ring. Cheap, poorly designed reel seats are a pet complaint of mine. I have fished rods that required me to keep tightening the rings while fighting a big gamefish, a terrible distraction when all of my attention should have been devoted to the sailfish or marlin. I vividly recall a 10-second sequence in which my client struck a sailfish, his reel fell off, and the fish exploded out of the blocks. The reel hissed and bounced around the transom like a drop of water in a pan of hot grease. I dove for the direct drive reel and, miracle of miracles, caught the edge of the reel opposite the rim control. As I held the reel, the big sail ran out nearly 200 yards of backing. When it paused for breath, I put the reel back on and cursed the rod manufacturer. Thirty minutes later, the sail was boated.

I should point out that reel manufacturers are also capable of producing reel feet so clunky that the reels don't fit properly in the fly rod's reel seat. Obviously, this kind of discovery should be made before leaving home.

FIGHTING BUTTS

Fighting butts should be built in and not require attachment after a fish is hooked. They don't need to be long—two inches is sufficient if the rod has been designed with an uplocking reel seat. This will usually place even five-inch-diameter reels at least the length of the fighting butt off your stomach.

FIGHTING BELTS

If a person is heavyset, the fighting butt can disappear into fat, leaving the reel's rim control to foul on the stomach, the shirt front, and whatever else hangs down. A fighting belt takes care of this problem, and protects anyone from a sore midsection. *Sometimes.* Fighting belts were not designed for fly rods, particularly not gimballed belts—those, that is, designed to accept the gimballed butt sections of rods deeply grooved four times, 90 degrees apart. These grooves fit into the socket of a fighting belt containing a heavy cross of wire in its base. Fly-rod butts are usually not gimballed, and they are often too large to fit into this arrangement. This applies in particular to 12-weight and larger rods. The exceptions: Sage's GFL 1390 and GFL 1489. Both rods come with a tight-fitting rubber butt cap that covers the hard plastic gimballed butt when it's not in use.

The fighting butts on fly rods often shear off because fly fishers jam the butts into the sockets of fighting belts, subjecting them to angles and stresses never intended by the manufacturer.

Gimballed big-game rods are pointed up and generally

kept above the horizontal when used in fighting chairs. Fly rods point down during the fight, never getting much above the horizontal. For this reason, fighting belts with sockets to accept the butts of fly rods—gimballed or otherwise—currently have limited application.

One satisfactory solution has been the leather or heavy nylon belts weightlifters use for back support. Once strapped on, such a belt can be turned around to provide a large, flat surface for the butt of the rod to rest against. The belts can be made even better if a thin layer of rubber padding is added to the hard surface. This lets the butt sink in a bit, preventing it from slipping during the fight. Another solution involves a fighting belt with a very shallow cup. This prevents the fighting butt from getting down so deeply that the rod angles necessary for fighting a fish are restricted or even denied.

CORK GRIPS AND FOREGRIPS

Cork grips should be constructed of cork of the highest quality and shaped to a full wells grip. Cheap, deeply pitted cork wears badly and is hard on the hands. A large, full wells grip, one that tapers to no more than ⅞ inch in diameter, and remains at least 1⅛ inches in diameter under the hand, helps prevent fatigue and cramping. Any tapering toward the end of the cork grip should be avoided.

Foregrips, usually built out of cork, are a fly-rod addition long associated with big gamefish. I've found them extremely desirable on two counts. When pumping up a big fish from the depths, the foregrip gives the hand—and hands—something substantial to grasp. This helps prevent the hand from cramping. (Fat foregrips are user friendly but unappealing aesthetically to fly fishers and manufacturers alike.) When a greyhounding billfish leaves hundreds of feet of slack line on the water, or when a captain is backing down the boat toward a billfish, a fly fisher must wind as fast and as hard as he can. Grasping a foregrip, rather than the rod, helps him steady the rod, prevent it from swinging back and forth as line is retrieved, and keep the line going onto the reel evenly.

A foregrip must be of sufficient diameter to do any real good; ⅞ inch is good, 1 full inch better. A skinny foregrip, one less than ¾ inch in diameter, causes the hand to cramp quickly. A temporary solution involves duct-taping foam rubber over the foregrip to increase its diameter, or over the rod itself if no foregrip exists. Another temporary foregrip can be shaped out of cork rings cut in half longitudinally, and taped in place on the rod.

FLY-ROD NOTES

ULTRALIGHT RODS AND 1 AND 2 KG (TWO- AND FOUR-POUND) CLASS TIPPETS

Taking any offshore gamefish on two- and four-pound class tippets remains among the sport's greatest challenges. I recall asking Dave Inks about the 5-pound, 14-ounce world record yellowfin tuna he took on a four-pound tippet.

"What special fish-fighting methods did you use, and how did you set up your tackle?"

He laughed and said, "If you try it, just bring lots of class tippets!" Inks broke off more than forty small yellowfin before bringing his record tuna to the net!

Inks's achievement is remarkable simply because a 5-pound yellowfin possesses sufficient speed and strength to break a 4-pound leader just by line drag. The reduction of that drag remains key to fishing these ultralight tippets.

Fly fishers use different methods to reduce drag and prevent break-offs. The IGFA does not stipulate how long a fly line must be and any length, even a foot, must meet its rules. However, the fly line must also be cast, and hopefully that prevents pure stunting. Shooting tapers of 10 or 12 feet can be cast. No effort should be made to match the shooting taper with the rod; underlining is both necessary and expected. Shooting line should be of a much finer monofilament than normal: 8- or 12-pound instead of 25 to 40. Backing is key; superthin gel-spun polyethylene lines in the lightest practical test should be used. (For example, Fenwick's cobwebby "Iron Thread" 8-pound has the diameter of 3-pound.) Rods must be soft and longer than normal to absorb the shock of the fish, yet must still be able to lift. I personally find the 10-foot 5-weights that fly fishers like to cast from float tubes about ideal for 4-pound class tippets and small schoolies, whether tuna, dorado, or bonito.

Selecting an appropriate reel becomes especially critical. I would choose a lightly built direct drive reel with a simple click mechanism (the Abel TR/3 is such a reel), or a saltwater rim control model with a superb, satin smooth drag backed almost completely off, the hand alone preventing the overrun. This recommendation leaves a large field. Success will depend in large measure on the fly fisher's ability, and whether he or she is able to follow the hooked fish.

Anglers delighted over the strength and length of runs delivered by 5-pound rainbows will be dumbfounded that a tuna about the size and shape of a football can blister off 50 yards of backing in several seconds.

7-WEIGHT RODS

A 7-weight rod is generally the lightest and least-used in my arsenal of offshore fly rods. I fish these rods with six- and eight-pound tippets where schooling tuna and dorado are dependably small. Examples include the three- and four-pound skipjack found around Hawaiian FAD buoys; black skipjack of up to five pounds that may school off headlands for weeks; and school dorado, which in places are consistently under 30 inches long, that is, 5 pounds or less. Where offshore and inshore fish mingle, I've been delighted to have my 7-weight along to cast for rainbow runners; a number of small jacks, including the ubiquitous green jack (*Caranx caballus*); school amberjack; Pacific barracuda; sierra mackerel (*Scomberamorus sierra*); bonito; pink salmon (humpback salmon); and even giant needlefish. Examples: Sage 709RPL-X Saltwater, Loomis FR1087, Thomas and Thomas HS 90 S.

8-WEIGHT RODS

I've used 8-weight rods with 8-pound tippets to take juvenile bigeye tuna from 7 to 11 pounds, numerous yellowfin tuna in the 5- to 10-pound range, and both black skipjack and kawakawa tuna of up to 11 pounds. In my view, any tuna over 10 pounds is really too much fish for an 8-weight. The 8-weight handles silver salmon (coho), chum salmon, and chinook salmon in the 8- to 15-pound range without difficulty. Like 7-weight rods, 8-weights have wide application for a variety of inshore gamefish. Examples: Sage 809RPL-X Saltwater, Loomis FR1028/9, Thomas and Thomas HS 908 S.

9-WEIGHT RODS

When school dorado are running up to 15 pounds, with the occasional bull topping 20 pounds, I like to set up two rods: a 10-weight for poppers, and a 9-weight for 2/0 Sea Habits, both Bucktails and Deceivers. The 9-weight does a decent job on tuna of up to 15 pounds. It is also an excellent one-rod choice for Pacific salmon in saltwater. Only when ocean chinook salmon regularly top 20 pounds do I feel a need to go to a heavier rod. Examples: Sage 909RPL-X Saltwater, Loomis 1028/9 Mega Taper Saltwater, Thomas and Thomas HS 909 S.

10-WEIGHT RODS

If I could fish only two rods for bluewater fly fishing, one would be a 10-weight, the other a 13-weight, and both would probably get the same amount of use. The 10-weight is an ideal choice for dorado and tuna of up to 20 pounds. (On a recent long-range fly-fishing trip, I landed a 28-pound yellowfin tuna on a 10-weight. The experience was not a lot of fun.) This is the lightest rod that I can use to cast my Mylar-covered, cork-bodied Gaines poppers I so like for dorado and tuna. The 10-weight is also my first choice when casting a full-sinking forward taper line for deep-running chinook salmon.

Using my Sage 10-weights, I have hooked several small sailfish, both Atlantics off West Africa and Pacifics in the Sea of Cortez. The rods were up to the task, for the fish weighed 50 pounds or so. Were I to go after billfish with 8-pound class tippets, I would choose to do so with a 10-weight rod.

I've fished every class tippet from 8- to 20-pound using 10-weight rods, but I've not always done so wisely. Once while fishing poppers on 20-pound tippets for 15- and 20-pound Atlantic jack crevalle, I broke two 10-weights on these bruisers in just a few minutes. I find that 8- and 12-pound tippets match my 10-weights perfectly. If recreating with dorado and midsized tuna while fishing 8 and 10 kg tippets, I do so knowing that if I lean hard enough on the fish the 10-weight rod will shatter.

Note: The Sage 10-weight in the RPL-X Saltwater Series can dead lift 12 pounds. Other examples: Loomis FR10210/11 Mega Taper Saltwater, Thomas and Thomas HS 910 S.

11-WEIGHT RODS

This is an odd size, and one not commonly used. That's unfortunate, because for many anglers, an 11-weight is just about the most powerful rod that can be cast continuously for long periods of time.

This is an excellent choice when fishing 12-pound tippets for Atlantic sailfish and wahoo. My big dorado sticks have always been 11-weights; one of my largest bulls, a 35-pounder, came on an old 11-weight Sage RP. Tuna of 25 pounds, whether blackfin, yellowfin, or albacore, will put tremendous stress on an 11-weight, but the rod is up to the task if the angler understands that it can be broken on a 16-pound tippet.

I find an 11-weight a very practical choice when fishing 12- and 16-pound tippets in heavy seaways. As the boat rises and falls a story at a time, the slightly softer and more forgiving 11-weight big-game stick, when teamed with a high quality reel, cushions the shock and helps prevent a broken tippet.

Note: The Sage 11-weight Graphite III RPL-X Saltwater rod can dead lift 16 pounds. Another example: Loomis FR10811/12 Meg Taper Saltwater.

12-WEIGHT RODS

For most fly fishers, the 12-weight is at just about the top end of what they can pick up, false cast, and actually make work as it was designed to work. For that reason alone, this rod has wide application. It's an ideal choice for chasing after tuna that regularly top 25 pounds—and may top 30; and for wahoo and dorado of any size, if fishing 16-pound class tippets. The 12-weight is generally my rod of choice for white marlin, the small black marlin found off Australia's Cape Bowling Green, Atlantic sailfish, and small Pacific sailfish such as those typically found in the Sea of Cortez. Examples: Sage 1209RPL-X Saltwater, Loomis FR10812/13 Mega Taper Saltwater, Thomas and Thomas HS 912 S.

13-WEIGHT RODS

When I first visited Costa Rica to fly fish for Pacific sailfish, the maximum class tippet the IGFA allowed was 8 kg (17.6 pounds), and I tied up my Bimini Twist class tippets with 15- or 16-pound Mason. (This leader typically had a breaking strength of about 17 pounds.) At the time, I thought of my Sage 12-weight as a *casting rod*, and my Sage 13-weight as a *fighting stick*, but either rod would break before the class tippet parted. How the two rods cast was never an issue because usually only a single back-cast was necessary to get a hookup. I fought sails with both, and more and more came to rely on the 13-weight because of its greater lifting power when pointing the rod down, leaning back, and lifting up on the foregrip *with both hands*. That is not to say that the 12-weight wouldn't get the job done. It would. But I found that the rod took a deeper set and forced me to keep my hands higher than did the 13-weight. In the end, because casting was such a minor part of my fishing, the 13-weight proved less fatiguing when fighting large Pacific sails and blue marlin on 8 kg class tippets.

When the IGFA added the 10 kg class tippet category in 1992, the Sage company beefed up its 12- and 13-weight rods, and then added a 14-weight model that was 8 feet, 9 inches long. The new 12-weight could dead lift 18 pounds. My impression was that that the new Sage "Saltwater Series" 12- and 13-weight rods were 1 weight more powerful than previous models.

Since its introduction, I have used the 13-weight Sage RPL-X more often than any other rod when fishing the new 10 kg class tippet for the largest offshore big gamefish. These included yellowfin tuna of over 40 pounds, Australia's black marlin, Baja California's striped marlin, both Atlantic and Pacific blue marlin, wahoo of over 50 pounds, and New Guinea's dogtooth tuna.

For a number of reasons, the Sage 13-weight has become my "all-purpose" big-game rod.

The 13-weight possess tremendous lifting power.

After a few broken rods, the angler gains a keen sense of exactly how much tension can be brought to bear without the rod breaking in half. I like a big-game rod to break just before the 10 kg class tippet goes. (This assumes that the class tippet has not been abraded, nicked, or otherwise weakened.) In this manner I can balance my maximum efforts against what the rod will take. As I become fatigued, and my fish-fighting techniques become sloppy and then downright spastic, I'm less likely to break my 10 kg tippet than I would be if using a more powerful rod—one that when put under maximum load could break off the fish.

The Sage 13-weight can be cast. This is extremely important when chasing after outsized tuna and schooled-up striped marlin, for many casts must be made, often for as much distance as possible.

The Sage 13-weight is otherwise user friendly. The rod has a rubber-covered gimballed butt, a large foregrip, and, as with all rods in the Sage Saltwater Series, comes in a three-piece model that can load into my carry-on rod tube.

Other examples, both superb: Loomis FR10213/15 Mega Taper Saltwater, and Thomas and Thomas HS 8613 S (8'6").

14/15-WEIGHT RODS

If stronger means better, then why not 14- and 15-weight rods? Why not 18-weight rods?

I believe such rods have their place, and more of them are sure to appear on the market in the years ahead. But I believe their application is limited, and generally misunderstood.

Fly rods are not ballistic whereby you pull a trigger, and the bigger the bore and bang, the larger the animal that keels over. Fly rods are more like bows—only more so. Whatever you shoot, you must be able to pull back and make perform. In short, an 18-weight rod is largely worthless in the hands of all but a very small percentage of fly fishers.

Extremely powerful rods require a very strong and able caster if they are to be used to cast a fly line (as opposed to trolling a fly). Placing these rods under heavy loads requires both strength and endurance on the part of the angler. That is another way of saying the rods place a premium on the angler's overall fitness. It's fine to giggle over the fact that a rod can dead lift 25 pounds. But so what? How long can a person hold even half that weight before the back and arms fizzle out? Try it for ten minutes! Never mind that a 100-pound yellowfin or a 200-pound blue marlin may take several hours to beat. And if you're not hunting for these fish with your 15- or 18-weight, *what are you fishing for?* More importantly, fully loading up such a rod can break a 10 kg class tippet, the strongest allowed by the IGFA. That means that as the rod loads up, the angler must be physically strong enough to hold a certain stress point on the rod, *but not go beyond that point*, and to do so through long periods of fatigue and pain as boat and gamefish endlessly change positions.

Such rods most definitely have a place in fly fishing. In my view they come into their own when extremely strong fish must be pumped up from great depths, or when the absolute maximum pressure must be applied to bring a timely end to a fight. Examples of the latter occurred on two recent long-range fly-fishing trips off Baja California. My companions and I boated over forty striped marlin using 14- to 17-weight rods and 10 kg class tippets. When we were able to lock up the drags and force the marlin to tow the rubber skiffs right after they had finished their initial jumping, we were able to so severely exhaust the fish that several were brought alongside for a safe release in under twenty minutes. Even marlin well over 100 pounds were being billed in under an hour. This kind of pressure would simply not have been possible with lighter rods.

Rods of these weights possessing gimballed butts can be used in conjunction with fighting belts and harnesses.

Offshore fly fishers need to get the rod tip as straight down as possible before lifting with both hands, so that the entire rod and the entire angler take the load of the lift. But fighting belts currently in use were not designed to be used with any rod in this position. However, if a harness can snap to the rod, and the rod be held horizontally, the rod should have sufficient strength in its upper half to stress a deep-holding big-game fish while providing time for the angler to rest the arms and hands. Circulation can be immediately improved, while cramping and muscle spasms can be put off, even avoided. When the fight continues, the angler unsnaps the harness, covers the gimballed butt with a rubber cap, and gets on with the business at hand.

Note: I personally do not use either a belt or a harness in my offshore fly fishing. Fighting belts designed specifically for fly fishers will likely appear on the market in the near future. I would be interested in trying one of these harnesses, particularly if going after large tuna and anticipating a long fight.

I would like to see 14- to 18-weight big-game fly rods of 7 to 7½ feet, sticks that reduce the leverage on the angler, and work more efficiently when "short stroking" a large gamefish to the surface.

REELS

The introduction of Tycoon/Fin-Nor and Seamaster reels in the early 1950s led directly to the development of bluewater fly fishing as we know it today. For the first time, large tuna, sailfish, and even marlin could be taken down by fly fishers. Fortunately, these reels from south Florida are still being manufactured. They currently have a lot of company, and not all of that company is wonderful.

I look for the following features in a reel I intend to fish offshore:

1. *Reliable drag.* Regardless of the material incorporated in the drag system, the breakaway torque—"start up" drag—should not exceed the pounds of drag setting. That is to say, if I want five pounds of drag, I don't want six pounds of initial inertia to be required to set those five pounds of drag in motion—to have no initial *stick* to get the drag going. Sound simple? Not so. Remarkably few reels can claim a drag so smooth.

2. *A drag with muscle.* The first revelation freshwater fly fishers experience when fishing the salt is how much drag is possible before the tippet breaks, especially if fishing an 8 kg or a 10 kg. Once a fish has settled down, I tell clients that if they can't pluck a tune on their backing, they're not in synch with the task at hand. That means at least 10 pounds of drag. Some otherwise fine reels have drags that either can't be set high enough, or else have a high setting that sticks, the breakaway torque exceeding the drag setting.

3. *A reel spool that won't distort when backing is wound on under load.* Dacron or monofilament, when stretched and wound on a reel, possesses enough energy to spread the flanges of lightly constructed spools. This is not something reel manufacturers like to discuss. If possible, ask anglers and charter boat captains who recreate and work at the cutting edge of offshore fly fishing. They'll have some horror stories to tell that you'll almost certainly find illuminating.

4. *Rim control.* Regardless of whether fishing antireverse or direct drive reels, you need to be able to instantly increase or decrease drag manually.

5. *Hard anodizing that goes deep into the metal and resists scratches.* Many offshore boats have a nonskid surface made up of volcanic sand mixed with gel coat. This surface can make a new reel look like an old reel in an afternoon.

6. *Aluminum bar stock construction: one-piece frame and spool.* Many of the best reels are milled from solid blocks of aluminum. This eliminates the posts and screws that connect to the side plates found in frame construction. All additional materials, mostly machine screws that hold handles, drags, reel seats, and so forth together, must be made of noncorrosive metals—stainless steel and bronze.

7. *Large reel handle.* Small Micky Mouse reel handles cause hand fatigue, and cause the forefinger to cramp.

DIRECT DRIVE AND ANTIREVERSE REELS

Fly reels come in two basic types: direct drive models, in which the handle turns with the spool, and antireverse models, in which the spool turns (pays out line) while the handle remains stationary. Each type has its advocates. Direct drive reels can be "knuckle busters," the run from an offshore fish causing the handle to turn into a blur. At such times, more than a few anglers have had fingers mauled, even broken. But this type of reel is ultimately positive, and clearly the superior choice when fishing light tippets. When the drag is backed nearly off antireverse reels to protect light tippets, the result is so much slippage that the reel becomes useless.

I like direct drive reels when I'm about to boat a large, still-unpredictable gamefish. I can back off the drag yet maintain any degree of pressure I wish by using the rim control reel. In this manner I can hold the fish's head up so that it can be billed—or gaffed, if a record—but remove my hand and instantly protect the tippet if the fish surges away.

If direct drive reels are used on long-running billfish, for which the drag setting must be repeatedly changed, it is critical that the reel has the drag knob opposite the handle side. If the handle and drag knob are on the same side, the drag setting can't be changed until the handle stops spinning.

I have used antireverse reels many times, and recommend them to clients, especially to those anglers who are not experienced with big-game fish. I find several advantages to their use. As the freshly hooked fish begins tearing away, any running line stripped in can be led to the reel without danger of the handle's sudden start-up causing injury. I can change the drag setting for clients, and for myself, depending on the behavior and fatigue of a billfish even as it takes out line. (Clients are often unaware of my participation, so mesmerizing is the sight of a jumping billfish.) If a high flying fish reverses itself when close in, and the angler is reeling, the antireverse prevents a break-off.

In my view the most notable downside of using antireverse reels occurs when the fish is nearly beaten, remains close in, and the angler has really set up the drag. If a fish suddenly comes to life and jumps, wallows, and surges, it is difficult if not impossible to immediately back off the drag—the drag wheel on some models require at least a 360-degree turn to reach the reduced level of resistance desired.

BACKING CAPACITY

Any reel with a sound drag system that has the capacity to hold 300 yards of 30-pound Dacron can withstand the *initial run* of almost any offshore gamefish a fly fisher is likely to ultimately beat. I should add that once a fish has 300 yards of backing on the water, control of the fight has pretty much passed to the fish. That being the case, why are reels capable of holding 600 yards, or even 1,000 yards? The answer is rate of retrieve. Fly reels have a 1:1 rate of retrieve. The obvious: The larger the diameter of the spool, the greater the rate of retrieve. This is all-important when a fish reverses itself and comes back at an angler; or when a captain is backing down on a billfish that seems intent on heading over the horizon; or when he is running down to bill a suddenly exhausted marlin. Bottom line: Rate of retrieve translates into control, and control translates into constant stress on the fish.

I recall some years ago when fishing for Pacific sailfish with a tarpon-sized antireverse reel. A very hot sail made an initial run that very nearly emptied the reel, and left me with a backing circle the size of a quarter. My rate of retrieve was reduced to less than three inches per reel turn. As I reeled, the captain backed down the boat, and the fish got rested. It took me a long time to get into position to again stress that sail. The entire business was sloppy.

Reel manufacturers are finally appreciating the fact that for offshore fishing, diameter and rate of retrieve matter more than capacity. It's not just reels that are increasing in diameter; in some case their arbors are increasing in diameter, too. That makes a lot of sense. Why pack on 300 yards of backing you'll never use and weight you don't need just to obtain a desirable diameter and a better rate of retrieve? It's much better to have 600 yards of backing on a reel 5 inches in diameter than to have the same amount on a wider model only 3¾ inches in diameter.

A secondary reason for favoring a relatively narrow, large-diameter reel involves the use of the superthin gel-spun polyethylene backing in which, for example, 50-pound is the same diameter as 12-pound braided Dacron. A lot of this backing can be in the water without radically changing the reel's rate of retrieve.

DRAG SYSTEMS

The compression or compression-disk drag, in which the reel spool is compressed against a contact surface of cork or cork composite remains the standard among the best reels currently being manufactured. What is added as a binder to the ground-up cork—the cork composite—can be a space-age, top secret kind of thing with the manufacturer. For this reason, no single servicing oil properly maintains all the drag systems in all saltwater reels. To avoid a drag system that suddenly gets cranky from improper lubrication, check with the manufacturer and follow the recommendations precisely.

Below are brief descriptions of a few of the best reels manufactured today that I have used personally.

SEAMASTER
4615 Le Jeune Road, Dept. SWS
Coral Gables (Miami), FL 33146

Bob McChristian, a part-time south Florida charter-boat captain from 1935 to 1941, quit his job as an Eastern Airline executive in the late 1940s and opened up Captain Mack's Tackle Shack in Miami. Legend has it that after his fly reel repeatedly failed on the big tarpon of Government Cut, he began working on designing a reel of his own. Two years of tinkering and field testing resulted in an antireverse reel a generation ahead of its time. McChristian would make a dozen reels to sell to friends, and lose money on every one. In the early 1950s, he closed his retail business and opened up a machine shop in Coral Gables. In 1953 McChristian marketed the first Seamaster reel.

No saltwater reel in the world today possesses the mystique of a Seamaster. Each handmade reel has doublesealed ball bearings, an anodized finish that rates a 9—out of a possible 10—on the Moh's scale (diamonds are a 10), and a large cork drag with absolutely no breakaway torque.

Seamasters are currently manufactured in direct drive and "dual mode" models, the latter antireverse when the fish is running, and direct drive when the angler is cranking. Offshore models in the dual mode include the "Mark III" (12-weight line and 300 yards of 30-pound backing); the "Marlin One" (12-weight line and 700 yards of 30-pound backing); and the "Marlin Two" (12-weight line and 1,000 yards of 30-pound backing).

TYCOON/FIN-NOR
2021 SW 31 Avenue
Hollandale, FL 33009

In the early 1930s, Fred Grieten, a mechanical wizard who worked at the Finley-Norwood Machine Shop in Miami, was asked by charter boat captain Tommy Gifford to produce a big-game reel that could handle the huge bluefin tuna and blue marlin that were destroying tackle off Bimini in the Bahamas. The result was the first Fin-Nor reel, a monster 18/0 milled from aluminum. These reels, in their characteristic gold color, were introduced to the public in 1935 and shortly became the standard for excellence in the big-game fishing market. From the beginning, the reels were marketed with Tycoon rods that the Biscayne Rod Company made in Miami, thus today's Tycoon/Fin-Nor Corporation.

In the early 1950s Gar Wood, Jr. designed a direct drive reel in a cage frame construction that proved so advanced that Fin-Nor picked up the patent. Production of Wood's prototype led to Fin-Nor's legendary series of gold "wedding cake" reels. Between 1955 and 1962, the Fin-Nor wedding cake reels were manufactured in four models, the No. 1 "Trout," the No. 2 "Salmon," the No. 3 "Tarpon," and the No. 4 "Marlin," a wide-spool version of the Tarpon.

Fin-Nor fly reels, No. 2 through No. 5, are offered in both direct drive and antireverse models. The two large offshore models are: No. 4 (12-weight line and 400 yards of 30-pound backing) and No. 5 (15-weight Scientific Anglers Billfish Taper and 700 yards of 30-pound backing).

BILLY PATE REELS/TED JURACSIK TOOL & DIE
900 NE 40th Court
Oakland Park, FL 33334

In 1975, World Wide Sportsman, Inc., owned by George Hommell and Billy Pate, received calls for more Seamaster reels than Bob McChristian could supply. Pate had ideas for a tarpon and billfish reel with features not yet available. This involved light weight and the least number of parts possible. Enter Ted Juracsik, a machinist in Oakland Park, Florida, who could translate Pate's design into a working reel. In honor of Pate, Juracsik called the prototype the "Billy Pate Tarpon." The resulting prototype for the "Tarpon" model was an immediate success, both because of its reliability, and because of the connection with Pate. Other models soon followed in both direct drive and antireverse: the "Bonefish," the "Salmon," and, most recently, the "Marlin."

Thanks to Ted Juracsik, when the Marlin first appeared on the market, I was able ultimately to get my hands on nine of them. For several seasons at Costa Rica's Bahía Pez Vela Lodge I equipped all my client with the antireverse model with rim control and never experienced a failure.

When I visited with Ted in the spring of 1994 at the International Sportsman's Expositions show in San Mateo, California, he showed me the prototype for his newest reel, the huge "Bluefin" model, sure to be a success among those fly fishers going after record tuna and marlin.

The two offshore models: the Tarpon (12-weight line and 300 yards of 30-pound backing) and the Marlin (12-weight line and 600 yards of 30-pound backing). Note: Three hundred yards of 30-pound backing on the Tarpon plus a 12-weight line makes for a very tight fit. The Tarpon becomes a much better offshore reel when 200 yards of 30-pound backing is topped off with 200 yards of one of the new superthin backing in either 40- or 50-pound test.

ABEL
165 Aviador Street
Camarillo, CA 93010

Steve Abel, a machinist from Camarillo, California, began working on developing a high quality fly reel in

1977. However, not until 1988 did he market the first Abel reel, the "2." Reels "O" through "5" soon followed; all were direct drive models. Despite a price tag more in keeping with the custom reels—the 5 initially retailed for $1,200—popularity for the Abel reels was immediate. Especially on the Pacific coast, the Abel reels dominated offshore fly-fishing circles after only a few years, a remarkable track record in the arcane high-end world of fly reels that are more the darling of collectors than fly fishers.

Abel succeeded for several reason. His reels are very attractive, possess one of the toughest anodized finishes in the business, and have drag systems that are satin smooth and dependable. Add the facts that Abel reels are readily available in fly shops around the country, and that the company has an excellent service records. (Regardless of how great a reel you make, if it takes political pull, a lot of money, and two years of waiting to get a reel, you're not a major player.)

I should comment on the Abel drag system. Abel experimented with cork composite, and cork-and-rubber composite, eventually determining the cork lubricated with *pure Neetsfoot oil* produced the smoothest drag. (Most across-the-counter Neetsfoot oil is cut with mineral oil. If you use this and the cork gets wet, the drag slips and grabs. Abel sells a lube kit that contains only pure Neetsfoot oil.)

I've fished offshore with Abel reels from the 2 to the 5. I've also fished a lot with Steve Abel, and we've had some great times together. But I buy my Abel reels, and Abel doesn't pay me to say nice things about them.

I'll list the backing capacities for Abel reels, and then describe how I set up the reels. Using 50-pound Spectra TUF line, by Western Filaments, Inc., I either top off the 30-pound Dacron backing, or fill the smaller narrow-diameter reels entirely with this backing. The manufacturer's backing figures have little relevance to me.

Abel 2 (8-weight line and 200 yards of 30-pound backing).

Abel 3N, the "N" for narrow (8-weight line and 225 yards of 20-pound backing): I pack nearly 400 yards of 50-pound ultrathin backing and a full-length 9-weight FT line, or shooting taper system, on this reel, turning it into a high-rate-of-retrieve bluewater giant killer and a remarkable reel for inshore gamefish. This has been my reel of choice when fishing the flats for permit.

Abel 3: Regardless of factory figures, the 3 actually has a greater capacity than the Billy Pate Tarpon. I pack on a 10-weight FT line and over 300 yards of 30-pound backing. When some of this Dacron is removed and replaced with 200 yards of 50-pound ultrathin gel-spun polyethylene backing, at least 400 yards of backing results.

Abel 4: A great reel but not my favorite; I would prefer more diameter, for a greater rate of retrieve, from such a muscle-bound reel. Capacity: 12-weight line and at least 350 yards of 30-pound backing. Because of its relatively small overall diameter, 3.375—identical to the 3—the wider 4 really shines when the 30-pound Dacron backing is topped off with 250 to 350 yards of 50-pound polyethylene backing.

Abel 4.5, (12-weight line and at least 450 yards of 30-pound backing): The star of the entire Abel line when fishing offshore. I fill the 4.5 with no more than 200 yards of Dacron backing, and then fill the reel with at least 400 yards of 50-pound polyethylene backing, resulting in over 600 total yards.

Abel 5: The first of the monster offshore reels, the Abel 5 offered anglers a huge drag surface and the kind of rate of retrieve that can make running down billfish almost enjoyable. The only problem anyone experienced was the spool spreading when Dacron or monofilament was wound on under extreme load. Following an initial production run, Abel brought out the 5 again in 1994 with a beefed-up spool. I recently boated several striped marlin using the "new" Abel 5, ultimately setting the drag at 18 pounds to bring the marlin to the surface. (The maximum drag setting is 22 pounds.) *This is a fabulous 10 kg reel.*

Late in 1994, Abel reels in antireverse became available.

ODYSSEY

The Orvis Company
Historic Route 7A
P. O. Box 798
Manchester, VT 05254-0798

In October 1990, Orvis hired Jim Lepage, a former Pratt and Whitney engineer whose specialty was metal joining, to design from scratch an entirely new "state-of-the-art" fly reel. The Odyssey, models "1," "2," "3," and "4," resulted from Lepage's years of research and development.

The somewhat futuristic Odyssey, with its rock-hard shiny black finish, features a tapered reel handle and recessed counterweight. After testing more than 200 drag materials, Lepage settled on a nitrate cork composite drag surface that can be lubed with just about any grease. The result is a satin smooth drag with no start-up inertia. Drag settings are infinite, with enough muscle left over to pop 10 kg tippets. On long runs under a hot tropical sun, the reel dissipates heat to the back side of the reel, and not to the rim control. Also, the reel can be easily changed from right- to left-handed. The Odyssey 3 holds 300 yards of 30-pound Dacron plus a 10-weight FT line. The Odyssey 4 holds 350 yards of 30-pound Dacron (or 650 yards of 50-pound Spectra TUF) plus a 12-weight FT line.

On a recent long-range fly-fishing trip out of Cabo San

Lucas, Mexico, I witnessed how well the Odyssey 4 performed. Jim Lepage and Steve Huff, the legendary Florida bonefish guide, were my shipmates. Each boated—and released—marlin using the Odyssey 4.

The four reel manufacturers thus far described market their reels approximately in the $450 to $1,500 range. Below are two additional reel manufacturers that have reels priced at less than $400.

STH Reels
P.O. Box 500816 (1000 15th Street)
Marathon, FL 33050-0816

STH reels are manufactured in Junin de los Andes, a small Patagonian village in the heart of Argentina's finest trout fishing. When I visited the area in 1988, I was fishing five STH freshwater reels and several of their company's newest saltwater models. Though I took many steelhead and a world record Pacific jack crevalle with one of the saltwater models, the reels were not without problems. The five freshwater reels, all sold through the Orvis Company, were as beautiful as their highly touted pawl system was ridiculous; on a hard strike, the reels went into free spool.

STH reels have come a long way since then. The company is now the largest manufacturer of machined fly reels in the world. Its entire line, from the "IM-Cassette" models starting at $100 (a favorite with many Alaskan guides), to the "Airweight Lever Drag" models at $250 (excellent for steelhead, salmon, and midsized inshore and offshore gamefish), to the "Grand Slam" models at $450 (beautifully engineered reels for big-game saltwater fish), are found in use worldwide. They are dependable, attractive, and a bargain.

Below are several STH models suitable for offshore fly fishing.

Caribbean (antireverse) and "Eliseo" (direct drive): 3½ inch, 8-weight line plus 220 yards of 20-pound backing; 3¾-inch, 10-weight line and 300 yards of 20-pound backing; 4-inch, 12-weight line and 350 yards of 30-pound backing.

Grand Slam (direct drive): 12-weight line and 350 yards of 30-pound backing.

Lamson
18080 NE 68th Street
Redmond, WA 98052

I was sent one of the first Lamson reels to come out of the Redmond, Washington plant to field test on British Columbia's Dean River. A year or so later, when John Harder joined Lamson as its chief design engineer, he loaned me reels for clients to fish in Costa Rica for Pa-

cific sailfish. The reels performed well and I've been a fan of Lamson ever since.

Four models in their Saltwater Series are suitable for offshore fishing: "Bonefish" (8-weight line and 250 yards of 20-pound backing), "Permit" (10-weight line and 250 yards of 30-pound backing), "Tarpon" (12-weight line and 300 yards of 30-pound backing), "Marlin" (13-weight line and 600 yards of 30-pound backing).

Lamson used a cork drag in all its saltwater reels. Each reel comes with a drag lubricant specific to the needs of these drags systems.

Based on comments from Lefty Kreh and Robert Trosset, I would add "Islander" and "Penn" fly reels to the above list. I personally have no experience with either reel.

CUSTOM REELS

I often think that every owner of a machine shop in the United States is at heart a custom crafter of fly reels. So many fly reels are now being milled in backyard shops that it seems like reel making has become a national cottage industry. Certainly the number of makes and models is far too vast to describe sufficiently in this text.

I have fished extensively with the reels of three manufacturers whose production remains small, but whose reels, like fine wines from small vintners, are destined to enter the mainstream of saltwater fly fishing through reputation alone.

Charleton
Outdoor Technologies, Inc.
1179-A Water Tank Road
Burlington, WA 98233

Jack Charleton, with a background in machining precision component parts for the medical and aerospace industries, entered the reel making business in 1992. His finely crafted reels, available in both aluminum and titanium, gained immediate acceptance, demand invariably exceeding production almost from the beginning.

These handsome reels, with bullet-proof black anodized finishes (aluminum), possess drag systems as smooth as any in the industry, thanks to six sealed stainless steel bearings. Each cork drag is completely sealed with a Vitron O-ring so that salt, grit, or water can't reach the drag to cause grief.

The Charleton Signature Series (the owner's signature is engraved into the sideplate) in both the "8500" (3.75-inch diameter in 0.8-, 1.2-, and 1.6-inch spool widths) and "8600" (4.75-inch diameter in 1³⁄₁₆-inch width) have wide application in offshore fly fishing. The 8600 is to die for: beautiful, functional, and the right size. I believe this reel will join the Abel 5 and 4.5, Billy Pate Marlin,

Seamaster's Marlin, and Fin-Nor's 5 as a standard of classic excellence for offshore big-game fish.

I have boated a variety of saltwater gamefish, from bonefish and permit, to striped marlin, on Charleton reels.

McNeese

McNeese Fishing Company
P.O. Box 21148
Salem, OR 97307

Dave McNeese, a longtime friend of mine from steelhead fly fishing, joined me several years ago in Costa Rica for a go at Pacific sailfish. When he arrived, the fly-shop owner from Salem, Oregon had brought along a box full of reels, handcrafted prototypes of the future McNeese reel that he hoped to manufacture. Before fishing one of his reels, I wondered why McNeese, big-bore hunter, expert with bow, tier of classic steelhead and salmon flies, dramatically fine fly caster, and generally all-around nice guy, would want to do this to himself, to bring out a reel under his own name in a market already glutted with just this kind of enterprise. The answer lay in McNeese, because whatever he set his mind to tended to be definitive, and his reels would be no exception. I took one, fished it hard, loaned it out, and by the end of a week it had kept on ticking through a dozen sailfish. The next year, same song. By that time, I'd become extremely fond of the reel, but as I was leaving Costa Rica's San Jose airport—zero security in this zoo—for Belize City, a primordial form of life raced away with my tackle bag and McNeese's reel. Insurance replaced the nine other reels stolen, but the McNeese prototype was one of a kind. I've been grieving over its loss ever since.

The McNeese antireverse reels for offshore fly fishing: the 3.2-inch "Bonefish" (9-weight line and 250 yards of 30-pound backing), the 4-inch "Tarpon" (12-weight line and 300 yards of 30-pound backing), and the 4.5-inch "Billfish" (600 yards of 30-pound backing).

Each reel has an oiled cork drag system and a spool insert of Dupont Vespel, a space age ceramic material that absorbs all the heat generated by the spool and remains forever corrosion-free.

Saracione

P.O. Box 372
Sandy, OR 97055

Joe Saracione builds reels that bring tears of nostalgia to salmon and steelhead fly fishers, modern reels masquerading as Vom Hoffs down to the last handcrafted screw. But Saracione can build a reel from the ground up, too, and his "Marlin" model, a 3 to 1 multiplier that weighs two pounds, holds any fly line you wish and 1,000 yards (and counting) of 30-pound whatever, and is probably the most powerful fly reel ever built. When I carted this reel to Mexico, I called it the "Black Death" and felt sorry for any fish that tried to eat a fly attached to it.

Saracione's entries into the saltwater sweepstakes are four old-style frame construction reels patterned after the "wedding cake" reels that Fin-Nor introduced forty years ago. With gold frames and black spools, and beefy cork drag systems, the reels will be instant collectibles for those who can't bring themselves to fish them. The reels are: "Bonefish" (3½-inch), "Permit" (3¾-inch), "Tarpon" (4-inch), and "Billfish" (4⅝-inch).

Saracione also manufactures a series of saltwater reels for Dave Inks. The Dave Inks Reels are essentially superbly machined copies of Seamaster reels, functional and collectible in every respect.

Based on comments from Ray Beadle, I would add Arculeta reels, by Bill Arculeta of Santa Rosa, California, to the above list of custom-built fly reels.

These billfish outfits were gathered from fly fishers participating in the 1994 Blue Water Fly Rod Invitational, a long-range fly-fishing trip that Ed Rice annually hosts. From left to right, the big-game reels: Billy Pate Marlin, Orvis Odyssey, Fin-Nor, McNeese Marlin, Abel 5, Abel 4.5, Arculeta, Seamaster, Charleton 8600.

FLY LINES, BACKING, LEADERS, KNOTS, AND ACCESSORIES

Whereas I happily pass weeks on British Columbia's steelhead-rich Skeena drainage with only three different fly lines, my saltwater lines would stock a fair-sized fly shop.

For offshore fishing, I typically fish rods from 7- to 15-weight, and lines that have sink rates from "II" (slow to medium), to "VI" (extremely fast), typified by Scientific Anglers Deep Water Express series of 550-, 700-, and 850-grain lines, which sink at rates of 7.5, 8.5, and 9.5 inches per second respectively.

Such an inventory requires careful organization. The following describes additional hybrid lines, how I prepare the various lines, when and how I use them, and how I keep the whole business organized.

FLY LINES

The reader should be aware that new saltwater fly lines are constantly appearing on the market, while lines of long standing are being improved by changes in tapers, core constructions, and line finishes. Though I try to get a jump on this ongoing technology by fishing experimental lines as part of the manufacturer's research and development programs, I still find the changes appearing at a

dizzying rate. As a result, I tend to describe lines somewhat generally, doing so in terms of line finishes, tapers, and sink rates, and how they relate to my fishing needs.

Regardless of line type and weight, I look for two attributes in lines for bluewater fly fishing. The first is stiffness. Stiff lines shoot better and are less likely to tangle, especially in tropical heat. The second is the toughness of the finish. Nonskid boat surfaces can be very abrasive. Fly lines with soft finishes can come up mangled after being ground underfoot on these areas. The latest generation of monocore lines is especially good at surviving this kind of rough treatment.

WF FLOATING

I do not use a floating line in bluewater fly fishing, ever, even when making long casts with poppers. Medium-sinking lines have a higher specific gravity, cut the wind better, and do not drag poppers down before a new cast must be made.

Carefully assembling one's tackle can result in successfully landing a magnificent gamefish such as this Pacific sailfish. Photograph by Neal Rogers.

WF Slow- to Medium-Sinking (II and III or about three to four inches/second)

I've fished two different stock lines that fall into this category. The first is Scientific Anglers orange-colored Mastery Series Ultra 2 Billfish line, a slow/medium sinker with a short belly, and an extremely steep front and back taper, so that lots of grains are as close as possible to the big, wind-resistant billfish flies and poppers being cast. Captains and anglers alike have complained about the orange color of the lines, but I've hooked *teased-in* white and blue marlin, and both Atlantic and Pacific sailfish, while using the lines, and I've never felt that the color discouraged the fish from eating the fly. Also, the orange line telegraphs the whereabouts and depth of a billfish, a fact that anglers new to the big-game field should appreciate. However, I do feel that the bright orange color and moderate sink rate are both distinct disadvantages when casting to free-swimming billfish, or to billfish that have broken off the tease and are being held with live chum, situations anglers are likely to experience on the LoPreste-Dunn long-range fly-fishing trips out of San Diego.

The second line I've used in this category is Scientific Anglers Mastery Series Tarpon Taper, a braided monocore line. This type of line doesn't have a single core. Instead, fine, loosely woven strands of monofilament are spread throughout the diameter of the line. The running line is pebbled to reduce line drag through the guides. This allows the lines to shoot extremely well. (The same finish also goes through skin like a saw, and an afternoon with big yellowfin tuna can leave you thinking you've been juggling razor blades.) I believe these are currently the best all-purpose, across-the-counter, full-length forward taper lines in bluewater fly fishing. I've taken countless tuna and dorado, and more than a dozen Pacific sailfish, with these lines, though they were not designed for billfish. I've found the lines especially useful when casting cork-bodied poppers to dorado and tuna working at or near the surface. If fishing one of these lines for billfish from offshore game boats where long casts aren't necessary, and where line drag remains a consideration, I cut 12 to 18 inches off the front end to get the large flies and poppers closer to more grains of line, and then cut the running line back so that the overall length of the line has been reduced from 110 feet to 60 feet. I attach this line directly to my backing.

WF Fast-sinking (IV and V or about four to six inches/second)

A weight forward line with a sink rate of IV or V is not wonderful to cast for distance because of the consider-able weight in the running line. However, the *fast-sinking running line gets the entire line down quickly*, and holds more of the line down in a horizontal curve. I think these lines have special application for inshore gamefish such as chinook salmon and yellowtail, tough fish not known for their long runs. However, high speed offshore fish put these lines under a tremendous amount of drag, the overall length and weight of the lines making them unsuitable for tuna, billfish, dorado, and wahoo. I would only use them as a last resort when fishing *10 kg class tippets* for deep-holding yellowfin tuna. I would then reduce the drag as much as possible by connecting the fly line *directly* to one of the ultrathin backings now available.

Teeny sink tip lines (28-foot sink tip)

The Teeny 300 and 400 with 24-foot sink tips, and the Teeny 500 with a 28-foot sink tip, have proven quite useful in my offshore fishing. The tips have Deep Water Express sink rates, and because of this, quickly take down even buoyant flies. I use the T-400 when serving up Sea Habit Bucktails for dorado, and the T-500 when going after big wahoo and billfish. Because the T-500 has a lot of grains near the huge flies I'm casting for marlin and sailfish, I'm able to turn the flies over and keep them motoring along on longer casts.

Jim Teeny's six new saltwater lines have widespread application in bluewater fly fishing. The 100-foot lines are color coded for easy identification, have 30-foot sink tips of Deep Water Express, and, beginning with the T-250, increase in weight at 100-grain increments up to the T-750. All the tips are dark green. The running lines are colored as follows: 250 (tan), 350 (red), 450 (green), 550 (purple), 650 (blue), 750 (orange).

Shooting taper lines

Shooting tapers—"shooting heads"—are manufactured in 30-foot lengths as floating lines, and as sinking lines with sink rates from I (intermediate) to VI. I most commonly use shooting tapers in two sink rates, a IV and a VI, the latter Scientific Anglers 550-grain Deep Water Express.

Because of the durability and shooting qualities of the opaque sinking monocore running lines in Scientific Anglers Mastery Series Bonefish and Tarpon lines, I save otherwise trashed lines solely for the running lines I can salvage from them. Using these lines as a starting point, I make up two basic shooting taper systems, one for the 10- to 11-weight rods I fish for school tuna and dorado of up to 35 pounds, the other for the 12- to 15- weight rods I fish for wahoo, large yellowfin, sailfish, and marlin.

Using 60 feet of running line cut from the Bonefish line, I secure 30-pound braided monocore loops at each end. I then loop this line to a 50-pound braided monocore loop attached to the butt end of a 26- to 28-foot 12- or 13-weight shooting taper, sink rate IV. The two to four feet I cut off comes from the back taper. To the front end of the shooting taper, I secure a 30-pound braided monocore loop that will, in turn, be looped to the tapered leader.

The 60 feet of Tarpon running line is prepared using 50-pound braided monocore loops at each end. I cut the 550-grain Deep Water Express shooting taper back to 26 feet, cutting 30 inches off the back taper and 18 inches off the front taper. This leaves a front taper of two to three feet, and very little back taper. I attach 50-pound braided monocore loops to each end of this line.

When casting either of these lines, I strip in the line until the shooting taper is in the tip-top guide and halfway down the rod. I roll cast the head out, letting a few feet of running line slip through my hand in the process. I then pick up the line, use the water to help load the rod, and, after one backcast, make my forward cast. No false casting is necessary. Almost the entire line shoots away on the forward cast.

It surprises many offshore fly fishers to discover that shooting tapers with sink rates of IV, V, and VI work quite well when fishing poppers. When casting either Edgewater's hard rubber poppers, or Gaines's cork-bodied poppers, with IV heads, I keep the rod tip up and rapidly strip back the popper. The line does hold down the face of the popper, but that only adds to its performance. In the case of Deep Water Express heads used on billfish, the foam head poppers in one-inch diameters usually get nailed by sailfish or marlin within a few seconds of their landings. Far more importantly, *the sinking head helps anchor the overbuoyant foam popper in place, providing a more stable target for the billfish to grab.*

If I find an especially deep sink is necessary, as when yellowfin are holding 60 or 70 feet down regardless of the amount of chum tossed their way, I can quickly switch to either the 700- or the 850-grain Deep Water Express head, cut back to 24 feet, and attach this head to a 150-foot running line of 25- or 30-pound monofilament.

I now use these combinations of monocore running line and heads, with sink rates of IV and VI, more than any other in my bluewater fly fishing.

The family of running lines currently commercially available, at diameters of about .029, are generally too limp and have too soft a finish for offshore work. However, on a recent trip to Florida, I fished a stiff, fast-shooting experimental monocore running line that tested 44 pounds. It proved superb. I believe that very shortly such monocore running lines in at least two diameters will be available commercially.

Organization of Fly Lines

Lefty Kreh's solution to this problem involves using an indelible marking pen and marking the tag end of the fly line, a long slash for a 5-weight line, with each short slash following designating the next line weight up. For example, a long slash followed by three short slashes would be an 8-weight line. As usual, Lefty has built a better mousetrap. With modifications, this system works well for my offshore fly fishing.

I use almost no full-length lines in offshore fly fishing of under 10-weight. If casting an 8-weight for school-sized bigeye tuna, I'll likely use a 10-weight shooting taper cut back to 26 to 28 feet. So to fill most of my needs, I must be able to quickly distinguish one shooting taper from another, plus know the weights of a few full-length monocore and billfish lines. Using Lefty's system, a single long slash in black (or whatever color you like), *made on the monocore loop*, stands for "10," a long slash followed by a short slash stands for "11," and so on. (This system can be duplicated for 5- to 9-weight lines by simply changing to another color.)

The series of Deep Water Express lines, and other super-fast-sinking lines, are often described solely in terms of grains, because they are so heavy that they fall outside the parameters of the number scale in grains established by the American Fishing Tackle Manufacturer's Association. To keep these specific lines from getting mixed, I use a different-colored slash on each monocore loop— blue for the 550-, red for the 700-, and green for the 850-grain Deep Water Express line. I do this regardless of how much I've cut back the line, for not only does the color indicate what line I've used, but it also tells me the sink rate and the grains per foot I'm casting.

When I get a new fly line, I break the spool apart, put a drop of Super Glue on the two halves, and fit them together again. Now the spool won't come apart when I'm winding line on or off. Using an indelible marker, I write the line I'm fishing on a piece of masking tape and place the tape on the underside of my reel seat. Another piece of identically marked tape identifies the plastic tool that carried the line. When I change that line, it goes back on the proper plastic spool. In this manner, I can check in and check out fly lines from a box holding dozens.

MONOFILAMENT RUNNING LINE

I don't commonly use monofilament in my offshore fly fishing, either as a running line, or as a shock-absorbing line between the fly line and the Dacron backing. My reasons are several.

Monofilament does not come off the reel memory-free. ("Amnesia" should refer to the angler who believes that it does, not to the monofilament with that name.) Unless an angler uses a stripping basket, mono blows all over the boat's transom area, gets in the way of other anglers, gets stepped on, and tangles. A nick in mono is fatal to its integrity. I've seen monofilament under tension break while being drawn through the thumb and forefinger of a gloved hand, the break occurring from the sudden build-up of heat.

I do use monofilament shooting line with Deep Water Express heads when the fish require an extremely fast and deep sink, when extra-long casts are necessary, or while carrying a stripping basket to wade in the surf or fish from rocky bays and headlands. I also use monofilament as a shooting line when putting together short shooting tapers for the 1 and 2 kg class tippet categories.

BACKING

I generally use 20-pound Dacron backing for single digit rods, and 30-pound Dacron for rods of 10-weight and up. But there is nothing hard and fast about this approach. If fishing 8- and 12-pound tippets (4 kg and 6 kg), I want the reduced drag that 20-pound backing provides. Conversely, the 10 kg class tippet calls for 30-pound backing because the class tippet would otherwise test higher than the backing.

I'm less than enthusiastic about braided Dacron backing because it wears so poorly. Almost any fly fisher who spends a lot of time offshore has a horror story to tell about his or her backing suddenly—and often mysteriously—parting.

Most often breaks occur at the connection to the fly line where wear is most severe. I've tried all sorts of connections, permanent and otherwise, including Bimini Twist loops. I don't like the Bimini Twist's large knot and twisted loop when I'm using 30-pound Dacron. I've also experienced line breaks at the point where I've sealed a four-turn Bimini "lock" with Super Glue. I've now settled on a loop made with a double surgeon's knot tied large enough to pass over a spool of fly line which facilitates a quick change of lines. When drawn tight, the double surgeon's knot is very small, makes a good square knot connection with the monocore loop at the end of the fly line, and passes easily through the rod. After a go at a couple of big gamefish, I cut off the loop and tie in another.

Because greyhounding billfish can break tippets simply from line drag, placing 100 to 200 feet of 30- or 40-pound monofilament between fly line and backing has been prescribed as an antidote. The monofilament is supposed to stretch, cushion the shock, and protect the tippet.

Really? Drag is caused by the resistance of line through the water, a product of diameter and weight. The drag of 30- and 40-pound monofilament through the water is not advantageous to that of straight 20- or 30-pound braided Dacron, for the two lines are approximately the same diameter. Braided Dacron has about thirteen percent stretch, while monofilament can have twice that amount, *but regardless of stretch, drag is drag.*

To reduce drag, one must reduce the diameter of the backing. This is most significantly accomplished by incorporating one of the new superthin gel-spun polyethylene lines into the backing system. As soon as it was available, I began using 50-pound Spectra TUF, by Western Filament, Inc., for all my reels destined to be fished on rods of 10-weight or higher, and 30-pound for rods of 9-weight and below. The 50-pound TUF Plus is smaller in diameter (.013) than either 12-pound Dacron or 15-pound monofilament; it is naturally waterproof, extremely abrasion resistant, and highly resistant to damage from sunlight. Stretch is but 2.7%, not really a factor, for the line knifes through the water with dramatically reduced drag.

I do not usually fill an entire reel with this backing for two reasons. The first is economy: I could easily wind a 1,000 yards on one of my big-game reels. That's far beyond anyone's ability to control and fight a fish with. The second reason relates to the problem of winding many yards of backing onto the reel under little or no tension, a sometime happening when a billfish runs right at an angler. This may or may not be a legitimate concern. But the superthin no-stretch backings can come back onto the reel grievously loose. If the line is then put under great tension, will it bury itself in the duff of the soft retrieve? Possibly.

I prefer to fill my big-game reels one-half to two-thirds full with 30-pound Dacron and then, depending on the reels' line capacities, top off the reels with 200 to 500 yards of the 50-pound TUF Plus. So thin is the backing that even with 200 yards out on my largest reels, little change occurs in my rate of retrieve.

I secure the *very slippery* backing to the braided Dacron backing with an Albright Knot, followed by a "lock." Using the Spectra, the lock is made by taking the tag end of the Albright and completing two half-hitches, and then taking eight turns around the standing line, pinning the tag end with thumb and forefinger at the end of the loop, and unwinding the eight turns on itself—creating, in effect, a nail knot—and gently pulling it tight. For additional security, I place a tiny drop of Super Glue on the lock, *and not on the single strand of Dacron.* When trimmed, the tiny knot passes easily through the guides.

When fishing 7- to 9-weight rods, I complete a Bimini Twist loop in the 35-pound Spectra backing and loop this to the fly line's 30-pound monocore loop. (Note: I lock the Bimini Twist and Super Glue it as described above.)

Terry Gunn showed me a clever way to prevent the loop of 35-pound Spectra from wearing excessively on the braided monocore loop. Before completing the Bimini Twist, he takes a two-inch length of Larva Lace (any color), passes a bobbin threader through it, and retrieves the tag end of the superthin backing. He then positions the Larva Lace to the end of the loop and completes a small Bimini Loop, and locks and seals it with Super Glue as described.

When fishing 10- to 15-weight rods, I Albright the Bimini Loop of 50-pound backing directly to the braided monocore loop, locking the knot with two half-hitches and a four-turn lock, and applying Super Glue to the connection as described above. This becomes a semi-permanent connection, but it prevents the backing loop from bearing and wearing directly on the monocore loop—a concern when fights with big-game fish go on for hours. To separate the backing from the fly line, I use a razor blade to carefully cut the backing free from the monocore loop.

The first fall I used this 50-pound TUF Plus backing, I fought seven white marlin, five striped marlin, a monster of an Atlantic blue marlin, and two wahoo of over 50 pounds without changing the backing connection and without a serious mishap. One of these striped marlin took me across the ocean for five hours, the backing banjo-string tight for much of the time. Whenever I retrieved line, I worked it well back and forth on the spool, spreading out the turns. Whether this was helpful, I cannot say. But the line did not bury itself under the extreme loads and it caused me no trouble.

A more dramatic view of the line's advantages occurred when I sailed on *Shogun*, a 92-foot, long-range LoPreste-Dunn fishing boat out of San Diego, California. On the fifth day at sea, I was free casting to a school of chummed-up striped marlin when the single Pacific sailfish in the group grabbed the fly. Captain Norm Nagato helped me run down the 90-pound fish, the first billfish ever taken while fly fishing on a long-range boat. From my vantage on the bow, and from Nagato's above me on the bridge, we saw how the superthin backing followed the fish with almost no deflection.

CONNECTIONS

MONOCORE LOOPS

When I began taking clients to Costa Rica's Bahía Pez Vela Lodge for Pacific sailfish, I would check out their equipment, first devoting critical attention to the manner in which they had connected their leader to their fly line, and then to how they had connected their fly line to their backing. Almost invariably they had borrowed from their freshwater experiences, and I would suggest changes. These I made myself, spending my first evening in camp cutting off leaders and terminating both ends of their fly lines with braided monocore loops. Completing these connections was tedious, but worth the effort. I've fought many saltwater gamefish using these monocore loops, including examples of five species that each ran over 100 pounds, and I've never had even one of these loops blow out. (Note: When fishing 10 kg class tippets for big-game fish, avoid having 30-pound braided monocore loops in your system. They won't blow out when tied as described below. Eventually, however, they'll break.)

Depending on the diameter of the fly line and the class tippet used, I make my own loops from either 30- or 50-pound Cortland Braided Mono by using a Matarelli Bobbin Threader. (A similar, less refined tool can be made by bending a six-inch piece of 30-pound single strand wire in half until if forms a flat loop at one end.) After cutting off six inches of monocore from the 100-foot spool, I insert the threader approximately two inches from the end, run it two inches up the center of the monocore, and then out the side. The other end of the monocore is then caught with the threader and pulled down into the center of the monocore, forming an even smaller loop until the threader is withdrawn. After the threader is removed, the small amount of monocore sticking out the side can be removed by pulling gently on the loop until this tag end has been drawn back into the center. I prefer to keep the loop small—½ inch or less. The result is a monocore loop three to four inches long that can be slipped nearly two inches over the fly line before the core of the loop butts against the fly line. After slipping the monocore loop over the fly line, I put a very small amount of Super Glue at the fly-line end of the loop, and where the fly line and the loop butt. This helps prevent the loop from slipping during the next two steps. After the Super Glue has thoroughly dried, I place a five-turn nail knot of eight-pound hard nylon over the end of the monocore loop, making the knot tight enough so that it digs slightly into the fly line, but does not cut through the finish. Using clippers, I trim off the two tag ends of the monofilament, and any bristles of monocore that stick out. I then place a hook in my fly-tying vise. (Clip off the eye first, for best results.) I place the monocore loop over the hook shank, pull down on the fly line until the loop is straight, and then, using a toothpick, cover the entire loop with a thin, even coat of Aquaseal, careful to work it deep into the braid. I finish off this step by carefully running a bead of Aquaseal around the nail knot at the very end of the loop. When done properly, the loop becomes opaque, contains no runs, and acts much like the fly line itself. If I'm working in a room temperature of 70 degrees or less, I like to blast the loop with a hair drier for a few seconds to drive the Aquaseal into all parts of the monocore. I otherwise let the fly line hang, loop down, for at least twelve hours to dry and cure.

To attach the leader butt to the fly line, I make a perfection loop at the end of the leader, pass the monocore loop through this loop, and then pass the end of the leader through the monocore loop. To form a tight square knot, I pinch each loop flat before I pull the two loops tight against each other.

Why so much attention to something so mundane? Alternatives are not nearly so dependable; nor do they resist wear so well, or pass so easily through the guides. To pump up tuna, one must get the rod tip straight down into the water. In the final stages of the fight, the line-to-leader connection may be repeatedly drawn back and forth through the tip-top guide, and smooth passage of the connection becomes critical. Billfish, especially, place great strain and wear on both ends of the fly line. Once the fish have settled down from their initial runs, the contest is often fought 50 to 100 feet from the angler, the backing connection passing back and forth through the guides dozens of times. While this is going on, the butt and class tippet of the leader are repeatedly abraded against the back of the fish.

Here are some commonly employed alternatives to braided monocore loops.

ATTACHING THE LEADER TO THE END OF THE FLY LINE WITH A NAIL KNOT

Don't even think about it. Under extreme load, the nail knot will come off with the fly-line finish. The nail knot must be coated with a fast-drying adhesive to pass easily through the guides, making the connection permanent, and preventing a quick change to a new leader or butt section.

ATTACHING THE LEADER, WITH A NAIL KNOT, TO THE END OF A FLY LINE THAT HAS BEEN DOUBLED BACK ON ITSELF

The connection is less likely to slip off, but the doubled line must be coated with an adhesive to pass through the guides, making the connection permanent. Still, with mid-sized gamefish there are no major problems with this arrangement.

CONNECTING THE LEADER TO THE FLY LINE WITH AN ALBRIGHT KNOT

This is a superb, pretty much bulletproof connection. Nevertheless, it's permanent. After a grueling fight, I change everything in front of the fly line, especially if I've been working on a billfish. The reason is twofold: The permanent butt section often comes back abraded; and the doubled Bimini Loop of extra-hard monofilament wears severely on the soft nylon perfection loop that terminates the permanent butt. I've seen 50-pound butts blow out when worn through by a Bimini's 15- or 20-pound doubled surgeon's loop of hard nylon. On one of these occasions, a 110-pound Pacific sailfish was almost beside the boat when it just swam off. This was my client's fifth or sixth sail on the same permanently fixed butt section.

STRIPPING THE FINISH OFF THE FLY LINE AND, BY USING THE BRAIDED CORE, WHIP-FINISHING A LOOP, AND COATING THE FINISH WITH AQUASEAL

This is the ultimate no-brainer. The braided core wears badly against the butt sections of the leader. I tell any fly fisher who will listen that one of the few Golden Rules of bluewater fly fishing is to never attach the leader in such a manner that it bears directly against the core of the fly line.

STRIPPING THE FINISH OFF THE FLY LINE AND, BY USING THE BRAIDED CORE FOR A BASE, WHIP-FINISHING A LOOP OF EXTRA-HEAVY BRAIDED DACRON

This is an excellent, labor-intensive solution, but why bother? A monocore loop is much easier to attach and is more resistant to wear.

WHIP-FINISHING A LOOP USING THE END OF A FLY LINE

The perfection loop in the leader soon cuts through the finish of the fly line, burying itself and obscuring the wear taking place against the core of the fly line. Eventually, the loop in the fly line blows out. Nevertheless, this approach has a lot of followers.

On a recent fly-fishing trip to Australia for black marlin, I watched Wendy Hanvold quickly set up several fly lines by securing a loop in the end of her line with three nail knots made with a Tie Fast tool. She had used this loop connection when taking several world record offshore gamefish, including a 136-pound striped marlin. I won't argue with success: Hanvold is savvy enough to check for wear, and typically travels with fifty fly lines. But I also saw one of these loops blow out for Lani Waller when we were fishing together for blue marlin off Baja's East Cape.

CREATING A PERMANENT BUTT SECTION USING A NEEDLE NAIL KNOT

This approach involves pulling the permanent leader butt a ½ inch up into the core of the fly line then out the side, where it is attached to the fly line with a nail knot. As a result, the leader comes out from the center of the fly line, rather than over to one side as it would in a conventional nail knot.

To manage this, the sharp end of a fine needle is run up the core of the line and out the side. To get the heavy monofilament through the eye of the needle, it must first be tapered with a razor blade. This is tricky, and some practice will be necessary to pull it off. With the curl of monofilament toward you, stroke the bitter end of the leader butt with the razor blade held at a 45-degree angle until an inch or so has been cut down and tapered to a fine point. Put this into the eye of the needle and, by using pliers, pull the needle and leader up into the core of the fly line and out the side until you have enough full-diameter monofilament to complete the nail knot. At this point I would coat the nail knot with Aquaseal to assure its smooth passage through the guides.

Permanent butt sections are fine for freshwater fishing, and okay for flats fishing, but should be avoided when fishing offshore, especially where double-digit rods are involved. Offshore fish simply put too much wear and tear on the entire leader system, including the butt section. I would argue in favor of placing a 30-pound braided monocore loop coated with Aquaseal at the end of the fly line even when using 7- to 9-weight rods for small dorado, bonito, and football-sized tuna. This would permit you to replace the entire leader at the first sign of wear.

CREATING AN EMERGENCY LEADER BUTT

Occasionally a break occurs very near the end of the fly line and emergency measures become necessary to quickly resume fishing. When this happens, I make a double overhand (figure eight) knot at the end of the fly line, and pass the butt of the new leader through both loops of this knot before drawing it snug—not tight. I then make a four-turn nail knot directly above the double overhand knot. I finish off the procedure by drawing the double overhand tight, snugging the nail knot down against the figure eight knot, and then drawing the nail knot tight. The downside of this approach: Even when carefully trimmed, the knots do not pass easily through the guides.

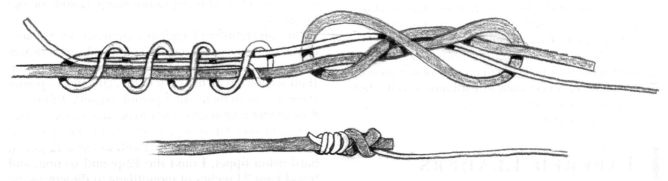

Emergency leader butt

LEADERS

Manufacturers market monofilament in varying degrees of stiffness, stretch, and resistance to abrasion. At one end of the scale are the "soft," pliable, copolymer, "high tenacity" monofilaments that have a 20 to 25% "elongation" (stretch) and great strength for their diameters. Examples include Jinkai, Ande, Stren, Rio (True Test), and Berkley—to name but a few of the very many. At the other end of the scale are primitive "hard" monofilaments (also used as toothbrush bristles) that possess less stretch, and are much more resistant to abrasion. Examples include Mason and Rio (Hard Nylon Saltwater). Monofilaments such as Climax and Maxima fall between the extremes; Momoi's Hi-Catch Fluoro-Carbon, distributed by the Tycoon Fin-Nor Corporation, leans toward the hard end of the scale, but remains less visible to fish in the water.

When a manufacturer claims that a particular mono tests 20 pounds, he means that *it will not test less than 20 pounds*. It may, in fact, test considerably more. For example, Mason's "20-pound" hard mono has been known to test as high as 25 pounds. That doesn't present a problem unless a fly fisher intends to fish one of the specific IGFA class tippet categories: 1, 2, 4, 6, 8, and 10 kg, or about two-, four-, eight-, sixteen-, and twenty-pound test. (A kilogram is just over 2.2 pounds, so that 10 kg class tippet would actually test 22.2 pounds.) If you were to submit a record application in the 10 kg category, and the tippet material tested 25 pounds, the record would be thrown out. Two solutions to this problem are offered. The material can be pretested. Some fly shops, such as World Wide Sportsman in Islamorada, Florida, offer this service. But you can gain the same information with a high quality hand scales. (After properly tying up a Bimini Twist, tie in doubled loops at each end using surgeon's knots. Place one end over a stick or dowel, and the other over the hook on the scales. While pulling slowly and evenly, a friend can read off the pounds of resistance until the leader breaks.) The second approach is to purchase leader material that the manufacturer guarantees to be rated IGFA accurate. For example, Rio's True Test is "Guaranteed IGFA."

I make leaders incorporating both soft and hard monofilament, or I make them entirely of soft mono. I do not make leaders entirely of hard mono, as the butt sections are too stiff and not in character with the casting properties in the fly line.

TAPERED LEADERS

I tie my own tapered leaders roughly following a 60% heavy butt, 20% tapered section, and 20% tippet config-

uration, doing so regardless of the leader's overall length. The butt section begins with 40- to 50-pound monofilament for 10-weight rods and higher, and 30- to 40-pound monofilament for 9-weight rods or lower. I generally connect all the parts of my tapered leaders with old-fashioned blood knots because the monofilament comes out of the knots absolutely straight, and because the knots, when trimmed close, won't catch on the guides.

Note that I use pounds of test, rather than diameter, as the criterion for my line selection. Diameter for a given breaking strength is not even remotely consistent among manufacturers. One example should suffice: Rio's class "20-pound" has a diameter of .018, while Mason's hard nylon "20-pound" has a diameter of .023. I have used several different leader brands, including Ande, Jinkai, Berkley, Climax, Rio, and Maxima. Whatever brand I use, I stick to throughout the construction of the leader. The exception occurs if I want to tie in a tippet using a more abrasion-resistant monofilament. Incidentally, working with lots of little spools makes me crazy; I try to purchase leader spools holding at least 100 yards of monofilament.

When I'm fishing for mid-sized gamefish, I generally prefer to cast an eight-foot leader. This is sufficiently long, particularly if the fish are being chummed up and in hot pursuit of anything thrown at them. Also, it has been my habit to replace, after a few bruising deepwater struggles, not just the tippet, but the entire tapered leader. I like to do this at the end of the day, making my loop-to-loop connection at the butt end of the fly line, tying on a new fly, stretching out the butt section so that it runs straight, and securing the fly in a rubber band I've placed around the reel seat. (I don't use hook keepers.) The leader, entirely outside the tip-top guide, can then be put under slight tension. In the morning I'll have a new, absolutely straight leader to fish.

If a longer leader is fished, it should still be stored outside the rod tip by bringing the fly around the reel and securing it in one of the stripping guides. If this is not done, the butt section of the leader will develop a hard-to-remove set from being drawn sharp against the tip-top guide.

Using an eight-foot length as a guideline, an 8-pound class tippet tapered leader configuration breaks down as follows: 36 inches of 40-pound, 16 inches of 30-pound (butt section); 6 inches each of 25-, 20-, and 15-pound (taper); and 20 inches of 8-pound (tippet). A tippet of 8-pound hard monofilament can be substituted directly, using a blood knot or surgeon's knot. If I'm keeping this basic leader configuration, but wish to fish a 12-pound hard nylon tippet, I omit the 12-pound section, and blood knot 24 inches of monofilament directly to the 6 inches of 15-pound. This move eats up most of the 6 inches; it doesn't matter.

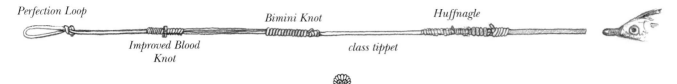

Perfection Loop   Bimini Knot   Huffnagle

Improved Blood
Knot   class tippet

Leader for billfish. The butt section terminates with a Perfection Loop. The butt section is then connected to the Bimini Loop with an Improved Blood Knot. This is followed by the Bimini Knot. The single line is the class tippet. The Bimini Knot and Bimini Loop is connected to the shock tippet with a Huffnagle.

A 10-foot leader tapered to a 12-pound tippet breaks down as follows: 48 inches of 40, 24 inches of 30 (butt); 8 inches each of 25, 20, and 15 (taper); and 24 inches of 12 (tippet). A switch to a tippet of 12-pound hard nylon can be made directly. If you wish to go up to a 16-pound hard nylon tippet, cut the leader back to the 30-pound butt section, blood knot in 24 inches of 25-pound test (taper), and surgeon knot in the 24 inches of 16-pound tippet.

If I'm putting together 8- to 10-foot leaders with 20-pound tippets for large tuna that are showing typical signs of leader shyness (this can happen even when live chum is used to attract), I taper my leader to a tippet of 20-pound hard nylon, choosing to use the less bulky surgeon's knot to tie on the tippet. If I'm using Jinkai for its fine diameter, my leader breaks down as follows: 48 inches of 50-pound, 24 inches of 40-pound, and 24 inches of 20-pound hard nylon tippet. If I'm seeking a finer diameter tippet, I tie the entire leader with Jinkai: 36 inches of 50-pound and 24 inches of 40-pound (butt); 12 inches of 30-pound and 12 inches of 25-pound (taper); and 24 inches of 20-pound (tippet). If the tippet fails, I tie in just enough 50- or 60-pound Jinkai shock with a surgeon's knot to protect the class tippet from the tuna's teeth. (Note: While a 40-pound yellowfin can have a mouthful of teeth, a 100-pound yellowfin can be almost toothless.)

BILLFISH LEADERS

My billfish leaders have an 18- to 24-inch butt of 50- to 60-pound soft monofilament. The butt has a small perfection loop at one end, which I loop to the monocore loop at the end of the fly line.

Several approaches are used to connect the butt to the class tippet. Tie in a perfection loop 1½ to 2 inches long at the class tippet end of the butt. This loop will be passed through the doubled surgeon's loop at the end of the Bimini Twist and passed over the fly or popper. The class tippet is then drawn through the loop until the perfection loop of the butt forms a square knot with the surgeon's loop at the end of the Bimini Twist.

To avoid loop-to-loop wear when I'm fishing for long-fighting tuna and marlin, I don't double the Bimini Loop. Instead, I use the single loop to make an improved

blood knot with the 50-pound butt section. This makes the butt-to-class-tippet connection permanent, and a quick change of flies isn't possible without setting up a new leader of butt/class tippet/shot. An alternative to connecting the Bimini Loop to the butt section is a double nail knot, an extremely strong and neat series of knots. (*See Improved Blood Knot and Double Nail Knot, pages 233 and 237.*)

When tying up class tippets for billfish, I always use hard, highly abrasion resistant monofilament.

The IGFA requires that the class tippet be at least 15 inches long between all knots. Because the class tippet is the weakest link between the angler and the fish, and is the part most vulnerable to abrasion from a billfish's bill, I keep the length short—15½ to 18 inches. The class tippet is permanently attached to the 12-inch shock tippet. Overall length of a typical billfish leader: 48 to 54 inches.

SHOCK TIPPETS

By the rules of the IGFA, monofilament of any test (a *shock tippet*) may be attached to the leader tippet (the *class tippet*), as long as the shock tippet and all connecting knots do not exceed 12 inches. This allowance permits anglers to hook and land rough-mouthed and sharp-toothed fish, such as tarpon, billfish, some tuna, and large dorado, that would otherwise abrade or cut through their leaders.

A shock tippet need only be heavier than the class tippet. Generally, I make my shock with hard monofilament when I'm fishing for mid-sized gamefish and trying to protect light class tippets. This may mean nothing more than connecting a 12-pound hard nylon shock with a surgeon's knot to a 4-, 6-, or 8-pound hard nylon class tippet if I'm fishing for 5- to 15-pound bonito, skipjack, little tunny, or yellowfin tuna. This may also mean a 20-pound hard nylon class tippet connected to a 30- or even 40-pound hard nylon shock with a surgeon's knot when I'm searching for really large bull dorado at first light. Beyond the 40-pound hard nylon, I switch to 60-pound soft monofilament, both for its smaller diameter and pliability.

Years ago I gave up using 100-pound hard nylon for billfish because I found it nearly impossible to seat a knot with the stuff, and I learned that the diameter was overkill for anything I expected to land. Besides, lengths of it had been boiled in water to kill their memory, and then stored in tubes, a lot of unnecessary aggravation.

I now purchase soft monofilament in 60-, 80-, 100-, and 150-pound test. I use the 60-pound for large dorado and for a number of inshore gamefish, including mid-sized tarpon. I like the 80-pound for Atlantic sailfish, regardless of their size, and for the 20- to 60-pound yearling black marlin found off Australia's Cape Bowling Green. The 100-pound monofilament would be my choice for Pacific sailfish and white marlin, and for black and striped marlin in the 100-pound range. I would go to 150-pound only when anticipating 200-pound blue, striped, and black marlin.

Because I use soft nylon for my billfish butts and shocks, I typically connect my class tippets permanently to both, coil the leaders up, and stow them in plastic envelopes that carry the date of the entry and a detailed description of the contents: "11/27/95: #50 Ande/#22 Rio/#100 Jinkai." *I do this before I go fishing.* When I want to tie on a billfish fly with a 3½-turn clinch knot, I measure 10½ to 10¾ inches from the class tippet end of the Huffnagle and make a soft kink in the shock at this point. I don't want much more than two inches of additional length to make the knot. I run the shock through the eye of the hook until the eye is against the kink in the shock. I then complete the 3½-turn clinch, running the turns on the tight side. When the knot is drawn tight—really tight, as it should be—the knot will slip to 11¾ inches. I want this extra ¼ inch for insurance against the slight slippage that might occur in the class tippet's Bimini Twist.

WIRE TRACES

The IGFA length rule of "12 inches including all knots" that applies to shock tippets applies as well to wire shocks, or wire traces. Other than billfish, only two species of gamefish featured in this book—the wahoo and the dogtooth tuna—require wire. The wahoo, with its row of razor-sharp teeth and its scissor-type bite, can cut through nearly anything except single strand wire. Typically, a haywire twist is used to connect a loop to the fly at one end and to a small swivel or ring at the other

end. In turn, a Palomar Knot connects the class tippet to the ring or swivel. A dogtooth tuna, with its mouthful of sharp-pointed, conical teeth, can be taken on plastic-coated braided wire, or on single strand wire. Braided wire—somewhat more user friendly than single strand wire—can be quickly secured to the fly with a figure eight knot, and can even be connected to a class tippet with a surgeon's knot. This works well for small "schoolie-sized" dogtooth tearing around near the surface, but my preference when working flies deep for fish in the 30- to 100-pound range is for single strand wire. The loop in the haywire twist allows the fly to dive for a more realistic presentation, while the wire itself can take a tremendous beating without breaking.

Regardless of which type of wire leader is used, length should be kept at 10 inches or more. Wahoo like to chew their way up a leader, and a really large wahoo can simply bite off a short leader. Dogtooth tuna flare out their gills and suck in the fly on the strike. If a large "doggie" takes a fly deep, you'll want all the wire trace the IGFA allows.

CRIMPING

In recent years, many offshore fly fishers have turned to crimping their shock tippets to their billfish flies. All that is required are some properly sized leader sleeves and crimping pliers. The length of the shock can be calculated precisely, and the entire crimping business takes but a few seconds. The same must be said for solid braided wire shocks: Each loop around the eye of the fly can be sized to perfection.

KNOTS

When I sailed on *Royal Star* out of San Diego, California for Ed Rice's first 10-day Blue Water Fly Rod Invitational, the company of anglers included such fly-fishing luminaries as Ray Beadle, Stu Apte, Steve Abel, Nick Curcione, Dave Whitlock, Peter Parker, Wendy Hanvold, Mike Wolverton, Dan Byford, Terry Gunn, and, of course, Rice himself. As we motored south down the Baja

Bimini Loop *single-strand class tippet* *black swivel* *Haywire Twist*

Improved Blood Knot *Palomar Knot* *Haywire Twist* *10-inch wire brace* *fly*

Leader for wahoo. Attach the Bimini Loop to the butt section with an Improved Blood Knot.

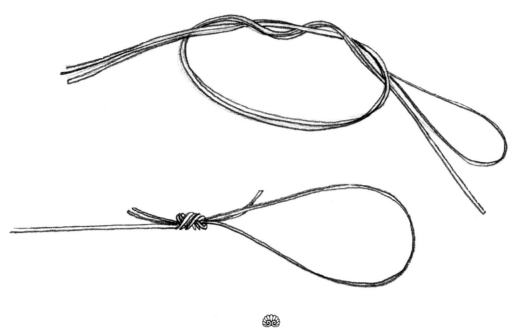

Surgeon's Loop

Peninsula, we found ourselves with at least a day and a half to spend swapping epic fishing tales of battles lost and won, and to complete the more mundane tasks like assembling our tackle and working on our tans. We did a little of all three, but mostly we discussed the knots—hours and hours of knots. Just as surely as trout fishers discuss hatches, offshore fly fishers discuss knots. No other type of fly fishing so depends on knots that will test as close to as possible to 100% of the line or leader's breaking strength.

The knots that I describe below represent my preferences. These are not the only knots—only those that have worked well for me.

SURGEON'S KNOT
(95% breaking strength)

I use the surgeon's knot to connect sections of leader material of substantially different diameters, whether replacing a tippet or attaching a light duty shock to the existing tippet. It is thus one of the most useful knots to know. Fortunately, it is dead easy to tie.

Note: This knot does not successfully connect a class tippet to a heavy duty shock—80-pound for example. The light monofilament simply does not have the strength to force the larger diameter nylon to form the knot.

1. Overlap the two length of leader material by at least four inches, as shown.

2. Make a half dollar–sized loop and tie in an overhand knot, and then tie in a second overhand knot.

3. Grasping one end in each hand, between thumb and forefinger, pull the knot tight. Now pull the standing lines tight, and then the tag ends tight. (For this I use two needle-nosed pliers that have no grooves in the jaw.)

Note: To make a double surgeon's knot, add one more overhand knot (three turns altogether). The monofilament comes out straighter when using this 95% breaking strength knot, but care must be used to make sure that two parts are drawn tight under equal tension.

I don't construct my entire leader using surgeon's knots because, even when trimmed as closely as possible, the knots do not pass so easily through the guides as blood knots that have been properly tied and trimmed even with the turns of the knot.

SURGEON'S LOOP
(95% breaking strength)

The surgeon's loop is formed as described above. Braided line or monofilament is doubled back to form a loop, and the knot is made. Add an extra turn and form a double surgeon's when you're tying in a loop using Dacron backing. If you're connecting braided line to your fly line, make the loop large enough to pass over the plastic cassette that holds the line.

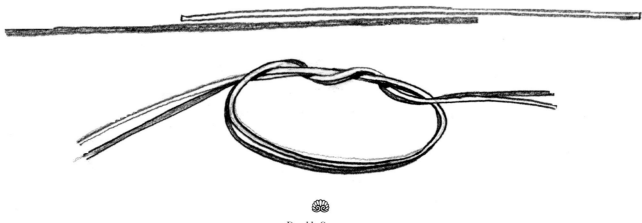

Double Surgeon

PERFECTION LOOP

The perfection loop uses only a single strand of monofilament to form the loop, rather than forming it with a doubled line. If the monofilament is drawn supertight, the result is a very small knot from which the tag end comes out at a right angle. When trimmed close, the knot passes easily through the guides. The stronger surgeon's loop is a larger knot from which the tag end emerges parallel to the standing line, where it can catch on the tip-top guide. The perfection loop is not a strong knot, but it doesn't need to be if it's used only in the heavy butt sections of offshore leaders.

1. Hold a loop between thumb and forefinger, with the tag end under the standing line.
2. With the tag end, pass a slightly smaller second loop around the first, and hold between thumb and forefinger.
3. Lay the tag end between the two loops.
4. Carefully draw the second loop through the first. As you draw the loop snug, the tag end should stand away from the knot at a right angle. *If the tag end doesn't stand away at a right angle, the knot is not tied properly, and it will slip.*

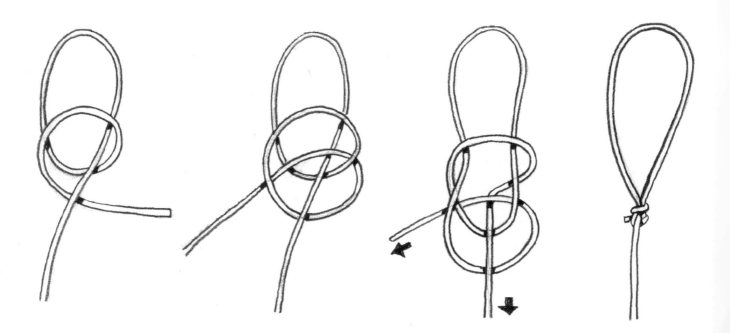

Perfection Loop

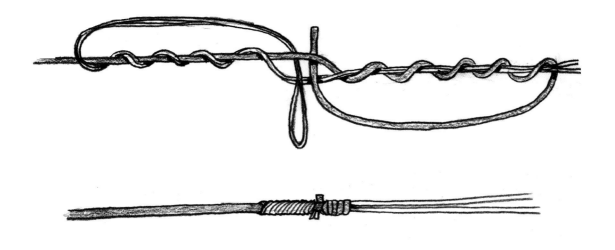

Improved Blood Knot. This knot connects the Bimini Loop and a single strand of monofilament. I most often use this knot when permanently connecting my class tippet to my butt section. I typically wind the class-tippet loop five times and the butt three times before pulling the knot tight when using a 50-pound butt and 15- to 20-pound class tippet. If the difference in strengths is not so great—as might be the case with fishing school tuna—the number of turns should be tied as illustrated.

IMPROVED BLOOD KNOT (95% breaking strength)

I use this knot to permanently connect the Bimini Loop of a class tippet to a 50-pound butt section. Long-fighting gamefish such as large tuna and marlin can cause the hard nylon, doubled Bimini Loop to cut, wear, and otherwise weaken the perfection loop in the butt section. This may or may not happen on a single fish. Eventually, however, new class tippets will take their toll on the old butt section. The improved blood knot prevents the ultimate failure of the loop-to-loop connection traditionally made between the class tippet and the butt section.

1. Cross the doubled line of the Bimini Loop, and the butt section, by several inches, and hold between thumb and forefinger at the V where they cross.

2. Wrap the doubled line over the butt section five times, bring back and across the V where the lines cross, and pin with thumb and forefinger.

3. Wrap the butt section 3½ times over the doubled line, and bring back and across the V in the direction opposite that of the doubled line. (If both tag ends come out on the same side, the knot will immediately slip.)

4. Pull both lines until the knot is firmly seated. (To help prevent the knot from slipping, I hold both tag ends in my teeth. Better yet, I have a friend hold the tag ends and draw on them slightly as I close the knot. As the knot

closes, I suddenly yank it tight. This helps prevent the loop from being drawn tight under unequal tension.) Trim close.

The standard blood knot is made exactly as described except that an equal number of turns (I do five) of single strand monofilament is made on each side. I hold the tag ends in my teeth, lubricate with saliva, and draw the knot really tight.

UNI-KNOT (95% breaking strength)

This simple, quickly tied knot has many uses, most notably for attaching a fly with or without a loop. Note: The loop closes down when under a load from struggling fish.

1. Run the leader through the eye of the fly, and bring the tag end back parallel to the standing line. Form a loop by bringing the tag end back to the eye of the hook and over the doubled line.

2. Make five to six turns around the doubled line, and pass through the loop formed by the tag end.

3. Lubricating with saliva, pull the tag end gently until the knot begins to form. Do not pull it tight. Pull on the standing line (leader) and slip the knot down to the eye of the hook. Now pull the tag end tight to form the loop.

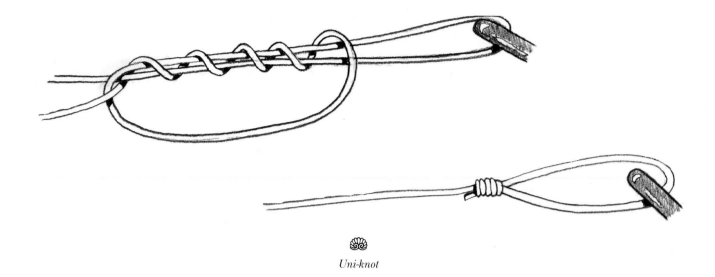

❀

Uni-knot

LEFTY KREH'S NONSLIP LOOP KNOT
(100% breaking strength)

1. Several inches from the end of the leader, form an overhand knot. Draw it down until the loop is about one-quarter inch in diameter.

2. Pass the end of the line through the eye of the fly and back through the overhand knot in the *same side of the loop it exited.*

3. Pass the tag end four to five times around the standing line before passing the tag end through the overhand knot. Draw the tag end slowly to tighten. To seat the wraps, and complete the knot, pull on the fly.

Charley Boillod, a longtime fishing companion of mine, showed me a neat variation of Lefty's nonslip loop knot. He omits step 2, instead passing the tag end through the eye of the hook, taking five turns, and passing the tag end through the overhand knot. He then completes the knot as described above. The result is a strong and tidy connection.

STEVE HUFF'S FIVE-TURN SURGEON'S LOOP KNOT
(100% breaking strength)

Steve Huff developed this fixed loop knot for permit fishing, but it has application for any gamefish not requiring a heavy shock. Note: *The knot is made with the tippet not yet tied to the leader.*

1. Pass the short tag end five to six inches through the eye of the fly.

2. Using both tag ends, make a loop, and pass both ends through the loop five times.

3. Work the loop down toward the fly by pulling on the loop nearest the eye. Pull the tag end and standing end at the same time until the "quadruple surgeon" is tight. Trim close. The result is an extremely neat and compact knot. The tippet can now be knotted to the leader.

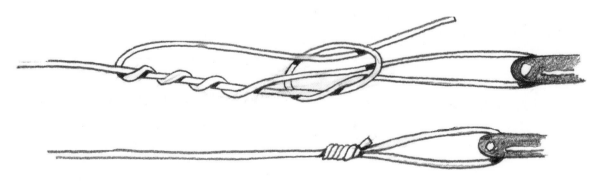

Lefty Kreh's Non-Slip Loop Knot

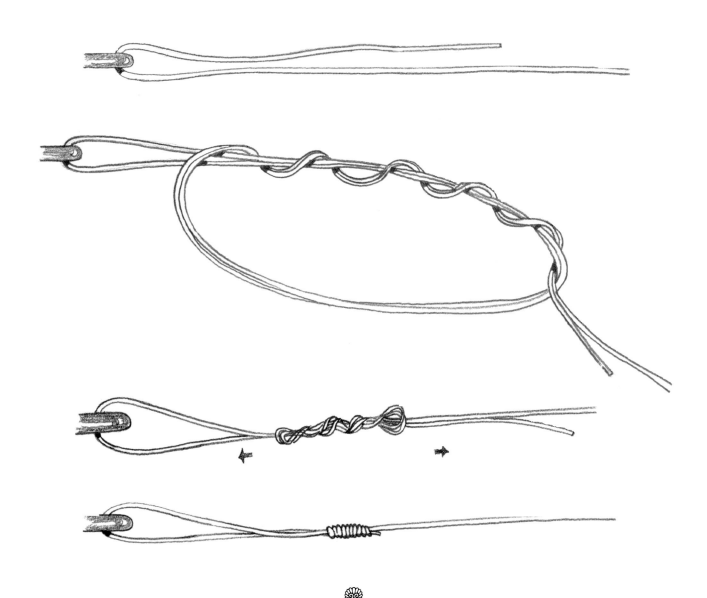

Steve Huff's Five-Turn Surgeon's Loop Knot

STEVE HUFF'S DOUBLE FIGURE EIGHT LOOP KNOT
(100% breaking strength)

This is the best knot to use when you're fishing heavy shock tippet and need to tie on a fly with a loop.

1. Attach the shock tippet to the Bimini Loop with a Huff-nagle.

2. From the start of the connection, measure 12¾ inches. Kink the monofilament at this point.

3. On the standing line above the kink, tie in a double over-hand (figure eight) and tighten until the "8" begins to form.

4. Take both loops and twist in the direction they want to go, forming a single loop. Run the tag end of the shock through the eye of the fly and pass through the loop you've just formed. Snug up the figure-eight knot.

5. Draw up the loop to the size desired and pull the figure-eight knot tight.

6. Pass the tag of the shock two times around the standing line, holding the turns close to the existing knot, and pass the tag end through the loops—the second figure-eight knot. Tighten and pull down on the first figure-eight knot.

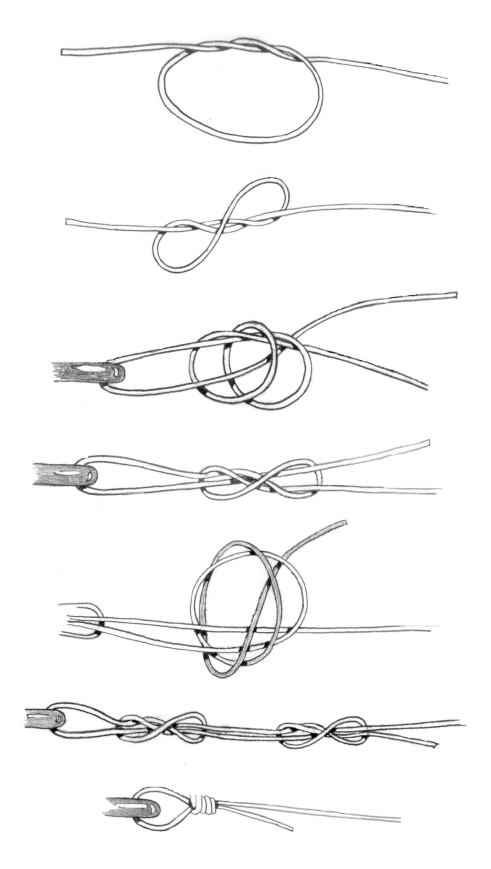

Steve Huff's Double Figure-Eight Loop Knot

NAIL KNOT
(95% breaking strength)

Most freshwater anglers use the nail knot solely to attach their leaders to their fly lines. However, among offshore fly fishers, the knot has a multitude of applications. I use it to attach my flies to my leader, to attach my shock tippet to my Bimini Twist loop, to connect monofilament shooting line to braided Dacron backing (double nail knot), and to finish off braided monocore loops.

To facilitate making the knot, I carry a stainless steel Tie Fast. (When offshore fly fishing, this tool keeps company with clippers and a Sharpie on a piece of fly line around my neck.)

To use the nail knot to form a loop connection to the fly:

1. Run the leader through the eye of the hook, and place the hook over the back slot of the Tie Fast. The tag end of leader that will be used to make the nail knot must be under the standing line.

2. Winding toward the hook, make four turns around the standing line, and pass the tag end through the Tie Fast and the turns.

3. This takes a little practice. But if you grasp the tag end between thumb and forefinger and *snap it off* the Tie Fast, the four turns will be perfectly formed, yet not overly tight. Lubricate the knot and the leader with saliva before drawing the nail knot down on the fly. (If you don't do this, the end of the leader will get pigtailed from being drawn through the knot.) When the knot is in place, pull the tag end tight.

DOUBLE NAIL KNOT
(95% breaking strength)

I use a Speed Tie to complete this knot when permanently connecting the single Bimini Loop of my class tippet to my 50-pound butt section.

1. Using the Speed Tie, make four turns with the Bimini Loop over the butt section. Snap off quickly so that the turns come off evenly. Pull snug.

2. Using the Speed Tie, make four turns with the butt section over the Bimini Loop. Snap off and pull snug. Pull the standing ends so that the two nail knots butt. Pull each knot tight. Again, pull the standing ends, and butt the knots against each other.

PALOMAR KNOT
(100% breaking strength)

I use the Palomar Knot when attaching a class tippet directly to a swivel or ring that has been connected to a wire leader and a fly with a haywire twist. The Palomar is also useful when I'm tying the tippet directly to the fly. Doubling the tippet gives the knot 100% breaking strength.

1. Double the single strand of class tippet back on itself to form a loop, and pass the loop through the eye of the swivel or ring.

2. Make an overhand knot in the tag end of the loop, so that the end of the loop points toward the eye of the fly.

3. Pass the loop over the fly. If passing the loop over a fly connected to a wire trace, be careful not to bend the wire so severely that a permanent kink is formed.

4. Pull both ends of the monofilament, making sure that all parts of the knot form on the tippet side. (When using small swivels and 20-pound hard nylon, you must carefully work the knot over the ring of the swivel.)

5. When the knot has been seated, pull the tag end again. Clip the tag end.

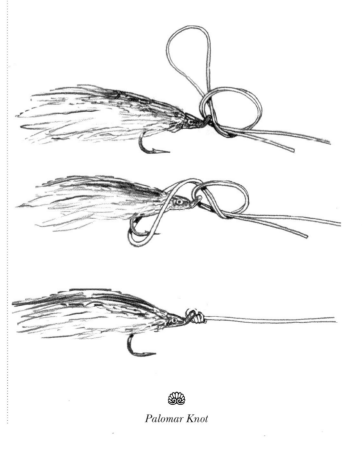

Palomar Knot

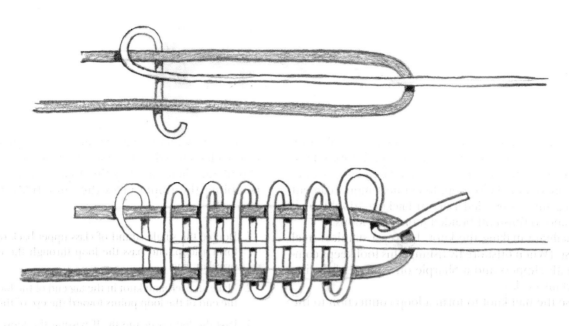

Albright Knot

ALBRIGHT KNOT
(95% plus breaking strength)

The Albright, named for famed Florida tarpon guide
Jimmie Albright, was originally designed to attach a class
tippet to a heavy shock. I use the Ablright for many purposes, but attaching my shock tippet is no longer one of
them. Most currently, I use the knot to attach superthin
and slippery gel-spun polyethylene backing to 30-pound
braided Dacron backing, and to attach this backing as a
Bimini Loop to a 30- or 50-pound monocore loop at the
end of the fly line. The knot is also useful for quickly and
permanently attaching a leader butt to a fly line.

Whether the connection involves a Bimini Loop, or a
single length of line, the procedure is identical.

1. Form a loop in the heavier line or leader. Pass the con-
    necting line (or loop, if you're connecting a loop of Spec-
    tra TUF backing to a monocore loop) through the loop.
    Pin the loop and connecting line between thumb and
    forefinger above the end of the loop. Begin making even

turns down the loop toward the bottom. If you're connecting a Bimini Loop or a double surgeon's loop, make
six to eight turns. If you're making the knot with a single
strand, complete ten turns. *Exit the loop in the direction you
entered.* Tighten the knot by pulling both ends evenly until the turns have come down nearly to the end of the
loop. I then pull down first on one line, then on the other,
and then on both, until the barrel of turns is flush against
the end of the loop.

I sometimes use this knot when I'm attaching a Bimini
Twist class tippet to a loop in my solid wire trace. To
avoid having the monofilament get cut by the wire, I take
the single Bimini Loop and connect it to 30-pound hard
monofilament using an Improved Blood Knot. I then
take the single strand of monofilament and connect it to
the wire loop with an Albright Knot. I keep the connecting knot as close as possible to the wire loop. As added
insurance, I put a drop of Aquaseal where the tag end
and standing end of the 30-pound hard monofilament
exit the wire loop of the haywire twist.

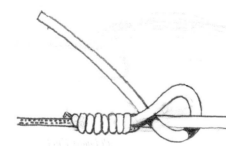

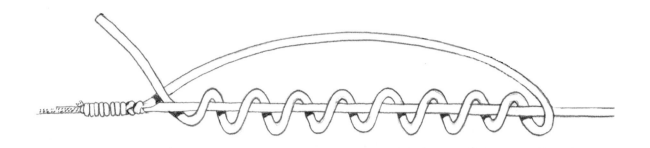

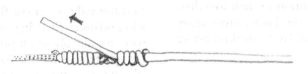

Albright, followed by a half hitch and an eight-turn reverse lock. This series of knots is useful for connecting braided Dacron backing to the superthin backings now being used by big-game fly fishers. The Dacron is used to form the Albright loop. After the knot is drawn tight, one or two half hitches are made with the super-thin backing. Follow this with an eight-turn lock. Pinch the loop where the tag end exits. Take the loop and wind the turns in reverse. When all the turns have been unwound, gently pull tight. Seal with Super Glue. Note: This same type of closure is employed when using monofilament as described in the Australian Connection (see page 245). When using monofilament, wet the knot well with saliva before pulling tight.

TRILENE KNOT (95% plus breaking strength)

This knot is used to attach a tippet to either a small black swivel or a small black ring that in turn has been connected to my single strand wire trace with a haywire twist. This is also an excellent knot when I'm tying on the fly without a loop.

1. Run the leader through the eye twice.

2. Pass the tag end four to five times around the standing line (leader), and pass the tag end through the two loops formed at the eye with the leader.

3. Moisten this knot with saliva before *slowly* drawing it tight; otherwise the monofilament will be scored and weakened.

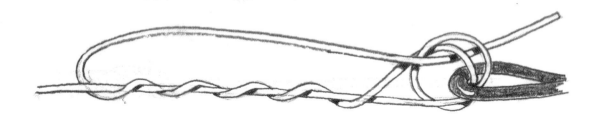

Trilene Knot

3½-TURN CLINCH KNOT (95% breaking strength)

No offshore fly-fishing knot is more used or more misunderstood. Anglers routinely use this knot to secure large flies to heavy billfish shock tippets. Too often they don't draw the knot tightly enough; this leaves enough play for the fly to swing around and get canted with the loop of the knot around the backside of the eye. To avoid this, I place the hook over something very secure and, by using both hands, pull on the shock tippet until the turns of the clinch knot seem almost to melt together. Besides locking the fly securely, the knot cannot allow shock tippet length, including all knots, to slip past 12 inches.

1. Pass the tag end through the eye of the hook.

2. Pass the tag end three times around the standing line and through the loop initially formed.

3. Pull on the standing line until the knot is snug. Pull on the tag end so that the turns are even. Pull extremely hard on the standing line until the knot is drawn as tight as possible.

IMPROVED CLINCH KNOT (95% breaking strength)

This is a quick, easily tied knot useful when connecting a light tippet to a fly without a loop.

1. Pass the tag end through the eye of the hook. Double

back and make five to six turns around the standing line.

2. Pass the tag end through the first loop at the end, and through the large return loop. Wet well with saliva and pull tight. Before trimming, I pull on the tag end with my teeth, and pull on the standing line one last time.

HAYWIRE TWIST (95% plus breaking strength)

Because wahoo can cut through plastic-coated braided wire, offshore fly fishers must depend on single strand wire, usually about 60-pound test, for these lightning-fast gamefish. I use the haywire twist at both ends of the wire trace, connecting one end to the fly, and the other to a black ring or swivel.

1. Pass the tag end through the eye of the hook for about three inches, crossing the wire so that a small loop is formed. *It is critical that the two lengths of wire are spread equally far apart.*

2. Hold the loop either between the thumb and forefinger, or with a pair of needle-nosed pliers. With the other hand, loosely twist the two lengths of wire five times.

3. Take the tag end and bend it up until it nearly makes a right angle to the wire shock. Still holding the loop of wire firmly, wind the tag end five to six times around the leader, forming closely spaced barrel wraps.

4. To break off the tag from the barrel wraps, make a "crank" with the tag end and turn in a circle parallel to the wire trace. Turn six or seven times in one direction, then reverse, and the wire tag should break off cleanly.

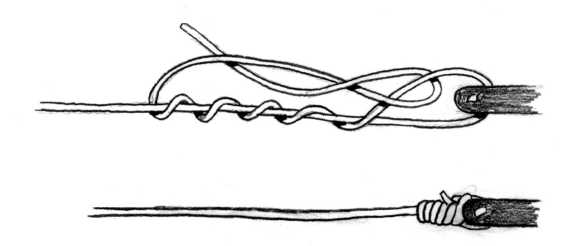

Improved Clinch Knot

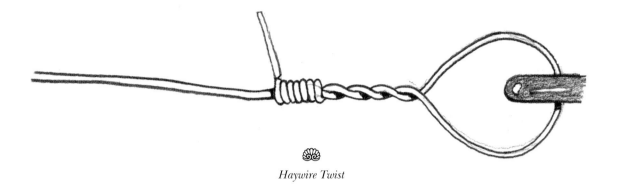

Haywire Twist

FIGURE-EIGHT KNOT
(95% plus breaking strength)

I use the figure-eight knot to secure a shock of braided wire to my fly. This type of wire protects the class tippet against gamefish with large conical teeth. Among the fish profiled in *Bluewater Fly Fishing*, only the dogtooth tuna fits this description. But in the course of pursuing offshore gamefish, I've encountered both great and Pacific barracuda, king mackerel, sierra mackerel, and narrow barred mackerel. All these toothy fish require a wire shock, either braided or solid.

1. Run the tag end of wire through the eye of the fly. Form a loop by passing the tag end under the standing part of the wire.

2. Pass the tag end over the standing part (forming one loop), then pass the tag end through the loop formed at the eye of the fly (the second loop and the figure eight).

3. Pull the standing part of the line to form and seat the knot.

Notes: 1. Plastic-coated braided wire can be quickly secured to the class tippet with a surgeon's knot. 2. A haywire twist can't be made using braided wire. 3. As with solid wire, braided wire can be sleeved and crimped to rings and swivels. The class tippet can then be secured to the plastic-coated braided wire with a Palomar Knot (my choice).

BIMINI TWIST
(100% breaking strength)

Before proceeding, I must point out several characteristics of the Bimini Twist—a knot of legend, mystique, and craftsmanship—and of the fly fishers who tie it and idiosyncratically claim it as their own.

Gear fishers and fly fishers generally tie the knot in the same way—or at least most begin in the same way—but they may make it with different numbers of turns and complete it, that is, *close* it, in a variety of ways. Even books on knots don't agree on the subject. (Don't look for absolution in what follows; regardless of what I recommend, I'll get letters of complaint on what is and what is not a "true" Bimini Twist and how I've violated those perceptions. Fly fishers who have time to write such letters should try to find a life.)

When "properly" tied, the Bimini Twist is a true 100% knot, the break occurring in the class tippet and never in any part of the Bimini Twist Knot.

The Bimini Twist begins with five to six feet of monofilament. The line is doubled back on itself at one end so that a loop is formed. Grasping the two ends, the tag end and standing end, in one hand between thumb and forefinger, use the two fingers of the other hand to make twists in the loop. How many? Traditionally, twenty. The Zen answer: How many do you need?

I never, ever, do twenty turns. Bad luck. For me. Overachievers go crazy over mind-numbing turns. Dan Byford does 100-turn Biminis for recreation. (We do not

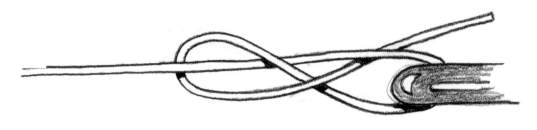

Figure-Eight Knot

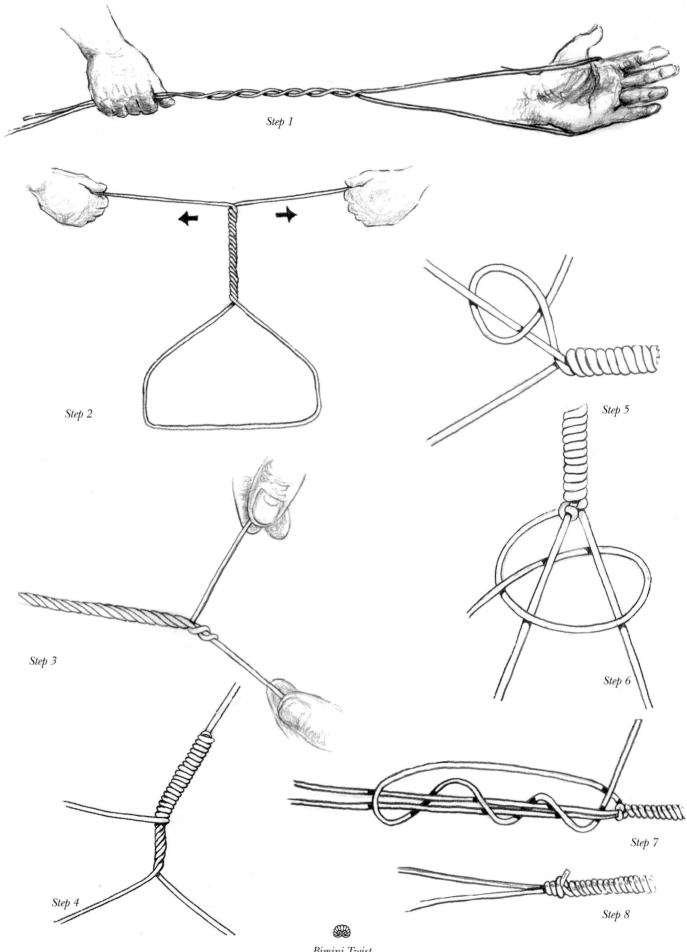

Step 1

Step 2

Step 3

Step 4

Step 5

Step 6

Step 7

Step 8

Bimini Twist

recreate together in this way.) I like seventeen and nine- teen turns, prime numbers that invite comment from my devil worshipping companions. Twenty-two is good luck for me. I'll take a chance with fifteen when fishing bill- fish, figuring that the shorter the knots, the longer the shock tippet. Besides, I believe that fifteen turns is about the minimum needed to assure a 100% knot.

For me, Biminis have become as intriguing as tarot cards. Books commonly illustrate the knot being tied on a person's knee, the loop of the knot underneath the tier's bare foot. This is an awful angle from which to tie this knot. If the tier can pass the loop over a peg about the diameter of a forefinger, and have the loop in a po- sition to look down on as the knot forms, a better job can be made of it. (Taking a 6-inch-square piece of board holding a ¾-inch dowel and clamping it to a table satis- fies this need.)

Begin the knot by holding the tag end in one hand and the standing line in the other hand and, using both hands, spreading the lines. This reduces the size of the loop and draws the twists up tighter. When the twists are tight, hold the standing line in one hand and push up on the V at the end of the loop with the middle finger of the other hand, while continuing to hold the tag end be- tween thumb and forefinger. Lift the tag end slightly, un- til it jumps over the first twist. Maintain tension on the turns by continuing to push up from below with the mid- dle finger, and holding the standing line firmly in the other hand. The tag end will wind down on the twists, be- coming ever shorter as it does. (Some practice is neces- sary to judge how much tag end is needed, for after winding down on the twists, the tag end will be used to lock the knot.)

I believe that the "jump" is the most critical part of the Bimini Twist. If the roll over the first twist is too tight, the Bimini Twist will likely break at that point, and not in the class tippet. For this reason, I make the initial jump over the twists wide and a little loose. Offshore fly fishers spend a lot of time discussing whether the entire Bimini Twist should be loose or tight, or whether it makes any difference. A loose Bimini Twist translates into length, which must be subtracted from the length of the shock tippet the IGFA allows—12 inches, including all connecting knots. This isn't much when fishing for billfish, and I want all the length I can get. I feel that as long as the first turn is loose, the additional turns can and should be closely spaced to create a shorter knot.

When the tag end has been run down all the twists, it must be temporarily secured between thumb and fore- finger while the free hand completes a half-hitch around the nearest line in the loop. This hitch locks the knot and prevents it from unraveling.

From this point on, some debate surrounds the Bimini Twist's completion. My own opinion on the matter was formed entirely from time in the field, where Bimini Twists must be tied up quickly so that they will not slip or come loose.

After the initial locking hitch has been made, I com- plete two additional hitches over both lines, always mak- ing the hitches in the same direction. I then make a final lock in which the tag end is passed four times around the double line (loop) and drawn tight. It's necessary to pull away the turns, to keep one from twisting on top of the other. Again, this takes some practice. But when fin- ished, the turns should run neatly side by side. Why four? This clinch-style knot binds most tightly on the first turn, and binds less and less on each turn that fol- lows. Using four turns, I can get the last turn to bind down enough to hold. Each turn after the fourth gets harder to tighten, and gets more and more suspect un- less the lock is secured with Super Glue. Also, it's more difficult to pull tight the additional turns, and to keep them from running over each other. For whatever it's worth, my approach has never failed me, and I like to clip my Bimini Knots close—⅛ inch at the most.

The other end of the Bimini Twist is completed as de- scribed. If you're making a loop-to-loop connection with the leader butt, the double Bimini Loop must be tied. To complete this, double the single loop, *making sure that both loops are exactly the same length.* Holding the base of the doubled loop very firmly, tie in a surgeon's knot. Still holding the base of the doubled loop, draw the knot tight by pulling on both loops equally. When it's tight, hold the doubled loops, and pull on the tag end, then the standing end. When completed, the two loops should be exactly the same length. If they're not, one loop will bear the full load of strain against the butt sec- tion. Trim the surgeon's knot close.

It sometimes becomes desirable to tie additional shock- absorbing qualities into the Bimini Loop. To accomplish this, make the Bimini Loop twice the normal length. Place twists in the loop by spinning the doubled line of the loop between your thumb and forefinger. When the twists have been run to the end of the loop, double the loop, and tie in a double surgeon's loop.

ATTACHING THE SINGLE LOOP OF THE BIMINI TWIST TO THE SHOCK TIPPET

This can be accomplished in a variety of ways using the Albright or Huffnagle. (Note: Nat Ragland, a Florida Keys fishing guide, named the Huffnagle for Steve Huff, one of saltwater fly fishing's premier flats guides, and the inventor of the connection.) The Albright has already been described. I prefer the Huffnagle to the Albright, when it's tied as described below.

HUFFNAGLE

1. To begin a Huffnagle, tie in a figure-eight knot (double overhand knot) and draw it up until it forms two loops. Pass the Bimini Loop through both loops until the Bimini Twist is against the figure-eight knot. Draw the figure-eight knot snug. Pull the Bimini Loop so that it again is against the Bimini Twist. Pull the figure-eight knot *tight*.

2. Using the Bimini Loop, complete two or three half-hitches over the shock tippet, all going in the same direction.

3. Using the Bimini Loop, and going in the same direction as that in which the half-hitches were completed, make four turns around the shock tippet and draw tight, being careful to make sure the turns run side by side. Complete this by pulling first on one side of the loop, then the other, watching carefully to be sure that all slack has been pulled from the lock. Trim, leaving about ⅛-inch of the tag end sticking out.

I make a slight change in this sequence. Instead of a figure-eight knot, I take a Tie Fast tool, place the shock tippet under the Bimini Loop, and complete a four-turn nail knot over the Bimini Loop. I draw this snug, making sure the loop is pulled through until the nail knot butts against the Bimini Twist. Then, using pliers, I pull the nail knot *tight*. I complete the knots as described above: two half-hitches and a four-turn lock, all going in the same direction. When properly done, this is a very neat-looking connection.

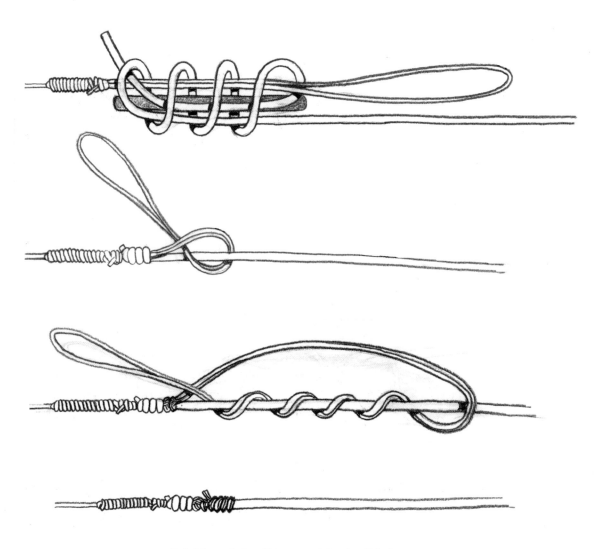

Pull tight and trim off the tag end, leaving ⅛ inch.

Huffnagle

AUSTRALIAN CONNECTION

With the seas empty of black marlin off Australia's Cape Bowling Green, Dean Butler, Alan "Fish" Philliskirk, and I began critiquing the various ways to connect a Bimini Loop to a shock tippet. The result was the Australian Connection—a different way to both lock a Bimini and connect the Bimini Loop to the shock tippet.

After making a twenty-two-turn twist (or whatever number of twists beyond fifteen that you prefer), lock the Bimini Loop with a single half-hitch on one side of the loop. This will prevent the Bimini from unraveling. Pass the tag end around the loop eight times (an eight-turn lock) and hold the tag end with the same thumb and forefinger that hold the Bimini turns. Gather up the loop with your free hand and unwind the turns—in effect, winding the turns over the tag end as in a nail knot. When this has been completed, pull gently on the tag end and draw the knot so that it is no longer loose, but still not tight. Then lubricate well with saliva and pull the tag end very tight. The tag end can be trimmed evenly with the turns, a neat closure, and a knot that will not slip or come loose. Note: If this knot is pulled tight without lubrication, the tag end will break somewhere inside the closure, thus destroying the integrity of the knot.

To connect this Bimini Loop to a shock tippet, use a Tie Fast to secure the shock tippet to the Bimini Loop with a four-turn nail knot. Using the tag end of the Bimini Loop, complete a single half-hitch. Continuing in the same direction, take seven turns around the shock as if making a lock, hold with thumb and forefinger, and unwind the turns as described above. Lubricate the turns and pull very tight. (Smooth-jawed needle-nosed pliers help here.) Again, because this is a nail knot-type closure, the tag end of the loop can be trimmed flush with the turns.

SPIDER HITCH

The spider hitch provides anglers with a double line knot that is quickly made and extremely strong but, I believe, does not absorb shock as well as the more elastic Bimini Twist. Nevertheless, it's a knot worth knowing.

1. Double the class tippet, forming a loop about 20 inches long.

2. Form a small loop, crossing the double line under the standing line. Pin this loop down with thumb and forefinger, thumb on top.

3. Pass the standing loop five to seven times around the thumb, then out through the loop.

4. Pulling on the standing loop, draw the loops off thumb, and tighten until a long, multiturn surgeon's knot forms.

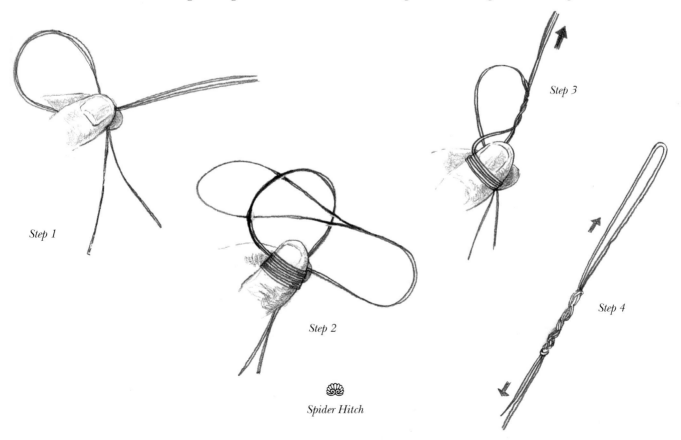

Step 1

Step 2

Step 3

Step 4

Spider Hitch

SUPERFAST SHOCK CONNECTION

Whether using a Bimini Twist or the spider hitch, an immediate connection to a shock that is up to three times the breaking strength of the class tippet can be made by using a surgeon's knot. You lose some shock length, and the result isn't terribly neat, but when speed is critical and the fish are not leader shy, this works well.

ACCESSORIES

Fly fishers, notorious for the piles of gear they wear and pack into the field, stagger to the streamside with more buttons, badges, and gizmos on their chests than Central American generals wear when reviewing their troops. Offshore anglers have far fewer needs. For example, clothing needs, the starting point of most fly fishers' buying sprees, can usually be satisfied by either sex with shorts, T-shirts, and tennis shoes. However scant the additional needs, they are critical.

MARK PACK'S "HIPPO RANGER" OR "LONG RANGER"

These nylon-covered tackle boxes with sliding trays hold a tremendous number of offshore flies, with plenty of room left over for extra reels and fly lines, plus many of the items listed below. Mark Pack also manufactures a heavy canvas cover for Rubbermaid's 18-gallon Keepers Rough Tote storage container. Both of the tackle boxes fit into this container, and it can then be safely checked at the airport with the other luggage. (Mark Pack Works, Oakland, CA 94607)

MONOCORE LOOP- AND LEADER-MAKING KIT

I carry a five-by-eight-inch plastic box that holds the following items:

2 pairs of 5-inch SS (stainless steel) pliers #8986 (G-LOX Products, 3302 Harrisburg Boulevard, Houston, TX 77003)

2 Matarelli stainless steel threader cleaners for bobbins

2 Tie Fast knot tiers

2 tubes of Duro Super Glue

1 tube of Aquaseal

Toothpicks

1 pair of extra-large clippers

1 pair of 3-inch Fiskars scissors

Lengths of Cortland's 30- and 50-pound braided monocore in plastic envelopes

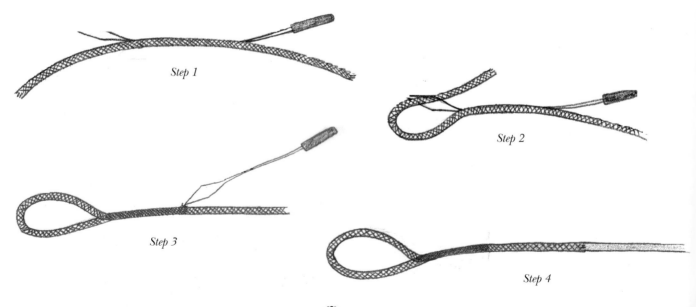

Monocore Loop

1 spool of 10-pound hard monofilament (for nail knots on monocore loops)

1 pair of 3X magnifier glasses (I carry at least one additional pair stowed elsewhere)

Note: I carry Super Glue and Aquaseal in tubes that have never been opened. I dump them at the end of the trip. This helps prevent their contents from leaking on the other items listed.

REEL MAINTENANCE KIT

Naphtha (or benzine) in a small plastic cosmetics bottle (I use this to clean grease off the cork drag surface.)

Pure Neetsfoot oil

Gun oil (or any fine machine oil)

1 can of compressed air (available in most photo stores)

1 rough pad from the back of a scrub sponge (for cleaning shafts, springs, etc., and for lightly wiping the cork drag surface after it has been cleaned)

1 can of Blue Grease, a waterproof grease not affected by salt water

Q-tips

400-grit wet/dry sandpaper (to remove corrosion and burrs on pawls when sand lacerates the inside of the reel)

1 Easydrive ratchet-type screwdriver (Creative Tools, Inc., Bennington, VT 05201)

GENERAL ITEMS

The Ultra Stretcher case, for setting up flies and shock tippets (contact Lee's Ferry Anglers at 602-355-2261)

Angler's Image Line Winder

Assorted heavy duty hook files

Donmar Big Game Hook Sharpener

A portable scale such as the Chatillon Brass scale in 60- and 100-pound capacity (Note: If you travel to remote areas and wish to apply for a world record with the IGFA, you or your companion must carry a scale certified for accuracy within a year of the date of the catch.)

Black barrel swivels in 30-pound test (for wahoo rigs)

No. 6 stainless steel wire in 58-pound (for wahoo)

Nylon-covered braided wire in 15- to 20-pound test (for sierra mackerel and Pacific barracuda)

Nylon-covered braided wire in 30- to 40-pound test (for barracuda)

Soft monofilament for shock tippets, in 60-, 80-, 100-, and 150-pound test

Soft monofilament for tapered leaders, in 50-, 40-, 30-, 25-, 20-, 15-, 12-, 10-, and 8-pound test

Hard monofilament for class tippets

2 pairs of dark glasses, amber lenses

Binoculars (extremely helpful when searching the horizon for working birds and schooling fish)

Hand towels

Extra-long needle-nosed or duck-billed pliers (for removing flies)

Band-Aids

Tape measure (for measuring record fish)

Flex wrap or gold gloves (for protecting fingers from line cuts)

Pocket knife

RIGGING AND STITCHING MATERIALS FOR TEASERS AND BAITS

The sleeves, crimping pliers, thimbles, rigging needles, rigging wire, knives, and so forth are discussed in chapter 19.

AROUND MY NECK

On a loop of fly line around my neck, I carry clips, a Sharpie hook sharpener, and Tie Fast nail knot tool.

CARRY-ON

D.B. Dun (2801 W. Idaho, Boise, ID 83702) custom-built for me a canvas-covered, leather trimmed, hard plastic carry-on tube 6 inches in diameter and 40 inches long. I can fit in any twelve three-piece saltwater rods of my choice.

ON BOARD

Boats carry a myriad of items that need not be discussed here. If fishing by the rules of the IGFA, a flying gaff is illegal; save yourself a lot of grief, and don't even have one on board. A fixed gaff may be no more than 8 feet long. Don't wait until you have a record marlin alongside the boat to discover that all the captain has on board is a 3-foot K Mart Special suitable for black bass.

BLUEWATER FLY PATTERNS

Saltwater fly tiers *who fish regularly* consider their flies to be in an ever-changing evolutionary process. Their research and development take place in the field—not in their imaginations at the fly-tying bench.

Saltwater gamefish do select one fly over another. My experiences on numerous long-range fly-fishing trips, where side-by-side anglers have cast their favorite flies, have illustrated this fact over and over again.

A billfish charging in after a teaser will, upon sudden removal of the teaser, attack just about any large fly tossed its way. The same billfish crashing balled-up sardines becomes far more selective, and a fly that swims well and resembles the baitfish is most likely to be taken. Dorado turned on with live chum are not the same gamefish that furtively hold under a kelp paddy and watch various flies go by. A school of tuna furiously driving baitfish to the surface will rush to take a white Deceiver slapped momentarily on the water. A single tuna cruising 70 feet down can be as picky as any brown trout.

The current generation of anglers matches baitfish more exactly and experiences fewer refusals. Their flies change as they incorporate the new synthetic tying materials that constantly appear. They visit their local fly shops and see the colors and textures in Hedron's FisHair, Flashabou, Saltwater Flashabou, Glo In The Dark Flashabou, and Krystal Flash; see the neon colors flashing from Gemmy Industries' Fire Fly, Tiewell's Reflections, and Cascade's Holographic Mylars; and find in Thompson's Ultra Hair, and Fiber Optic's Super Hair, subtle opaque colors not available in natural furs. They mix this wealth with Mylar piping and braids, glitter paints, and bucktail in endless colors both normal and fluorescent. These other materials challenge them to achieve new and ever more realistic imitations of baitfish and squid.

The flies assembled for this book represent but a small sampling of the patterns now used offshore. They are, however, proven in the field, represent the most effective flies currently available, and provide fly fishers with examples of the basic tying approaches used in bluewater fly fishing. Hopefully, anglers' experiences in the field will build upon these patterns, and enhance the sport with new and even better saltwater flies in the years ahead.

HOOKS

In many fly-fishing books, the treatment of hooks used for saltwater fly fishing begins with the traditional spiel on the importance of sharp hooks, and ends with a description of how to make them sharp. Usually these are stainless steel hooks that come out of the box on a sharpness scale ranging from "dull" to "worthless." After placing the hook in a vise, a large file is used to dress it on each side at a 45-degree angle until a razor-sharp cutting edge has been left on the barb. This produces a spear point that is triangular shaped in cross section. Additional filing on the outside produces a second cutting edge for even greater penetration. In the larger hook sizes, it's necessary to file both sides until the barb is reduced in size by half, and until the actual diameter of the hook from the point to the bend has been reduced. Fly fishers who fail to do this find it difficult to drive a 7/0 or 8/0 hook into a marlin's mouth unless the hook penetrates the soft spot in the roof of the mouth. Even when sharpened to perfection, the spear point can cut through a lot of tissue during a long fight, eventually falling out.

Several years ago I switched over from such conventional hooks as the Mustad 34007, and began tying my flies on chemically sharpened offset bait hooks with upturned eyes. I didn't want them offset—that is, twisted out of the horizontal at the bend—and I didn't really want them upturned either, but the hooks had short, thin, rolled points elliptical in cross section, as well as short barbs. I thought these attributes mattered a lot more than traditional style and conventional wisdom. Besides, halibut and salmon anglers swore by them because they penetrated so well, and held far out of proportion to their diameter. As a result of the change, my hookup ratio rose dramatically. And once the billfish or wahoo was hooked, the hook rarely came out.

I experimented with a number of hooks of this type, eventually settling on the Gamakatsu "Octopus," and the Owner SSW. I fished the Gamakatsu hooks just as they came out of the box. I used pliers to open the gaps of the Owner hooks. Because of its shorter point, I came to use the Gamakatsu as the lead hook in tandem hook setups. The Owner had a wider, flatter, and longer point, held extremely well in the roof of a billfish's mouth, and took a terrific hold in soft-mouthed species such as yellowfin tuna. Both hooks were chrome plated, and rusted when salt water penetrated their finishes. I found it necessary to rinse my flies in fresh water at the end of each fishing day.

I tied my flies on two other Owner hooks, the "Spinnerbait" in 5/0, a great sailfish and large-tuna fly, and the "Flyliner" in 1/0, an incredibly strong hook for midsized gamefish. (The Owner "Gorilla" and "Gorilla Big Game" are really too massive for fly fishing; I leave them for gear fishers.)

These bait hooks do not represent the ultimate bluewater fly-fishing hooks. I would like to see their basic design be stainless steel, without being offset, and with a ring eye. I believe such hooks will be forthcoming as more and more fly fishers look offshore for their sport.

STEVE ABEL

At his plant in Camarillo, California, Steve Abel oversees the production of fly reels as ruggedly dependable and attractively finished as any in the world. Everything he puts his name to, whether reels, pliers, knives, or even tackle bags and luggage, sets a new standard of excellence. His Abel Anchovy is no exception. In recent years this easy-to-tie dressing has become one of the most popular flies in saltwater fly fishing, both as an inshore and as an offshore pattern. Belizean guides swear by it when blind casting for tarpon. Abel routinely takes chummed-up blue and mako sharks with the Abel Anchovy, and he has world records for both species. Long-range fly fishers use it for every offshore species except billfish—though in larger sizes it would doubtless be effective for these fish, too. Because the large hot-glue head sends the fly diving on a slack line, and the silver Flashabou produces a crippled baitfish scale fall effect, I think it is one of the three best wahoo flies ever conceived.

When I tie the fly, I first tie in a short clump of bucktail at the throat to help prevent the fly from fouling.

Abel first tied the fly in the late 1980s using epoxy in the head, an application he found messy and time consuming. He discovered that by using a rotary vise and a glue gun, a large head could be made that would quickly give the fly a baitfish contour.

When tied three to four inches long, the fly suggests an anchovy; at four to five inches, it becomes a sardine; at five to seven inches, it can pass for a mackerel. Abel makes the head especially large when seeking to imitate a mullet.

Late in 1994, Abel added the Abel Mackerel and the Abel Sardine to the Abel family of flies for billfish, large tuna, and wahoo. I observed how very effective these flies were in January 1995 during a long-range fly-fishing trip to "the ridge" for striped marlin.

ABEL ANCHOVY

Body: None necessary. *Wing:* White bucktail (50%), green bucktail (25%), and blue bucktail (25%). *Topping:* Silver Flashabou and peacock herl. *Typical sizes:* 1/0 to 5/0. *Eyes:* The eyes are dropped onto the head and pressed into place while the glue is still hot. *Construction notes:* The Abel Anchovy can be tied entirely with FisHair, Ultra Hair, or even Krystal Flash. Tarpon fishers often tie

Steve Abel used an Abel Anchovy to take this 60-pound-plus wahoo on "the ridge" off Baja, California. Photograph by Terry Gunn.

in the wing at the bend of the hook, build up a long-nosed head of tying thread, and epoxy 7mm doll eyes to each side at the rear edge of the head.

ABEL MACKEREL

Hook: 6/0 to 8/0. *Tying thread:* Chartreuse. *Hot-glue color:* Clear. *Belly:* A bunch of any white synthetic hair mixed with pearl Krystal Flash tied under the hook, full length, to produce an 8-inch fly. Repeat on top of the hook. On top, tie in a large bunch of blue-green holographic Mylar. Tie in over with pearl and then silver saltwater Flashabou. *Topping:* Peacock herl. To complete the body, tie in a grizzly hackle dyed blue to run along each side dorsally. *Throat:* Red hackle fibers or fur. *Eyes:* Red plastic. Cut the stems down and set into the head before the glue hardens.

ABEL SARDINE

Hook: 4/0 to 6/0. *Tying thread:* Chartreuse. *Hot-glue color:* Clear. *Belly:* A bunch of any white synthetic hair mixed with gold holographic Mylar to body length, about 6 inches. Repeat on top without the gold. Tie in over with green and silver holographic Mylar. On top, tie in gold holographic Mylar. *Topping:* Peacock herl. *Down each side dorsally:* Grizzly saddle hackle dyed green. *Shoulder:* Two gold strips of saltwater Flashabou down each side. *Throat:* Red hackle fibers or fur. *Eyes:* Red plastic. Cut the stems down and set into the head before the glue hardens.

RON AYOTTE

When I first met Ron Ayotte of Port Orchard, Washington at an International Sportsman's Exposition show, he was representing Charleton reels and continuing to experiment with Mylar-bodied flies in a seemingly endless variety. Though Ayotte had used the flies mostly on Puget Sound salmon, both silver and blackmouth (sexually immature kings), we could see their much broader application for mid-sized inshore and offshore gamefish and green saddle hackles. Wind the tying thread forward. Tie in a bunch of yellow bucktail mixed with gold and pearl Flashabou on the bottom of the hook. On top, tie in green bucktail mixed with green, yellow, and blue Krystal Flash. Working forward, repeat the application of yellow bucktail below and green bucktail above two more times. *Head:* Color the top half of the head with a blue marking pen. The head is otherwise completed as described under "Goatfish" (*page 254*).

BLUE MACKEREL

Hooks: 7/0 Mustad 3407. Prepare the hooks and secure in tandem as described under "Goatfish." All tying is done on the forward hook. *Tying instructions:* At the bend of the hook, tie in a bunch of white bucktail. *All hackles are tied flared out.* Tie in eight 7- to 8-inch-long white saddle hackles on each side. Above the white saddle hackles, tie in two 7- to 8-inch-long blue grizzly hackles on each side. Wind forward, and tie in a bunch of white bucktail mixed with silver and pearl Flashabou under the hook. On top, tie in a bunch of blue bucktail mixed with pearl blue, light blue, and smolt blue Krystal Flash. Working forward, repeat the application of white bucktail below and blue bucktail above two more times. *Head:* Color the top half of the head with a blue marking pen. The head is otherwise completed as described under "Goatfish" (*page 254*).

GREEN-BACK MACKEREL

Hooks: 7/0 Mustad 3407. Prepare the hooks and secure in tandem as described under "Goatfish" (*page 254*). All tying is done on the forward hook. *Tying instructions:* At the bend of the hook, tie in a bunch of white bucktail. *All hackles are tied flared out.* Tie in eight 7- to 8-inch white saddle hackles on each side. Above the white saddle hackles, tie in two 7- to 8-inch green grizzly saddle hackles on each side. Wind forward and tie in a bunch of white bucktail mixed with pearl and silver Flashabou under the hook. On top, tie in green bucktail mixed with lime green, green, and olive Krystal Flash. Working forward, repeat the application of white bucktail below and green bucktail on top two more times. *Head:* Color the top half of the head with a green marking pen. The head is otherwise completed as described under "Goatfish" (*page 254*).

BLACK SKIPJACK

Hooks: 7/0 Mustad 3407. Prepare the hooks and secure in tandem as described under "Goatfish" (*page 254*). All tying is done on the forward hook. *Tying instructions:* At the bend of the hook, tie in a bunch of white bucktail. *All hackles are tied flared out.* Tie in eight 7- to 8-inch saddle hackles on each side. Above these, tie in two 7- to 8-inch magenta grizzly saddle hackles on each side. Wind

forward and tie in a bunch of white bucktail mixed with pearl and silver Flashabou on the bottom of the hook. On top, tie in a large bunch of magenta bucktail mixed with purple and pink Krystal Flash. Working forward, repeat the application of white bucktail below and magenta bucktail on top two more times. *Head:* Color the top half of the head with a purple marking pen. The head is otherwise completed as described under "Goatfish" (*page 254*).

DAN BLANTON

Dan Blanton, a pioneer in west coast saltwater fly fishing, developed the Sar-Mul-Mac in 1971. Named for three different saltwater baitfish hunted by marine gamefish, the sardine, mullet, and mackerel, Blanton says the Sar-Mul-Mac can be tied to imitate many other baitfish, such as anchovies, herring, ballyhoo, and jack smelt, by changing the colors of materials used. While fishing this fly on trips to Mexico's Sea of Cortez, to Central America, to the Carribean, and to backyard hot spots in San Francisco Bay, Blanton has taken many species of inshore and offshore gamefish including dorado, skipjack, striped bass, bonito, and roosterfish.

I personally believe the Sar-Mul-Mac is one of the best half-dozen offshore flies ever developed. My reasons for this opinion are several. The general construction of the fly is Deceiver oriented, with long, supple white hackles supplying plenty of action. The heavy plastic eyes make the entire fly head-heavy. If the Sar-Mul-Mac is tied on with any of several loop knots, the fly tips down on any slack between strips, giving it a diving action, too. The fly possesses the dense, general contour of a baitfish—a fly truly three dimensional from any angle. Like Lefty's Deceiver, the fly lends itself to numerous modifications depending on the size and species of baitfish the fly fisher seeks to imitate.

SAR-MUL-MAC

Hook: Mustad 34007, sizes 2/0 to 4/0. *Tying thread:* White. The entire fly will be tied using only the forward half of the hook shank. *Tail:* White bucktail, length optional to match saddle hackles. *Hackle:* Three white saddle hackles to each side, with five strips of silver Flashabou to half the length of the hackles. Pull the hackles so they splay out. This provides a more pronounced action. *Overwing:* Dyed grizzly saddles, one to each side, as long or longer than the white hackles. *Throat:* Red or Maroon marabou fluff. *Shoulder:* Gray marabou fluff. *Cheeks:* Teal flank feather. *Head topping:* Loop of gray chenille. *Eyes:* 8mm amber glass eyes attached to a wire stem. *Head:* A single ring of red chenille followed by white chenille. *Construction notes:* The blue, green, or yellow grizzly hackles simulate the dorsal areas of baitfish. After tying in the teal flank, coat the base of the feather with head cement to keep the fibers married. To form the topping for the head of the fly, tie in the ends of a loop of gray chenille in front of the gray marabou, and then move the loop out of the way. Bend the soft wire stem of the eyes at a 90-degree angle, and tie down the stem to the head on each side. Cut off any excess wire. Coat with head cement. Tie in medium white chenille behind the eyes, wind forward, and figure-eight it around the eyes to build a full, tapered head. Tie off the white chenille. Now bring the loop of gray chenille forward over the top of the head and tie off. Whip-finish.

GEORGE "CHAPPIE" CHAPMAN

For as long as anyone can remember, Chappie Chapman's signature fly has been a balsa popper. Inspired by the Quilby Minnow, a crappie popper made with a goose quill, Chapman made his first balsa poppers in the late 1950s and fished them for smallmouth bass on Virginia's Potomac River. When he moved to California in the 1970s, he enlarged the poppers, added pearlescent tape, and fished them for striped bass. He says, "The first time I saw Mylar piping, I flipped out. I knew exactly how I was going to use the stuff."

Chapman's Mylar-covered poppers have taken numerous offshore and inshore species of gamefish. The pearlescent model with the red head has proven especially effective on bonito. It was at Gary LaFontaine's suggestion that Chapman left a Mylar skirt at the shoulders to suggest gills.

(Chapman's technique of covering poppers with Mylar piping and coating the result with 5-Minute epoxy inspired Lani Waller to use the same approach with Gaines poppers. See Lani Waller, *page 278.*)

MYLAR POPPERS
Chapman finishes all of his Mylar poppers in the following manner regardless of their size. The body is sanded to shape. A shallow slot is cut for the hook and held in place with Zap-a-Gap. Coat the body twice with sanding sealer, sanding after each coat. Spray with white lacquer. Paint on the eye. (To keep the paint from sagging, Chapman mounts the poppers on an electric rotisserie.) Slip on the Mylar piping and tie down on the body behind the eyes. Coat the piping with 5-Minute epoxy.

When tying extra-large poppers for billfish, Chapman ties in feathers flared out and cocked up at the bend of the hook. The rear end of the popper sinks down from the weight of the hook, but the feathers stay on the surface. He does not cover these poppers with Mylar piping.

TREY COMBS

SEA HABIT FLIES
After spending several days epoxying Mylar piping over cork popper bodies, I sent samples of the piping to Mark Waslick in Middlebury, Vermont. Waslick, one of the country's most brilliant fly tiers—his full-dressed Atlantic salmon flies sell for hundreds of dollars—quickly saw its application elsewhere. A week later I received some flies from Waslick in which the Mylar piping had been slipped over the head of the fly, and epoxied in place. The result was a very lifelike scaled effect. I tried this approach on my offshore flies and discovered that most of the time-consuming hassles of finishing off the head of a fly with tying thread could be eliminated. I simply tied down the materials, giving the butt ends a shot of Super Glue, and trimmed the head to shape. I then slipped the Mylar piping over the head, tied it down just behind the eye, and coated it with 5-Minute epoxy. The epoxy soaked through the piping and into the head, making the entire business nearly indestructible. After the epoxy had cured, I took a single-edged razor blade and trimmed away the extra piping that extended over the eye. I tried all sorts of paints and marking pens for a dorsal color, but I was never satisfied with the results until hitting upon Scribbles "Soft Fashion Paint," a tough, flexible glitter paint used on clothing. I found many colors useful, especially "Pacific Blue," "Clover Green," "Confetti," and "Night Star," the latter color matching the peacock herl that I often used as a topping in my flies. After the initial coat of epoxy, I stuck on Witchcraft eyes, applied a heavy coat of Scribbles, and let it dry overnight. The heavy application of Scribbles helped smooth out the taper of the head, and gave the head the deep translucence of an actual baitfish.

Bob Popovics showed me a neat trick for putting on the Witchcraft eyes. To prevent them from sticking out like hubcaps from the side of the head, he creased the eyes between thumb and forefinger and stuck them on the head with the crease horizontal to the hook shank. The eyes stuck to the curve of the head until the Scribbles paint dried. I then applied a heavy second coat of 5-Minute epoxy over the entire head. This filled in any gaps, increased the size of the head, and sealed the eyes.

I called the result "Sea Habit" flies, and I at first concentrated on the tube flies I'd already been fishing offshore for tuna and dorado. A tube fly easily lent itself to a head of Mylar piping, and otherwise had both good and bad points. When the hook in the tube fly became damaged, the hook could be replaced and the fly used again. The fly itself could be dressed with translucent Mylar piping around a tube body—a very supple, life-suggesting combination. But because the tube extends the overall length of the hook, the fly was given to fouling. This was no big deal if fishing inshore water for cruising salmon, but a very big deal if getting off a single cast on a school of tuna streaking by, for gamefish would reject the fly whenever the wing fouled on the hook. A simple way to get around this was to lengthen the tube beyond the length of the body materials. This made a great trolling fly for silver salmon to take from behind, but pelagic saltwater gamefish often took the fly at the head and impaled themselves outside their mouths. My other option was to construct the tube as short as possible and use a short shanked hook.

Regardless of the length of the tube, if I tied in body materials that extended beyond the hook, I tied the fly with a belly of short, stiff bucktail. This gave a better baitfish contour while helping prevent more flexible materials such as FisHair from fouling.

I tie all my Sea Habit flies, whether Tubes, Bucktails, Deceivers, or Billfish flies, with an underbody of pearl Flashabou. The larger and more massive the fly, the more Flashabou I use. The reasons are several. With a heavy underbody of Flashabou, the bucktail need not be applied so heavily to obtain the same bulk. This allows more water and light to pass through the lighter-built fly, giving it better action and more flash. The fly carries less water when I pick it up on the cast, and sheds water more easily on the start of the forward cast.

The other approach I use is to tie the basic fly almost entirely in white. Dorsal colors are added over the white as a veiling. They are not achieved by stacking one color over another. This difference cannot really be appreciated until the fly is swimming, for then the fly turns translucent and seems to glow with life.

Note: Many tiers substitute other materials for the Krystal Flash and Flashabou described, but still try to get the colors approximately as I've noted.

SEA HABIT TUBES

Small: For tube flies three to four inches long, use ⅛-inch OD Nylaflow tubing set inside ³⁄₁₆-inch OD, ⅛-inch ID vinyl tubing. *Medium:* For tube flies four to five inches long, use ⅛-inch OD Nylaflow tubing set inside ¼-inch OD, ⅛-inch ID vinyl tying. The total length of the vinyl tubing need not be more than 1¼ inches. The Nylaflow tubing insert should be no more than ¾ inch long. Coat half the length of the Nylaflow tubing with epoxy and push inside the vinyl tubing. This will cause a bead of epoxy to form around the rim of the vinyl tubing. Set the tube upright on a toothpick while the epoxy cures. If tying a ballyhoo imitation, leave the Nylaflow tubing long to suggest the elongated lower jaw of the ballyhoo.

Regardless of the pattern, all the tube flies begin identically. *Underbody:* Tie in strands of pearl Flashabou around the entire tube three-quarters the length of the intended fly. Tie in several strands of silver Flashabou on

what will be the dorsal side. (Note: The vinyl tubing comes packed in coils and thus has a natural curve. I try to make sure the top of the curve becomes the dorsal part of the fly.) *Overbody 1:* Tie in white bucktail on the belly half the length of the fly. Tie in a bunch of white bucktail on each side the full length of the fly. Tie in a bunch of bucktail on top four-fifths the length of the fly. Do not stack the bucktail. The uneven ends help give the tube fly a minnow shape. If using white FisHair instead of bucktail, tie in white bucktail on the belly as described to help prevent the FisHair from fouling on the hook. Substitute FisHair, or any other synthetic hair, in the colors as described as "bucktail."

ANCHOVY
Overbody 2: Above the midline, tie in lime green Krystal Flash, with a few strands of lime green bucktail over. On top, tie in a bunch of pearl blue Krystal Flash, followed by a few strands of blue bucktail. *Topping:* Peacock Krystal Flash or peacock herl. Finish with five to six strands of silver Krystal Flash on each side. *Head:* Pearl Mylar coated with epoxy. *Eyes:* Witchcraft. *Dorsal head color:* Scribbles "Night Star."

FLYING FISH
Overbody 2: Above the midline, tie in pearl blue Krystal Flash, with a few strands of pale blue bucktail over. Tie in a bunch of pearl Krystal Flash on top, followed by a few strands of blue bucktail. *Topping:* Royal blue Krystal Flash and several strands of black FisHair or black bucktail. Finish with five to six strands of silver Krystal Flash on each side. *Head:* As above. *Dorsal head color:* Scribbles "Pacific Blue."

SARDINE
Overbody 2: Above the midline, tie in olive and pearl blue Krystal Flash, followed with a small amount of lime green bucktail. On top, tie in a small bunch of pearl Krystal Flash, followed by a few strands of green bucktail. *Topping:* Peacock herl. Finish with a few strands of silver Krystal Flash on each side. You may add a longer midline strand of orange Krystal Flash on each side. *Head:* As above. *Dorsal head color:* Olive green.

BALLYHOO
Overbody 2: Above the midline, tie in pearlescent purple and pearl blue Krystal Flash, thickly followed with a pale blue bucktail. On top, tie in a mixed bunch of gray ghost and pearl blue Krystal Flash and cover lightly with gray bucktail. *Topping:* a few strands of black bucktail. Shoulder with five to six strands each of silver and pink Krystal Flash on each side. *Dorsal head color:* Scribbles "Confetti."

LARGE SEA HABIT TUBES

To tie large, 6- to 10-inch tube flies, set the tube up as you would a medium tube fly, the ⅛-inch OD Nylaflow

tubing set inside ¼-inch OD and ⅛-inch ID vinyl tubing. *Over the vinyl tubing, epoxy in place a ½-inch length of PVC tubing, ¼-inch ID, ⅜-inch OD.* The PVC provides a large-diameter base upon which to begin the tying. This prevents having to initially pile on bucktail or FisHair to gain bulk. If tying a ballyhoo pattern, extend the length of the Nylaflow tubing to 2 inches to simulate the fish's long lower jaw. On some species of ballyhoo this lower jaw is red. This is easily imitated by coloring the Nylaflow tubing with an indelible red marking pen.

I never tie large flies entirely with FisHair. The material holds too much water, and it can snarl into a balled-up mess on the stinger hook when fishing a tandem hook setup. If tying with FisHair, or any of the older synthetic hairs, I suggest alternating the synthetics with bucktail well larded with Flashabou. This works quite well even when tying a 10-inch fly, the shorter bucktail and Flashabou providing bulk, the FisHair and matching Flashabou providing length. Any of the tube fly patterns described above work equally well on sailfish, marlin, large tuna, and wahoo when tied extra-large on this tube/coupler combination. My first fly-caught wahoo and Colombian Pacific sailfish came on the Ballyhoo tube pattern tied large.

SEA HABIT BILLFISH POPPERS

To setup a tube/coupler for one-inch-diameter foam head poppers, use the tube combination described above for ballyhoo dressings. The Nylaflow tubing will stick out of the foam head approximately ¾ inch. (If setting up a tube/coupler for foam head poppers with diameters of 9/16 inch to ¾ inch, the extra PVC tube can be omitted.)

When fishing poppers for billfish, I have relied principally on just three patterns, often fishing the Pink Squid for Pacific sailfish, the Green Machine for blue marlin, and the Flying Fish for all billfish species. However, I have hooked many sailfish on the Green Machine, and hooked a half-dozen blue marlin on huge Flying Fish poppers.

I prefer to cast these poppers on a fast-sinking line like Scientific Anglers 550 Deep Water Express, the Teeny

500, or Teeny's new saltwater series of lines in the 500- and 650-grain sizes. The sinking line tends to anchor the popper and keep it from being pushed away by the waves created by the rising sailfish or marlin.

PINK SQUID

Underbody: Tie in a medium bunch of white bucktail (the longer the better), mixed with strands of pink and pearl Flashabou. Tie in an additional bunch of white bucktail above and to each side, mixed as described. This sequence gives a pie silhouette and leaves a wide tying platform upon which to build the balance of the fly. On top tie in a six- to eight-inch bunch of white FisHair mixed with pink Flashabou. Tie in on top a bunch of pink bucktail mixed with pink Flashabou. Top with hot pink FisHair. Tie in a medium bunch of pink bucktail and again top with hot pink FisHair. *Overbody:* Four long, hot pink saddle hackles on each side, horizontal to the hook. Tie four additional hot pink saddle hackles on each side above the first. The second bunch of saddle hackles almost comes together along the dorsal part of the fly. Shoulder the fly with a large bunch of hot pink Flashabou or Krystal Flash on each side, one-third the length of the hackles. Do not bother with carefully tying off the materials. Just trim off the excess and prepare the popper head. *Popper head:* one-inch-diameter, closed cell foam coated with fluorescent "Neon Pink" Scribbles paint, and final coating with "Crystal Pink Lemonade" Scribbles paint. (Note: No paint will permanently attach to closed cell foam, and a billfish will remove the paint on the take. I believe it is more important that the eyes—not the paint—stay on the head. However, some anglers mask off the eyes and body, and give the head a quick shot of spray paint.) *Eyes:* ⅝-inch-diameter doll eyes *set to the rear edge of the head.* I want the eyes as close to the lead hook as possible, for the eyes are where the billfish is going to grab the popper. Secure with Aquaseal. Because the Aquaseal takes hours to dry, I do one side at a time. If purchasing the kind of doll eyes that can be sewn on, a needle threaded with single strand floss can be used to bind the eyes down to the unpainted head. *Head:* To seat the tube in the foam head, run a needle completely through the foam head from the front end about two-thirds of the way down from the top of the head. Place a piece of Nylaflow tubing over the point of the needle, and push the tubing through the foam while withdrawing the needle. Remove the tubing. Take tying scissors and carefully cut out a cone-shaped channel large enough to accept the fly's head. Coat the head with Aquaseal and jam the fly into the head. Stand the popper with the head down and let dry overnight.

GREEN MACHINE

Prepare tube/coupler as for the Pink Squid. *Underbody:* White bucktail mixed with pearl Flashabou. Tie in three times, with the second and third bunches tied on each

Fly tiers: Steve Abel, The Orvis Company (Nick Curcione), Trey Combs, Bill Hayes. Rows 1 and 2: Abel Sardine, Abel Anchovy, Abel Anchovy (tarpon-style), Abel Mackerel. Row 3: Curcione's Big Game Fly, Curcione's Flasher. Row 4, Sea Habit Tube Flies: Anchovy, Ballyhoo Billfish. Row 5, Sea Habit Tube Flies: Sardine, Flying Fish, Ballyhoo.

Bob and Gloria Harper pose with a Pacific sailfish that hit a Pink Squid popper tied by the author. Captain Calin Canales and Mate Curpin Mendez join the fun.

side and slightly above the first. This will help create a strong silhouette. Top with alternate layers of chartreuse bucktail and fluorescent lime green FisHair. Top first with medium green bucktail, and then with blue FisHair mixed with blue Flashabou to 8 inches. *Outer body:* Up to ten hot chartreuse saddle hackles on each side. Top on each side with two medium blue saddle hackles set high. Shoulder with a pearl blue, smolt blue, and chartreuse Krystal Flash one-third the length of the fly.

FLYING FISH

Prepare tube/coupler as for the Pink Squid. *Underbody:* tie in a large clump of white bucktail and follow with an additional clump of white bucktail on each side. Mix the white bucktail well with pearl Flashabou. Top with royal blue FisHair mixed heavily with royal blue Krystal Flash. *Outer body:* six to fifteen white saddle hackles on each side. Above the white saddle hackles, tie in one or two fluorescent chartreuse saddle hackles, two to three silver doctor blue saddle hackles, and two royal blue saddle hackles. *Cheeks:* Pearl, silver, and pearl blue Krystal Flash. *Popper head:* undercoating—"Matte White" Scrib-

bles; outer coat—"Glittering Crystal" below, "Crystal Pacific Blue" above; eyes—⅜- to ⅝-inch doll eyes sewn in place and glued with Aquaseal. Note: I find that a ring of Aquaseal around the entire front and edge of the painted foam head helps prevent the paint from coming loose.

SEA HABIT BUCKTAILS

The general tying approach used for the Sea Habit Bucktails is identical to that used when tying the tube flies—that is, a fly with an underbody of pearl Flashabou, and an overbody of white bucktail, with the dorsal colors applied by veiling over the white. I tie these flies in sizes from 4 to 5/0, and fish them for everything from Alaska's Bristol Bay rainbow trout to billfish. I generally like short shank hooks for these flies, and I often use bait hooks by Owner and Gamakatsu. They are offset, have rolled points, and upturned eyes, and penetrate and hold extremely well. (I open up the Owner stringer hook to increase the gap and give the hook a better bit.) While certainly atypical of offshore fly hooks, they do not prevent the fly from properly tracking on the strip. A notable exception to this preference is Owner's Spinnerbait hook with a straight eye and nickel finish in 5/0, a hook that is at least 2X long. If using this hook on flies to be fished for either billfish or large tuna, I generally don't include a stinger hook.

Underbody: Tail: Tie ten to fifteen strands of pearl Flashabou approximately twice the shank length on hooks 1 to 2/0. Tie in bucktail at least three times the hook length and heavily mix with pearl Flashabou on hooks 3/0 to 5/0. Wind tying thread forward and, depending on the hook size, stop ¼ to ¾ inch from the eye. Turn the hook upside down and tie in a heavy throat of pearl Flashabou followed by white bucktail. Both should extend just beyond the bend of the hook. Turn hook right side up. Tie in a clump of pearl Flashabou on both sides, and on top, so that it extends two-thirds of the way to the end of the tail. Wind forward and repeat the application of pearl Flashabou in larger sizes, 3/0 to 5/0. The fly should take on a general minnow shape just from the pearl Flashabou. Tie in bucktail the same length along each side over the Flashabou. Keep the bucktail somewhat thin, so that when the fly is wet, the pearl Flashabou will show through. Tie in strands of silver and pearl Flashabou over the bucktail, and tie in one or two longer clumps of white bucktail on top, as needed for bulk. This should complete the overall body shape. When the dorsal colors are added, they should be slightly shorter than the last clump of white bucktail. Note: Do not use a stacker to even out the lengths of bucktail. Cut off the bucktail and directly tie in place. This helps give the fly a minnow shape. Beginning with this basic all-white, single hook fly, the following patterns can be tied.

ANCHOVY BLUE

Veil: Shoulder on each side with lime green and olive Krystal Flash, followed by a very small bunch of lime green bucktail on each side to hold the Krystal Flash in place. Tie over a bunch of pearl blue Krystal Flash, and a small bunch of blue bucktail (I prefer turquoise blue). *Topping:* Peacock herl. *Shoulder:* Silver Krystal Flash. *Dorsal head color:* Scribbles "Glittering Night Star."

ANCHOVY GREEN

Substitute green bucktail for turquoise blue bucktail. The fly is otherwise identical to the blue in every respect.

HERRING

Veil: Above the midline on each side tie in a few strands of lime green Krystal Flash. Tie in gray ghost Krystal Flash above. Veil with a few strands of light blue bucktail. Tie in a large bunch of pearl blue Krystal Flash on top. Tie over a very thin bunch of blue bucktail. *Topping:*

Peacock herl. *Shoulder:* Silver Krystal Flash. *Dorsal head color:* Scribbles "Glittering Night Star."

SARDINE

Veil: On each side, lime green and olive Krystal Flash, mixed, followed by a *very small bunch* of lime green bucktail. *Topping:* Olive and pearl blue Krystal Flash topped with a few strands of green bucktail. *Topping:* Peacock herl. (In the smallest sizes, I often substitute a few strands of moss FisHair.) *Shoulder:* Silver Krystal Flash. Run a couple of strands of orange Krystal Flash down the midline on each side. *Head:* Any dark green color applied lightly. Note: The Sardine suggests one of many off-green baitfish. It doesn't look like much, but it often takes school tuna more successfully than any other Sea Habit Bucktail.

I tie a variation of the Sardine in the Deceiver style that imitates the Pacific sand lance. *Pacific Sand Lance:* Tie in a few strands of bucktail mixed with pearl Flashabou at the tail. Tie in two to three thin white saddle hackles on each side. Tie in an underbody of pearl Flashabou as described above. Tie in white bucktail as described above. Tie in a few strands of lime green and olive Krystal Flash above the midline. Tie in a few strands of lime green bucktail. Top with olive Krystal Flash. *Topping:* Moss FisHair. Shoulder with a few strands of silver Krystal Flash. *Head:* Color the Sea Habit head with any glitter paint or marking pen that matches the moss FisHair.

FLYING FISH

Veil: On each side, pearl Krystal Flash and a few strands of light blue bucktail. On top, tie in a bunch of pearl blue Krystal Flash. Tie over a thin clump of blue bucktail. *Topping:* Several strands of royal blue Krystal Flash, and *a few strands* of black bucktail. *Shoulder:* Silver Krystal Flash. *Head:* Scribbles "Glittering Pacific Blue." Note: The flying fish found off Baja California have an especially deep blue dorsal color. Perhaps for this reason, the dorado that continually hunt them seem to take this blue-over-white fly better than do other gamefish.

SEA HABIT BUCKTAILS FOR WAHOO

Any of the above patterns in sizes 3/0 to 5/0 works well for wahoo. The only change I make is to mix silver Flashabou with the pearl Flashabou when tying in the underbody, and then to heavily shoulder the fly with silver Flashabou. Because the fly is fished first on a slack drift, the fluttering strands of silver Flashabou suggest a scale from a wounded baitfish.

SEA HABIT BUCKTAILS FOR SAILFISH

If tying these flies tandem style for billfish, I first tie in white bucktail heavily mixed with pearl Flashabou at the upturned stinger hook. After this is completed, I coat the head with 5-Minute epoxy, and tie the balance of the fly on the lead hook as described above. If length greater than the bucktail is needed, alternate bucktail with longer bunches of FisHair.

SEA HABIT DECEIVER

I tie the same patterns for Sea Habit Deceivers that I tie for Sea Habit Bucktails. The only difference is that the tail of white bucktail is well mixed with pearlescent Flashabou, and the two to six white saddle hackles are set on each side over the bucktail. I then shoulder these hackles on each side with a bunch of pearlescent Flashabou mixed with a few strands of silver Flashabou. Just as for the Sea Habit Bucktails, I tie in a heavy underbody of pearl Flashabou. These construction features aren't appreciated until the fly is wet, for then the Flashabou comes through to really bring the fly to life.

For specific patterns, see Sea Habit Bucktails in the Anchovy Blue, Anchovy Green, Herring, Sardine, and Flying Fish patterns.

I typically fish these variations of Lefty's Deceiver in sizes 1 to 7/0. As with the Sea Habit Bucktails, I usually tie the fly on Owner and Gamakatsu bait hooks, and the Owner Spinnerbait hook in 5/0. As tied with a Sea Habit head of Mylar piping that has been twice coated with 5-Minute epoxy, the fly is head-heavy. If connected to the leader with a loop knot, the fly will tip head down between strips. If given slack, the fly dives dramatically, the long saddle hackles and pearl and silver Flashabou fluttering behind. In this attitude, the Sea Habit Deceiver in the Anchovy Blue pattern loaded with silver Flashabou is the most effective fly I've ever used for wahoo and large tuna.

In sizes 1 to 3/0, I use Witchcraft decal-type eyes. In sizes 4/0 to 7/0, as single hook patterns, I epoxy on doll eyes, either 7mm round eyes or 10mm oval eyes. These eyes don't prevent the fly from diving, and they keep the fly on an even keel when it is stripped in.

I tie a Sea Habit Deceiver in two patterns—the Green Machine and the Dorado—that are not listed among Sea Habit Bucktails, because I tie them only in the Deceiver style. As a single hook dressing, the Green Machine is a pattern worth tying for dorado, dogtooth tuna, and a variety of inshore gamefish. As a tandem hook fly, it's an excellent billfish pattern. The Dorado pattern in 3/0 to 5/0 fishes well for both inshore and offshore gamefish.

GREEN MACHINE
Hook: Owner 5/0. *Tail:* A medium bunch of white bucktail mixed with pearl Flashabou. Tie in a bunch of chartreuse Krystal Flash on each side. Tie in, on each side, two long saddle hackles, two each of white, chartreuse,

and hot green (twelve saddle hackles in all). Tie in an underbody of pearl Flashabou as described above. Tie in a short bunch of white bucktail at the throat. Tie in a bunch of chartreuse and olive Krystal Flash on each side, and tie chartreuse bucktail over. Repeat up the side with longer bunches of chartreuse bucktail. Tie over, on each side above the midline, a bunch of pearl blue Krystal Flash. Tie over a few strands of blue bucktail. Tie on top a bunch of pearl blue Krystal Flash. Tie over a thin bunch of blue bucktail. *Topping:* Royal blue Krystal Flash and peacock herl. *Shoulder:* A few strands of silver Flashabou and a bunch of chartreuse and pearl blue Krystal Flash. *Head:* 10mm oval doll eyes. *Dorsal head color:* Scribbles "Night Star."

DORADO
Tail: White bucktail mixed with pearl Flashabou. Tie in long saddle hackles on each side of the white bucktail in the following sequence: two yellow, two chartreuse, one hot green, and one silver doctor blue. Set the last two hackles higher off the hook than the previous hackles. Tie in, at the head, an underbody of pearl and chartreuse Krystal Flash. Tie in a short bunch of yellow bucktail under the hook. Extend the length of the bucktail with each additional application. Tie in, on each side above the midline, a small bunch of chartreuse bucktail. Tie in on top a bunch of pearl Krystal Flash and a thin bunch of turquoise blue bucktail or peacock blue FisHair. *Topping:* Peacock herl (optional). *Shoulder:* Pearl blue Krystal Flash.

SEA HABIT BILLFISH

I tie the Sea Habit Billfish flies with a 7/0 Gamakatsu bait hook forward, and a 6/0 Owner stinger hook up, connecting the two hooks with 150-pound monofilament with no more than 2 inches between the hooks. The overall length of the flies runs from 9 to 10 inches. *Tying instructions:* To the 6/0 stinger, tie in a long clump of bucktail mixed with pearl Flashabou, and four long white saddle hackles to each side. To each side of the hackles, tie in a clump of pearl and silver Flashabou one-third of the length of the hackles. At the bend of the 7/0

Sea Habit Deceivers, left row, top to bottom: Dorado, Ballyhoo (wahoo), Anchovy Green, Flying Fish (wahoo), Anchovy Blue. Middle row: Green Machine (Sea Habit Deceiver), Sea Habit Bucktail Billfish (Anchovy Blue patterns with a single hook), Sea Habit Billfish (double hook), Sea Habit Bucktail Wahoo. (Almost any bright dorsal color will work as long as the basic fly is white and contains a lot of silver flash.) Sea Habit Bucktails, right row, top to bottom: Wahoo (purple dorsal), Flying Fish, Sardine, Anchovy Blue, Ballyhoo, Anchovy Green.

hook, tie in a large clump of white bucktail mixed with pearl Flashabou on each side, so that the two sides partially enclose the stinger hackles. Outside of the bucktail tie in four to six white saddle hackles to a side, shouldering the tie with a mix of silver and pearl Flashabou that extends back to the hackles on the stinger hook. Wind forward. Around the hook, tie in thick bunches of pearl Flashabou that extend slightly past the forward hackles. Tie in a short bunch of bucktail under the hook. Tie in white bucktail on each side over this throat, and repeat, each tie longer than the previous. When the general contour of the baitfish has been achieved in white, tie the patterns as described below. Note: When using doll eyes ¼ inch or larger on these tandem hook flies, the eyes will prevent the fly from sinking and it will swim unnaturally. *It is then necessary to puncture the eyes and force water into them before fishing the fly.*

ANCHOVY BLUE

Above the midline, tie in strands of olive and lime green Krystal Flash on each side, over the white bucktail. Tie in a small bunch of lime green bucktail over the Krystal Flash (Don't worry if the dorsal bunches of bucktail don't extend the full length of the fly.) On top, tie in a bunch of pearl blue Krystal Flash and follow with a bunch of peacock blue FisHair in the 10-inch length, mixed with a few strands of smolt blue Krystal Flash. This application can be as long as you wish. Repeat with turquoise blue bucktail mixed with smolt blue Krystal Flash. *Topping:* Peacock herl. *Shoulder:* Silver Flashabou on each side.

If you wish to tie an *Anchovy Green* billfish pattern (a good mackerel imitation), substitute green bucktail mixed with green Krystal Flash.

FLYING FISH

Above the midline, tie in strands of pearl and pearl blue Krystal Flash over the white bucktail. Top with light blue bucktail. Tie in a bunch of pearl blue Krystal Flash. Tie on top a thin bunch of blue bucktail. Repeat twice. On the last application of blue bucktail, mix with royal blue Krystal Flash. *Topping:* Peacock herl. *Shoulder:* Silver Flashabou on each side.

BALLYHOO

Above the midline, tie in a mix of pearl, chartreuse, and pink Krystal Flash, over the white bucktail. Tie on each side a bunch of light blue bucktail. Tie on top a large bunch of pearl blue Krystal Flash. Tie over on top a bunch of medium gray bucktail or FisHair mixed with gray ghost Krystal Flash. Repeat as needed for size and bulk. *Topping:* Peacock herl. *Shoulder:* Silver Flashabou on each side. Note: This pattern also suggests a mullet, a baitfish commonly rigged as a teaser for billfish.

I've hooked six species of billfish and boated five using these flies. This includes at least a half-dozen free-swimming striped marlin. Though teased-in billfish will come from a longer distance to hammer a large popper, these flies have a much better hookup ratio. On a recent trip, two companions and I were fishing my flies tied on the Gamakatsu and Owner hooks as described. We hooked ten striped marlin, lost one when the fly came out on a jump, lost two well into the fight due to broken class tippets, and boated seven legal by the rules of the IGFA.

The upturned stinger hook throws the fly somewhat out of balance, and makes it much less head-heavy. As a result, if you cast one of these flies dry, it will at first float, or swim on its side. I soak the fly for at least fifteen minutes in seawater before casting it, to make sure it begins swimming upright the moment it comes under tension.

NICK CURCIONE

Nick Curcione has been my fishing companion in offshore Mexican waters and on remote rivers of New Guinea. These experiences remain among my fondest fly-fishing memories, as much for Curcione's companionship as for the knowledge and skill he brings to the sport. When not traveling to remote fly-fishing destinations, Curcione gives talks and casting demonstrations, and writes articles for national fly-fishing magazines. I found his recent book, *The Orvis Guide to Saltwater Fly Fishing*, tremendously informative on a remarkable variety of gamefish.

Curcione recommends the following flies for inshore and offshore gamefish.

TUNA TONIC 2/0

Body: Gold Mylar piping. *Wing:* White marabou mixed with pearl Flashabou. *Topping:* Pearl blue Krystal Flash. *Eyes:* Red plastic eyes. Apply clear 5-Minute epoxy around the eyes.

SARDINE 2/0

Body: None. *Wing:* Matching white saddle hackles. Tie in blue saddle hackles along each side, setting slightly above the white hackles. Shoulder with pearl Flashabou. *Topping:* Pearl blue Krystal Flash. *Eyes:* Red plastic eyes. Apply 5-Minute epoxy around the eyes.

CURCIONE'S BUSHWACKER

Hook: 4/0. Extend the body to three times the hook length by lashing down a length of 300-pound monofilament to the hook shank. To the end of the monofilament, tie in eight to twelve white saddle hackles. Tie in a marabou plume and wind it around the monofilament. Cover the monofilament with marabou in a white/blue/white sequence. *Body:* Cactus chenille on the hook shank. *Eyes:* Red plastic eyes. Apply 5-Minute epoxy around the eyes.

CURCIONE'S FLASHER

Body: None. *Wing:* Ocean Hair, pale blue over white. Top with large bunch of pearl Krystal Flash. Cover the wing with Flashabou, a mix of blues and golds.

CURCIONE'S BIG GAME FLY NO. 2

Hooks: 7/0 Mustad 3407 and 6/0 Owner bait hook for the stinger. Lash down a loop of 90-pound Sevenstrand wire to the forward hook by running the doubled wire through the eye and down the shank of the hook. Leave the loop about 3 inches long. All tying is completed on the forward hook. *Tying instructions:* Tie in a large bunch of white Ocean Hair. Tie in four saddle hackles on each side over the Ocean Hair. Tie in two grizzly hackles dyed blue on each side of the white hackles. *Topping:* A lavish mix of Flashabou: bronze, dark blue, and various electric blues, violets, and purples.

CHICO FERNANDEZ

Chico Fernandez, a pioneer in American saltwater fly fishing and a popular writer, lecturer, and casting instructor, lives in Miami, Florida where an enormous variety of offshore, inshore, and flats gamefish are only minutes away. His Big Fish Fly represents one of the earliest uses of FisHair for billfish.

I like the fly much better when the FisHair is spaced and opened up with shorter bucktail of the same color. I also like to put small doll eyes on the fly to help keel it; and I like to build up the head with epoxy so that the fly dives between strips.

FERNANDEZ'S BIG FISH FLY

Hook: 4/0 to 6/0. *Tying instructions:* The entire fly is constructed from FisHair. Tie in a large bunch of white FisHair 7 to 8 inches long. This represents at least half the fly. Top with shorter lengths of light green and blue FisHair. Shoulder on each side with strands of silver Flashabou to the length of the blue and green FisHair.

ROD HARRISON

Rod Harrison, my "mate" on trips to Mexico, Australia, and Papua New Guinea, has been a leading proponent of saltwater fly fishing in Australian waters. When not fishing, he keeps constantly on the go with video projects, writing assignments, and speaking engagements. In local waters, he fishes Rod's Billfish Fly for black marlin and Pacific sailfish.

ROD'S BILLFISH FLY

Hook: 6/0 front, 4/0 stinger. *Tying thread:* Blue. Secure hooks together with heavy braided wire and set about one-and-a-half inches apart. Tie in a bunch of white FisHair to the stinger hook. Tie four to six white saddles hackles to each side. At the front hook, tie in a large bunch of white bucktail. To each side of the bucktail tie in eight to ten saddle hackles. (The number of saddle hackles depends on their length and quality. If the hackles are long and full, fewer need to be used.) Tie in strands of pearl Flashabou to each side. *Topping:* Blue bucktail mixed with blue Flashabou. *Cheek and eye:* Mallard breast feather. Epoxy to each side a large-diameter Mylar eye. *Beard:* Red marabou.

KATE & BILL HOWE

Kate and Bill Howe, commercial fly tiers and fly-fishing instructors of national prominence, manage Hat Creek Ranch, a private waters property owned by The Fly Shop in Redding, California. Both have been Master Fly Tiers in the Fly Tying Theater at International Sportsman's Expositions shows for many years. There they demonstrate their skills at tying a variety of flies, including what has become their signature fly—the ALF.

When not fishing the West's finest trout waters, or stalking bonefish on Mexican flats, they fish inshore and offshore waters with ALF (an acronym for "Any Little Fellow"), from tiny wisps of ALFs ("Fry" and "Stir Fry") to tandem hook 7/0 monster ALFs for dogtooth tuna and billfish. Like a Lefty's Deceiver, an ALF in any size or color works on just about anything that swims.

The ALF is a type of fly and tying approach rather than a specific pattern. The Howes' description of the Blue ALF is tediously detailed only to illustrate how remarkable the shadings of color are that can be constructed into an ALF dressing. They invite you to try your hand at ALF that satisfy your local needs, whether you're sight fishing for Florida tarpon, working deep running lines for yellowfin tuna, or casting for silver salmon in Washington's Puget Sound.

BLUE ALF

Hook: 3/0 TMC 800. *Thread:* "A" white monocord. *Tying instructions:* The basic ALF tying approach involves tying down small bunches of Ultra Hair from a point over the barb, and winding forward with the tips pointing over the eye of the hook, then folding the Ultra Hair back over and tying it down. Each subsequent bunch is tied down a couple of wraps farther forward. The Ultra Hair is trimmed to length as the fly is constructed. By blending many different colors of Ultra Hair, the Howes create an extremely lifelike effect. Wind thread down the hook shank until it's over the barb. Tie down fifteen strands of white Super Hair, wrap forward, and fold back. Repeat. Trim so that the ends are ¼ inch longer than the first bunch of white Super Hair. Tie in eight strands of smoke Super Hair, fold back, and trim so that the longest strands run just past the longest white. Tie in eight strands of clear yellow Ultra Hair, fold over, and trim to the length of the smoke Ultra Hair. Tie in six strands of smoke Ultra Hair, fold over, and trim so that the longest strands are slightly longer than the yellow Ultra Hair. Tie in six to eight strands of silver Flashabou, of uneven lengths, the longest strands ½ inch longer than any of the Ultra Hair. Purple Ultra Hair, six strands, tie down, fold back, trim even with the Flashabou. Olive Ultra Hair, six strands, tie down, trim to ½ inch longer than the Flashabou. Light blue Ocean Hair, twelve strands, tie down, fold back, tie down and trim no longer than the body length. (The Howes feel that the slightly stiffer Ocean Hair helps stabilize the softer Ultra Hair and Flashabou.) Gray ghost Krystal Flash, six strands, tie down, fold over, and tie down. Trim to the length of the silver Flashabou. Olive Ultra Hair, six strands, tie down, fold back, and tie down. Trim to the body length. Peacock Krystal Flash, four strands, tie down, fold over, and tie down. Red Ocean Hair, twenty-five strands on each side, extending to the bend of the hook to simulate "bleeding gills." White Ocean Hair, twenty-five strands, tied on each side along the bottom of the hook at the point where you tied in the first bunch of Ocean Hair. On top, royal blue Ultra Hair, fifteen strands, tie down, fold back, and tie down. Trim ½ inch shorter than the body length. Mixed color Krystal Flash, twelve strands, tie down, fold back, and tie down. Trim to the length of the blue Ultra Hair. Polar bear Ultra Hair, thirty strands on each side. Tie down along the underside, extend to halfway between the first belly section and the length of blue Ultra Hair. Black Ocean Hair—the topping—twelve strands, tie down, fold back, and tie down. Attach 10mm doll eyes above the hook shank in line with the red gills. (Kate and Bill Howe use Hot Stuff Special T Glue with Kick-It accelerator.) Color the top of the head with a brown marking pen.

CALAMARI

The Calamari, a Kate Howe squid imitation, has been successfully used in the 4/0 size, on Costa Rican sailfish. In sizes down to 1/0, the fly has caught a variety of inshore and offshore species. *Hook:* Tiemco 800S 2/0 to 4/0. Open the gap with pliers. Extend the shank to at least twice the hook length with 60-pound braided wire crimped at the hook and at the loop. *Thread:* Monocord, color to match the pattern. Wind thread several times around the hook shank for a heavy thread base. At the bend of the hook, tie in a small bunch of white, then purple, Ultra Hair, mixed with lavender and blue Flashabou; holographic Mylar; and Lite Brite. Tie four saddle hackles flared out on each side, and eight to ten rubber legs (Sili Legs) the length of the hackles. *Eyes:* 12mm to 15mm doll eyes. Reduce the post length by half and connect the eyes together with a plastic tubing sleeve

and 5-Minute epoxy. Place the joined eyes on top of the hook shank and secure with figure eight wraps. The shank of the hook is wrapped with a string of white rabbit. Tie in the rabbit at the bend of the hook, undercoat with rubber cement, and wrap around the eyes. Stop and tie in a small bunch of Lite Brite, and lavender and blue Flashabou. Coat with rubber cement and again wrap with the strip of rabbit. Continue this sequence until the hook and braided wire have been covered with rabbit, Flashabou and Lite Brite added into each inch. *Head:* At the head, tie in a short bunch of purple Ultra Hair on each side to simulate the fins of the mantle. Apply purple and dark brown dots to the hackles and the head with marking pens.

DAVE INKS

Dave Inks, president of Outdoor Enterprises, Inc., "commutes" between his offices in Santa Rosa, California, and Missoula, Montana where his Watermaster float tube–style rafts are manufactured. An experienced offshore fly fisherman, he has used the following patterns for many species of pelagic gamefish, including two world record yellowfin tuna. His offshore destinations have included Mexico, Belize, Panama, Florida, and California.

DINK'S MACKEREL

Tying thread: White single strand floss. *Body:* Tie in polar bear Ultra Hair above and below the hook. Mix with a few strands of pearl Flashabou. Tie in on top a bunch of chartreuse Ultra Hair. Top with small bunches of smoke and blue Ultra Hair. Shoulder with a single grizzly saddle hackle extending to nearly the full length of the fly.

DINK'S ANCHOVY

Tying thread: White single strand floss. *Body:* Tie in pearl Flashabou and then white bucktail under the hook to the full length of the body. On top of the hook, tie in a small bunch of smoke Ultra Hair slightly shorter than the bucktail. Tie in small bunches of pearl Flashabou, lime green bucktail, and blue bucktail. *Eyes:* Yellow iris, black pupil.

DINK'S RED HEAD MINNOW

Hook: 2/0 to 4/0. *Tying thread:* White single strand floss. *Body:* Tie in, under the hook, white bucktail, long, to the full length of the body. Tie in, on top of the hook, sparse brown bucktail half the length of the white bucktail. Over the brown bucktail, tie in smoke Ultra Hair three-quarters the length of the body. Tie over with white bucktail to the full length of the fly. *Topping:* Peacock herl. *Shoulder:* Grizzly saddle hackle on each side tied in to run along the upper application of white bucktail. *Head:* Red.

Fly tiers: Dan Blanton, Ralph Kanz, Bill Howe, Dave Inks. Left row, top to bottom: Blanton's Sal-Mul-Sac (2), Kanz's Mylar Monnow (2), Bill Howe's ALF (3) in sizes for tuna, tarpon, etc. Right row: Dave Ink's Dink's Read Head Minnow, Dink's Mackerel, Dink's Anchovy (3), Bill Howe's ALF in sizes and colors for offshore schoolies.

RALPH KANZ

Ralph Kanz's Mylar-laden flies have become enormously popular in recent years. I've seen them attract gamefish from rainbow runners and giant trevally to striped and black marlin. On long-range fly-fishing trips, Kanz's Mylar Minnow has accounted for more wahoo than any other pattern. This is one of those few "must have" flies when fishing offshore.

LITTLE FLASH

Hook: Eagle Claw 66SS 1/0 to 3/0. *Eyes:* 4mm glass eyes attached to soft wire. *Thread:* Silver Mylar. *Tail:* Bucktail. (Optional—tie in if you want a fuller-looking fly.) *Body:* Silver Mylar braid. *Underwing:* Silver Flashabou. *Wing:* Bucktail in preferred colors. You can also use FisHair and other synthetics. *Tying instructions:* Take the offset out of the hook and sharpen. (On small hooks, if the offset isn't removed, the fly will swim on its side.) Start the thread at the midpoint of the shank and wind forward to a point ¹⁄₁₆ the length of the shank. Bend the wire flat to the eyes and tie down with the wire toward the bend of the hook. The wire should extend about two-thirds of the way down the shank of the hook. Tie in the tail of bucktail. Tie in a doubled piece of Mylar braid just behind the eyes. Wind to the tail and back, and tie off, making sure the Mylar fills in behind the eyes. Whip-finish and tie off. Coat the body and eyes with Flex-Cote or Classic Rod Coat finish. (Kanz normally completes a dozen bodies at a time in this manner.) When dry, tie in the thread in front of the eyes; tie in a bunch of Flashabou on top of the hook and taper-cut half to three-quarters the length of the fly. Repeat directly under the eyes so that the two bunches match up. Tie on top a bunch of Mylar half the length of the body. Repeat below. Tie on top a bunch of Mylar one-third the length of the body. Repeat below. The Mylar has now formed the basic shape of the fly. Tie in a bunch of bucktail on top with the end facing forward. Tie in a contrasting bunch of bucktail below, with the tip points toward the tail. Pull the top bucktail back and secure with several wraps and a whip-finish. Coat the head of the fly with the same finish used on the body. Run the finish up against the eyes to additionally secure them.

KANZ'S MYLAR MINNOW

Hook: Single or double, the size depending on the application. For billfish, 7/0 to 8/0. *Thread:* Silver Mylar. *Eyes:* Glass, 6mm or larger, with soft wire stems attached. *Underwing:* Silver Mylar. *Lateral line:* Iridescent Mylar. *Cheeks:* Red hackle fibers. *Wing:* FisHair. *Tying instructions:* Attach the thread and wind back to the bend of the hook. Tie in the first bunch of Mylar and trim to the total length of the fly. Tie in a bunch of Mylar on each side and trim to half the length of the fly. Add three more bunches of Mylar as you work forward, until you reach the spot where the eyes will be attached, about ¹⁄₁₆ the total length of the fly. Tie in the lateral line on each side of the hook. Tie in the red hackle cheeks. Bend the wires as described under "Little Flash." Tie in the eyes, the wire extending to the barb of the hook. Whip-finish the fly and coat with either Flex-Cote or Classic Rod Coat finish. When the fly is dry, reattach the thread at the head, and add three more bunches of Mylar on top and two on the bottom. Tie in FisHair on the top and bottom. Coat the head with rod finish, paint it to match the colors of the wing, and coat it again.

KANZ'S BUCKTAIL BAITFISH

Use the same tying approach described under "Mylar Minnow." The base of the fly is constructed with bucktail and Mylar. Tie in a tail of FisHair and add a bunch of bucktail on each side. Tie in a bunch of silver Mylar, with a bunch of bucktail on top, halfway between the tail tie-in point and the spot where the eyes will be tied in. Move forward and repeat just behind the spot where the eyes will be tied in. Tie in the lateral line, cheeks, and eyes. Cement around the eyes. Forward of the eyes, tie in Mylar and bucktail. Tie in FisHair top and bottom. Finish the head as described in "Mylar Minnow." This is a somewhat fuller fly than the Mylar Minnow. I prefer this Kanz fly when casting for billfish.

LEFTY KREH

Lefty Kreh, the world's best known and most popular fly fisherman, developed Lefty's Deceiver, the best all-purpose fly in saltwater fly fishing. The fly, now more than forty years young and the subject of a United States postage stamp, is a type that Lefty has continually refined, and one that others have used as a starting point for their own fly designs. The reasons for the fly's popularity are several. Long matching hackles are tied at the bend of the hook. If the hackles are relatively narrow and fine stemmed, the fly produces terrific action. Tied in this manner, the hackles make the fly almost always foul-free, an extremely important consideration when you may get only one shot at a fast-moving saltwater gamefish. When you combine the basic tail of white hackles with the myriad of bucktail colors, Flashabous, and Krystal Flashes, you can create a number of baitfish-imitating patterns. Change the wing to yellow, chartreuse, hot green, or pale gray hackles; or mix these with white; or shoulder the nearly completed fly with barred grizzly dyed a variety of colors, and you have Lefty's Deceivers in an endless variety good for offshore and inshore gamefish.

Below are a few of the many Lefty's Deceivers that Kreh offers in his book *Salt Water Fly Patterns*, the only book I take with me everywhere I travel.

OLIVE DECEIVER

Wing: six to twelve white saddle hackles, with an olive-dyed grizzly saddle on each side. Add strands of lime or gold Krystal Flash. *Body:* Silver Mylar or none. *Beard:* Red Krystal Flash or rabbit fur ½ inch long. *Collar:* White bucktail with a short olive-dyed grizzly hackle on each side. *Topping:* ten to fifteen strands of peacock herl mixed with strands of lime green Krystal Flash. *Head:* Green. *Eyes:* Yellow iris, black pupil (optional).

ORANGE DECEIVER

Identical to the Olive Deceiver, except orange grizzly is substituted for olive.

YELLOW DECEIVER

Tie as you would the Olive Deceiver, except substitute yellow saddle hackles and yellow-dyed grizzly hackles, and tie in a collar of yellow bucktail. *Head:* Yellow.

WHITE DECEIVER

If tied with extra-long saddle hackles, this all-white Deceiver is a great billfish fly. I add a topping of peacock herl, shoulder it with pearl and silver Flashabou, and epoxy doll eyes just behind the head to each side of the bucktail collar, then add some 5-Minute epoxy around the head for weight.

BIG-EYED DECEIVER

Wing: eight to sixteen saddle hackles shouldered with pearl Krystal Flash. *Collar:* White bucktail. *Topping:* Peacock herl. On each side of the collar behind the head, tie in a teal or mallard breast feather that has been coated with Flexament. *Eyes:* Yellow iris, black pupil, large, painted in on breast feather.

WINSTON MOORE

Winston Moore of Boise, Idaho has quite possibly taken more IGFA legal Pacific sailfish on the fly than any other fly fisher in history. Today, Moore is at least as well known for his skills at flats fishing for permit. His billfish flies, made entirely of FisHair, are easily tied and very effective on teased-in sailfish.

Hooks are usually 5/0, front and rear, secured with 90-pound monofilament. Using pliers, increase the gap of the rear hook. (This is especially helpful if the hook takes hold in the billfish's palate.) Length of the flies is about 6 inches. Cover the shank of the front hook with silver Mylar. Tie all flies entirely from the front hook. Colors are green/blue/white (baitfish imitation); chartreuse/yellow (dorado imitation); orange and red/white (pure attractor). Moore often uses a tapered foam head dyed red, the smaller end in the lead, in conjunction with these flies. He does not attach eyes to the foam head.

PETE PARKER

Pete Parker, a master fly tier from Indian Hills, Colorado, manages the Fly Tying Theater at Ed Rice's International Sportsman's Exposition shows. As a result, he knows every tier and the details of every tricked-out fly heading for the salt. Parker offers the following flies for fishing mid-sized offshore gamefish, from bonito and dorado to wahoo. Parker and I have fished for weeks together on Ed Rice's Blue Water Invitationals, long-range fly-fishing trips off Baja California, and I can testify to the effectiveness of his saltwater flies.

Parker finishes the heads of all his "glitter head" flies in the following manner: Cover the thread wraps with a thin coat of hot glue. Dip the head in a container of silver glitter. Make sure all surfaces are covered. Moisten your fingers and shape the head into a basic arrow point. Color the top of the head to match the dorsal color of the fly. Place a small drop of hot glue on each side where you want the eyes. Press the Witchcraft decal-type eye, or doll eye, in place. Add the red gill stripe. Cover the entire head with 5-Minute epoxy. To keep the epoxy from running, you can turn the fly around in your hand, or use a rotator vise.

PETE'S ANCHOVY

Hook: 3/0 or 4/0 TMC 811S. *Tying thread:* 3/0 Dynacord. Color is not important. *Body:* A bunch of white Super Hair under the hook and a second bunch tied over. Taper the bundles by clipping to 7 inches. (Do not clip at a 90-degree angle. Clip with the point of the scissors horizontal to the wing.) As the tying in of the wing continues, make sure all bunches are stacked on top of each other, and tapered with scissors to maintain the basic color and shape of a baitfish. Tie in a bunch of smoke Super Hair on top. Tie in fifteen to twenty strands each of copper and green Fire Fly for a lateral line. Tie in a bunch of lime green Super Hair. Tie in, separately, two bunches of olive Super Hair mixed with peacock Flashabou. *Gills:* ten to twelve strands of red Super Hair tied short just behind the head. *Eyes:* 10mm doll eyes. Finish with "glitter head" as described above.

PETE'S FLASH CHOVIE

Hook: 1/0 or 2/0 Tiemco 811S. *Tying thread:* 3/0 Dynacord. *Body:* A small bunch of smoke Super Hair and pearl Flashabou mixed 50/50. Follow with olive Super Hair and peacock Flashabou mixed 50/50. *Gills:* Red Super Hair, short, tied as a beard. *Eyes:* Witchcraft, white iris, black pupil. *Markings:* Lightly bar the sides with a black permanent marking pen.

PETE'S CHOVIE

Hook: 2/0 or 3/0 Tiemco 800S. *Tying thread:* 3/0 Dynacord. *Body:* Small bunches of white, smoke, chartreuse, olive, and peacock Super Hair. *Eyes:* 7mm plastic. *Head:* "Glitter head." *Markings:* Bar lightly with a black permanent marking pen.

PETE'S MACKEREL

Hook: 3/0 to 4/0 Tiemco 811S. *Tying thread:* 3/0 Dynacord. Color is not important. *Body:* Two bunches of white Super Hair tied above and below the hook. Taper with scissor cuts to about 7 inches from the hook eye. Tie in on top a bunch of smoke Super Hair. Tie in, separately, two bunches of olive Super Hair mixed with peacock Flashabou. *Topping:* twenty to thirty strands of peacock Flashabou. *Gills:* ten to twelve strands of red Super Hair tied short on the side of the head. *Eyes:* 8mm oval doll eyes. Finish with "glitter head." *Markings:* Using a black permanent marker, apply irregular marks on the back, like those found on mackerel.

PETE'S SIDE POPPER

Hook: 2/0 Mustad 33900. *Tying thread:* 3/0 Dynacord. *Body:* Drive a sharpened 9/16-inch copper tube through a 1½-inch-thick balsa block, creating a balsa dowel. Cut and sand the balsa to the popper shape. Using a Dremel tool, hollow out the head to a concave shape. Cut a groove along the flat side of the body to accept the hook shank. Epoxy the hook shank to the body. Fill the slot with sanding sealer. Sand smooth. Apply a thin coat of 5-Minute epoxy over the dorsal half of the body. Sprinkle silver glitter over the epoxy. Coat the glitter with blue fingernail polish. *Eyes:* Witchcraft, one on top, one on the bottom. Draw in red gill slits with a red marking pen. *Tail:* White over blue Super Hair. Cover the tail wraps with two turns of pearl spike or cactus chenille.

PETE'S SLIDER

Hook: Eagle Claw 66S 4/0. *Tying thread:* Dynacord. *Body:* Polyfoam caulksaver. Cut into one-inch lengths. Drive a hole down the middle of the foam cylinder and push onto the hook shank. Slide Mylar piping over the foam. Leave about one-half inch of hook shank at the rear end. Tie down both ends so that you have a beer-can shape. *Tail:* Olive over chartreuse Super Hair mixed with peacock Flashabou. Cover with two wraps of green spike or cactus chenille. *Eyes:* Witchcraft. Draw in gill slits.

BILLY PATE

Joe Howell, the owner of the Blue Heron Fly Shop on the banks of the North Umpqua River in Idleyld Park, Oregon, ties these flies to Billy Pate's specifications. Using these two patterns, Pate has boated many Pacific sailfish and hooked several blue marlin.

The hooks are snelled in tandem with 100-pound monofilament. The monofilament continues from the lead hook and become the shock tippet. (If the fly survives a hookup with a billfish, just clip off the damaged shock tippet, and tie in a new shock with a 3½-turn clinch knot.)

Hooks: Forward hook, Owner Spinnerbait 5/0; stinger hook, Owner 5/0 black chrome bait hook. (The stinger hook is offset and has an upturned eye.) *Tying instructions:* Tying begins on the stinger hook. Tie in a bunch of pearl Krystal Flash and eight matching saddle hackles on each side (sixteen hackles in all). Shoulder with a bunch of pearl Krystal Flash on each side. Coat the head with epoxy. Go to the forward hook and tie in eight saddle hackles on each side. Shoulder with bunches of pearl Krystal Flash on each side. Tie in bunches of magenta bucktail below the hook, to obtain a baitfish contour. Split a peacock sword and tie in to run dorsally down the fly. Over this, tie in heavy bunches of peacock Krystal Flash. Color the dorsal part of the head with a dark blue marking pen. Attach doll eyes with epoxy. Apply epoxy a second time and fill the area between the eyes.

If tying the hot chartreuse fly, shoulder the saddle hackles on both the stinger and forward hook with green saltwater Flashabou. Along the dorsal length, mix pearl, blue, green, and chartreuse Krystal Flash. Color the dorsal part of the head with a dark green marking pen. Complete the head as described above.

BOB POPOVICS

Whoever said there was nothing new in fly tying obviously hadn't heard of Bob Popovics. Popovics, who owns Shady Rest Pizza Parlour in Bayville, New Jersey, resides in nearby Seaside Park in the heart of some of North America's best inshore fly fishing. Bluefish and striped bass almost at his doorstep provide a proving grounds for his saltwater flies, easily among the most original—and effective—to be found anywhere on the fly-fishing scene.

SURF CANDY

When tied with pale green or olive over white, the Surf Candy imitates a spearing (also called "silversides"). The same fly with tan over white imitates a baitfish called "rainfish" along the New Jersey coast, and "bay anchovy" along New England's coastline.

(Note: Popovics uses Larva Lace "fine" nylon thread, manufactured by D. H. Thompson, and a rotating-style vise, when tying all of his epoxy flies.) *Body:* Silver Mylar piping. (When this is given two coats of epoxy, it looks exactly like the silver-lined stomach of a baitfish.) Tie in a clump of white Super Hair. Tie in a length of silver Mylar piping that extends beyond the Super Hair. Remove the core, flatten, and slip the stem end of a short section

Fly tiers: Jow Howell, Billy Pate, Rod Harrison. Attractor-style flies designed to be cast to teased-in billfish. Top to bottom: Flies (2) tied by Howell for Pate, white tandem-hook fly tied by Pate, whited tandem-hook fly tied by Harrison for Australia's black marlin.

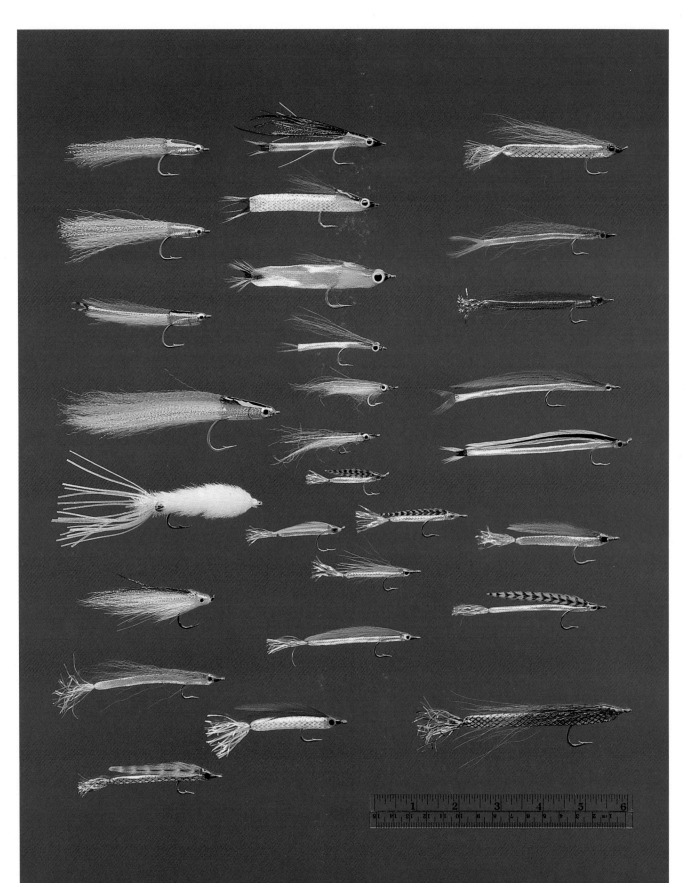

of grizzly saddle hackle and fix with Super Glue. This imitates the tail. Coat Mylar piping with clear fingernail polish to stiffen it and prevent it from fouling. Tie in the dorsal color, using Super Hair. Tie in a bunch of silver Flashabou at the head, twist, and wind around the head. Tie off and trim so that the head is a silver ball. Mark the dorsal part of the head with a marking pen that matches the dorsal color of Super Hair. Coat the entire body with Devcon 5-Minute epoxy. Lift the dorsal clump of Super Hair to give the body some bulk and keep the epoxy from matting down the hair. Rotate the fly to keep the epoxy from dripping. When the epoxy has hardened, paint in the red gill stripe with a marking pen, and apply the silver Witchcraft eyes, 3mm. (Bend the eyes in half horizontally to keep them lying flat.) Liberally apply a second coat of epoxy, again rotating the vise until the epoxy has hardened. (Popovics more commonly ties the fly without the midline of silver Mylar piping.) The final shape of the Surf Candy is achieved by trimming the Super Hair dorsally and ventrally at a 45-degree angle until the entire body tapers toward the tail.

SEA CANDY
The larger Sea Candy imitates herring, or even a mullet. It is tied as described above, but with the addition of silver Flashabou along each side. Keep this to the body length so that the individual strands can be spread when the first coat of epoxy is applied. Then trim the Flashabou to half the body length.

3-D SQUID
The 3-D Squid, so named because Popovics ties it fully in the round, is sure to become one of the most used of squid-type flies. Though the example Popovics ties is white, materials are available to tie it in any number of hot colors such as pink or red. Tie down a piece of stiff 20-pound monofilament to the hook shank, and temporarily secure the other end. On the monofilament, approximately three-quarters inch beyond the bend of the hook, tie in and wind on a ball of pearl cactus chenille. Tie in twelve to fifteen Sili Legs over the ball of chenille. (The ball spreads out the legs.) Complete a second ball of cactus chenille. Attach Witchcraft eyes to the second

Fly tiers: Bob Popoviks, Richard Stoll, Ron Ayotte, Trey Combs (single fly). Left row, top to bottom: Popovik's Surf Candy (3), Sea Candy, and 3-D Squid; Comb's Sea Habit Bucktail Sardine used on school tuna and Pacific salmon; Ayotte's Maylar Baitfish (2). Middle row: Stoll's Mylar Candlefish and Fluorescent Herring (second from top), Ayotte's Maylar Baitfish (8). Right row: Ayotte's Mylar Baitfish (8).

ball. *Body:* From the head, spin on a circle of white Ultra Hair at 5 to 6 tie-in points. Trim to shape—widest at the eye of the hook, tapered to the head. Seen head on, the overall shape is oval, the 3-D Squid about half as deep as it is wide.

STEVE PROBASCO
Steve Probasco, a nationally known outdoor writer from Raymond, Washington, pursues salmon off the coasts of Washington and British Columbia using the following patterns.

SALTWATER BAITFISH
Hook: TMC 800S 4/0. *Thread:* White monocord. *Tail:* White SLF hanks. *Body:* Pearl braid. *Wing:* White SLF hanks, then white Krystal Flash, blue Krystal Flash, green Fiber Optic Super Hair. *Topping:* Peacock herl. *Sides:* Silver Krystal Flash. *Gills:* Red SLF hanks. *Eyes:* Witchcraft, pearl iris, black pupil. *Head:* Clear epoxy.

SALTWATER FRY
Hook: Mustad 34011 2/0. *Thread:* White monocord. *Tail:* Golden-pheasant green neck feather. *Body:* Silver Mylar tubing. *Wing:* White Super Hair under, a bunch of peacock herl over. *Throat:* Lite Brite. *Sides:* Silver Krystal Flash. *Eyes:* Witchcraft, silver iris, black pupil.

RICHARD STOLL
(Northwest Angler, 26682 Edgewater Boulevard, NW, Poulsbo, WA 98370)

Richard Stoll owns Northwest Angler in Poulsbo, Washington, a Puget Sound beachfront town with year-round salmon fishing. No one in the area better understands the movements of silver and chinook salmon. While he describes his methods of presentation in terms of salmon, they work equally well on mid-sized inshore and offshore gamefish.

Stoll has been my fishing companion for permit and bonefish on the flats of Mexico's Ascension Bay. I wouldn't be caught on any saltwater trip without a few of his Mylar baitfish flies.

MYLAR CANDLEFISH
Most often this fly does not work well when stripped back like a streamer. Along beaches it should be fished on a floating line or Type II sink tip. I allow the fly to fall and drift in the current in and around schools of candlefish, herring, and smelt. If action is needed to elicit a re-

sponse, making a few short strips and letting the fly fall between strips is all that is necessary. Most of the time, the fly will be picked up by salmon on the fall.

Hook: Daiichi 2546, sizes 1 to 4. *Tail/Body:* Flattened pearl Mylar tubing with a badger hackle section Super Glued in as a tail fin. "I prefer Zap-a-Gap and use Zip-Kicker to mist the glue for instant setting. Go very light on misting the glue. Too much Zip-Kicker will cause the catalytic reaction to go too far, resulting in a poor-looking and weak glue joint." Thread the debarbed hook through the tubing. A piece of 25-pound fluorescent red Amnesia is threaded down the center of the Mylar tubing and tied in at the head. This acts as a stiffener and adds a red fluorescent blood line to the fly. Tie the tubing in at the head. *Wing:* Blue, green, brown, and gray dun bucktail to imitate the brownish green–gray coloration of candlefish. Tie in very sparsely and only two-thirds the length of the body. *Eyes:* Wapsi white solid plastic eyes. The stems of these eyes must first be clipped off with scissors. Lay the eyes backside up on the edge of the table. Place a tiny drop of Zap-a-Gap on the back of each eye. Mist the head of the fly with Zip-Kicker. Touch the misted fly to one of the eyes in the location where the eye should attach. Turn the fly over and repeat to attach the second eye. Fill in around the two eyes and head with Zap-a-Gap and mist with Zip-Kicker.

FLUORESCENT HERRING

The Fluorescent Herring incorporates Everglow tubing rather than pearlescent Mylar piping in the body. This tubing glows in the dark, making the fly extremely effective early in the morning and late in the evening.

This is not an impressionistic fly, but rather an actual imitation of an injured candlefish, herring, or smelt. It should be fished directly in and around schools of these baitfish.

Flies coated with Aquaseal have an entirely different action. They tend to sink head first. These flies should be worked alternately with short strips and slack line falls to be most effective.

I have also fished the larger Aquaseal version on lead core lines in water as deep as 100 feet with success for large chinook salmon.

Hook: Daiichi 2546, sizes 2/0 to 2. *Tail/Body:* Identical to the Mylar Candlefish except for the use of fluorescent pearl Everglow tubing. *Wing:* Blue and green bucktail, mixed, two-thirds the length of the body. *Eyes:* Same as the Mylar Candlefish. *Throat:* Red hackle fibers. *Head:* Aquaseal neoprene wader glue accelerated with Cotol. After coating, put the fly on an electric rotating rod finishing tool. This will keep the Aquaseal level as it hardens. Aquaseal gives a soft texture and is not as heavy as epoxy.

BOB VEVERKA

Avid fly tiers worldwide know Bob Veverka of Underhill, Vermont as the consummate tier of full-dressed Atlantic salmon flies and of lavishly complex steelhead flies. But Veverka turns to the salt for his sport, too, and not surprisingly, his flies for inshore and offshore gamefish are as attractive as they are effective. He fishes these patterns on New England waters for striped bass, bluefish, and Atlantic bonito, and off Florida and Baja California for school tuna and dorado.

CALAMARI EXPRESS

Hook: 3X long, 1/0 to 4/0. *Tail:* A few strands of white polar bear. Mix over white marabou, and a few strands of pink and pearl Fire Fly. Shoulder with two white neck hackles on each side, tied to flare out. Tie in glass eyes at the base of the hackles. *Body:* Lite Brite Pearl Dubben. At the front cross section, gather, glue, and flatten, using Cellaine head cement. Cut the leading edge of the body to the shape of an arrowhead. Coat the flat part of the mantle with epoxy.

BONITO BULLET ("YELLOW" AND "WHITE")

The Bullet doesn't represent a specific baitfish, but is nevertheless deadly on a variety of gamefish when they're feeding on small baitfish. *Hook:* Short shank, 1, 2, and 4. *Wing:* Yellow or white goat hair, sparse, mixed with pearl Fire Fly. Tie in a single white neck hackle on each side. *Body:* Opal Essence braided tubing. Draw in a red gill slit using a fine marking pen. *Eyes:* Witchcraft, white iris, black pupil. Coat the entire body with epoxy.

SAND EEL

The Sand Eel (known on the West Coast as "Pacific sand lance," "needlefish," and "candlefish") fill East Coast waters from spring until fall and become the prime food source for many saltwater gamefish. Veverka's Sand Eel effectively imitates this baitfish and reliably takes striped bass, bluefish, bonito, and little tunny when they're feeding on sand eels. *Hook:* 3X long hook. *Wing:* Tie in white bucktail mixed with a few strands of pearl Fire Fly at the

Fly tiers: Bob Veverka, Ralph Kanz, Steve Probasco, The Orvis Company (Nick Curcione), Westbank Anglers (Steve Vletas). Left row: Veverka's Baby Bunker, Bonito Special, Sand Eel, Baby Sand Eel, Ballyhoo, Calamari Express; Probasco's Saltwater Baitfish. Middle row: Veverka's Blue Water Express, Bonito Bullet (2), Spearing, Sardine, Tuna Special; Probasco's Saltwater Fly. Right row: Veverka's Anchovy, Vleta's WBA Sardina (3), Kanz's Mylar Minnow (2), including a "bend back" model, Curcione's Tuna Tonic, Curcione's Sardine.

bend of the hook. Cover with olive marabou. *Body:* Opal Essence braided tubing over the hook shank. Draw in a red gill slit. *Eyes:* Witchcraft, silver iris, black pupil. Coat entire body with epoxy.

BABY SAND EEL

Hook: Short shank 2 and 4. The construction details of the fly are otherwise identical to the Sand Eel.

SIMULATOR SERIES

In Bob Veverka's Simulator Series, the body is tied with a double row of Opal Essence braided tubing. After the wing is tied in place, the tubing is tied down on top at the front and at the back. With the thread at the back, tie in a second piece of braided tubing and bring it forward under the hook. Before tying it in at the eye of the hook, pinch it flat to form the belly of a baitfish. Draw in a red gill slit with a marking pen. Stick on Witchcraft eyes. Coat the entire body with epoxy.

BONITO SPECIAL

Hook: Short shank 1, 2, and 4. *Wing:* White bucktail mixed with silver Fire Fly. Cover with white marabou and veil with pearl Fire Fly. *Body:* As above.

SARDINE

Hook: Short shank 4 to 3/0. *Wing:* White bucktail mixed with silver Fire Fly. Cover with white marabou and veil with pearl Fire Fly. Top with olive marabou mixed with a few strands of chartreuse Fire Fly. *Eyes:* Witchcraft, gold iris, black pupil. *Body:* As above.

ANCHOVY

Veverka fishes the Anchovy and the Tuna Special in Baja's East Cape waters to take both yellowfin tuna and dorado. *Hook:* Short shank 4 to 3/0. *Wing:* White bucktail mixed with silver Fire Fly; chartreuse marabou mixed with chartreuse Fire Fly; blue marabou mixed with both green and blue Fire Fly. *Eyes:* Witchcraft, gold iris, black pupil. *Body:* As above.

TUNA SPECIAL

Hook: Short shank 2 to 5/0. *Wing:* White bucktail mixed with silver Fire Fly. Cover with white marabou veiled with pearl Fire Fly. *Eyes:* Witchcraft, silver iris, black pupil. *Body:* As above.

BLUE WATER EXPRESS

Veverka uses the Blue Water Express as an all-purpose inshore and offshore fly for many different gamefish. The fly is especially effective on dorado. *Hook:* Short shank 2 to 5/0. *Wing:* White bucktail mixed with silver Fire Fly.

Cover with white marabou veiled with pearl Fire Fly, and blue marabou veiled with blue and green Fire Fly. *Eyes:* Witchcraft, silver iris, black pupil.

SPEARING

The baitfish called "spearing" in New Jersey is the "silversides" in Long Island and Rhode Island. Whatever its name, Veverka's Spearing imitates it closely enough to take striped bass and bonito. *Hook:* Short shank 2 and 1. *Wing:* White goat hair mixed with pearl Fire Fly tied at the bend of the hook. Tie in olive green goat hair at the front of the hook so that it extends over the hook eye. Tie in several strands of silver Flashabou tinsel to each side. Pull back the wing of olive goat hair and hold it in place as the epoxy is applied. This will provide both depth to the fly, and the desired dorsal color. Draw in a red gill with a fine marking pen. *Eyes:* Witchcraft, hot green iris, black pupil. After the eyes go on, apply a second coat of epoxy.

BABY BUNKER

Veverka ties the Baby Bunker to imitate the Atlantic menhaden, called the "pogy" off Maine and the Vineyard, and "mossbunker" elsewhere. The Baby Bunker is especially effective in late spring and early summer when the menhaden are the size of the fly described. *Hook:* Short shank 2 to 2/0. *Wing:* White goat hair mixed with silver Flashabou. Top with lavender and blue goat hair. Veil with pearl Fire Fly. At the eye, tie in black goat hair so that it extends over the hook eye. Pull back over the body, hold in place, and coat with epoxy. Draw in red gill slits with a fine marking pen. *Eyes:* Witchcraft, silver iris, black pupil.

STEPHEN VLETAS

(Westbank Anglers, P.O. Box 523, Teton Village, WY 83025)

Stephen Vletas's Westbank Anglers Sardina series (thus "WBA") matches the changing colors of sardines during the year along the Baja California peninsula from La Paz to Cabo San Lucas and north to the Chicken Ranch. In this intensely fish rich area, Vletas has caught roosterfish to 40 pounds, jack crevalle, wahoo, dorado, and school tuna including yellowfin, black skipjack, and skipjack. He especially likes the all-white Sardina for roosterfish (4/0) and sierra mackerel (2/0).

WBA SARDINA WHITE

Tail: Pearl Krystal Flash and a small amount of white bucktail. *Body:* Snap top from a pop can, cut exactly in half, placed against a 4/0 hook, and tied in place with wraps at each end. Cover with Mylar piping, and coat

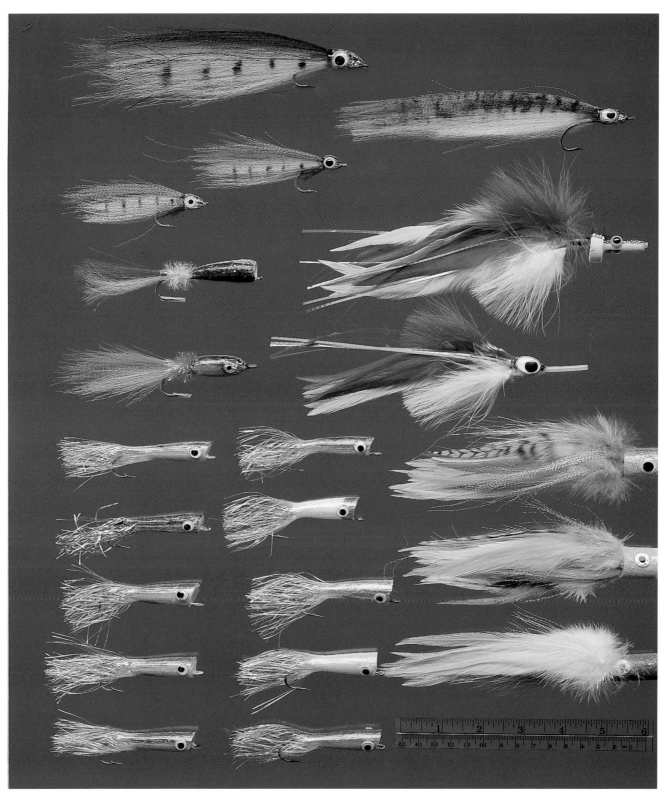

Fly tiers: Pete Parker, Trey Combs, Lani Waller, Cam Sigler Company. Top four: Pete's Anchovy, Pete's Mackerel, Pete's Flash Chovie, Pete's Chovie. Left row: Pete's Side Popper, Pete's Slider; Gaine's Poppers covered with Mylar piping by Trey Combs (5). Note the second popper, a Silver Bullet covered with silver Mylar. This is a low-light favorite of the author for dorado and tuna. Middle row: Waller's Mylar Popper (5). Right row: Cam Sigler's Big Game Tube Flies (Blue Mackerel), Combs's ethafoam poppers in the Air Africque, Green Machine, and Pink Squid patterns in sizes for sailfish.

with 5-Minute epoxy. *Wing:* White bucktail. *Topping:* Peacock herl. For the WBA Sardina Green and Blue, divide the wing equally between white and green or blue, before tying in a topping.

LANI WALLER

Inspired by Chappie Chapman of pencil popper fame, Lani Waller began epoxying large-diameter pearl Mylar to the 2/0 Gaines Saltwater poppers some ten years ago. The transformation was dazzling: The Mylar changed the black-over-pearl body to one of deep green and pearl; the body of light-blue-over-pearl remained true, but with green highlights to resemble a flying fish; the black-over-yellow resulted in a fantastic likeness to a baby dorado. Gamefish found the popper irresistible. Waller recalls that he once came upon dorado balling up sardines and watched a bull leave the real bait for the Mylar popper. During trips to Baja he took yellowfin tuna and bonito on the poppers. When he began hosting trips to Belize, he found the popper effective on tarpon, barracuda, and snappers. Waller has even raised a couple of sailfish to the poppers!

I've been an avid fan of these poppers ever since Waller gave me a handful. I've since fished them on jungle rivers, on flats, inshore, and offshore, and still find them the most effective poppers around. Five years ago I be-

gan covering them with silver Mylar piping and coating the dorsal area with a number of different Scribbles Soft Fashion Paints containing glitter. The results were fantastic low-light poppers that everything from jack crevalle to skipjack tuna jumped on.

MYLAR POPPERS

Tying instructions: Cut a 5-inch length of large-diameter Mylar piping and remove the core. Slip over the popper from the hook end, until the piping is slightly past the head. Using a toothpick, apply a small amount of 5-Minute epoxy around the head. When the epoxy has hardened, pull the Mylar piping back so that it is flush against the popper body. Apply 5-Minute epoxy to the entire body. I like to actually coat the Mylar a little past the body—in effect, extending the body. Trim the Mylar so that it extends about one body length past the body. Trim flush to the head. Using 5-Minute epoxy, secure 7mm doll eyes to each side. Note: Large and powerful gamefish can straighten the long shank 2/0 hook used in these poppers. To purchase only the painted popper bodies, ask your local fly shop to contact The Gaines Company, Box 35, Gaines, PA 16921.

Lani Waller poses with captain and mate and his 16-pound yellowfin tuna that took a fly off the Palmas de Cortez resort on Baja California's East Cape.

INDEX